NELSON PHILIP American Compact Atlas

Edited by
HAROLD FULLARD, M. SC.,
Cartographic Editor

THOMAS NELSON INC., PUBLISHERS
GEORGE PHILIP & SON LTD.

ISBN 8407-4063-8

**Published by
Thomas Nelson Inc., Publishers
in Nashville, Tennessee**

© 1978 George Philip & Son Ltd., London

**Prepared in Great Britain by George Philip Printers Ltd.
Printed in Hong Kong**

Contents

Maps 1–72

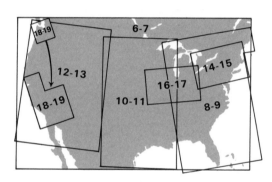

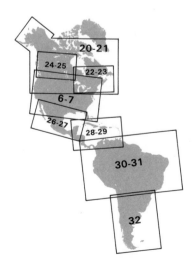

Contents–II

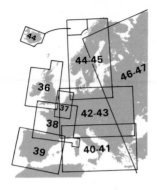

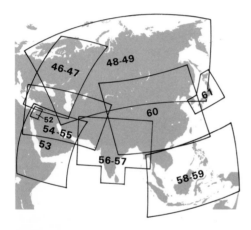

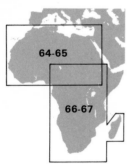

Population of Countries

Country	Area in thousands of square km	Population in thousands	Density of population per sq. km	Capital Population in thousands
Afghanistan	647	19 280	30	Kabul (534)
Albania	29	2 482	86	Tiranë (175)
Algeria	2 382	16 776	7	Algiers (943)
Angola	1 247	6 761	5	Luanda (475)
Argentina	2 777	25 383	9	Buenos Aires (8 925)
Australia	7 687	13 507	2	Canberra (185)
Austria	84	7 523	90	Vienna (1 615)
Bangladesh	144	76 815	533	Dacca (1 730)
Belgium	31	9 796	321	Brussels (1 075)
Belize	23	140	6	Belmopan (3)
Benin	113	3 112	27	Porto-Novo (104)
Bhutan	47	1 173	25	Thimphu (10)
Bolivia	1 099	5 634	5	Sucre (107) / La Paz (661)
Botswana	600	691	1	Gaborone (18)
Brazil	8 512	107 145	13	Brasilia (517)
Brunei	6	147	26	Bandar Seri Begawan (41)
Bulgaria	111	8 722	79	Sofia (962)
Burma	677	31 240	46	Rangoon (2 055)
Burundi	78	3 763	135	Bujumbura (79)
Cameroon	475	6 398	13	Yaoundé (178)
Cambodia	181	8 110	45	Phnom Penh (2 000)
Canada	9 976	22 831	2	Ottawa (626)
Central Africa	623	1 716	3	Bangui (187)
Chad	1 284	4 030	3	Ndjamena (179)
Chile	757	10 253	14	Santiago (3 263)
China	9 597	838 803	87	Peking (5 000)
Colombia	1 139	29 717	22	Bogota (2 855)
Congo	342	1 345	4	Brazzaville (250)
Costa Rica	51	1 968	39	San José (395)
Cuba	115	9 090	79	Havana (1 751)
Cyprus	9	639	69	Nicosia (116)
Czechoslovakia	128	14 802	116	Prague (1 096)
Denmark	43	5 059	117	Copenhagen (1 328)
Djibouti	22	106	5	Djibouti (62)
Dominican Republic	49	4 697	96	Santo Domingo (818)
Ecuador	284	6 733	24	Quito (565)
Egypt	1 001	37 233	37	Cairo (5 715)
El Salvador	21	4 007	190	San Salvador (337)
Equatorial Guinea	28	310	11	Rey Malabo (37) / Bata (27)
Ethiopia	1 222	27 946	23	Addis Ababa (1 161)
Fiji	18	577	32	Suva (80)
Finland	337	4 707	14	Helsinki (822)
France	547	52 913	97	Paris (9 108)
French Guiana	91	60	1	Cayenne (25)
Gabon	268	526	2	Libréville (57)
Gambia	11	524	46	Banjul (48)
Germany, East	108	16 850	156	East Berlin (1 094)
Germany, West	249	61 832	249	Bonn (283)
Ghana	239	9 866	41	Accra (738)
Greece	132	9 046	69	Athens (2 101)
Greenland	2 176	54	0.02	Godthaab (4)
Guatemala	109	5 540	51	Guatemala (707)
Guinea	246	4 416	18	Conakry (197)
Guyana	215	791	4	Georgetown (195)
Haiti	28	4 584	165	Port-au-Prince (494)
Honduras	112	3 037	27	Tegucigalpa (302)
Hong Kong	1	4 367	4 179	Victoria (849)
Hungary	93	10 540	113	Budapest (2 051)
Iceland	103	218	2	Reykjavik (99)
India	3 288	598 097	182	Delhi (3 647)
Indonesia	1 904	136 044	71	Djakarta (4 576)
Iran	1 648	33 019	20	Tehran (4 002)
Iraq	435	11 124	26	Baghdad (2 969)
Irish Republic	70	3 127	44	Dublin (650)
Israel	21	3 371	162	Jerusalem (344)
Italy	301	55 810	185	Rome (2 868)
Ivory Coast	322	4 885	15	Abidjan (420)
Jamaica	11	2 029	185	Kingston (573)
Japan	372	110 953	298	Tokyo (11 623)
Jordan	98	2 702	28	Amman (598)
Kenya	583	13 339	23	Nairobi (630)
Korea, North	121	15 852	132	Pyongyang (1 500)
Korea, South	98	33 949	345	Seoul (5 433)
Kuwait	18	996	56	Kuwait (295)
Laos	237	3 303	14	Vientiane (174)
Lebanon	10	2 869	276	Beirut (939)
Lesotho	30	1 039	34	Maseru (29)
Liberia	111	1 708	15	Monrovia (110)
Libya	1 760	2 444	1	Tripoli (332)
Luxembourg	3	357	138	Luxembourg (78)
Madagascar	587	6 750	12	Tananarive (378)
Malawi	118	5 044	43	Zomba (20)
Malaysia	330	12 093	37	Kuala Lumpur (452)
Mali	1 240	5 697	5	Bamako (197)
Malta	0.3	300	1 949	Valletta (14)
Mauritania	1 031	1 318	1	Nouakchott (104)
Mauritius	2	899	440	Port Louis (141)
Mexico	1 973	60 145	30	Mexico (11 340)
Mongolia	1 565	1 444	1	Ulan Bator (287)
Morocco	447	17 305	39	Rabat (597)
Mozambique	783	9 239	12	Maputo (384)
Nepal	141	12 572	89	Katmandu (333)
Netherlands	41	13 653	334	Amsterdam (996)
New Zealand	269	3 087	11	Wellington (142)
Nicaragua	130	2 155	17	Managua (399)
Niger	1 267	4 600	4	Niamey (130)
Nigeria	924	62 925	68	Lagos (1 477)
Norway	324	4 007	12	Oslo (645)
Oman	212	766	4	Muscat (25)
Pakistan	804	70 260	87	Islamabad (77)
Panama	76	1 668	22	Panama (404)
Papua New Guinea	462	2 756	6	Port Moresby (76)
Paraguay	407	2 647	7	Asunción (473)
Peru	1 285	15 839	12	Lima (3 303)
Philippines	300	42 513	142	Quezon City (995)
Poland	313	34 020	109	Warsaw (1 400)
Portugal	92	8 762	95	Lisbon (1 612)
Puerto Rico	9	3 087	347	San Juan (695)
Rhodesia	391	6 420	16	Salisbury (502)
Rumania	238	21 178	89	Bucharest (1 566)
Rwanda	26	4 198	159	Kigali (54)
Saudi Arabia	2 150	8 966	4	Riyadh (300)
Senegal	196	4 136	21	Dakar (581)
Sierra Leone	72	2 729	38	Freetown (214)
Singapore	1.6	2 250	3 872	Singapore (2 250)
Somali Republic	638	3 170	5	Mogadishu (230)
South Africa	1 221	25 471	21	Pretoria (562) / Cape Town (1 097)
S. W. Africa	824	888	1	Windhoek (60)
Spain	505	35 472	70	Madrid (3 520)
Sri Lanka	66	13 986	213	Colombo (618)
Sudan	2 506	17 757	7	Khartoum (648)
Surinam	163	422	3	Paramaribo (182)
Swaziland	17	494	28	Mbabane (14)
Sweden	450	8 195	18	Stockholm (1 353)
Switzerland	41	6 403	155	Berne (288)
Syria	185	7 355	40	Damascus (923)
Taiwan	36	16 150	449	Taipei (1 922)
Tanzania	945	15 155	16	Dar es Salaam (517)
Thailand	514	42 277	82	Bangkok (1 867)
Togo	56	2 222	40	Lomé (193)
Trinidad and Tobago	5	1 074	214	Port of Spain (68)
Tunisia	164	5 772	35	Tunis (648)
Turkey	781	39 180	50	Ankara (1 554)
Uganda	236	11 549	49	Kampala (331)
United Arab Emirates	84	222	3	Dubai (70)
U.S.S.R.	22 402	254 382	11	Moscow (7 632)
United Kingdom	244	56 149	229	London (7 168)
United States	9 363	213 611	23	Washington (2 861)
Upper Volta	274	6 032	22	Ouagadougou (125)
Uruguay	178	3 064	17	Montevideo (1 230)
Venezuela	912	11 993	13	Caracas (2 175)
Vietnam	333	45 211	136	Hanoi (920)
Western Samoa	2.8	159	56	Apia (33)
Yemen (Sana)	195	6 668	34	Sana (120)
Yemen (South)	333	1 690	5	Aden (285)
Yugoslavia	256	21 352	23	Belgrade (775)
Zaire	2 345	24 902	11	Kinshasa (2 008)
Zambia	753	4 896	7	Lusaka (448)

Population of Cities

The population figures used are from censuses or more recent estimates and are given in thousands for towns and cities over 500 000 (over 600 000 in China and U.S.S.R.). Where possible the population of the metropolitan area is given e.g. Greater London, Greater New York, etc.; if this is not possible however, city proper figures are shown, and these are indicated by an asterisk alongside the country name.

AFRICA

ALGERIA (1966)
Algiers 943

EGYPT (1974)
Cairo 5 715
Alexandria 2 259
El Giza 854

ETHIOPIA (1975)*
Addis Ababa 1 161

GHANA (1970)
Accra 738

KENYA (1973)
Nairobi 630

MOROCCO (1973)
Casablanca 1 753
Rabat-Salé 597

NIGERIA (1975)*
Lagos 1 477
Ibadan 847

RHODESIA (1973)
Salisbury 502

SENEGAL (1969)
Dakar 581

SOUTH AFRICA (1970)
Johannesburg 1 433
Cape Town 1 097
Durban 843
Pretoria 562

TANZANIA (1975)*
Dar es Salaam 517

TUNISIA (1966)
Tunis 648

ZAÏRE (1972-74)*
Kinshasa 2 008
Kananga 601

ASIA

AFGHANISTAN (1973)
Kabul 534

BANGLADESH (1974)
Dacca 1 730
Chittagong 890

BURMA (1973)*
Rangoon 2 055

CAMBODIA (1973)
Phnom Penh 2 000

CHINA (1970)*
Shanghai 10 820
Peking 7 570
Tientsin 4 280
Shenyang 2 800
Wuhan 2 650
Canton 2 500
Chungking 2 400
Nanking 1 750
Harbin 1 670
Lü-ta 1 650
Sian 1 600
Lanchow 1 450
Taiyuan 1 350
Tsingtao 1 300
Chengtu 1 250
Changchun 1 200
Kunming 1 100
Tsinan 1 100
Fushan 1 080
Anshan 1 050
Chengchow 1 050
Hangchow 960
Tangshan 950
Paotow 920
Tzepo 850

Changsha 825
Shihkiachwang 800
Tsitsihar 760
Soochow 730
Kirin 720
Suchow 700
Foochow 680
Nanchang 675
Kweiyang 660
Wusih 650
Hofei 630
Hwainan 600
Penki 600

HONG KONG (1971)
Kowloon 2 195
Victoria 849

INDIA (1971)
Calcutta 7 031
Bombay 5 971
Delhi 3 647
Madras 3 170
Hyderabad 1 796
Ahmedabad 1 742
Bangalore 1 654
Kanpur 1 275
Pune 1 135
Nagpur 930
Lucknow 814
Coimbatore 736
Madurai 712
Agra 635
Jaipur 637
Varanasi 607
Indore 561
Jabalpur 535
Allahabad 513

INDONESIA (1971)*
Jakarta 4 576
Surabaya 1 556
Bandung 1 202
Semerang 647
Medan 636
Palembang 583

IRAN (1973)*
Tehran 4 002
Esfahan 605
Mashhad 592
Tabriz 510

IRAQ (1970)
Baghdad 2 969

ISRAEL (1974)
Tel Aviv-Jaffa 1 157

JAPAN (1974)
Tokyo 11 623
Osaka 2 780
Yokohama 2 620
Nagoya 2 080
Kyoto 1 460
Kobe 1 360
Sapporo 1 240
Kitakyushu 1 060
Kawasaki 1 020
Fukuoka 1 000
Hiroshima 761
Sakai 716
Chiba 614
Sendai 576
Amagasaki 538

JORDAN (1974)*
Amman 598

KOREA, NORTH (1970)
Pyongyang 1 500

KOREA, SOUTH (1970)*
Seoul 5 433
Pusan 1 842

Taegu 1 064
Inchon 634

LEBANON (1970)
Beirut 939

PAKISTAN (1972)*
Karachi 3 499
Lahore 2 165
Lyallpur 822
Hyderabad 628
Rawalpindi 615
Multan 542

PHILIPPINES (1975)*
Manila 1 438
Quezon City 995
Davao 591

SINGAPORE (1975)
Singapore 2 250

SRI LANKA (1973)
Colombo 618

SYRIA (1970)
Damascus 923
Aleppo 639

TAIWAN (1970-73)
Taipei 1 922
Kaohsiung 915

THAILAND (1970)*
Bangkok 1 867
Thonburi 628

TURKEY (1973)
Istanbul 3 135
Ankara 1 554
Izmir 819

VIETNAM (1966-71)*
Ho Chi Minh City ..1 825
Hanoi 920

EUROPE

AUSTRIA (1971)*
Vienna 1 615

BELGIUM (1971)
Brussels 1 075
Antwerp 673

BULGARIA (1974)
Sofia 962

CZECHOSLOVAKIA (1974)*
Prague 1 096

DENMARK (1974)
Copenhagen 1 328

FINLAND (1973)
Helsinki 822

FRANCE (1975)
Paris 9 108
Lyon 1 167
Marseille 1 004
Lille 922
Bordeaux 589

GERMANY, EAST (1975)*
East Berlin 1 094
Leipzig 569
Dresden 508

GERMANY, WEST (1974)
West Berlin 2 048
Hamburg 1 752
Münich 1 337
Cologne 832
Essen 674
Frankfurt am Main ..663
Dortmund 632

Düsseldorf 628
Stuttgart 625
Bremen 584
Nürnberg 515
Hannover 505

GREECE (1971)
Athens 2 101
Thessaloniki 557

HUNGARY (1974)*
Budapest 2 051

IRELAND (1971)
Dublin 650

ITALY (1975)*
Rome 2 868
Milano 1 731
Napoli 1 224
Torino 1 202
Genova 806
Palermo 663

NETHERLANDS (1974)
Rotterdam 1 036
Amsterdam 996
s'Gravenhage 682

NORWAY (1974)
Oslo 645

POLAND (1974)*
Warsaw 1 400
Lódz 784
Kraków 663
Wroclaw 565
Poznan 503

PORTUGAL (1974)
Lisbon 1 612
Oporto 1 315

RUMANIA (1974)
Bucharest 1 566

SPAIN (1974)
Madrid 3 520
Barcelona 1 810
Valencia 713
Sevilla 589

SWEDEN (1974)
Stockholm 1 353
Göteborg 688

SWITZERLAND (1975)
Zürich 721

U.S.S.R. (1975)*
Moscow 7 632
Leningrad 4 311
Kiyev 1 947
Tashkent 1 595
Baku 1 383
Kharkov 1 357
Gorkiy 1 283
Novosibirsk 1 265
Kuybyshev 1 164
Sverdlovsk 1 147
Minsk 1 147
Tbilisi 1 006
Odessa 1 002
Chelyabinsk 969
Omsk 968
Dnepropetrovsk 958
Donetsk 950
Kazan 946
Perm 939
Volgograd 900
Yerevan 899
Ufa 895
Rostov 888
Alma-Ata 836
Saratov 834
Riga 796
Krasnoyarsk 748
Voronezh 746

Zaporozhye 744
Krivoy Rog 628
Lvov 617

UNITED KINGDOM (1974)
London 7 168
Birmingham 1 003
Glasgow 816
Liverpool 561
Manchester 516
Sheffield 507

YUGOSLAVIA (1971)*
Belgrade 775
Zagreb 566

NORTH AMERICA

CANADA (1974)
Montréal 2 798
Toronto 2 741
Vancouver 1 137
Ottawa 626
Winnipeg 570
Edmonton 529
Hamilton 520

CUBA (1970)
Havana 1 751

DOMINICAN REP. (1970)
Santo Domingo 818

GUATEMALA (1973)*
Guatemala City 707

MEXICO (1974)
Mexico City 11 340
Guadalajara 1 963
Monterrey 1 638
Ciudad Juárez 521

PUERTO RICO (1970)
San Juan 695

UNITED STATES (1973)
New York 11 571
Los Angeles 7 032
Chicago 6 979
Philadelphia 4 818
Detroit 4 200
San Francisco 3 110
Washington 2 861
Boston 2 754
Pittsburgh 2 401
St Louis 2 363
Baltimore 2 071
Cleveland 2 064
Houston 1 985
Newark 1 857
Minneapolis-
St. Paul 1 814
Dallas 1 556
Seattle 1 422
Anaheim-
Santa Ana 1 420
Milwaukee 1 404
Atlanta 1 390
Cincinnati 1 385
San Diego 1 358
Paterson 1 359
Buffalo 1 349
Miami 1 268
Kansas City 1 254
Denver 1 228
San Bernardino 1 143
Indianapolis 1 110
San Jose 1 065
New Orleans 1 046
Tampa-
St. Petersburg 1 013
Portland 1 009
Phoenix 968
Columbus 916

Providence 911
Rochester 883
San Antonio 864
Dayton 850
Louisville 827
Sacramento 801
Memphis 770
Fort Worth 762
Birmingham 739
Albany 722
Toledo 693
Norfolk 681
Akron 679
Hartford 664
Oklahoma City 641
Syracuse 636
Gary 633
Honolulu 629
Fort Lauderdale 620
Jersey City 609
Greensboro 604
Salt Lake City 558
Jacksonville 548
Allentown 544
Nashville 541
Grand Rapids 539
Youngstown 536
Springfield 530

SOUTH AMERICA

ARGENTINA (1970)
Buenos Aires 8 925
Rosario 811
Córdoba 799
La Plata 506

BOLIVIA (1975)
La Paz 661

BRAZIL (1970)
São Paulo 5 241
Rio de Janeiro 4 316
Belo Horizonte 1 126
Recife 1 070
Salvador 1 018
Pôrto Alegre 887
Belém 572
Fortaleza 530
Brasília 517

CHILE (1975)
Santiago 3 263
Valparaíso 592

COLOMBIA (1972-73)
Bogotá 2 855
Medellin 1 417
Cali 923
Barranquilla 727

ECUADOR (1972)*
Guayaquil 861
Quito 565

PERU (1972)
Lima 3 303

URUGUAY (1975)*
Montevideo 1 230

VENEZUELA (1971)
Caracas 2 175
Maracaibo 652

AUSTRALASIA

AUSTRALIA (1973)
Sydney 2 874
Melbourne 2 584
Brisbane 911
Adelaide 868
Perth 739

Geographical Terms—I

This is a list of some of the geographical words from foreign languages which are found in the place names on the maps and in the index. Each is followed by the language and the English meaning.

Afr. afrikaans	*Chin.* chinese	*Gae.* gaelic	*It.* italian	*Nor.* norwegian	*Ser.-Cr.* serbo-croat
Alb. albanian	*Cz.* czechoslovakian	*Ger.* german	*Jap.* japanese	*Pash.* pashto	*Siam.* siamese
Amh. amharic	*Dan.* danish	*Gr.* greek	*Kor.* korean	*Pers.* persian	*Sin.* sinhalese
Ar. arabic	*Dut.* dutch	*Heb.* hebrew	*Lapp.* lappish	*Pol.* polish	*Som.* somali
Ber. berber	*Fin.* finnish	*Hin.* hindi	*Lith.* lithuanian	*Port.* portuguese	*Span.* spanish
Bulg. bulgarian	*Flem.* flemish	*I.-C.* indo-chinese	*Mal.* malay	*Rum.* rumanian	*Swed.* swedish
Bur. burmese	*Fr.* french	*Ice.* icelandic	*Mong.* mongolian	*Russ.* russian	*Tib.* tibetan
					Turk. turkish

A. (Ain) *Ar.* spring
–á *Ice.* river
a *Dan., Nor., Swed.* stream
–abad *Pers., Russ.* town
Abyad *Ar.* white
Ad. (Adrar) *Ar., Ber.* mountain
Ada, Adasi *Tur.* island
Addis *Amh.* new
Adrar *Ar., Ber.* mountain
Ain *Ar.* spring
Ākra *Gr.* cape
Akrotiri *Gr.* cape
Alb *Ger.* mountains
Albufera *Span.* lagoon
–ålen *Nor.* islands
Alpen *Ger.* mountain pastures
Alpes *Fr.* mountains
Alpi *It.* mountains
Alto *Port.* high
–älv, –älven *Swed.* stream, river
Amt *Dan.* first-order administrative division
Appennino *It.* mountain range
Arch. (Archipiélago) *Span.* archipelago
Arcipélago *It.* archipelago
Arq. (Arquipélago) *Port.* archipelago
Arr. (Arroyo) *Span.* stream
–Ås, –åsen *Nor., Swed.* hill
Autonomna Oblast *Ser.-Cr.* autonomous region
Ayios *Gr.* cape
Ayn *Ar.* well, waterhole

B(a). (Baía) *Port.* bay
B. (Baie) *Fr.* bay
B. (Bahía) *Span.* bay
B. (Ben) *Gae.* mountain
B. (Bir) *Ar.* well
B. (Bucht) *Ger.* bay
B. (Bugt.) *Dan.* bay
Baai, –baai *Afr.* bay
Bâb *Ar.* gate
Bäck, –bäcken *Swed.* stream
Back, backen, *Swed.* hill
Bad, –baden *Ger.* spa
Bâdiya,-t *Ar.* desert
Baek *Dan.* stream
Baelt *Dan.* strait
Bahía *Span.* bay
Bahr *Ar.* sea, river
Bahra *Ar.* lake
Baía *Port.* bay
Baie *Fr.* bay
Bajo, –a, *Span.* lower
Bakke *Nor.* hill
Bala *Pers.* upper
Baltă *Rum.* marsh, lake
Banc *Fr.* bank
Bander *Ar., Mal.* port
Bandar *Pers.* bay
Banja *Ser. Cr.* spa resort
Barat *Mal.* western
Barr. (Barrage) *Fr.* dam
Barracão *Port.* dam, waterfall
Bassin *Fr.* bay
Bayt *Heb.* house, village
Bazar *Hin.* market, bazaar
Be'er *Heb.* well
Beit *Heb.* village
Belo-, Belyy, Belaya,

Beloye, *Russ.* white
Ben *Gae.* mountain
Bender *Somal.* harbour
Berg,(e) –berg(e) *Afr.* mountain(s)
Berg, –berg *Ger.* hill, mountain, rock
–berg, –et *Nor., Swed.* hill, mountain, rock
Bet *Heb.* house, village
Bir, Bîr *Ar.* well
Birket *Ar.* lake, bay, marsh
Bj. (Bordj) *Ar.* port
–bjerg *Dan.* hill, point
Boca *Span.* river mouth
Bodden *Ger.* bay, inlet
Bogaz, Boğaz, –ı *Tur.* strait
Boka *Ser.-Cr.* gulf, inlet
Bol. (Bolshoi) *Russ.* great, large
Bordj *Ar.* fort
–borg *Dan., Nor., Swed.* castle, fort
–botn *Nor.* valley floor
bouche(s) *Fr.* mouth
Br. (Burnu) *Tur.* cape
Brațul *Rum.* distributary stream
–breen *Nor.* glacier
–bruck *Ger.* bridge
–brunn *Swed.* well, spring
Bucht *Ger.* bay
Bugt, –bugt *Dan.* bay
Buheirat *Ar.* lake
Bukit *Mal.* hill
Bukten *Swed.* bay
–bulag *Mong.* spring
Bûr *Ar.* port
Burg. *Ar.* fort
Burg, –burg *Ger.* castle
Burnu *Tur.* cape
Burun *Tur.* cape
Butt *Gae.* promontory
–by *Dan., Nor., Swed.* town
–byen *Nor., Swed.* town

C. (Cabo) *Port., Span.* headland, cape
C. (Cap) *Fr.* cape
C. (Capo) *It.* cape
Cabeza *Span.* peak, hill
Camp *Port., Span.* land, field
Campo *Span.* plain
Campos *Span.* upland
Can. (Canal) *Fr., Span.* canal
Canale *It.* canal
Canalul *Ser.-Cr.* canal
Cao Nguyên *Thai.* plateau, tableland
Cap *Fr.* cape
Capo *It.* cape
Cataracta *Sp.* cataract
Cauce *Span.* intermittent stream
Causse *Fr.* upland (limestone)
Cayi *Tur.* river
Cayo(s) *Span.* rock(s), islet(s)
Cerro *Span.* hill, peak
Ch. (Chaîne)) *Fr.* mountain range(s)
Ch. (Chott) *Ar.* salt lake
Chaco *Span.* jungle
Chaîne(s) *Fr.* mountain range(s)
Chap. (Chapada) *Port.* hills, upland

Chapa *Span.* hills, upland
Chapada *Port.* hills, upland
Chaung *Bur.* stream, river
Chen *Chin.* market town
Ch'eng *Chin.* town
Chiang *Chin.* river
Ch'ih *Chin.* pool
Ch'ŏn *Kor.* river
–chŏsuji *Kor.* reservoir
Chott *Ar.* salt lake, swamp
Chou *Chin.* district
Chu *Tib.* river
Chung *Chin.* middle
Chute *Fr.* waterfall
Co. (Cerro) *Span.* hill, peak
Coch. (Cochilla) *Port.* hills
Col *Fr., It.* Pass
Colline(s) *Fr.* hill(s)
Conca *It.* plain, basin
Cord. (Cordillera) *Span.* mountain chain
Costa *It., Span.* coast
Côte *Fr.* coast, slope, hill
Cuchillas *Spain* hills
Cu-Lao *I.-C.* island

D. (Dolok) *Mal.* mountain
Dágh *Pers.* mountain
Dağ(ı) *Tur.* mountain(s)
Dağları *Tur.* mountain range
Dake *Jap.* mountain
–dal *Nor.* valley
–dal, -e *Dan., Nor.* valley
–dal, –en *Swed.* valley, stream
Dalay *Mong.* sea, large lake
–dalir *Ice.* valley
–dalur *Ice.* valley
–damm, –en *Swed.* lake
Danau *Mal.* lake
Dao *I.-O.* island
Dar *Ar.* region
Darya *Russ.* river
Daryācheh *Pers.* marshy lake, lake
Dasht *Pers.* desert, steppe
Daung *Bur.* mountain, hill
Dayr *Ar.* depression, hill
Debre *Amh.* hill
Deli *Ser.-Cr.* mountain(s)
Denizi *Tur.* sea
Dépt. (Département) *Fr.* first-order administrative division
Desierto *Span.* desert
Dhar *Ar.* region, mountain chain
Dj. (Djebel) *Ar.* mountain
Dō *Jap., Kor.* island
Dong *Kor.* village, town
Dong *Thai.* jungle region
–dorf *Ger.* village
–dorp *Afr.* village
–drif *Afr.* ford
–dybet *Dan.* marine channel
Dzong *Tib.* town, settlement

Eil.-eiland(en) *Afr., Dut.* island(s)
–elv *Nor.* river
–'emeq *Heb.* plain, valley
'erg *Ar.* desert with dunes
Estrecho *Span.* strait
Estuario *Span.* estuary

Étang *Fr.* lagoon
–ey(jar) *Ice.* island(s)

F. (Fiume) *It.* river
F. Folyó *Hung.* river
Fd. (Fjord) *Nor.* Inlet of sea
–feld *Ger.* field
–fell *Ice.* mountain, hill
–feng *Chin.* mountain
Fiume *It.* river
Fj. (–fjell) *Nor.* mountain
–fjall *Ice.* mountain(s), hill(s)
–fjäll(et) *Swed.* hill(s), mountain(s), ridge
–fjällen *Swed.* mountains
–fjard(en) *Swed.* fjord, bay, lake
Fjeld *Dan.* mountain
–fjell *Nor.* mountain, rock
–fjord(en) *Nor.* inlet of sea
–fjorden *Dan.* bay, marine channel
–fjörður *Ice.* fjord
Fl. (Fleuve) *Fr.* river
Fl. (Fluss) *Ger.* river
–flói *Ice.* bay, marshy country
Fluss *Ger.* river
foce, –i *It.* mouth(s)
Folyó *Hung.* river
–fontein *Afr.* fountain, spring
–fors, –en, *Swed.* rapids, waterfall
Foss *Ice., Nor.* waterfall
–furt *Ger.* ford
Fylke *Nor.* first-order administrative division

G. (Gebel) *Ar.* mountain
G. (Gebirge) *Ger.* hills, mountains
G. (Golfe) *Fr.* gulf
G. (Golfo) *It.* gulf
G. (Gora) *Bulg., Russ., Ser.-Cr.* mountain
G. (Gunong) *Mal.* mountain
–gang *Kor.* river
Ganga *Hin., Sin.* river
–gat *Dan.* sound
–gau *Ger.* district
Gave *Fr.* stream
–gawa *Jap.* river
Geb. (Gebirge) *Ger.* hills, mountains
Gebel *Ar.* mountain
Geziret *Ar.* island
Ghat *Hin.* range of hills
Ghiol *Rum.* lake
Ghubbat *Ar.* bay, inlet
Gji *Alb.* bay
Gl. (Glava) *Ser.-Cr.* mountain, peak
Glen. *Gae.* valley
Gletscher *Ger.* glacier
Gobi *Mong.* desert
Gol *Mong.* river
Golfe *Fr.* gulf
Golfo *It., Span.* gulf
Gomba *Tib.* settlement
Gora *Bulg., Russ., Ser.-Cr.* mountain(s)
Góry *Pol.* mountains
Gölü *Tur.* lake
–gorod *Russ.* small town
Grad *Bulg., Russ., Ser-Cr.* town, city

Grada *Russ.* mountain range
Guba *Russ.* bay
–Guntō *Jap.* island group
Gunong *Mal.* mountain
Gură *Rum.* passage

H. Hadabat *Ar.* plateau
–hafen *Ger.* harbour, port
Haff *Ger.* bay
Hai *Chin.* sea
Haihsia *Chin.* strait
–hale *Dan.* spit, peninsula
Hals *Dan., Nor.* peninsula, isthmus
Halvø *Dan.* peninsula
Halvøya *Nor.* peninsula
Hämad, Hamada,
Hammādah *Ar.* stony desert, plain
–hamn *Swed., Nor.* harbour, anchorage
Hämün *Ar.* plain
Hāmūn *Pers.* low-lying marshy area
–Hantō *Jap.* peninsula
Harju *Fin.* hill
Hassi *Ar.* well
–haug *Nor.* hill
Hav *Swed.* gulf
Havet *Nor.* sea
–havn *Dan., Nor.* harbour
Hegyseg *Hung.* forest
Heide *Ger.* heath
Hi. (hassi) *Ar.* well
Ho *Chin.* river
–hø *Nor.* peak
Hochland *Afr.* highland
Hoek, –hoek *Afr., Dut.* cape
Höfn *Ice.* harbour, port
–hög, –en, –högar,
–högarna *Swed.* hill(s), peak, mountain
Höhe *Ger.* hills
Holm *Dan.* island
–holm, –holme, –holzen, *Swed.* island
Hon *I.-C.* island
Hora *Cz.* mountain
–horn *Nor.* peak
Hory *Cz.* mountain range, forest
–hoved *Dan.* point, headland, peninsula
Hráun *Ice.* lava
–hsi *Chin.* mountain, stream
–hsiang *Chin.* village
–hsien *Chin.* district
Hu *Chin.* lake
Huk *Dan., Ger.* point
Huken *Nor.* head

I. (Île) *Fr.* island
I. (Ilha) *Port.* island
I. (Insel) *Ger.* island
I. (Isla) *Span.* island
I. (Isola) *It.* island
Idehan *Ar., Ber.* sandy plain
Île(s) *Fr.* island(s)
Ilha *Port.* island
Insel(s) *Ger.* island(s)
Irmak *Tur.* river
Is. (Inseln) *Ger.* islands
Is. (Islas) *Span.* islands
Is. (Isola) *It.* island
Isola, –e *It.* island(s)
Istmo *Span.* isthmus

J. (Jabal) *Ar.* mountain
J. (Jazira) *Ar.* island
J. (Jebel) *Ar.* mountain
J. (Jeziora) *Pol.* lake
Jabal *Ar.* mountain, range
–jaur *Swed.* lake
–järvi *Fin.* lake, bay, pond
Jasovir *Bulg.* reservoir
Jazā'ir *Ar.* islands
Jazira *Ar.* island
Jazireh *Pers.* island
Jebel *Ar.* mountain
Jezero *Ser.-Cr.* lake
Jezioro *Pol.* lake
–Jima *Jap.* island
Jøkelen *Nor.* glacier
–joki *Fin.* stream
–jökull *Ice.* glacier
Jūras Līcis *Lat.* bay, gulf

K. (Kap) *Dan.* cape
K (Khalīg) *Ar.* gulf
K. (Kiang) *Chin.* river
K. (Kuala) *Mal.* confluence, estuary
Kaap *Afr.* cape
Kai *Jap.* sea
Kaikyō *Jap.* strait
Kamennyy *Russ.* stony
Kampong *Mal.* village
Kan. (Kanal) *Ser.-Cr.* channel, canal
Kanaal *Dut., Flem.* canal
Kanal *Dan.* channel, gulf
Kanal *Ger., Swed.* canal, stream
kanal *Ser.-Cr.* channel, canal
Kang *Kor.* river, bay
Kangri *Tib.* mountain glacier
Kap *Dan., Ger.* cape
Kapp *Nor.* cape
Kas *I.-C.* island
–kaupstaður *Ice.* market town
–kaupunki *Fin.* town
Kavir *Pers.* salt desert
Kébir *Ar.* great
Kéfar *Heb.* village, hamlet
–ken *Jap.* first-order administrative division
Kep *Alb.* cape
Kepulauan *Mal.* archipelago
Ketjil *Mal.* lesser, little
Khalīg, Khalīj *Ar.* gulf
khamba, –ídg *Tib.* source, spring
Khawr *Ar.* wadi
Khirbat *Ar.* ruins
Kho Khot *Thai.* isthmus
Khōr *Pers.* creek, estuary
Khrebet *Russ.* mountain range
Kiang *Chin.* river
–klint *Dan.* cliff
–Klintar *Swed.* hills
Kloof *Afr.* gorge
Knude *Dan.* point
Ko *Jap.* lake
Ko *Thai.* island
Kohi *Pash.* mountains
Kol *Russ.* lake
Kolymskoye *Russ.* mountain range
Kólpos *Gr., Tur.* gulf, bay
Kompong *Mal.* landing place
–kop *Afr.* hill

Geographical Terms—II

–köping *Swed.* market town
Körfezi *Tur.* gulf
Kosa *Russ.* spit
–koski *Fin.* cataract, rapids
–kraal *Afr.* native village
Krasnyy *Russ.* red
Kryash *Russ.* ridge, hills
Kuala *Mal.* confluence, estuary
kuan *Chin.* pass
Kuh –hha *Pers.* mountains
Kul *Russ.* lake
Kulle *Swed.* hill, shoal
Kum *Russ.* sandy desert
Kumpu *Fin.* hill
Kurgan *Russ.* mound
Kwe *Bur.* bay, gulf
Kyst *Dan.* coast
Kyun, –zu, –umya *Bur.* island(s)

L. (Lac) *Fr.* lake
L. (Lacul) *Rum.* lake
L. (Lago) *It.*, *Span.* lake, lagoon
L. (Lagoa) *Port.* lagoon
L. (Límni) *Gr.* lake
L. (Loch) *Gae.* (lake, inlet)
L. (Lough) *Gae.* (lake, inlet)
La *Tib.* pass
La (Lagoa) *Port.* lagoon
–laagte *Afr.* watercourse
Lääni *Fin.* first-order administrative division
Län *Swed.* first-order administrative division
Lac *Fr.* lake
Lacul *Rum.* lake, lagoon
Lago *It.*, *Span.* lake, lagoon
Lagoa *Port.* lagoon
Laguna *It.*, *Span.* lagoon, intermittent lake
Lagune *Fr.* lake
Lahti *Fin.* bay, gulf, cove
Lakhti *Russ.* bay, gulf
Lampi *Fin.* lake
Land *Ger.* first-order administrative division
–land *Dan.* region
–land *Afr.*, *Nor.* land, province
Lido *It.* beach, shore
Liehtao *Chin.* islands
Lilla *Swed.* small
Límni *Fin.* lake
Ling *Chin.* mountain range, ice
Linna *Fin.* historical fort
Llano *Span.* prairie, plain
Loch *Gae.* (lake)
Lough *Gae.* (lake)
Lum *Alb.* river
Lund *Dan.* forest
–lund, –en *Swed.* wood(s)

M. (Maj, Mai) *Alb.* mountain, peak
M. (Mont) *Fr.* mountain peak
M. (Mys) *Russ.* cape
Madîna(h) *Ar.* town, city
Madiq *Ar.* strait
Maj *Alb.* peak
Mäki *Fin.* hill, hillside
Mal *Alb.* mountain
Mal *Russ.* little, small
Mal/a, –i, –o *Ser.-Cr.* small, little
Man *Kor.* bay
Mar *Span.* lagoon, sea
Mare *Rum.* great
Marisma *Span.* marsh
–mark *Dan.*, *Nor.* land
Marsâ *Ar.* anchorage, bay, inlet
Masabb *Ar.* river mouth
Massif *Fr.* upland, plateau
Mato *Port.* forest
Mazar *Pers.* shrine, tomb
Meer *Afr.*, *Dut.*, *Ger.* lake sea

Mi., Mti. (Monti) *It.* mountains
Miao *Chin.* temple, shrine
Midbar *Heb.* wilderness
Mif. (Massif) *Fr.* upland, plateau
Misaki *Jap.* cape, point
–mo *Nor.*, *Swed.* heath, island
–mon *Swed.* heath
Mong *Bur.* town
Mont *Fr.* hill, mountain
Montagna *It.* mountain
Montagne *Fr.* hill, mountain
Montaña *Span.* mountain
Monte *It.*, *Port.*, *Span.* mountain
Monti *It.* mountains
More *Russ.* sea
Mörön *Hung.* river
Mt. (Mont) *Fr.* mountain
Mt. (Monti) *It.* mountain
Mt. (Montaña) *Span.* mountain range
Mte. (Monte) *It.*, *Port.*, *Span.* mountain
Mţi. (Munţii) *Rum.* mountain
Mts. (Monts) *Fr.* mountains
Muang *Mal.* town
Mui *Ar.*, *I.-C.* cape
Mull *Gae.* (promontory)
Mund, –mund *Afr.* mouth
Munkhafed *Ar.* depression
Munte *Rum.* mount
Munţi(i) *Rum.* mountain(s)
Muong *Mal.* village
Myit *Bur.* river
Myitwanya *Bur.* mouths of river
–mýri *Ice.* bog
Mys *Russ.* cape

N. (Nahal) *Heb.* river
Naes *Dan.* point, cape
Nafûd *Ar.* sandy desert
Nahal *Heb.* river
Nahr *Ar.* river, stream
Najd *Ar.* plateau, pass
Nakhon *Thai.* town
Nam *I.-C.* river
–nam *Kor.* south
–näs *Swed.* cape
–nes *Ice.*, *Nor.* cape
Ness, –ness *Gae.* promontory, cape
Nez *Fr.* cape
–niemi *Fin.* cape, point, peninsula, island
Nizhne, –iy *Russ.* lower
Nizmennost *Russ.* plain, lowland
Nísos, Nisoi *Gr.* island(s)
Nor *Chin.* lake
Nor *Tib.* peak
Nos *Bulg.*, *Russ.* cape, point
Nudo *Span.* mountain
Nuruu *Mong.* mountain range
Nuur *Mong.* lake

O. (Ostrov) *Russ.* island
O (Ouâdî, Oued) *Ar.* wadi
–ö *Swed.* island, peninsula, point
–öar, (–na) *Swed.* islands
Oblast *Russ.* administrative division
Öbor *Mong.* inner
Occidental *Fr.*, *Span.* western
Odde *Dan.*, *Nor.* point, peninsula, cape
Oji *Alb.* bay
Ojo *Span.* spring
Oki *Jap.* bay
–ön *Swed.* island peninsula
Ondör *Mong.* high, tall

–ör *Swed.* island, peninsula, point
Oraşul *Rum.* city
Ord *Gae.* point
Öri *Gr.* mountains
Oriental *Span.* eastern
Órmos *Gr.* bay
Óros *Gr.* mountain
Ort *Ger.* point, cape
Ostrov(a) *Russ.* island(s)
Otok(–i) *Ser.-Cr.* island(s)
Ouadi, –edi *Ar.* dry watercourse, wadi
Ouzan *Pers.* river
Ova (–si) *Tur.* plains, lowlands
–øy, (–a) *Nor.* island(s)
Oya *Hin.* point
Oya *Sin.* river
Oz. (Ozero, a) *Russ.* lake(s)

P. (Passo) *It.* pass
P. (Pasul) *Rum.* pass
P. (Pico) *Span.* peak
P. (Prokhod) *Bulg.* pass
–pää *Fin.* hill(s), mountain
Pahta *Lapp.* hill
Pampa, –s *Span.* plain(s) salt flat(s)
Pan. (Pantano) *Span.* Reservoir
Pantao *Chin.* peninsula
Parbat *Urdu* mountain
Pas *Fr.* gap
Paso *Span.* pass, marine channel
Pass *Ger.* pass
Passo *It.* pass
Pasul *Rum.* pass
Patam *Hin.* small village
Patna, –patnam *Hin.* small village
Pegunungan *Mal.* mountain, range
Pei, –pei *Chin.* north
Pélagos *Gr.* sea
Pen. (Península) *Span.* peninsula
Peña *Span.* rock, peak
Península *Span.* peninsula
Per. (Pereval) *Russ.* pass
Pertuis *Fr.* channel
Peski *Russ.* desert, sands
Phanom *I.-C.*, *Thai.* mountain
Phnom *I.-C.* mountain
Phu *I.-C.* mountain
Pic *Fr.* peak
Pico(s) *Span.* peak(s)
Pik *Russ.* peak
Piz., pizzo *It.* peak
Pl. (Planina) *Ser.-Cr.* mountain, range
Plage *Fr.* beach
Plaine *Fr.* plain
Planalto *Span.* plateau
Planina *Bulg.*, *Ser.-Cr.* mountain, range
Plat. (Plateau) *Fr.* level upland
Plato *Russ.* plateau
Playa *Span.* beach
P-ov. (Poluostrov) *Russ.* peninsula
Pointe *Fr.* point, cape
Pojezierze *Pol.* lakes plateau
Polder *Dut.* reclaimed farmland
–pólis *Gr.* city, town
Poluostrov *Russ.* peninsula
Połwysep *Pol.* peninsula
Pont *Fr.* bridge
Ponta *Port.* point, cape
Ponte *It.* bridge
Poort *Afr.* passage, gate
–poort *Dut.* port
Porta *Port.* gate
Porţil, –e *Rum.* gate
Portillo *Span.* pass
Porto *It.* port
Porto *Port.*, *Span.* port

Pot. (Potámi, Potamós) *Gr.* river
Poulo *I.-C.* island
Pr. (Prŭsmyk) *Cz.* pass
Pradesh *Hin.* state
Presa *Span.* reservoir
Presqu'île *Fr.* peninsula
Prokhod *Bulg.* pass
Proliv *Russ.* strait
Prusmyk *Cz.* pass
Pso. (Passo) *It.* pass
Pta. (Ponta) *Port.* point, cape
Pta. (Punta) *It.*, *Span.* point, cape, peak
Pte. (Pointe) *Fr.* point cape
Puerto *Span.* port, pass
Puig *Cat.* peak
Pulau *Mal.* island
Puna *Span.* desert plateau
Punta *It.*, *Span.* point, peak
Puy *Fr.* hill

Qal'at *Ar.* fort
Qanal *Ar.* canal
Qasr *Ar.* fort
Qiryat *Heb.* town
Qolleh *Pers.* mountain

Ramla *Ar.* sand
Rann *Hin.* swampy region
Rao *I.-C.* river
Ras *Amh.* cape, headland
Râs *Ar.* cape, headland
Recife(s) *Port.* reef(s)
Reka *Bulg.*, *Cz.*, *Russ.* river
Repede *Rum.* rapids
Represa *Port.* dam
Reshteh *Pers.* mountain range
–Rettō *Jap.* group of islands
Ría *Span.* estuary, bay
Ribeirão *Port.* river
Rijeka *Ser.-Cr.* river
Rio *Port.* river
Río *Span.* river
Riv. (Riviera) *It.* coastal plain, coast, river
Riviera *It.* coast
Rivière *Fr.* river
Roche *Fr.* rock
Rog *Russ.* horn
–rück *Ger.* ridge
Rüd *Pers.* stream, river
Rudohorie *Cz.* ore mountains
Rzeka *Pol.* river

S. (Sungei) *Mal.* river
Sa. (Serra) *It.*, *Port.* range of hills
Sa. (Sierra) *Span.* range of hills
–saari *Fin.* island
Sadd *Ar.* dam
Sagar, –ara *Hin.*, *Urdu* lake
Saharâ *Ar.* desert
Sahrâ *Ar.* desert
Sa'id *Ar.* highland
Sakar *Fin.* mountain
–Saki *Jap.* point
Sal. (Salar) *Span.* salt pan
Salina(s) *Span.* salt (flat)s
–salmi *Fin.* strait, sound, lake, channel
Saltsjöbad *Swed.* resort
Sammyaku *Jap.* mountain, range
Samut *Thai.* gulf
–San *Jap.* hill, mountain
Sap. (Sapadno) *Russ.* west
Sasso *It.* mountain
Se, Sé *I.-C.* river
Sebkha, –kra *Ar.* salt flats
See *Ger.* lake
–see *Ger.* sea
–şehir *Turk.* town
Selat *Mal.* strait
–selkä *Fin.* bay, lake, sound, ridge, hills

Selva *Span.* forest, wood
Seno *Span.* bay, sound
Serîr *Ar.* desert of small stones
Serra *It.*, *Port.* range of hills
Serranía *Span.* mountains
Sev. (Severo) *Russ.* north
–shahr *Pers.* city, town
Shan *Chin.* hills, mountains, pass
Shan-mo *Chin.* mountain range
Shatt *Ar.* river
–Shima *Jap.* island
Shimâli *Ar.* northern
–Shotō *Jap.* group of islands
Shuik'u *Chin.* reservoir
Sierra *Span.* hill, range
Sjö, sjön *Swed.* lake, bay, sea
Sjøen *Dan.* sea
Skär *Swed.* island, rock, cape
Skog *Nor.* forest
–skog, –skogen *Swed.* wood(s)
–skov *Dan.* forest
Slieve *Gae.* range of hills
–sø *Dan.*, *Nor.* lake
Sør *Nor.* south, southern
Solonchak *Russ.* salt lake, marsh
Souk *Ar.* market
Spitze *Ger.* peak, mountain
–spruit *Afr.* stream
–stad *Afr.*, *Nor.*, *Swed.* town
–stadt *Ger.* town
Staður *Ice.* town
Stausee *Ger.* reservoir
Stenón *Gr.* strait, pass
Step *Russ.* plain
Str. (Stretto) *It.* strait
–strand *Dan.*, *Nor.* beach
–strede *Nor.* straits
Strelka *Russ.* spit
–strete *Nor.* straits
Stretto *It.* strait
Stroedet *Dan.* strait
–ström, –strömmen *Swed.* stream(s)
–stroom *Afr.* large river
Suidō *Jap.* strait, channel
Sûn *Bur.* cape
Sund *Dan.* sound
–sund, –sundet *Swed.* sound, estuary, inlet
–sund(et) *Nor.* sound
Sungai, –ei *Mal.* river
Sungei *Mal.* river
Sur *Span.* south, southern
Sveti *Bulg.* pass
Syd *Dan.*, *Swed.* south

Tai –tai *Chin.* tower
Tal *Mong.* plain, steppe
–tal *Ger.* valley
Tall *Ar.* hills, hummocks
Tandjung *Mal.* cape, headland
Tao *Chin.* island
Tassili *Ar.* rocky plateau
Tau *Russ.* mountain, range
Taung *Bur.* mountain, south
Taunggya *Bur.* pass
Tělok *I.-C.*, *Mal.* bay, bight
Teluk *Mal.* bay, gulf
Tg. (Tandjung) *Mal.* cape, headland
–thal *Ger.* valley
Thok *Tib.* town
Tierra *Span.* land, country
–tind *Nor.* peak
Tjärn, –en, –et *Swed.* lake
Tong *Nor.* village, town
Tong *Bur.*, *Thai.* mountain range
Tonle *I.-C.* large river, lake
–träsk *Swed.* bog, swamp
Tsangpo *Tib.* large river
Tso *Tib.* lake

Tsu *Jap.* entrance, bay
Tulur *Ar.* hill
T'un *Chin.* village
Tung *Chin.* east
Tunnel *Fr.* tunnel
Tunturi *Fin.* hill(s), mountain(s), ridge

Uad *Ar.* dry watercourse, wadi
Udjung *Mal.* cape
Udd, udde, udden *Swed.* point, peninsula
Uebi *Somal.* river
Us *Mong.* water
Ust *Russ.* river mouth
Uul *Mong.*, *Russ.* mountain, range

V. (Volcán) *Span.* volcano
–vaara *Fin.* hill, mountain, ridge, peak
–våg *Nor.* bay
Val *Fr.*, *It.* valley
Valea *Rum.* valley
–vall, –vallen *Swed.* mountain
Valle *Span.* valley
Vallée *Fr.* valley
Valli *It.* lake, lagoon
Väst *Swed.* west
–vatn *Ice.*, *Nor.* lake
Vatten *Swed.* lake
Vdkhr. (Vodokhranilishche) *Russ.* reservoir
–ved, –veden *Swed.* range, hills
Veld, –veld *Afr.* field
Velik/a, –e, –i, –o *Ser.Cr.* large
–vesi *Fin.* water, lake, bay sound, strait
Vest *Dan.*, *Nor.* west
Vf. (vîrful) *Rum.* peak, mountain
–vidda *Nor.* plateau
Vig *Dan.* bay, inlet, cove, lagoon, lake, bight
–vik, –vika, –viken *Nor.*, *Swed.* bay, cove, gulf, inlet, lake
Vila *Port.* small town
Villa *Span.* town
Ville *Fr.* town
Vinh *I.-C.* bay
Virful *Rum.* peak, mountain
–vlei *Afr.* pond, pool
Vodokhranilishche *Russ.* reservoir
Vol. (Volcán) *Span.* volcano, mountain
Vorota *Russ.* gate
Vostochnyy *Russ.* eastern
Vozyshennost *Russ.* heights, uplands
Vrata *Bulg.* gate, pass
Vrchovina *Cz.* mountainous country
Vrchy *Cz.* mountain range
Vung *I.-C.* gulf
–vuori *Fin.* mountain, hill

W. (Wâdi) *Ar.* dry watercourse
Wâhât *Ar.* oasis
Wald *Ger.* wood, forest
Wan *Chin.*, *Jap.* bay
Webi *Amh.* river
Woestyn *Afr.* desert

Yam *Heb.* sea
Yang *Chin.* ocean
Yazovir *Bulg.* reservoir
Yoma *Bur.* mountain range
–yüan *Chin.* spring

Zaki *Jap.* peninsula
Zalew *Pol.* lagoon, swamp
Zaliv *Russ.* bay
Zan *Jap.* mountain
Zatoka *Pol.* bay
Zee *Dut.* sea
Zemlya *Russ.* land, island(s)

Chart of the Stars

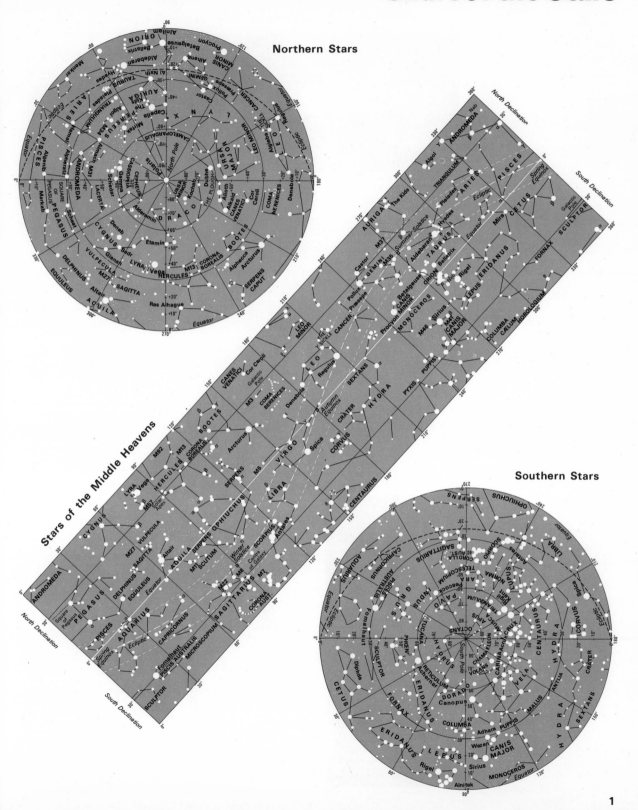

Northern Stars

Stars of the Middle Heavens

Southern Stars

The Solar System

The Solar System is a minute part of one of the innumerable galaxies that make up the universe. Our Galaxy is represented in the drawing to the right and The Solar System (S) lies near the plane of spiral-shaped galaxy, but 27 000 light-years from the centre. The System consists of the Sun at the centre with planets, moons, asteroids, comets, meteors, meteorites, dust and gases revolving around it. It is calculated to be at least 4 700 million years old.

The Solar System can be considered in two parts: the Inner Region planets- Mercury, Venus, Earth and Mars - all small and solid; the Outer Region planets - Jupiter, Saturn, Uranus and Neptune - all gigantic in size, and on the edge of the system the smaller Pluto.

Our galaxy

Inner region planets

Outer region planets

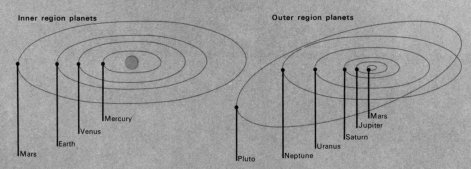

Mars
Earth
Venus
Mercury

Pluto
Neptune
Uranus
Saturn
Jupiter
Mars

The planets

All planets revolve round the Sun in the same direction, and mostly in the same plane. Their orbits are shown (left) - they are not perfectly circular paths.

The table below summarizes the dimensions and movements of the Sun and planets.

The Sun

The Sun has an interior with temperatures believed to be of several million °C brought about by continuous thermo-nuclear fusions of hydrogen into helium. This immense energy is transferred by radiation into surrounding layers of gas the outer surface of which is called the chromosphere. From this "surface" with a temperature of many thousands °C "flames" (solar prominences) leap out into the diffuse corona which can best be seen at times of total eclipse (see photo right). The bright surface of the Sun, the photosphere, is calculated to have a temperature of about 6 000 °C, and when viewed through a telescope has a mottled appearance, the darker patches being called sunspots - the sites of large disturbances of the surface.

Total eclipse of the sun

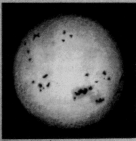

The sun's surface

	Equatorial diameter in km	Mass (earth=1)	Mean distance from sun in millions km	Radii of orbit (earth=1)	Orbital inclination	Sidereal period	Period of rotation on axis	Number of satellites
Sun	1 392 000	333 434	–	–	–	–	25 days 9hrs	–
Mercury	4 840	0·04	58	0·39	7°	88d	59 days	0
Venus	12 300	0·83	108	0·72	3°24'	225d	244 days	0
Earth	12 756	1·00	150	1·00	–	1 year	23hrs 56m	1
Mars	6 790	0·11	228	1·52	1°51'	1y 322d	24hrs 37m	2
Jupiter	143 200	318	778	5·20	1°18'	11y 315d	9hrs 50m	12
Saturn	119 300	95	1 427	9·54	2°29'	29y 167d	10hrs 14m	10
Uranus	47 100	15	2 870	19·19	0°46'	84y 6d	10hrs 49m	5
Neptune	51 000	17	4 497	30·07	1°46'	164y 288d	15hrs 48m	2
Pluto	5 900	0·06	5 950	39·46	17°06'	247y 255d	6d 9hrs 17m	–

The Sun's diameter is 109 times greater than that of the Earth.

58	Mercury
108	Venus
150	Earth
228	Mars
778	Jupiter
1427	Saturn
2870	Uranus
4497	Neptune
5950	Pluto

Mercury is the smallest planet and nearest to the Sun. It is composed mostly of metals and probably has an atmosphere of heavy inert gases.

Venus is similar in size to the Earth, and probably in composition. It is, however, much hotter and has a dense atmosphere of carbon dioxide which obscures our view of its surface.

Earth is the largest of the inner planets. It has a dense iron-nickel core surrounded by layers of silicate rock. The surface is approximately ⅖ land and ⅗ water, and the lower atmosphere consists of a mixture of nitrogen, oxygen and other gases supplemented by water vapour. With this atmosphere and surface temperatures usually between −50°C and +40°C, life is possible.

Mars, smaller than the Earth, has a noticeably red appearance. Recent photographs sent back by satellite show clearly the cratered surface and the ice areas at the poles made from condensed carbon dioxide.

The Asteroids orbit the Sun mainly between Mars and Jupiter. They consist of thousands of bodies of varying sizes with diameters ranging from yards to hundreds of miles.

Jupiter is the largest planet of the Solar System. It shines brightly in the sky (magnitude −2·5), and is notable for its cloud belts and the Great Red Spot.

Saturn, the second largest planet consists of hydrogen, helium and other gases. Its density is less than that of water. It is unique in appearance because of its equatorial rings believed to be made of ice-covered particles.

Uranus was discovered in 1781 by Herschel. It is extremely remote yet faintly visible to the naked eye. Methane in its atmosphere gives it a slightly green appearance.

Neptune, yet more remote than Uranus and larger. It is composed of gases and has a bluish green appearance when seen in a telescope. As with Uranus, little detail can be observed on its surface.

Pluto No details are known of its composition or surface. The existence of this planet was firstly surmised in a computed hypothesis, which was tested by repeated searches by large telescopes until in 1930 the planet was found.

The Earth

Seasons, Equinoxes and Solstices

The Earth revolves around the Sun once a year and rotates daily on its axis, which is inclined at 66½° to the orbital plane and always points into space in the same direction. At midsummer (N.) the North Pole tilts towards the Sun, six months later it points away and half way between the axis is at right angles to the direction of the Sun (right).

Earth data

Maximum distance from the Sun (Aphelion) 152 007 016 km
Minimum distance from the Sun (Perihelion) 147 000 830 km
Obliquity of the ecliptic 23° 27′ 08″
Length of year - tropical (equinox to equinox) 365.24 days
Length of year - sidereal (fixed star to fixed star) 365.26 days
Length of day - mean solar day 24h 03m 56s
Length of day - mean sidereal day 23h 56m 04s

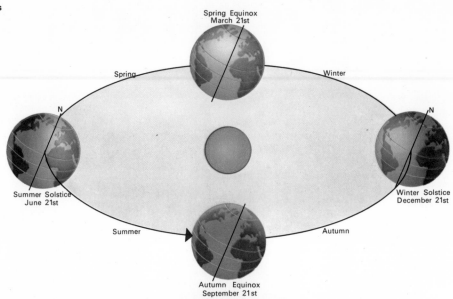

Length of day and night

At the summer solstice in the northern hemisphere, the Arctic has total daylight and the Antarctic total darkness. The opposite occurs at the winter solstice. At the equator, the length of day and night are almost equal all the year, at 30° the length of day varies from about 14 hours to 10 hours and at 50° from about 16 hours to 8 hours.

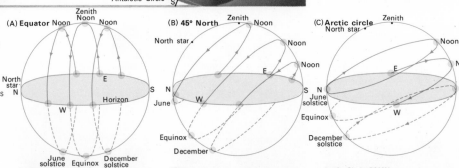

Apparent path of the Sun

The diagrams (right) illustrate the apparent path of the Sun at A the equator, B in mid latitudes say 45°N, C at the Arctic Circle 66½° and D at the North Pole where there is six months continuous daylight and six months continuous night

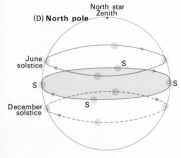

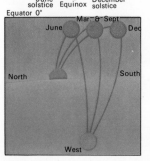

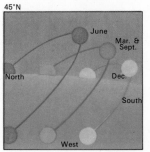

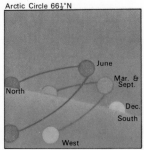

The Moon

The Moon rotates slowly making one complete turn on its axis in just over 27 days. This is the same as its period of revolution around the Earth and thus it always presents the same hemisphere ('face') to us. Surveys and photographs from space-craft have now added greatly to our knowledge of the Moon, and, for the first time, views of the hidden hemisphere.

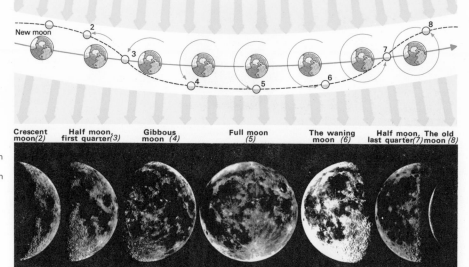

New moon 2 3 4 5 6 7 8

Phases of the Moon

The interval between one full Moon and the next is approximately $29\frac{1}{2}$ days - thus there is one new Moon and one full Moon every month. The diagrams and photographs (right) show how the apparent changes in shape of the Moon from new to full arise from its changing position in relation to the Earth and both to the fixed direction of the Sun's rays.

Crescent moon (2) | Half moon, first quarter (3) | Gibbous moon (4) | Full moon (5) | The waning moon (6) | Half moon, last quarter (7) | The old moon (8)

Moon data
Distance from Earth 356 410 km
to 406 685 km
Mean diameter 3 473 km
Mass approx. $\frac{1}{81}$ of that of Earth
Surface gravity $\frac{1}{6}$ of that of Earth
Atmosphere - none, hence no clouds, no weather, no sound.
Diurnal range of temperature at the Equator +200°C

Landings on the Moon
Left are shown the landing sites of the U.S. Apollo programme.
Apollo 11 Sea of Tranquility (1°N 23°E) 1969
Apollo 12 Ocean of Storms (3°S 24°W) 1969
Apollo 14 Fra Mauro (4°S 17°W) 1971
Apollo 15 Hadley Rill (25°N 4°E) 1971
Apollo 16 Descartes (9°S 15°E) 1972
Apollo 17 Sea of Serenity (20°N 31°E) 1972

Eclipses of Sun and Moon
When the Moon passes between Sun and Earth it causes a partial eclipse of the Sun (right 1) if the Earth passes through the Moon's outer shadow (P), or a total eclipse (right 2), if the inner cone shadow crosses the Earth's surface.
In a lunar eclipse, the Earth's shadow crosses the Moon, and gives either total or partial eclipses.

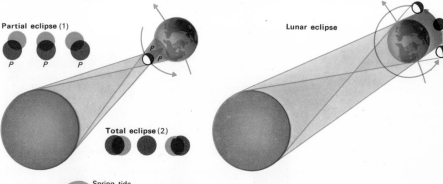

Partial eclipse (1)

P P P

Total eclipse (2)

Lunar eclipse

Tides
Ocean water moves around the Earth under the gravitational pull of the Moon, and, less strongly, that of the Sun. When solar and lunar forces pull together - near new and full Moon - high spring tides result. When solar and lunar forces are not combined - near Moon's first and third quarters - low neap tides occur.

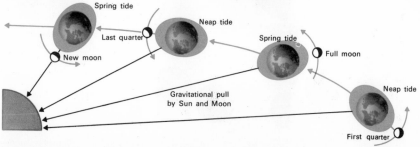

Spring tide
Neap tide
Last quarter
New moon
Spring tide
Full moon
Neap tide
Gravitational pull by Sun and Moon
First quarter

Time

Time measurement
The basic unit of time measurement is the day, one rotation of the earth on its axis. The subdivision of the day into hours and minutes is arbitrary and simply for our convenience. Our present calendar is based on the solar year of 365¼ days, the time taken for the earth to orbit the sun. A month was anciently based on the interval from new moon to new moon, approximately 29½ days - and early calendars were entirely lunar.

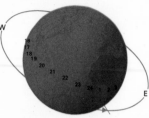
Rotation of the Earth

Greenwich Observatory

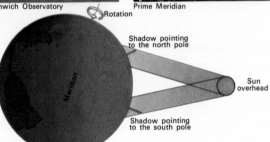
Prime Meridian

Rotation

Meridian

Shadow pointing to the north pole

Sun overhead

Shadow pointing to the south pole

The International Date Line
When it is 12 noon at the Greenwich meridian, 180° east it is midnight of the same day while 180° west the day is only just beginning. To overcome this the International Date Line was established, approximately following the 180° meridian. Thus, for example, if one travelled eastwards from Japan (140° East) to Samoa (170° West) one would pass from Sunday night into Sunday morning.

Time zones
The world is divided into 24 time zones, each centred on meridians at 15° intervals which is the longitudinal distance the sun appears to travel every hour. The meridian running through Greenwich passes through the middle of the first zone. Successive zones to the east of Greenwich zone are ahead of Greenwich time by one hour for every 15° of longitude, while zones to the west are behind by one hour.

Night and day
As the earth rotates from west to east the sun appears to rise in the east and set in the west: when the sun is setting in Shanghai on the directly opposite side of the earth New York is just emerging into sunlight. Noon, when the sun is directly overhead, is coincident at all places on the same meridian with shadows pointing directly towards the poles.

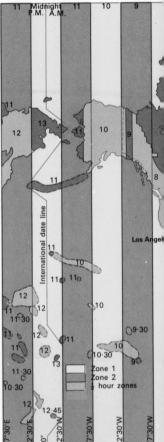

Solar time
The time taken for the earth to complete one rotation about its own axis is constant and defines a day but the speed of the earth along its orbit around the sun is inconstant. The length of day, or 'apparent solar day', as defined by the apparent successive transits of the sun is irregular because the earth must complete more than one rotation before the sun returns to the same meridian.

approx. 1°
approx. 10''

Earth's orbit

Sidereal time
The constant sidereal day is defined as the interval between two successive apparent transits of a star, or the first point of Aries, across the same meridian. If the sun is at the equinox and overhead at a meridian on one day, then the next day the sun will be to the east by approximately 1°; thus the sun will not cross the meridian until about 4 minutes after the sidereal noon.

Towards Aries

Earth's orbit

Astronomical clock, Delhi

Sundials
The earliest record of sundials dates back to 741 BC but they undoubtedly existed as early as 2000 BC although probably only as an upright stick or obelisk. A sundial marks the progress of the sun across the sky by casting the shadow of a central style or gnomon on the base. The base, generally made of stone, is delineated to represent the hours between sunrise and sunset.

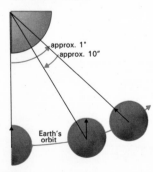

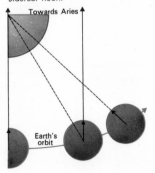
Kendall's chronometer

Chronometers
With the increase of sea traffic in the 18th century and the need for accurate navigation clockmakers were faced with an intriguing problem. Harrison, an English carpenter, won a British award for designing a clock which was accurate at sea to one tenth of a second per day. He compensated for the effect of temperature changes by incorporating bi-metallic strips connected to thin wires and circular balance wheels.

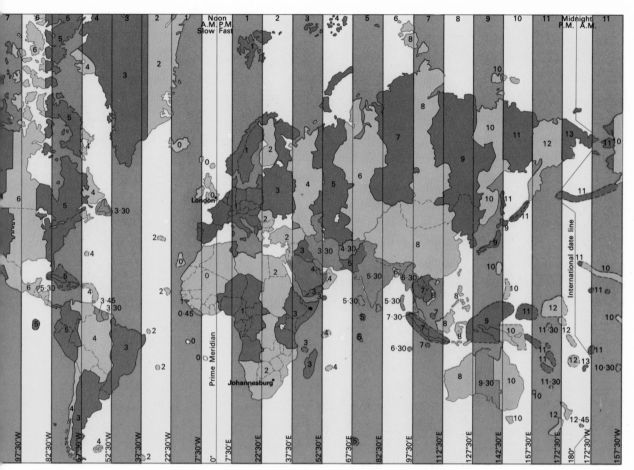

World time zone map showing hour differences from GMT. Column labels along top: Noon A.M. P.M. Slow Fast, Midnight P.M. A.M. Longitude markers along bottom: 97°30'W, 82°30'W, 67°30'W, 52°30'W, 37°30'W, 22°30'W, 7°30'W, 0°, 7°30'E, 22°30'E, 37°30'E, 52°30'E, 67°30'E, 82°30'E, 97°30'E, 112°30'E, 127°30'E, 142°30'E, 157°30'E, 172°30'E, 180°, 172°30'W, 157°30'W. Prime Meridian labelled. International date line labelled. Cities marked: London, Johannesburg.

Progress of the accuracy of timekeepers

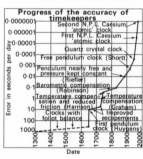

Graph — Error in seconds per day (0·000001 to 1000) versus Date (1300 to 2000), showing:
- Second N.P.L. Caesium 'atomic' clock
- First N.P.L. Caesium 'atomic' clock
- Quartz crystal clock
- Free pendulum clock (Shortt)
- Pendulum nearly free and pressure kept constant (Riefler)
- Barometric compensation (Robinson)
- Temperature compensation and reduced friction (Harrison)
- Temperature compensation (Graham)
- Improved escapements
- Clocks with foliot balance
- First pendulum clock (Huygens)

Vibration of quartz ring

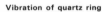

Chronographs

The invention of the chronograph by Charles Wheatstone in 1842 made it possible to record intervals of time to an accuracy of one sixtieth of a second. The simplest form of chronograph is the stopwatch. This was developed to a revolving drum and stylus and later electrical signals. A recent development is the cathode ray tube capable of recording to less than one ten-thousandth of a second.

Quartz crystal clocks

The quartz crystal clock, designed originally in America in 1929, can measure small units of time and radio frequencies. The connection between quartz clocks and the natural vibrations of atoms and molecules mean that the unchanging frequencies emitted by atoms can be used to control the oscillator which controls the quartz clock. A more recent version of the atomic clock is accurate to one second in 300 years.

Time difference when travelling by air

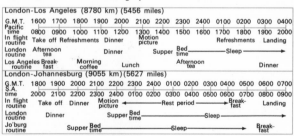

London-Los Angeles (8780 km) (5456 miles)

G.M.T.	1600	1700	1800	1900	2000	2100	2200	2300	2400	0100	0200	0300	0400
Pacific time	0800	0900	1000	1100	1200	1300	1400	1500	1600	1700	1800	1900	2000
In flight routine	Take off	Refreshments	Dinner		Motion picture					Refreshments		Landing	
London routine	Afternoon tea		Dinner			Supper		Bed time	Sleep				
Los Angeles routine	Break-fast		Morning coffee		Lunch			Afternoon tea			Dinner		

London-Johannesburg (9055 km) (5627 miles)

G.M.T.	1800	1900	2000	2100	2200	2300	2400	0100	0200	0300	0400	0500	0600	0700
S.A. time	2000	2100	2200	2300	2400	0100	0200	0300	0400	0500	0600	0700	0800	0900
In flight routine	Take off	Dinner	Motion picture			Rest period						Break-fast		Landing
London routine	Dinner			Supper	Bed time		Sleep							
Jo'burg routine			Supper	Bed time			Sleep						Break-fast	

International date line

Gain a day

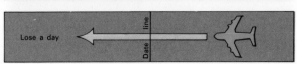

Lose a day

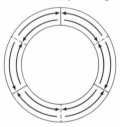

The Atmosphere and Clouds

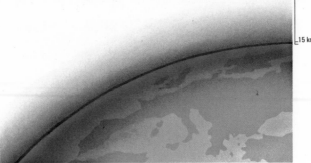

Earth's thin coating *(right)*
The atmosphere is a blanket of protective gases around the earth providing insulation against otherwise extreme alternations in temperature. The gravitational pull increases the density nearer the earth's surface so that 5/6ths of the atmospheric mass is in the first 15 kms. It is a very thin layer in comparison with the earth's diameter of 12 680 kms., like the cellulose coating on a globe.

Exosphere *(1)*
The exosphere merges with the interplanetary medium and although there is no definite boundary with the ionosphere it starts at a height of about 600 kms. The rarified air mainly consists of a small amount of atomic oxygen up to 600 kms. and equal proportions of hydrogen and helium with hydrogen predominating above 2 400 kms.

Ionosphere *(2)*
Air particles of the ionosphere are electrically charged by the sun's radiation and congregate in four main layers, D, E, F1 and F2, which can reflect radio waves. Aurorae, caused by charged particles deflected by the earth's magnetic field towards the poles, occur between 65 and 965 kms. above the earth. It is mainly in the lower ionosphere that meteors from outer space burn up as they meet increased air resistance.

Stratosphere *(3)*
A thin layer of ozone contained within the stratosphere absorbs ultra-violet light and in the process gives off heat. The temperature ranges from about -55°C at the tropopause to about -60°C in the upper part, known as the mesosphere, with a rise to about 2°C just above the ozone layer. This portion of the atmosphere is separated from the lower layer by the tropopause.

Troposphere *(4)*
The earth's weather conditions are limited to this layer which is relatively thin, extending upwards to about 8 kms. at the poles and 15 kms. at the equator. It contains about 85% of the total atmospheric mass and almost all the water vapour. Air temperature falls steadily with increased height at about 1°C for every 100 metres above sea level.

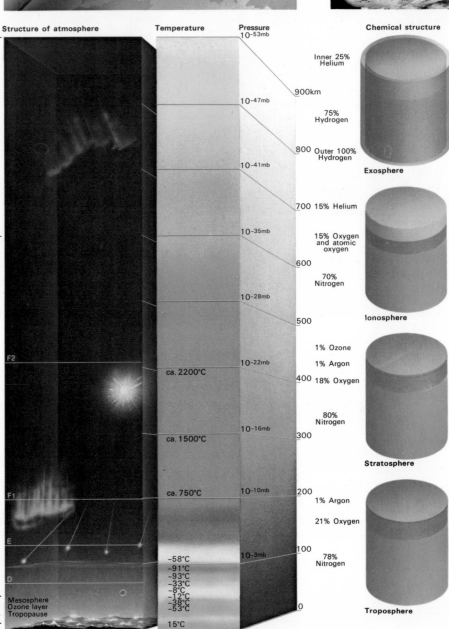

Structure of atmosphere

Temperature

Pressure

Chemical structure

600 km

15 km

1

2

F2

F1

E

D

3
4

Mesosphere
Ozone layer
Tropopause

ca. 2200°C

ca. 1500°C

ca. 750°C

-58°C
-91°C
-93°C
-33°C
-8°C
-12°C
-38°C
-53°C

15°C

10^{-53}mb

10^{-47}mb

10^{-41}mb

10^{-35}mb

10^{-28}mb

10^{-22}mb

10^{-16}mb

10^{-10}mb

10^{-3}mb

10^3mb

900km

800

700

600

500

400

300

200

100

0

Inner 25% Helium

75% Hydrogen

Outer 100% Hydrogen

Exosphere

15% Helium

15% Oxygen and atomic oxygen

70% Nitrogen

Ionosphere

1% Ozone

1% Argon

18% Oxygen

80% Nitrogen

Stratosphere

1% Argon

21% Oxygen

78% Nitrogen

Troposphere

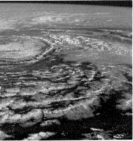

Pacific Ocean
Cloud patterns over the Pacific show the paths of prevailing winds.

Circulation of the air

Circulation of the air
Owing to high temperatures in equatorial regions the air near the ground is heated, expands and rises producing a low pressure belt. It cools, causing rain, spreads out then sinks again about latitudes 30° north and south forming high pressure belts.

High and low pressure belts are areas of comparative calm but between them, blowing from high to low pressure, are the prevailing winds. These are deflected to the right in the northern hemisphere and to the left in the southern hemisphere (Corolis effect). The circulations appear in three distinct belts with a seasonal movement north and south following the overhead sun.

Cloud types
Clouds form when damp air is cooled, usually by rising. This may happen in three ways: when a wind rises to cross hills or mountains; when a mass of air rises over, or is pushed up by another mass of denser air; when local heating of the ground causes convection currents.

Cirrus *(1)* are detached clouds composed of microscopic ice crystals which gleam white in the sun resembling hair or feathers. They are found at heights of 6 000 to 12 000 metres.

Cirrostratus *(2)* are a whitish veil of cloud made up of ice crystals through which the sun can be seen often producing a halo of bright light.

Cirrocumulus *(3)* is another high altitude cloud formed by turbulence between layers moving in different directions.

Altostratus *(4)* is a grey or bluish striated, fibrous or uniform sheet of cloud producing light drizzle.

Altocumulus *(5)* is a thicker and fluffier version of cirro cumulus, it is a white and grey patchy sheet of cloud.

Nimbostratus *(6)* is a dark grey layer of cloud obscuring the sun and causing almost continuous rain or snow.

Cumulus *(7)* are detached heaped up, dense low clouds. The sunlit parts are brilliant white while the base is relatively dark and flat.

Stratus *(8)* forms dull overcast skies associated with depressions and occurs at low altitudes up to 1 500 metres.

Cumulonimbus *(9)* are heavy and dense clouds associated with storms and rain. They have flat bases and a fluffy outline extending up to great altitudes.

High clouds
Middle clouds
Low clouds

Thousands of metres

1 Cirrus

2 Cirrostratus

3 Cirrocumulus

4 Altostratus

5 Altocumulus

6 Nimbostratus

7 Cumulus

8 Stratus

9 Cumulonimbus

Climate and Weather

All weather occurs over the earth's surface in the lowest level of the atmosphere, the troposphere. Weather has been defined as the condition of the atmosphere at any place at a specific time with respect to the various elements: temperature, sunshine, pressure, winds, clouds, fog, precipitation. Climate, on the other hand, is the average of weather elements over previous months and years.

Climate graphs *right*
Each graph typifies the kind of climatic conditions one would experience in the region to which it is related by colour to the map. The scale refers to degrees Celsius for temperature and millimetres for rainfall, shown by bars. The graphs show average observations based over long periods of time, the study of which also compares the prime factors for vegetation differences.

Development of a depression *below*
In an equilibrium front between cold and warm air masses (i) a wave disturbance develops as cold air undercuts the warm air (ii). This deflects the air flow and as the disturbance progresses a definite cyclonic circulation with warm and cold fronts is created (iii). The cold front moves more rapidly than the warm front eventually overtaking it, and occlusion occurs as the warm air is pinched out (iv).

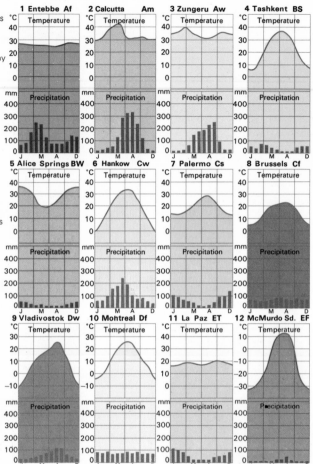

1 Entebbe Af
2 Calcutta Am
3 Zungeru Aw
4 Tashkent BS
5 Alice Springs BW
6 Hankow Cw
7 Palermo Cs
8 Brussels Cf
9 Vladivostok Dw
10 Montreal Df
11 La Paz ET
12 McMurdo Sd. EF

Af Equatorial forest
Am Monsoon forest
Aw Savanna

Tropical climates

| Af | Am | Aw |

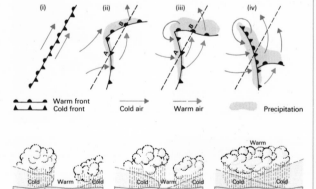

Warm front
Cold front
Cold air
Warm air
Precipitation

Frontal cloud

Precipitation

The upper diagrams show in plan view stages in the development of a depression.
The cross sections below correspond to stages (ii) to (iv).

Kinds of precipitation
Rain The condensation of water vapour on microscopic particles of dust, sulphur, soot or ice in the atmosphere forms water particles. These combine until they are heavy enough to fall as rain.

Frost Hoar, the most common type of frost, is precipitated instead of dew when water vapour changes directly into ice crystals on the surface of ground objects which have cooled below freezing point.

Hail Water particles, carried to a great height, freeze into ice particles which fall and become coated with fresh moisture. They are swept up again and refrozen. This may happen several times before falling as hail-stones.

Snow is the precipitation of ice in the form of flakes, or clusters, of basically hexagonal ice crystals. They are formed by the condensation of water vapour directly into ice.

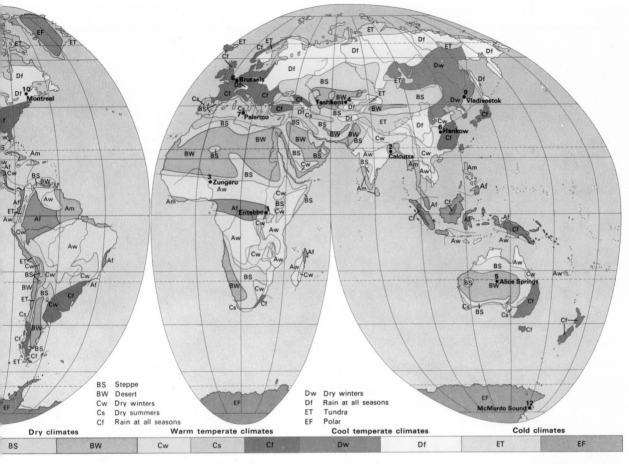

BS Steppe
BW Desert
Cw Dry winters
Cs Dry summers
Cf Rain at all seasons

Dw Dry winters
Df Rain at all seasons
ET Tundra
EF Polar

Dry climates			Warm temperate climates			Cool temperate climates		Cold climates	
BS	BW	Cw	Cs	Cf	Dw	Df	ET	EF

Tropical storm tracks *below*
A tropical cyclone, or storm, is designated as having winds of gale force (60 kph) but less than hurricane force (120 kph). It is a homogenous air mass with upward spiralling air currents around a windless centre, or eye. An average of 65 tropical storms occur each year, over 50% of which reach hurricane force. They originate mainly during the summer over tropical oceans.

Extremes of climate & weather *right*
Tropical high temperatures and polar low temperatures combined with wind systems, altitude and unequal rainfall distribution result in the extremes of tropical rain forests, inland deserts and frozen polar wastes. Fluctuations in the limits of these extreme zones and extremes of weather result in occasional catastrophic heat-waves and drought, floods and storms, frost and snow.

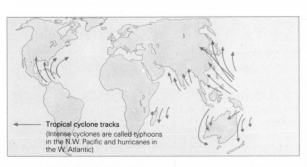

Tropical cyclone tracks
(Intense cyclones are called typhoons in the N.W. Pacific and hurricanes in the W. Atlantic)

Hurricane devastation

Hot desert

Tornado

Arctic dwellings

The Earth from Space

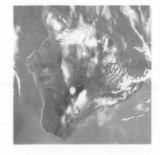

Mount Etna, Sicily *left*
Etna is at the top of the photograph, the Plain of Catania in the centre and the Mediterranean to the right. This is an infra-red photograph; vegetation shows as red, water as blue/black and urban areas as grey. The recent lava flows, as yet with no vegetation, show up as blue/black unlike the cultivated slopes which are red and red/pink.

Hawaii, Pacific Ocean *above*
This is a photograph of Hawaii, the largest of the Hawaiian Islands in the Central Pacific. North is at the top of the photograph. The snowcapped craters of the volcanoes Mauna Kea (dormant) in the north centre and Mauna Loa (active) in the south centre of the photograph can be seen. The chief town, Hilo, is on the north east coast.

River Brahmaputra, India *left*
A view looking westwards down the Brahmaputra with the Himalayas on the right and the Khasi Hills of Assam to the left.

Szechwan, China *right*
The River Tachin in the mountainous region of Szechwan, Central China. The lightish blue area in the river valley in the north east of the photograph is a village and its related cultivation.

New York, U.S.A. *left*
This infra-red photograph shows the western end of Long Island and the entrance to the Hudson River. Vegetation appears as red, water as blue/black and the metropolitan areas of New York, through the cloud cover, as grey.

The Great Barrier Reef, Australia *right*
The Great Barrier Reef and the Queensland coast from Cape Melville to Cape Flattery. The smoke from a number of forest fires can be seen in the centre of the photograph.

Eastern Himalayas, Asia
above left
A view from Apollo IX looking
north-westwards over the
snowcapped, sunlit mountain
peaks and the head waters of
the Mekong, Salween,
Irrawaddy and, in the distance,
with its distinctive loop, the
Brahmaputra.

Atacama Desert, Chile
above right
This view looking eastwards
from the Pacific over the
Mejillones peninsula with the
city of Antofagasta in the
southern bay of that peninsula.
Inland the desert and salt-pans
of Atacama, and beyond, the
Andes.

The Alps, Europe *right*
This vertical photograph shows
the snow-covered mountains
and glaciers of the Alps along
the Swiss-Italian-French
border. Mont Blanc and the
Matterhorn are shown and, in
the north, the Valley of the
Rhône is seen making its sharp
right-hand bend near Martigny.
In the south the head waters
of the Dora Baltea flow
towards the Po and, in the
north-west, the Lac d'Annecy
can be seen.

The Evolution of the Continents

The origin of the earth is still open to much conjecture although the most widely accepted theory is that it was formed from a solar cloud consisting mainly of hydrogen. Under gravitation the cloud condensed and shrank to form our planets orbiting around the sun. Gravitation forced the lighter elements to the surface of the earth where they cooled to form a crust while the inner material remained hot and molten. Earth's first rocks formed over 3500 million years ago but since then the surface has been constantly altered.

Until comparatively recently the view that the primary units of the earth had remained essentially fixed throughout geological time was regarded as common sense, although the concept of moving continents has been traced back to references in the Bible of a break up of the land after Noah's floods. The continental drift theory was first developed by Antonio Snider in 1858 but probably the most important single advocate was Alfred Wegener who, in 1915, published evidence from geology, climatology and biology. His conclusions are very similar to those reached by current research although he was wrong about the speed of break-up.

The measurement of fossil magnetism found in rocks has probably proved the most influential evidence. While originally these drift theories were openly mocked, now they are considered standard doctrine.

The jigsaw
As knowledge of the shape and structure of the earth's surface grew, several of the early geographers noticed the great similarity in shape of the coasts bordering the Atlantic. It was this remarkable similarity which led to the first detailed geological and structural comparisons. Even more accurate fits can be made by placing the edges of the continental shelves in juxtaposition.

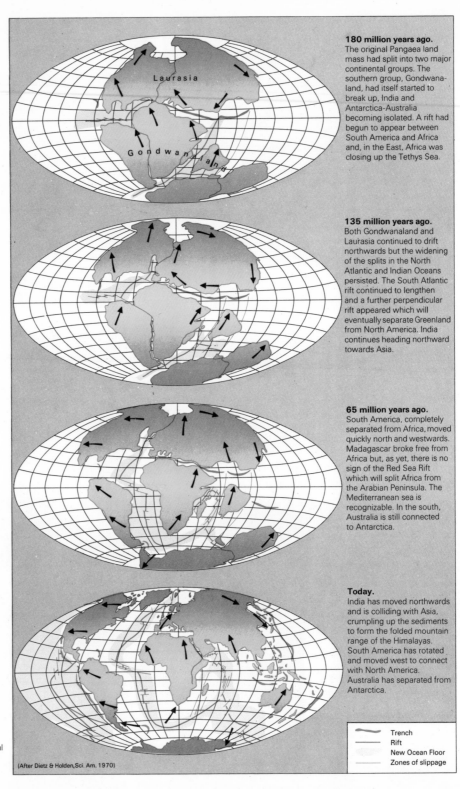

(After Dietz & Holden, Sci. Am. 1970)

180 million years ago.
The original Pangaea land mass had split into two major continental groups. The southern group, Gondwana-land, had itself started to break up, India and Antarctica-Australia becoming isolated. A rift had begun to appear between South America and Africa and, in the East, Africa was closing up the Tethys Sea.

135 million years ago.
Both Gondwanaland and Laurasia continued to drift northwards but the widening of the splits in the North Atlantic and Indian Oceans persisted. The South Atlantic rift continued to lengthen and a further perpendicular rift appeared which will eventually separate Greenland from North America. India continues heading northward towards Asia.

65 million years ago.
South America, completely separated from Africa, moved quickly north and westwards. Madagascar broke free from Africa but, as yet, there is no sign of the Red Sea Rift which will split Africa from the Arabian Peninsula. The Mediterranean sea is recognizable. In the south, Australia is still connected to Antarctica.

Today.
India has moved northwards and is colliding with Asia, crumpling up the sediments to form the folded mountain range of the Himalayas. South America has rotated and moved west to connect with North America. Australia has separated from Antarctica.

	Trench
	Rift
	New Ocean Floor
	Zones of slippage

Plate tectonics

The original debate about continental drift was only a prelude to a more radical idea; plate tectonics. The basic theory is that the earth's crust is made up of a series of rigid plates which float on a soft layer of the mantle and are moved about by convection currents in the earth's interior. These plates converge and diverge along margins marked by earthquakes, volcanoes and other seismic activity. Plates diverge from mid-ocean ridges where molten lava pushes upwards and forces the plates apart at a rate of up to 30mm. a year. Converging plates form either a trench, where the oceanic plate sinks below the lighter continental rock, or mountain ranges where two continents collide. This explains the paradox that while there have always been oceans none of the present oceans contain sediments more than 150 million years old.

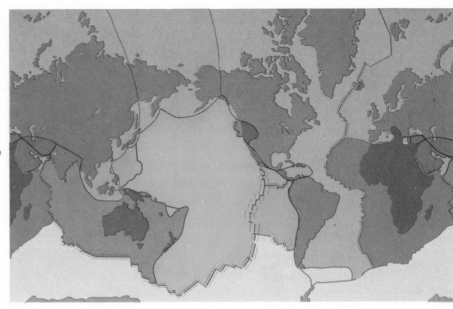

Trench boundary

The present explanation for the comparative youth of the ocean floors is that where an ocean and a continent meet the ocean plate dips under the less dense continental plate at an angle of approximately 45°. All previous crust is then ingested by downward convection currents. In the Japanese trench this occurs at a rate of about 120mm. a year.

Transform fault

The recent identification of the transform, or transverse, fault proved to be one of the crucial preliminaries to the investigation of plate tectonics. They occur when two plates slip alongside each other without parting or approaching to any great extent. They complete the outline of the plates delineated by the ridges and trenches and demonstrate large scale movements of parts of the earth's surface

Ridge boundary

Ocean rises or crests are basically made up from basaltic lavas for although no gap can exist between plates, one plate can ease itself away from another. In that case hot, molten rock instantly rises from below to fill in the incipient rift and forms a ridge. These ridges trace a line almost exactly through the centre of the major oceans.

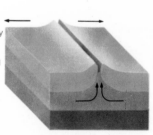

Destruction of ocean plates.

As the ocean plate sinks below the continental plate some of the sediment on its surface is scraped off and piled up on the landward side. This sediment is later incorporated in a folded mountain range which usually appears on the edge of the continent, such as the Andes. Similarly if two continents collide the sediments are squeezed up into new mountains.

Sea floor spreading

Reversals in the earth's magnetic field have occured throughout history. As new rock emerges at the ocean ridges it cools and is magnetised in the direction of the prevailing magnetic field. By mapping the magnetic patterns either side of the ridge a symmetrical stripey pattern of alternating fields can be observed (see inset area in diagram). As the dates of the last few reversals are known the rate of spreading can be calculated.

The Unstable Earth

The earth's surface is slowly but continually being rearranged. Some changes such as erosion and deposition are extremely slow but they upset the balance which causes other more abrupt changes often originating deep within the earth's interior. The constant movements vary in intensity, often with stresses building up to a climax such as a particularly violent volcanic eruption or earthquake.

The crust *(below and right)*
The outer layer or crust of the earth consists of a comparatively low density, brittle material varying from 5 to 50 kilometres deep beneath the continents. Under this is a layer of rock consisting predominately of silica and aluminium; hence it is called 'sial'. Extending under the ocean floors and below the sial is a basaltic layer known as 'sima', consisting mainly of silica and magnesium.

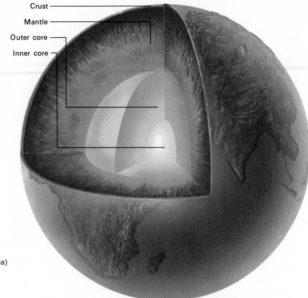

Crust
Mantle
Outer core
Inner core

Continental crust
Ocean crust

Sediment
Granite rock (sial)
Basaltic layer (sima)
Mantle

Volcanoes *(right, below and far right)*
Volcanoes occur when hot liquified rock beneath the crust reaches the surface as lava. An accumulation of ash and cinders around a vent forms a cone. Successive layers of thin lava flows form an acid lava volcano while thick lava flows form a basic lava volcano. A caldera forms when a particularly violent eruption blows off the top of an already existing cone.

The mantle *(above)*
Immediately below the crust, at the mohorovicic discontinuity line, there is a distinct change in density and chemical properties. This is the mantle - made up of iron and magnesium silicates - with temperatures reaching 1600°C. The rigid upper mantle extends down to a depth of about 1000 km., below which is the more viscous lower mantle which is about 1 900 km. thick.

The core *(above)*
The outer core, approximately 2100 km. thick, consists of molten iron and nickel at 2000°C to 5000°C possibly separated from the less dense mantle by an oxidised shell. About 5000 km. below the surface is the liquid transition zone, below which is the solid inner core, a sphere of 2740 km. diameter where rock is three times as dense as in the crust.

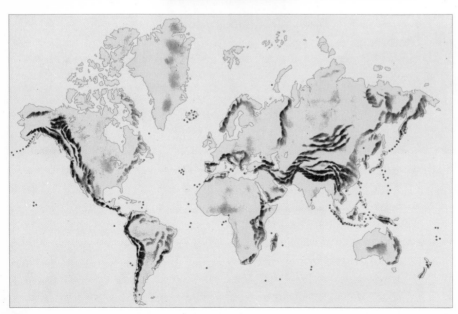

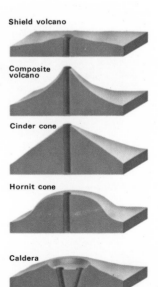

Shield volcano

Composite volcano

Cinder cone

Hornit cone

Caldera

Major earthquakes in the last 100 years	numbers killed
1896 Japan (tsunami)	22 000
1906 San Francisco	destroyed
1906 Chile, Valparaiso	22 000
1908 Italy, Messina	77 000
1920 China, Kansu	180 000
1923 Japan, Tokyo	143 000
1930 Italy, Naples	2 100
1931 Napier	destroyed
1931 Nicaragua, Managua	destroyed
1932 China, Kansu	70 000
1935 India, Quetta	60 000
1939 Chile, Chillan	20 000
1939/40 Turkey, Erzincan	30 000
1948 Japan, Fukui	5 100
1956 N. Afghanistan	2 000
1957 W. Iran	2 500
1960 Morocco, Agadir	12 000
1962 N.W. Iran	10 000
1963 Yugoslavia, Skopje	1 000
1966 U.S.S.R., Tashkent	destroyed
1970 N. Peru	66 800
1972 Nicaragua, Managua	7 000
1974 N. Pakistan	10 000
1975 Turkey, Lice	2 300
1976 China, Tangshan	650 000
1976 Turkey, Van	3 800

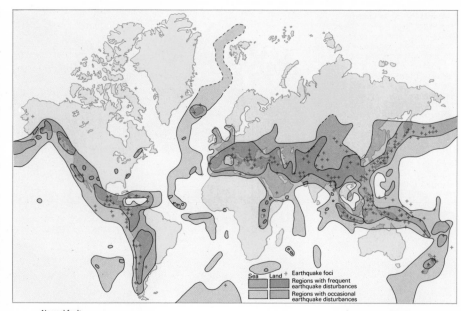

Earthquake foci +
Sea   Land
Regions with frequent earthquake disturbances
Regions with occasional earthquake disturbances

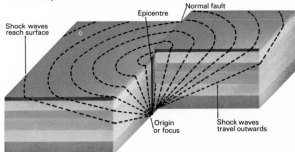

Shock waves reach surface
Epicentre
Normal fault
Origin or focus
Shock waves travel outwards

Earthquakes (right and above)
Earthquakes are a series of rapid vibrations originating from the slipping or faulting of parts of the earth's crust when stresses within build up to breaking point. They usually happen at depths varying from 8-30 km. Severe earthquakes cause extensive damage when they take place in populated areas destroying structures and severing communications. Most loss of life occurs due to secondary causes i.e. falling masonry, fires or tsunami waves.

Alaskan earthquake, 1964

Tsunami waves (left)
A sudden slump in the ocean bed during an earthquake forms a trough in the water surface subsequently followed by a crest and smaller waves. A more marked change of level in the sea bed can form a crest, the start of a Tsunami which travels up to 60 kph with waves up to 60 metres high. Seismographic detectors continuously record earthquake shocks and warn of the Tsunami which may follow it.

Wave travel times in hours

Seismic Waves (right)
The shock waves sent out from the epicentre of an earthquake are of three main kinds each with distinct properties. Primary (P) waves are compressional waves which can be transmitted through both solids and liquids and therefore pass through the earth's liquid core. Secondary (S) waves are shear waves and can only pass through solids. They cannot pass through the core and are reflected at the core-mantle boundary taking a concave course back to the surface. The core also refracts the P waves causing them to alter course, and the net effect of this reflection and refraction is the production of a shadow zone at a certain distance from the epicentre, free from P and S waves. Due to their different properties P waves travel about 1·7 times faster than S waves. The third main kind of wave is a long (L) wave, a slow wave which travels along the earth's surface, its motion being either horizontal or vertical.

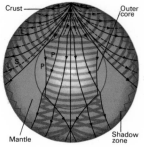

Crust
Outer core
Mantle
Shadow zone

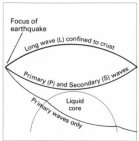

Focus of earthquake
Long wave (L) confined to crust
Primary (P) and Secondary (S) waves
Liquid core
Primary waves only

Horizontal
D M P

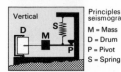

Vertical
D M S P

Principles of seismographs (left)
M = Mass
D = Drum
P = Pivot
S = Spring

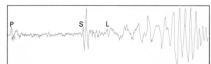

P   S   L

Seismographs
are delicate instruments capable of detecting and recording vibrations due to earthquakes thousands of miles away. P waves cause the first tremors. S the second, and L the main shock.

The Making of Landscape

The making of landscape

The major forces which shape our land would seem to act very slowly in comparison with man's average life span but in geological terms the erosion of rock is in fact very fast. Land goes through a cycle of transformation. It is broken up by earthquakes and other earth movements, temperature changes, water, wind and ice. Rock debris is then transported by water, wind and glaciers and deposited on lowlands and on the sea floor. Here it builds up and by the pressure of its own weight is converted into new rock strata. These in turn can be uplifted either gently as plains or plateaux or more irregularly to form mountains. In either case the new higher land is eroded and the cycle recommences.

A Peneplain

Uplifted peneplain

Rivers

Rivers shape the land by three basic processes: erosion, transportation and deposition. A youthful river flows fast eroding downwards quickly to form a narrow valley (1). As it matures it deposits some debris and erodes laterally to widen the valley (2). In its last stage it meanders across a wide flat flood plain depositing fine particles of alluvium (3).

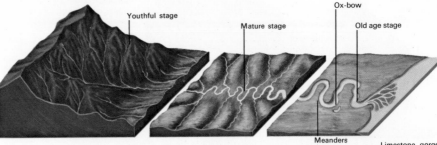

Youthful stage

Mature stage

Ox-bow

Old age stage

Meanders

Underground water

Water enters porous and permeable rocks from the surface moving downward until it reaches a layer of impermeable rock. Joints in underground rock, such as limestone, are eroded to form underground caves and caverns. When the roof of a cave collapses a gorge is formed. Surface entrances to joints are often widened to form vertical openings called swallow holes.

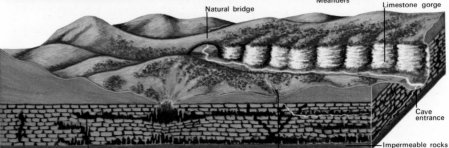

Natural bridge

Limestone gorge

Cave entrance

Impermeable rocks

Cave with stalactites and stalagmites

River disappears down swallow hole

Wind

Wind action is particularly powerful in arid and semi-arid regions where rock waste produced by weathering is used as an abrasive tool by the wind. The rate of erosion varies with the characteristics of the rock which can cause weird shapes and effects (right). Desert sand can also be accumulated by the wind to form barchan dunes (far right) which slowly travel forward, horns first.

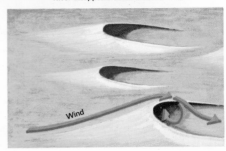

Wind

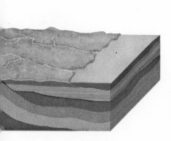

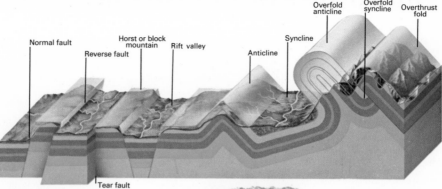

Normal fault
Reverse fault
Horst or block mountain
Rift valley
Anticline
Syncline
Overfold anticline
Overfold syncline
Overthrust fold
Tear fault

Folding and faulting

A vertical displacement in the earth's crust is called a fault or reverse fault; lateral displacement is a tear fault. An uplifted block is called a horst, the reverse of which is a rift valley. Compressed horizontal layers of sedimentary rock fold to form mountains. Those layers which bend up form an anticline, those bending down form a syncline : continued pressure forms an overfold.

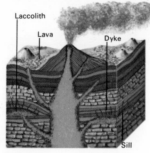

Laccolith
Lava
Dyke
Sill

Volcanic activity

When pressure on rocks below the earth's crust is released the normally semi-solid hot rock becomes liquid magma. The magma forces its way into cracks of the crust and may either reach the surface where it forms volcanoes or it may collect in the crust as sills dykes or laccoliths. When magma reaches the surface it cools to form lava.

Waves

Coasts are continually changing, some retreat under wave erosion while others advance with wave deposition. These actions combined form steep cliffs and wave cut platforms. Eroded debris is in turn deposited as a terrace. As the water becomes shallower the erosive power of the waves decreases and gradually the cliff disappears. Wave action can also create other features (far right).

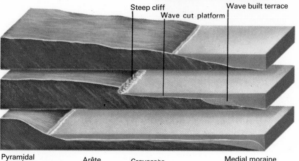

Steep cliff
Wave cut platform
Wave built terrace

Ice

These diagrams (right) show how a glaciated valley may have formed. The glacier deepens, straightens and widens the river valley whose interlocking spurs become truncated or cut off. Intervalley divides are frost shattered to form sharp arêtes and pyramidal peaks. Hanging valleys mark the entry of tributary rivers and eroded rocks form medial moraine. Terminal moraine is deposited as the glacier retreats.

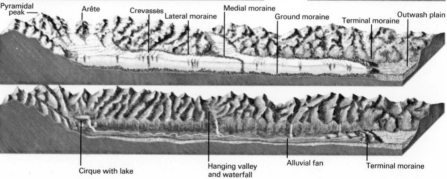

Pyramidal peak
Arête
Crevasses
Lateral moraine
Medial moraine
Ground moraine
Terminal moraine
Outwash plain
Cirque with lake
Hanging valley and waterfall
Alluvial fan
Terminal moraine

Subsidence and uplift

As the land surface is eroded it may eventually become a level plain - a peneplain, broken only by low hills, remnants of previous mountains. In turn this peneplain may be uplifted to form a plateau with steep edges. At the coast the uplifted wave platform becomes a coastal plain and in the rejuvenated rivers downward erosion once more predominates.

Rock debris forms sedimentary rock

The Earth: Physical Dimensions

Its surface
Highest point on the earth's surface: Mt. Everest, Tibet - Nepal boundary 8 848 m
Lowest point on the earth's surface: The Dead Sea, Jordan below sea level 395 m
Greatest ocean depth,: Challenger Deep, Mariana Trench 11 022 m
Average height of land 840 m
Average depth of seas and oceans 3 808 m

Dimensions
Superficial area	510 000 000 km²
Land surface	149 000 000 km²
Land surface as % of total area	29·2 %
Water surface	361 000 000 km²
Water surface as % of total area	70·8 %
Equatorial circumference	40 077 km
Meridional circumference	40 009 km
Equatorial diameter	12 756·8 km
Polar diameter	12 713·8 km
Equatorial radius	6 378·4 km
Polar radius	6 356·9 km
Volume of the Earth	1 083 230 x 10⁶ km³
Mass of the Earth	5·9 x 10²¹ tonnes

The Figure of Earth
An imaginary sea-level surface is considered and called a geoid. By measuring at different places the angles from plumb lines to a fixed star there have been many determinations of the shape of parts of the geoid which is found to be an oblate spheriod with its axis along the axis of rotation of the earth. Observations from satellites have now given a new method of more accurate determinations of the figure of the earth and its local irregularities.

Land and Sea Hemispheres.
About 85% of the total land area is contained in the hemisphere centred on a point between Paris and Brussels.

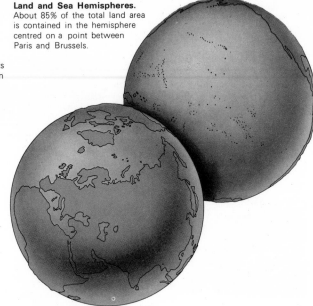

Oceans and Seas
Area in 1000 km²

Pacific Ocean	165 721	North Sea	575
Atlantic Ocean	81 660	Black Sea	448
Indian Ocean	73 442	Red Sea	440
Arctic Ocean	14 351	Baltic Sea	422
Mediterranean Sea	2 966	Persian Gulf	238
Bering Sea	2 274	St. Lawrence, Gulf of	236
Caribbean Sea	1 942	English Channel & Irish Sea	179
Mexico, Gulf of	1 813	California, Gulf of	161
Okhotsk, Sea of	1 528		
East China Sea	1 248		
Hudson Bay	1 230		
Japan, Sea of	1 049		

Lakes and Inland Seas
Areas in 1000 km²

Caspian Sea, Asia	424·2	Lake Ontario, N.America	19·5
Lake Superior, N.America	82·4	Lake Ladoga, Europe	18·4
Lake Victoria, Africa	69·5	Lake Balkhash, Asia	17·3
Aral Sea (Salt), Asia	63·8	Lake Maracaibo, S.America	16·3
Lake Huron, N.America	59·6	Lake Onega, Europe	9·8
Lake Michigan, N.America	58·0	Lake Eyre (Salt), Australia	9·6
Lake Tanganyika, Africa	32·9	Lake Turkana (Salt), Africa	9·1
Lake Baikal, Asia	31·5	Lake Titicaca, S.America	8·3
Great Bear Lake, N.America	31·1	Lake Nicaragua, C.America	8·0
Great Slave Lake, N.America	28·9	Lake Athabasca, N.America	7·9
Lake Nyasa, Africa	28·5	Reindeer Lake, N.America	6·3
Lake Erie, N.America	25·7	Issyk-Kul, Asia	6·2
Lake Winnipeg, N.America	24·3	Lake Torrens (Salt), Australia	6·1
Lake Chad, Africa	20·7	Koko Nor (Salt), Asia	6·0
		Lake Urmia, Asia	6·0
		Vänern. Europe	5·6

Longest rivers

	km.
Nile, Africa	6 690
Amazon, S.America	6 280
Mississipi - Missouri, N.America	6 270
Yangtze, Asia	4 990
Zaïre, Africa	4 670
Amur, Asia	4 410
Hwang Ho (Yellow), Asia	4 350
Lena, Asia	4 260
Mekong, Asia	4 180
Niger, Africa	4 180
Mackenzie, N.America	4 040
Ob, Asia	4 000
Yenisei, Asia	3 800

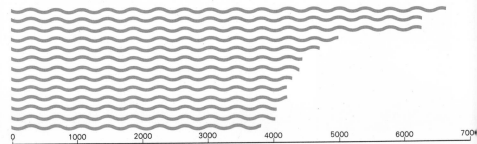

0	1000	2000	3000	4000	5000	6000	7000

The Highest Mountains and the Greatest Depths.

Mount Everest defied the world's greatest mountaineers for 32 years and claimed the lives of many men. Not until 1920 was permission granted by the Dalai Lama to attempt the mountain, and the first successful ascent came in 1953. Since then the summit has been reached several times. The world's highest peaks have now been climbed but there are many as yet unexplored peaks in the Himalayas some of which may be over 7 600 m.

The greatest trenches are the Puerto Rico deep (9 200m). The Tonga (10 822 m) and Mindanao (10 497 m) trenches and the Mariana Trench (11 022 m) in the Pacific. The trenches represent less than 2% of the total area of the sea-bed but are of great interest as lines of structural weakness in the Earth's crust and as areas of frequent earthquakes.

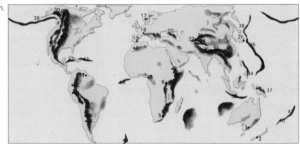

High mountains

Bathyscaphe

Waterfall

Dam

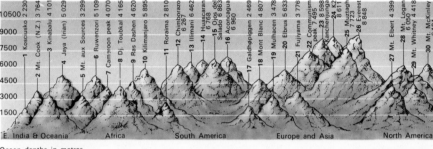

Mountain heights in metres

1 Kosciusko 2 230 · 2 Mt. Cook (N.Z.) 3 764 · 3 Kinabalu 4 101 · 4 Jaya (Irian) 5 029 · 5 Mt. aux Sources 3 299 · 6 Ruwenzori 5 109 · 7 Cameroon peak 4 070 · 8 Dj. Toubkal 4 165 · 9 Ras Dashen 4 620 · 10 Kilimanjaro 5 895 · 11 Roraima 2 810 · 12 Chimborazo 6 267 · 13 Illimani 6 462 · 14 Huascaran 6 768 · 15 Ojos del Salado 6 863 · 16 Aconcagua 6 960 · 17 Galdhøpiggen 2 469 · 18 Mont Blanc 4 807 · 19 Mulhacen 3 478 · 20 Elbrus 5 633 · 21 Fujiyama 3 776 · 22 Communism peak 7 495 · 23 8 598 · Kanchenjunga 8 848 · 24 K2 8 611 · 25 Muztagh 7 723 · 26 Everest 8 848 · 27 Mt. Elbert 4 399 · 28 Mt Logan 6 050 · 29 Mt. Whitney 4 418 · 30 Mt. McKinley 6 194

E. India & Oceania | Africa | South America | Europe and Asia | North America

Ocean depths in metres — Sea level

31 Mauritius basin 6 400 · 32 W. Australian basin 6 459 · 33 Java trench 7 450 · 34 Mindanao trench 10 497 · 35 Mariana trench 11 022 · 36 Japan trench 10 554 · 37 Bougainville deep 9 140 · 38 Kuril trench 10 542 · 39 Aleutian trench 7 822 · 40 Kermadec trench 10 047 · 41 Tonga trench 10 822 · 42 Cayman trough 7 680 · 43 Puerto Rico trough 9 200 · 44 S. Sandwich trench 8 428 · 45 Romanche deep 7 758

Indian Ocean | Pacific Ocean | Atlantic Ocean

Notable Waterfalls
heights in metres

Angel, Venezuela	980
Tugela, S. Africa	853
Mongefossen, Norway	774
Yosemite, California	738
Mardalsfossen, Norway	655
Cuquenan, Venezuela	610
Sutherland, N.Z.	579
Reichenbach, Switzerland	548
Wollomombi, Australia	518
Ribbon, California	491
Gavarnie, France	422
Tyssefallene, Norway	414
Krimml, Austria	370
King George VI, Guyana	366
Silver Strand, California	356
Geissbach, Switzerland	350
Staubbach, Switzerland	299
Trümmelbach, Switzerland	290
Chirombo, Zambia	268
Livingstone, Zaïre	259
King Edward VIII, Guyana	256
Gersoppa, India	253
Vettifossen Norway	250
Kalambo, Zambia	240
Kaieteur, Guyana	226
Maletsunyane, Lesotho	192
Terui, Italy	180
Murchison, Uganda	122
Victoria, Rhodesia - Zambia	107
Cauvery, India	97
Stanley, Zaïre	61
Niagara, N.America	51
Schaffhausen, Switzerland	30

Notable Dams
heights in metres
Africa

Cabora Bassa, Zambezi R. (under construction)	168
Akosombo Main Dam, Volta R.	141
Kariba, Zambezi R.	128
Aswan High Dam, Nile R.	110

Asia

Nurek, Vakhsh R., U.S.S.R.	317
Bhakra, Sutlej R., India	226
Kurobegawa, Kurobe R. , Jap.	186
Charvak, Chirchik R., U.S.S.R.	168
Okutadami, Tadami R., Jap.	157
Bhumiphol, Ping R., Thai.	154

Australasia

Warragamba, N.S.W., Australia	137
Eucumbene, N.S.W., Australia	116

Europe

Grande Dixence, Switz.	284
Vajont, Vajont, R., Italy	261
Mauvoisin, Drance R., Switz.	237
Contra , Verzasca R., Switz.	230
Luzzone, Brenno R., Switz.	208
Tignes, Isère R., France	180
Amir Kabir, Karadj R., U.S.S.R.	180
Vidraru, Arges R., Rum.	165
Kremasta, Acheloos R., Greece	165

North America

Oroville, Feather R.,	235
Hoover, Colorado R.,	221
Glen Canyon, Colorado R.,	216
Daniel Johnson, Can.	214
New Bullards Bar, N. Yuba R.	194
Mossyrock, Cowlitz R.,	184
Shasta, Sacramento R.,	183
W.A.C. Bennett, Canada.	183
Don Pedro, Tuolumne R.,	178
Hungry Horse, Flathead R.,	172
Grand Coulee, Columbia R.,	168

Central and South America

Guri, Caroni R., Venezuela.	106

Distances

Kms

Lower-left values are in kilometres. Upper-right values (in miles) are shown in the second table.

Kilometres

	Berlin	Bombay	Buenos Aires	Cairo	Calcutta	Caracas	Copenhagen	Chicago	Darwin	Hong Kong	Honolulu	Johannesburg	Lagos	London	Los Angeles
Berlin															
Bombay	6288														
Buenos Aires	11909	14925													
Cairo	2890	4355	11814												
Calcutta	7033	1664	16524	5699											
Caracas	8435	14522	5096	10203	15464										
Copenhagen	357	6422	12067	3206	7072	8392									
Chicago	7084	12953	9011	9860	12839	4027	6840								
Darwin	12946	7257	14693	11612	6047	18059	12903	15065							
Hong Kong	8754	4317	18478	8150	2659	16360	8671	12526	4271						
Honolulu	11764	12914	12164	14223	11343	9670	11407	6836	8640	8921					
Johannesburg	8870	6974	8088	6267	8459	11019	9225	13984	10639	10732	19206				
Lagos	5198	7612	7916	3915	9216	7741	5530	9612	14222	11845	16308	4505			
London	928	7190	11131	3508	7961	7507	952	6356	13848	9623	11632	9071	5017		
Los Angeles	9311	14000	9852	12200	13120	5812	9003	2804	12695	11639	4117	16676	12414	8758	
Lisbon	2311	8018	9600	3794	9075	6509	2478	6424	15114	11028	12587	8191	3799	1588	912
Mexico City	9732	15656	7389	12372	15280	3586	9514	2726	14631	14122	6085	14585	11071	8936	249…
Moscow	1610	5031	13477	2902	5534	9938	1561	8000	11350	7144	11323	9161	6254	2498	97…
Nairobi	6370	4532	10402	3536	6179	11544	6706	12883	10415	8776	17282	2927	3807	6819	155…
New York	6385	12541	8526	9020	12747	3430	6188	1145	16047	12950	7980	12841	8477	5572	393…
Paris	876	7010	11051	3210	7858	7625	1026	6650	13812	9630	11968	8732	4714	342	90…
Peking	7822	4757	19268	7544	3269	14399	7202	10603	6011	1963	8160	11710	11457	8138	100…
Reykjavik	2385	8335	11437	5266	8687	6915	2103	4757	13892	9681	9787	10938	6718	1887	69…
Rio de Janeiro	10025	13409	1953	9896	15073	4546	10211	8547	16011	17704	13342	7113	6035	9299	101…
Rome	1180	6175	11151	2133	7219	8363	1531	7739	13265	9284	12916	7743	4039	1431	101…
Singapore	9944	3914	15879	8267	2897	18359	9969	15078	3349	2599	10816	8660	11145	10852	141…
Sydney	16096	10160	11800	14418	9138	15343	16042	14875	3150	7374	8168	11040	15519	16992	120…
Tokyo	8924	6742	18362	9571	5141	14164	8696	10137	5431	2874	6202	13547	13480	9562	88…
Vancouver	7980	12267	11294	10838	11445	6701	7646	2851	12215	10246	4357	16452	11951	7582	17…
Wellington	18140	12370	9981	16524	11354	13122	17961	13451	5325	9427	7513	11761	16050	18814	108…

Upper-right values (miles)

From	Bombay	Buenos Aires	Cairo	Calcutta	Caracas	Copenhagen	Chicago	Darwin	Hong Kong	Honolulu	Johannesburg	Lagos	London	Los Angeles
Berlin	3907	7400	1795	4370	5241	222	4402	8044	5440	7310	5511	3230	557	578
Bombay		9275	2706	1034	9024	3990	8048	4510	2683	8024	4334	4730	4467	870
Buenos Aires			7341	10268	3167	7498	5599	9130	11481	7558	5025	4919	6917	612
Cairo				3541	6340	1992	6127	7216	5064	8838	3894	2432	2180	758
Calcutta					9609	4395	7978	3758	1653	7048	5256	5727	4946	815
Caracas						5215	2502	11221	10166	6009	6847	4810	4664	361
Copenhagen							4250	8017	5388	7088	5732	3436	592	559
Chicago								9361	7783	4247	8689	5973	3949	174
Darwin									2654	5369	6611	8837	8605	788
Hong Kong										5543	6669	7360	5980	723
Honolulu											11934	10133	7228	258
Johannesburg												2799	5637	1030
Lagos													3118	771
London														544

Distance chart (Miles). The upper-right triangle is shown with column headers given by the diagonal city labels; row labels appear at the right. The leftmost value in each of the Berlin–Los Angeles rows is partially cropped (leading digit cut off).

Lisbon	Mexico City	Moscow	Nairobi	New York	Paris	Peking	Reykjavik	Rio de Janeiro	Rome	Singapore	Sydney	Tokyo	Vancouver	Wellington	City
436	6047	1000	3958	3967	545	4860	1482	6230	734	6179	10002	5545	4959	11272	Berlin
982	9728	3126	2816	7793	4356	2956	5179	8332	3837	2432	6313	4189	7622	7686	Bombay
964	4591	8374	6463	5298	6867	11972	7106	1214	6929	9867	7332	11410	7018	6202	Buenos Aires
358	7687	1803	2197	5605	1994	4688	3272	6149	1325	5137	8959	5947	6734	10268	Cairo
639	9494	3438	3839	7921	4883	2031	5398	9366	4486	1800	5678	3195	7112	7055	Calcutta
044	2228	6175	7173	2131	4738	8947	4297	2825	5196	11407	9534	8801	4164	8154	Caracas
540	5912	970	4167	3845	638	4475	1306	6345	951	6195	9968	5403	4751	11160	Copenhagen
992	1694	4971	8005	711	4132	6588	2956	5311	4809	9369	9243	6299	1771	8358	Chicago
391	9091	7053	6472	9971	8582	3735	8632	9948	8243	2081	1957	3375	7590	3309	Darwin
853	8775	4439	5453	8047	5984	1220	6015	11001	5769	1615	4582	1786	6367	5857	Hong Kong
821	3781	7036	10739	4958	7437	5070	6081	8290	8026	6721	5075	3854	2708	4669	Honolulu
089	9063	5692	1818	7979	5426	7276	6797	4420	4811	5381	6860	8418	10223	7308	Johannesburg
360	6879	3886	2366	5268	2929	7119	4175	3750	2510	6925	9643	8376	7426	9973	Lagos
987	5552	1552	4237	3463	212	5057	1172	5778	889	6743	10558	5942	4711	11691	London
668	1549	6070	9659	2446	5645	6251	4310	6310	6331	8776	7502	5475	1078	6719	Los Angeles
	5391	2427	4015	3369	903	6007	1832	4805	1157	7385	11295	6928	5149	12163	Lisbon
		6664	9207	2090	5717	7742	4635	4780	6365	10321	8058	7024	2451	6897	Mexico City
			3942	4666	1545	3600	2053	7184	1477	5237	9008	4651	5097	10283	Moscow
				7358	4029	5727	5395	5548	3350	4635	7552	6996	8917	8490	Nairobi
					3626	6828	2613	4832	4280	9531	9935	6741	2425	8951	New York
						5106	1384	5708	687	6671	10539	6038	4923	11798	Paris
							4897	10773	5049	2783	5561	1304	5292	6700	Peking
								6135	2048	7155	10325	5469	3540	10725	Reykjavik
									5725	9763	8389	11551	6983	7367	Rio de Janeiro
										6229	10143	6127	5587	11523	Rome
											3915	3306	7971	5298	Singapore
												4861	7767	1383	Sydney
													4694	5762	Tokyo
														7304	Vancouver
															Wellington

Miles

Lower-left triangle (row labels cropped at left; partial values visible along the diagonal staircase, left to right):

- 676 (Paris)
- 906, 10724 (Peking)
- 6461, 14818, 6344 (Reykjavik)
- 422, 3364, 7510, 11842 (Rio de Janeiro)
- 454, 9200, 2486, 6485, 5836 (Rome)
- 668, 12460, 5794, 9216, 10988, 8217 (Singapore)
- 948, 7460, 3304, 8683, 4206, 2228, 7882 (Sydney)
- 734, 7693, 11562, 8928, 7777, 9187, 17338, 9874 (Tokyo)
- 861, 10243, 2376, 5391, 6888, 1105, 8126, 3297, 9214 (Vancouver)
- 886, 16610, 8428, 7460, 15339, 10737, 4478, 11514, 15712, 10025 (Wellington)
- 178, 12969, 14497, 12153, 15989, 16962, 8949, 16617, 13501, 16324, 6300
- 149, 11304, 7485, 11260, 10849, 9718, 2099, 8802, 18589, 9861, 5321, 7823
- 287, 3945, 8203, 14351, 3903, 7923, 8516, 5698, 11238, 8991, 12829, 12501, 7554
- 575, 11100, 16549, 13664, 14405, 18987, 10782, 17260, 11855, 18545, 8526, 2226, 9273, 11754

Water Resources and Vegetation

Water resources and vegetation
Fresh water is essential for life on earth and in some parts of the world it is a most precious commodity. On the other hand it is very easy for industrialised temperate states to take its existence for granted, and man's increasing demand may only be met finally by the desalination of earth's 1250 million cubic kilometres of salt water. 70% of the earth's fresh water exists as ice.

The hydrological cycle
Water is continually being absorbed into the atmosphere as vapour from oceans, lakes, rivers and vegetation transpiration. On cooling the vapour either condenses or freezes and falls as rain, hail or snow. Most precipitation falls over the sea but one quarter falls over the land of which half evaporates again soon after falling while the rest flows back into the oceans.

Distribution of water

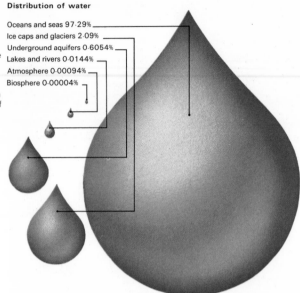

Oceans and seas 97·29%
Ice caps and glaciers 2·09%
Underground aquifers 0·6054%
Lakes and rivers 0·0144%
Atmosphere 0·00094%
Biosphere 0·00004%

Tundra

Mediterranean scrub

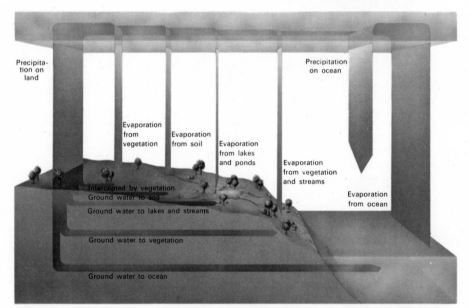

Precipitation on land

Precipitation on ocean

Evaporation from vegetation

Evaporation from soil

Evaporation from lakes and ponds

Evaporation from vegetation and streams

Evaporation from ocean

Intercepted by vegetation
Ground water to soil

Ground water to lakes and streams

Ground water to vegetation

Ground water to ocean

Domestic consumption of water
An area's level of industrialisation, climate and standard of living are all major influences in the consumption of water. On average Europe consumes 636 litres per head each day of which 180 litres is used domestically. In the U.S.A. domestic consumption is slightly higher at 270 litres per day. The graph (right) represents domestic consumption in the U.K. in 1970.

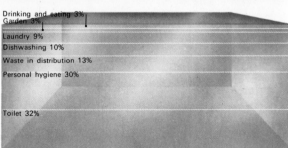

Drinking and eating 3%
Garden 3%
Laundry 9%
Dishwashing 10%
Waste in distribution 13%
Personal hygiene 30%
Toilet 32%

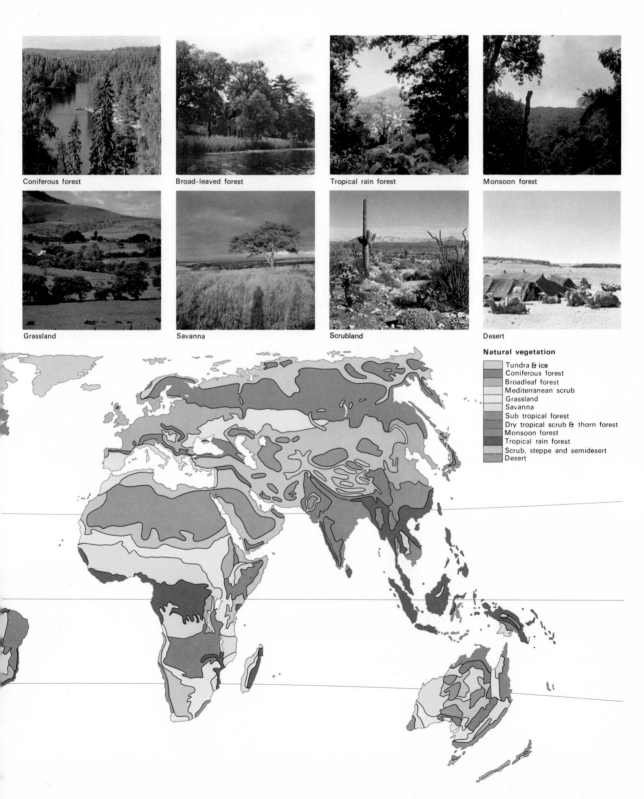

Coniferous forest

Broad-leaved forest

Tropical rain forest

Monsoon forest

Grassland

Savanna

Scrubland

Desert

Natural vegetation

Tundra & ice
Coniferous forest
Broadleaf forest
Mediterranean scrub
Grassland
Savanna
Sub tropical forest
Dry tropical scrub & thorn forest
Monsoon forest
Tropical rain forest
Scrub, steppe and semidesert
Desert

Population

Population distribution
(right and lower right)
People have always been unevenly distributed in the world. Europe has for centuries contained nearly 20% of the world's population but after the 16-19th century explorations and consequent migrations this proportion has rapidly reduced. In 1750 the Americas had 2% of the world's total: in 2000 AD they are expected to contain 16%.

The most densely populated regions are in India, China and Europe where the average density is between 100 and 200 per square km. although there are pockets of extremely high density elsewhere. In contrast Australia has only 1·5 people per square km. The countries in the lower map have been redrawn to make their areas proportional to their populations.

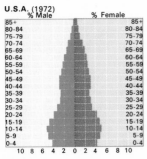

U.S.A. (1972)

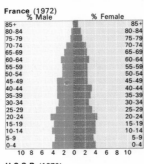

France (1972)

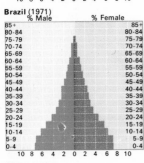

Brazil (1971)

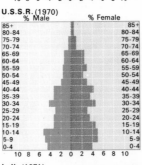

U.S.S.R. (1970)

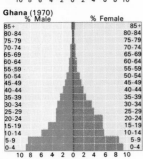

Ghana (1970)

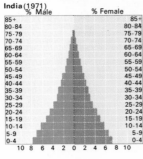

India (1971)

Age distribution
France shows many demographic features characteristic of European countries. Birth and death rates have declined with a moderate population growth - there are nearly as many old as young. In contrast, India and several other countries have few old and many young because of the high death rates and even higher birth rates. It is this excess that is responsible for the world's population explosion.

World population increase
Until comparatively recently there was little increase in the population of the world. About 6000 BC it is thought that there were about 200 million people and in the following 7000years an increase of just over 100 million. In the 1800's there were about 1000 million; at present there are over 3500 million and by the year 2000 if present trends continue there would be at least 7000 million.

1650   1700   1750   1800

World population distribution

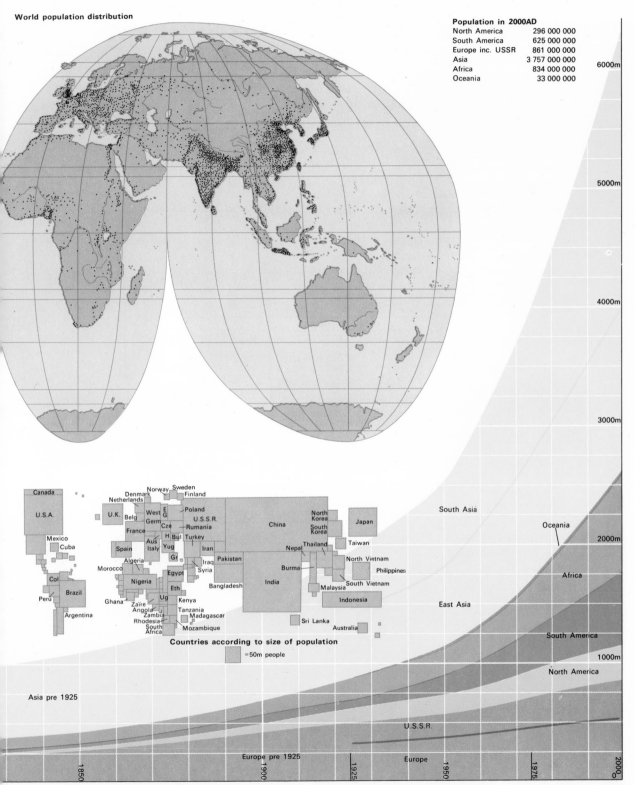

Population in 2000AD

North America	296 000 000
South America	625 000 000
Europe inc. USSR	861 000 000
Asia	3 757 000 000
Africa	834 000 000
Oceania	33 000 000

6000m

5000m

4000m

3000m

South Asia

Oceania

Africa

East Asia

South America

2000m

North America

1000m

Countries according to size of population

= 50m people

Asia pre 1925

U.S.S.R.

Europe pre 1925   Europe

1850   1900   1925   1950   1975   2000

Language

Languages may be blamed partly for the division and lack of understanding between nations. While a common language binds countries together it in turn isolates them from other countries and groups. Thus beliefs, ideas and inventions remain exclusive to these groups and different cultures develop.

There are thousands of different languages and dialects spoken today. This can cause strife even within the one country, such as India, where different dialects are enough to break down the country into distinct groups.

As a result of colonization and the spread of internationally accepted languages, many countries have superimposed a completely unrelated language in order to combine isolated national groups and to facilitate international understanding, for example Spanish in South America, English in India.

Assyrian (carved)

Ancient Hebrew (painted)

Egyptian hieroglyphic (painted)

Some modern non-latin type faces

Greek
ΑΒΓΔΕΖΗΘΙΚΛΜΝΞΟΠΡΣΤΥΦΧΨΩς

Cyrillic
АБВГДЕЖЗИЙІКЛМНОПРСТУФХЦЧШ

Arabic
فى عام ١٨٩٧ وصل إلى إنجلترا أ نموذج

Bengali
১৮৯৭ খ্রীস্টাব্দে আধুনিক মডেলের একটি

Telugu
నిన్న న్యూయాంటకీ వచ్చిన యుథిఫ యేమియు

Japanese
国土の位置と地形

Chinese
父獨子出有之限地位司，
司在提印芬刷奥業司上有

Related languages

Certain languages showing marked similarities are thought to have developed from common parent languages for example Latin. After the retreat of the Roman Empire wherever Latin had been firmly established it remained as the new nation's language. With no unifying centre divergent development took place and Latin evolved into new languages.

Calligraphy

Writing was originally by a series of pictures, and these gradually developed in styles which were influenced by the tools generally used. Carved alphabets, such as that used by the Sumerians, tended to be angular, while those painted or written tended to be curved, as in Egyptian hieroglyphics development of which can be followed through the West Semitic, Greek and Latin alphabets to our own.

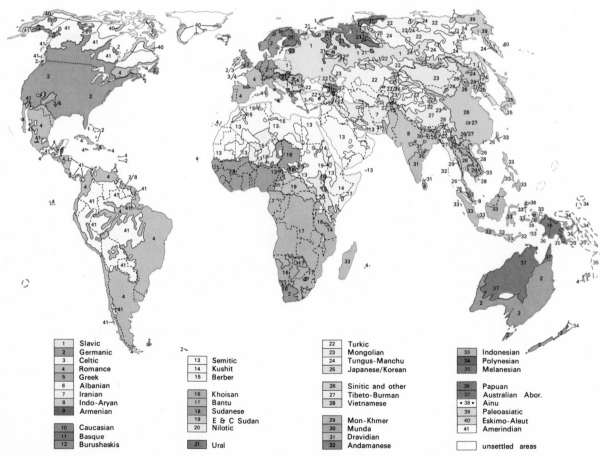

1	Slavic	22	Turkic
2	Germanic	23	Mongolian
3	Celtic	24	Tungus-Manchu
4	Romance	25	Japanese/Korean
5	Greek		
6	Albanian	26	Sinitic and other
7	Iranian	27	Tibeto-Burman
8	Indo-Aryan	28	Vietnamese
9	Armenian		
		29	Mon-Khmer
10	Caucasian	30	Munda
11	Basque	31	Dravidian
12	Burushaskis	32	Andamanese
13	Semitic	33	Indonesian
14	Kushit	34	Polynesian
15	Berber	35	Melanesian
16	Khoisan	36	Papuan
17	Bantu	37	Australian Abor.
18	Sudanese	38	Ainu
19	E & C Sudan	39	Paleoasiatic
20	Nilotic	40	Eskimo-Aleut
21	Ural	41	Amerindian

unsettled areas

Religion

Throughout history man has had beliefs in supernatural powers based on the forces of nature which have developed into worship of a god and some cases gods.

Hinduism honours many gods and goddesses which are all manifestations of the one divine spirit, Brahma, and incorporates beliefs such as reincarnation, worship of cattle and the caste system.

Buddhism, an offshoot of Hinduism, was founded in north east India by Gautama Buddha (563-483 BC) who taught that spiritual and moral discipline were essential to achieve supreme peace.

Confucianism is a mixture of Buddhism and Confucius' teachings which were elaborated to provide a moral basis for the political structure of Imperial China and to cover the already existing forms of ancestor worship.

Judaism dates back to c. 13th century B.C. The Jews were expelled from the Holy Land in AD70 and only reinstated in Palestine in 1948.

Christian monastery

Jewish holy place

Hindu temple

Islam, founded in Mecca by Muhammad (570-632 AD) spread across Asia and Africa and in its retreat left isolated pockets of adherent communities.

Christianity was founded by Jesus of Nazareth in the 1st century AD The Papal authority, established in the 4th century, was rejected by Eastern churches in the 11th century. Later several other divisions developed eg. Roman Catholicism, Protestantism.

Mohammedan mosque

Buddhist temple

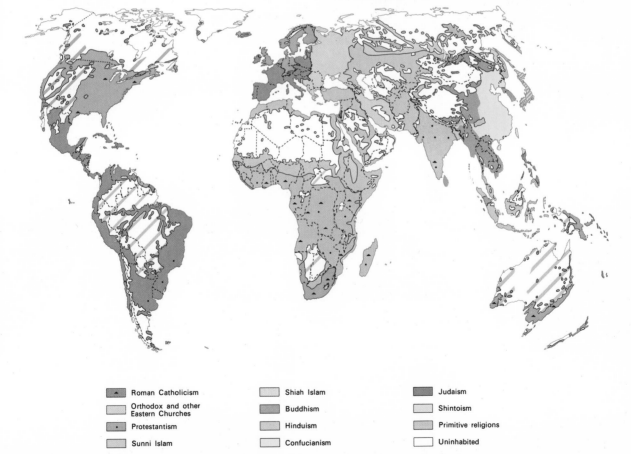

Roman Catholicism
Orthodox and other Eastern Churches
Protestantism
Sunni Islam
Shiah Islam
Buddhism
Hinduism
Confucianism
Judaism
Shintoism
Primitive religions
Uninhabited

The Growth of Cities

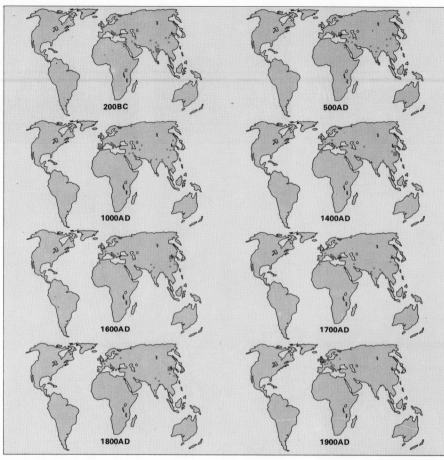

200BC

500AD

1000AD

1400AD

1600AD

1700AD

1800AD

1900AD

Cities through history
The evolution of the semi-perm
anent Neolithic settlements into a
city took from 5000 until 3500 BC.
Efficient communications and
exchange systems were developed
as population densities increased
as high as 30 000 to 50 000 per
square kilometre in 2000BC
in Egypt and Babylonia,
compared with New York
City today at 10 000.

■ The largest city in
the world

· The twenty five
largest cities in
the world

São Paulo

Increase in urbanisation
The increase in urbanisation is
a result primarily of better
sanitation and health resulting in
the growth of population and
secondarily to the movement of
man off the land into industry and
service occupations in the cities.
Generally the most highly
developed industrial nations are the
most intensely urbanised although
exceptions such as Norway and
Switzerland show that rural
industrialisation can exist.

Increase in urbanisation
1 Norway
2 Japan
3 Switzerland
4 Sweden
5 Canada
6 England and
 Wales
7 U.S.A.

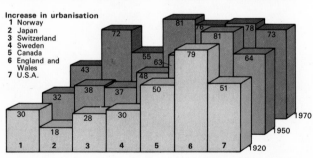

1970
1950
1920

Metropolitan areas
A metropolitan area can be
defined as a central city linked
with surrounding communities
by continuous built-up areas
controlled by one municipal
government. With improved
communications the neighbouring
communities generally continue
to provide the city's work-force.
The graph (right) compares the
total populations of the world's
ten largest cities.

City populations		
1	Shanghai (1973)	12 000 000
2	Tokyo (1973)	11 612 000
3	New York (1970)	11 571 000
4	Mexico City (1974)	10 767 000
5	Paris (1975)	9 108 000
6	Peking (1973)	7 570 000
7	Moscow (1975)	7 528 000
8	London (1974)	7 168 000
9	Los Angeles (1970)	7 032 000
10	Calcutta (1971)	7 031 000

Major cities
Normally these are not only
major centres of population and
wealth but also of political power
and trade. They are the sites of
international airports and
characteristically are great ports
from which imported goods are
distributed using the roads and
railways which focus on the city.
Their staple trades and industries
are varied and flexible and depend
on design and fashion rather
than raw material production.

New York

Sydney

Moscow

Tokyo

Hong Kong

London

Bombay

Cairo

Rio de Janeiro

Rome

Cities over 5 000 000 inhabitants

2 000 000-5 000 000 inhabitants

1 000 000-2 000 000 inhabitants

250 000-1 000 000 inhabitants

Food Resources: Vegetable

Cocoa, tea , coffee

These tropical or sub-tropical crops are grown mainly for export to the economically advanced countries. Tea and coffee are the world's principal beverages. Cocoa is used more in the manufacture of chocolate.

- Cocoa
- Tea
- Coffee

Sugar beet, sugar cane

Cane Sugar - a tropical crop - accounts for the bulk of the sugar entering into international trade. Beet Sugar, on the other hand, demands a temperate climate and is produced primarily for domestic consumption.

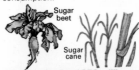

- Sugar beet
- Sugar cane

World production 1973 million tons

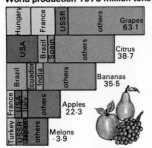

Grapes 63·1
Citrus 38·7
Bananas 35·5
Apples 22·3
Melons ·3·9

Vegetable oilseeds and oils

Despite the increasing use of synthetic chemical products and animal and marine fats, vegetable oils extracted from these crops grow in quantity, value and importance. Food is the major use- in margarine and cooking fats.

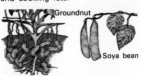

Groundnuts are also a valuable subsistence crop and the meal is used as animal feed. Soya-bean meal is a growing source of protein for humans and animals. The Mediterranean lands are the prime source of olive oil.

Cereals

Cereals include those members of the grain family with starchy edible seeds - wheat, maize, barley, oats, rye, rice, millets and sorghums.

Cereals and potatoes (not a cereal but starch-producing) are the principal source of food for our modern civilisations because of their high yield in bulk and food value per unit of land and labour required. They are also easy to store and transport, and provide food also for animals producing meat, fat, milk and eggs. Wheat is the principal bread grain of the temperate regions in which potatoes are the next most important food source. Rice is the principal cereal in the hotter. humid regions. especially in Asia. Oats, barley and maize are grown mainly for animal feed; millets and sorghums as main subsistence crops in Africa and India.

Fruit, wine

With the improvements in canning, drying and freezing, and in transport and marketing, the international trade and consumption of deciduous and soft fruits, citrus fruits and tropical fruits has greatly increased. Recent developments in the use of the peel will give added value to some of the fruit crops.

Over 80% of grapes are grown for wine and over a half in countries bordering the Mediterranean.

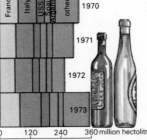

1970
1971
1972
1973

0   120   240   360 million hectolitres

- Groundnuts
- Soya beans

- Rape seed
- Sunflower seed

32

Maize (or Corn)

Needs plenty of sunshine, summer rain or irrigation and frost free for 6 months. Important as animal feed and for human food in Africa, Latin America and as a vegetable and breakfast cereal.

World production 320·6 million tonnes

Barley

Has the widest range of cultivation requiring only 8 weeks between seed time and harvest. Used mainly as animal-feed and by the malting industry.

World production 157·1 million tonnes

Oats

Widely grown in temperate regions with the limit fixed by early autumn frosts. Mainly fed to cattle. The best quality oats are used for oatmeal, porridge and breakfast foods.

World production 50·5 million tonnes

Rice

Needs plains or terraces which can be flooded and abundant water in the growing season. The staple food of half the human race. In the husk, it is known as paddy.

World production 342·9 million tonnes

Wheat

The most important grain crop in the temperate regions though it is also grown in a variety of climates e.g. in Monsoon lands as a winter crop.

World production 362·6 million tonnes

Rye

The hardiest of cereals and more resistant to cold, pests and disease than wheat. An important foodstuff in Central and E. Europe and the U.S.S.R.

World production 26·0 million tonnes

Millets

The name given to a number of related members of the grass family, of which sorghum is one of the most important. They provide nutritious grain.

World production 52·3 million tonnes

Potato

Δ

An important food crop though less nutritious weight for weight than grain crops. World production is over 300 million tonnes.

World production 301·6 million tonnes

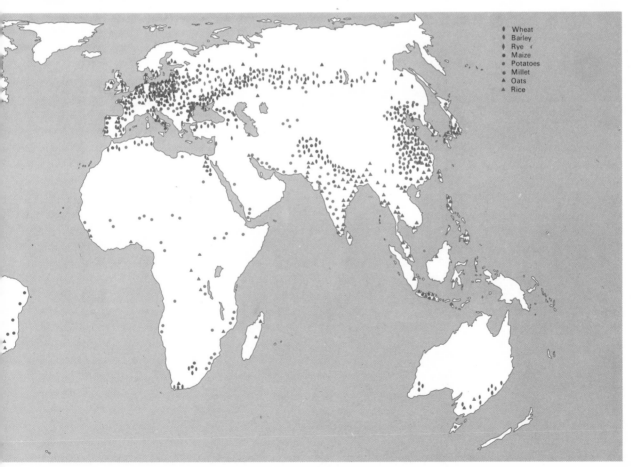

- Wheat
- Barley
- Rye
- Maize
- Potatoes
- Millet
- Oats
- Rice

Food Resources: Animal

Food resources: Animal
Meat, milk and allied foods are prime protein-providers and are also sources of essential vitamins. Meat is mainly a product of continental and savannah grasslands and the cool west coasts, particularly in Europe. Milk and cheese, eggs and fish - though found in some quantity throughout the world - are primarily a product of the temperate zones.

Beef cattle
Australia, New Zealand and Argentina provide the major part of international beef exports. Western U.S.A. and Europe have considerable production of beef for their local high demand.

World production 978·8 million head

Dairy Cattle
The need of herds for a rich diet and for nearby markets result in dairying being characteristic of densely-populated areas of the temperate zones - U.S.A., N.W. Europe, N.Zealand and S.E. Australia.

World production 200·0 million head

Cheese
The principal producers are the U.S.A., India, W. Europe, U.S.S.R., and New Zealand and principal exporters Netherlands, New Zealand, Denmark and France.

World production 10·7 million tonnes

Sheep
Raised mostly for wool and meat, the skins and cheese from their milk are important products in some countries. The merino yields a fine wool and crossbreds are best for meat.

World production 1 046·2 million head

Pigs
Can be reared in most climates from monsoon to cool temperate. They are abundant in China, the corn belt of the U.S.A. N.W. and C. Europe, Brazil and U.S.S.R.

World production 674·3 million head

Fish
Commercial fishing requires large shoals of fish of one species within reach of markets. Freshwater fishing is also important. A rich source of protein, fish will become an increasingly valuable food source.

World catch 65·7 million tonnes

Butter
The biggest producers are U.S.S.R., W. Europe, U.S.A., New Zealand and Australia.

World production 6·3 million tonnes

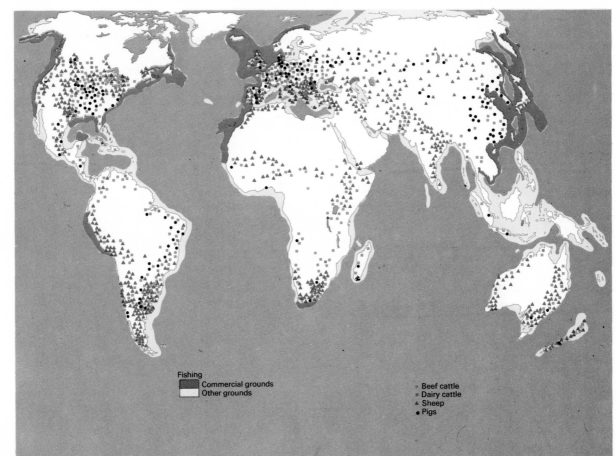

Fishing
- Commercial grounds
- Other grounds

- ■ Beef cattle
- ■ Dairy cattle
- ▲ Sheep
- ● Pigs

Nutrition

Foodstuffs fall, nutritionally, into three groups - providers of energy, protein and vitamins. Cereals and oil-seeds provide energy and second-class 'protein'; milk, meat and allied foods provide protein and vitamins, fruit and vegetables provide vitamins, especially Vitamin C, and some energy. To avoid malnutrition, a minimum level of these three groups of foodstuffs is required: the maps and diagrams show how unfortunately widespread are low standards of nutrition and even malnutrition.

Comparison of daily diets

3 000 calories
2 000 calories
1 000 calories
0 calories

Supplies Require-ments   Supplies Require-ments
Far East, Near East, Africa & Latin America   Europe, Oceania & North America

Vitamin deficiences

Vitamin A
Vitamin B
Vitamin C
Vitamin D

Proportions of calories

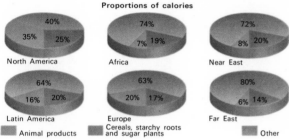

North America — 40% / 35% / 25%
Africa — 74% / 7% / 19%
Near East — 72% / 8% / 20%
Latin America — 64% / 16% / 20%
Europe — 63% / 20% / 17%
Far East — 80% / 6% / 14%

Animal products
Cereals, starchy roots and sugar plants
Other

People and tractors engaged in agriculture

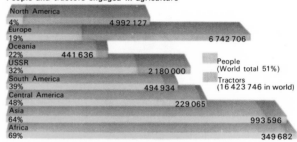

North America 4% — 4 992 127
Europe 19% — 6 742 706
Oceania 22% — 441 636
USSR 32% — 2 180 000
South America 39% — 494 934
Central America 48% — 229 065
Asia 64% — 993 596
Africa 69% — 349 682

People (World total 51%)
Tractors (16 423 746 in world)

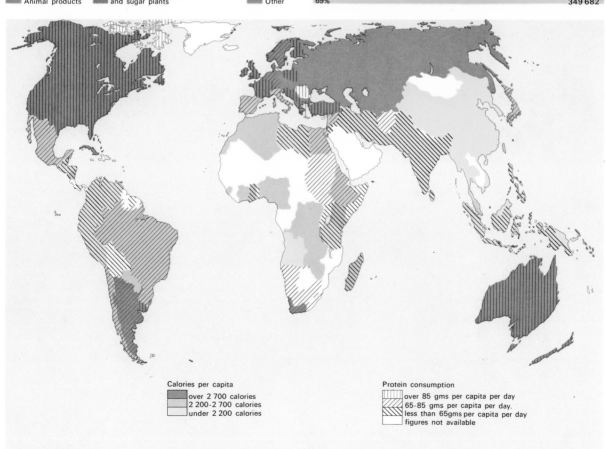

Calories per capita
- over 2 700 calories
- 2 200-2 700 calories
- under 2 200 calories

Protein consumption
- over 85 gms per capita per day
- 65-85 gms per capita per day.
- less than 65gms per capita per day
- figures not available

Mineral Resources I

Primitive man used iron for tools and vessels and its use extended gradually until iron, and later steel, became the backbone of the Modern World with the Industrial Revolution in the late 18th Century. At first, local ores were used, whereas today richer iron ores in huge deposits have been discovered and are mined on a large scale, often far away from the areas where they are used; for example, in Western Australia, Northern Sweden, Venezuela and Liberia. Iron smelting plants are today increasingly located at coastal sites, where the large ore carriers can easily discharge their cargo.

Steel is refined iron with the addition of other minerals, ferro-alloys, giving to the steel their own special properties; for example, resistance to corrosion (chromium, nickel, cobalt), hardness (tungsten, vanadium), elasticity (molybdenum), magnetic properties (cobalt), high tensile strength (manganese) and high ductility (molybdenum).

Production of Ferro-alloy metals

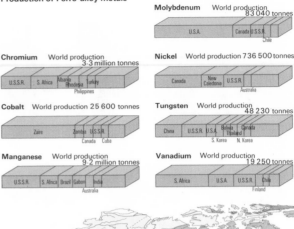

Chromium World production 3·3 million tonnes

Cobalt World production 25 600 tonnes

Manganese World production 9·2 million tonnes

Molybdenum World production 83 040 tonnes

Nickel World production 736 500 tonnes

Tungsten World production 48 230 tonnes

Vanadium World production 19 250 tonnes

Iron and Steel Industry of Western Europe

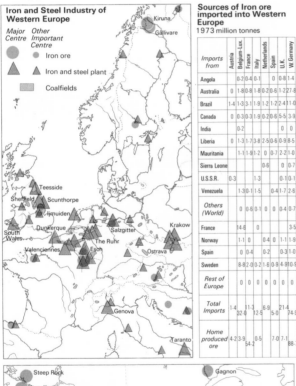

Major Centre ● / Other Important Centre ● Iron ore

▲ Major / ▲ Other — Iron and steel plant

Coalfields

Sources of Iron ore imported into Western Europe

1973 million tonnes

Imports from	Austria	Belgium-Lux.	France	Italy	Netherlands	Spain	U.K.	W Germany
Angola		0·2	0·4	0·1		0	0·8	1·4
Australia	0	1·8	0·8	1·8	0·2	0·6	1·2	27·8
Brazil	1·4	1·3	3·1	1·9	1·2	1·2	2·4	11·0
Canada	0	0·3	0·3	1·9	0·2	0·6	5·5	3·9
India		0·2				0	0	
Liberia	0	1·3	1·7	3·4	2·5	0·6	0·9	8·5
Mauritania		1·1	1·9	1·2	0	0·7	2·2	1·0
Sierra Leone				0·6		0	0·7	
U.S.S.R.	0·3		1·3			0·1	0·1	
Venezuela		1·3	0·1	1·5		0·4	1·7	2·6
Others (World)	0	0·6	0·1	0	0	0·4	0·7	
France		14·8	0				3·5	
Norway	1·1	0		0·4	0	1·1	1·9	
Spain	0	0·4		0·2		0·3	1·0	
Sweden	8·8	2·0	0·2	1·6	0·9	4·9	10·9	
Rest of Europe	0	0	0	0	0	0	0	
Total Imports	1·4 / 32·0	11·3	12·5 / 6·9	5·0	21·4 / 74·9			
Home produced ore	4·2 / 54·2	3·9	0·5	7·0 / 88·7	7·1			

Iron and Steel Industry of Eastern North America

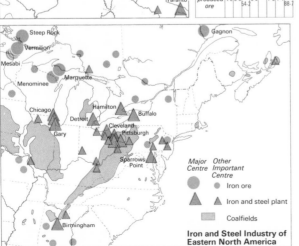

Major Centre ● / Other Important Centre ● Iron ore

▲ Major / ▲ Other — Iron and steel plant

Coalfields

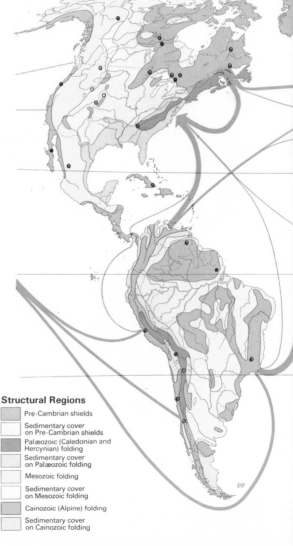

Structural Regions

- Pre-Cambrian shields
- Sedimentary cover on Pre-Cambrian shields
- Palæozoic (Caledonian and Hercynian) folding
- Sedimentary cover on Palæozoic folding
- Mesozoic folding
- Sedimentary cover on Mesozoic folding
- Cainozoic (Alpine) folding
- Sedimentary cover on Cainozoic folding

World production of Pig iron and Ferro-alloys

Total World production 1972: 461·9 M tonnes

Lux. 1%
Rumania 1%
S. Africa 1%
Brazil 1%
Spain 1%
Australia 1%
India 1·5%
Poland 1·5%
Czech. 2%
Canada 2%
Italy 2%
Belg. 2·5%
U.K. 3%
France 4%
China 6%
W. Germany 7%
Japan 16%
U.S.A. 18%
U.S.S.R. 20%
Others 8·5%

Growth of World production of Pig iron and Ferro-alloys

M tonnes

1938
1946
1951
1956
1961
1966
1974

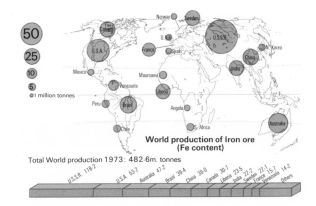

World production of Iron ore (Fe content)

Total World production 1973: 482·6m. tonnes

U.S.S.R. 118·2 · U.S.A. 53·2 · Australia 41·2 · Brazil 39·4 · China 39·0 · Canada 30·7 · Liberia 23·5 · India 22·2 · Sweden 22·1 · France 15·7 · Venezuela 14·2 · Others

50
25
10
5
1 million tonnes

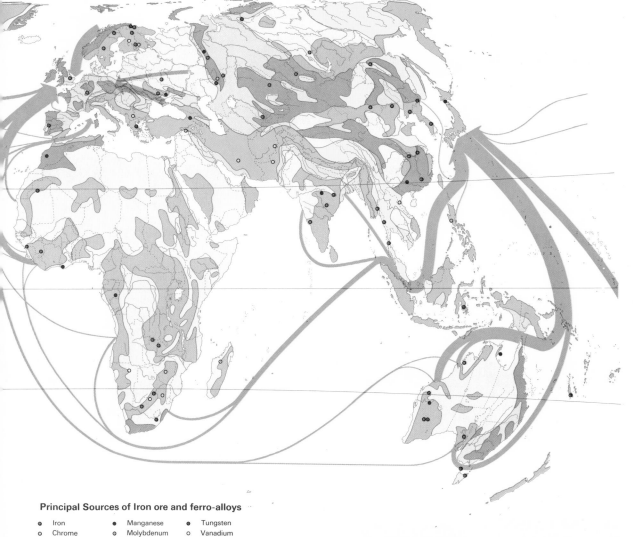

Principal Sources of Iron ore and ferro-alloys

- Iron
- Chrome
- Cobalt
- Manganese
- Molybdenum
- Nickel
- Tungsten
- Vanadium
- Iron ore trade flow

Mineral Resources II

Antimony – imparts hardness when alloyed to other metals, especially lead.
Uses: type metal, pigments to paints, glass and enamels, fireproofing of textiles.

World production 78 478 tonnes

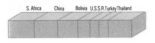

S. Africa   China   Bolivia   U.S.S.R. Turkey Thailand

Lead – heavy, soft, malleable, acid resistant.
Uses: storage batteries, sheeting and piping, cable covering, ammunition, type metal, weights, additive to petrol.

World production 3·57 million tonnes

U.S.A.   U.S.S.R.   Australia Canada

Tin – resistant to attacks by organic acids, malleable.
Uses: canning, foils, as an alloy to other metals (brass and bronze).

World production 217 200 tonnes

Malaysia   Bolivia   Indonesia   China Thailand

Aluminium – light, resists corrosion, good conductor.
Uses: aircraft, road and rail vehicles, domestic utensils, cables, makes highly tensile and light alloys.

World production 81·22 million tonnes (of Bauxite)

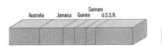

Australia   Jamaica   Surinam Guinea   U.S.S.R.

Gold – untarnishable and resistant to corrosion, highly ductile and malleable, good conductor. The pure metal is soft and it is alloyed to give it hardness.
Uses: bullion, coins, jewellery, gold-leaf, electronics.

World production 1135 tonnes

S. Africa   U.S.S.R.

Copper – excellent conductor of electricity and heat, durable, resistant to corrosion, strong and ductile.
Uses: wire, tubing, brass (with zinc and tin), bronze (with tin), (compounds) – dyeing.

World production 7·89 million tonnes

U.S.A.   U.S.S.R.   Chile Canada Zambia Zaire

Mercury – the only liquid metal, excellent conductor of electricity.
Uses: thermometers, electrical industry, gold and silver ore extraction, (compounds) – drugs, pigments, chemicals, dentistry.

World production 8932 tonnes

U.S.S.R.   Spain   China   Italy   Mexico

Zinc – hard metal, low corrosion factor.
Uses: brass (with copper and tin), galvanising, diecasting, medicines, paints and dyes.

World production 5·89 million tonnes

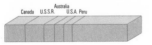

Canada   U.S.S.R.   Australia   U.S.A. Peru

Diamonds – very hard and resistant to chemical attack, high lustre, very rare.
Uses: jewellery, cutting and abrading other materials.

World production 44·63 million carats

Zaire   U.S.S.R.   S. Africa Ghana Botswana

Silver – ductile and malleable, a soft metal and must be alloyed for use in coinage.
Uses: coins, jewellery, photography, electronics, medicines.

World production 9306 tonnes

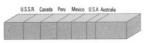

U.S.S.R.   Canada   Peru   Mexico   U.S.A Australia

	1949/51	1963/65	1971/73	
Copper				52% from scrap
reserves	181	140	298 m.t.	
Lead				42% from scrap
reserves	36	29	108 m.t.	
Zinc				21% from scrap
reserves	45	64	101 m.t.	

million tonnes (0 1 2 3 4 5 6 7 8)

Nickel	1949/51	1963/65	1971/73
reserves	14	28	33 m.t.
Tin	26% from scrap		
reserves	5·1 5·1 3·6 m.t.		

tonnes (0 100 200 300 400 500 600 000)

Aluminium	1949/51	1963/65	21% from scrap 1971/73
reserves	no figures		

million tonnes (0 5 10 15)

World consumption of non-ferrous metals

These diagrams show the average yearly world consumption of certain refined metals for 1949/51, 1963/65 and 1971/73 and also the percentage of the latter produced from scrap. The figures beneath each diagram show estimates made in 1950, 1964 and 1973 of reserves in the Western World.

While indicating that the reserves are by no means infinite the figures show how widely these estimates have differed over 10 years and take no account of unknown reserves, particularly in the sea-bed, or advances in mining technology which will make it economic to mine low-content ores.

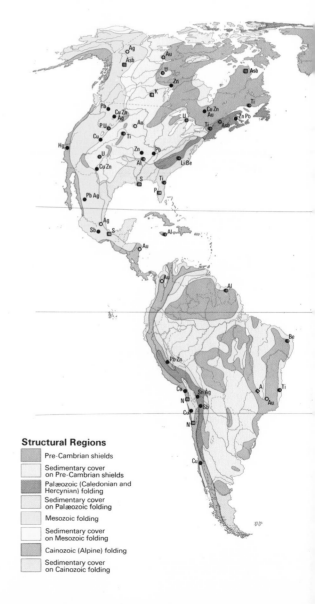

Structural Regions

- Pre-Cambrian shields
- Sedimentary cover on Pre-Cambrian shields
- Palæozoic (Caledonian and Hercynian) folding
- Sedimentary cover on Palæozoic folding
- Mesozoic folding
- Sedimentary cover on Mesozoic folding
- Cainozoic (Alpine) folding
- Sedimentary cover on Cainozoic folding

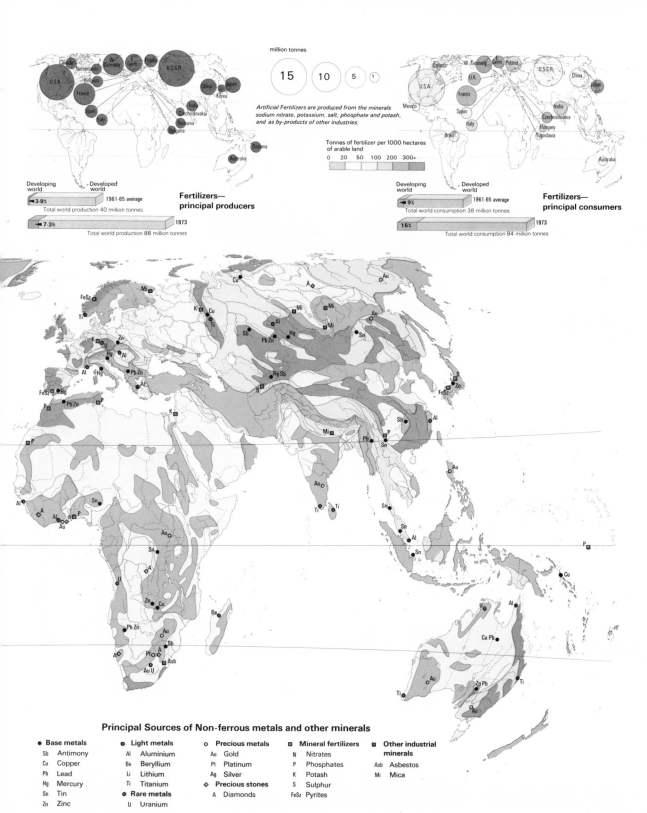

million tonnes

15   10   5 1

Artificial Fertilizers are produced from the minerals
sodium nitrate, potassium, salt, phosphate and potash,
and as by-products of other industries.

Tonnes of fertilizer per 1000 hectares
of arable land

0 20 50 100 200 300+

Fertilizers—principal producers

Developing world · Developed world

◄ 3·9%   1961-65 average
Total world production 40 million tonnes

◄ 7·3%   1973
Total world production 88 million tonnes

Fertilizers—principal consumers

Developing world · Developed world

◄ 9%   1961-65 average
Total world consumption 38 million tonnes

15%   1973
Total world consumption 84 million tonnes

Principal Sources of Non-ferrous metals and other minerals

● Base metals		● Light metals		○ Precious metals		■ Mineral fertilizers		■ Other industrial minerals	
Sb	Antimony	Al	Aluminium	Au	Gold	N	Nitrates		
Cu	Copper	Be	Beryllium	Pt	Platinum	P	Phosphates	Asb	Asbestos
Pb	Lead	Li	Lithium	Ag	Silver	K	Potash	Mi	Mica
Hg	Mercury	Ti	Titanium	◇ Precious stones		S	Sulphur		
Sn	Tin	● Rare metals		A	Diamonds	FeSz	Pyrites		
Zn	Zinc	U	Uranium						

39

Fuel and Energy

Coal

Coal is the result of the accumulation of vegetation over millions of years. Later under pressure from overlying sediments, it is hardened through four stages: peat, lignite, bituminous coal, and finally anthracite. Once the most important source of power, coal's importance now lies in the production of electricity and as a raw material in the production of plastics, heavy chemicals and disinfectants.

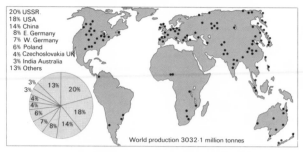

20% USSR.
18% USA
14% China
8% E. Germany
7% W. Germany
6% Poland
4% Czechoslovakia UK
3% India Australia
13% Others

World production 3032·1 million tonnes

Coal mine

Oil

Oil is derived from the remains of marine animals and plants, probably as a result of pressure, heat and chemical action. It is a complex mixture of hydrocarbons which are refined to extract the various constituents. These include products such as gasolene, kerosene and heavy fuel oils. Oil is rapidly replacing coal because of easier handling and reduced pollution.

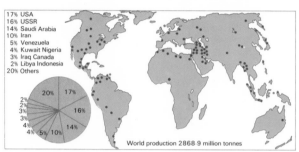

17% USA
16% USSR
14% Saudi Arabia
10% Iran
5% Venezuela
4% Kuwait Nigeria
3% Iraq Canada
2% Libya Indonesia
20% Others

World production 2868·9 million tonnes

Oil derrick

Natural gas

Since the early 1960's natural gas (methane) has become one of the largest single sources of energy. By liquefaction its volume can be reduced to 1/600 of that of gas and hence is easily transported. It is often found directly above oil reserves and because it is both cheaper than coal gas and less polluting it has great potential.

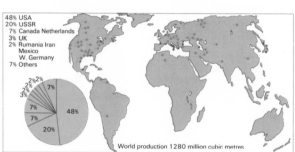

48% USA
20% USSR
7% Canada Netherlands
3% UK
2% Rumania Iran
Mexico
W. Germany
7% Others

World production 1280 million cubic metres

North sea gas rig

Water

Hydro-electric power stations use water to drive turbines which in turn generate electricity. The ideal site is one in which a consistently large volume of water falls a considerable height, hence sources of H.E.P. are found mainly in mountainous areas. Potential sources of hydro-electricity using waves or tides are yet to be exploited widely.

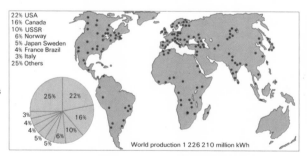

22% USA
16% Canada
10% USSR
6% Norway
5% Japan Sweden
4% France Brazil
3% Italy
25% Others

World production 1 226 210 million kWh

Water power

Nuclear energy

The first source of nuclear power was developed in Britain in 1956. Energy is obtained from heat generated by the reaction from splitting atoms of certain elements, of which uranium and plutonium are the most important. Although the initial installation costs are very high the actual running costs are low because of the slow consumption of fuel.

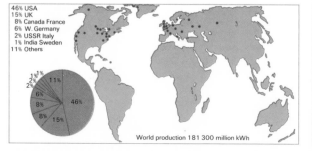

46% USA
15% UK
8% Canada France
6% W. Germany
2% USSR Italy
1% India Sweden
11% Others

World production 181 300 million kWh

Nuclear power station

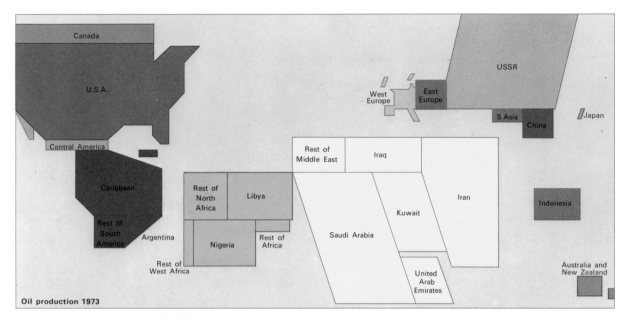

Oil production 1973

Labels within image: Canada, U.S.A., Central America, Caribbean, Rest of South America, Argentina, Rest of West Africa, Rest of North Africa, Libya, Nigeria, Rest of Africa, Rest of Middle East, Iraq, Saudi Arabia, Kuwait, United Arab Emirates, Iran, West Europe, East Europe, USSR, S Asia, China, Japan, Indonesia, Australia and New Zealand

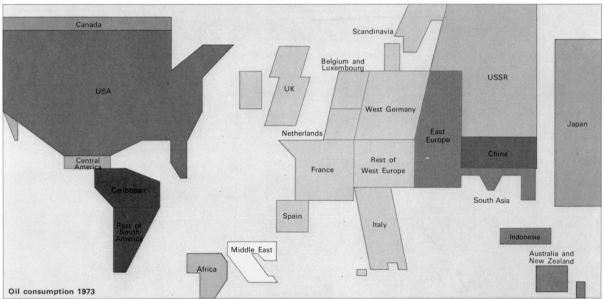

Oil consumption 1973

Labels within image: Canada, USA, Central America, Caribbean, Rest of South America, Africa, Middle East, UK, Netherlands, France, Spain, Belgium and Luxembourg, Scandinavia, West Germany, Rest of West Europe, Italy, East Europe, USSR, China, South Asia, Japan, Indonesia, Australia and New Zealand

Oil's new super-powers *above*
When countries are scaled according to their production and consumption of oil they take on new dimensions. At present, large supplies of oil are concentrated in a few countries of the Caribbean, the Middle East and North Africa, except for the vast indigenous supplies of the U.S.A. and U.S.S.R. The Middle East, with 55% of the world's reserves, produces 37% of the world's supply and yet consumes less than 3%. The U.S.A.,

despite its great production, has a deficiency of nearly 300 million tons a year, consuming 30% of the world's total. Estimates show that Western Europe, at present consuming 747 million tons or 27% of the total each year, may by 1980 surpass the U.S. consumption. Japan is the largest importer of crude oil with an increase in consumption of 440% during the period 1963-73.

Energy balance

millions of tons of coal equivalent

- −500 to −200
- −200 to −50
- −50 to 0
- 0 to +50
- +50 to +200
- +200 to +500

The figures indicate whether a surplus or deficit exists between home production and home consumption.

Occupations

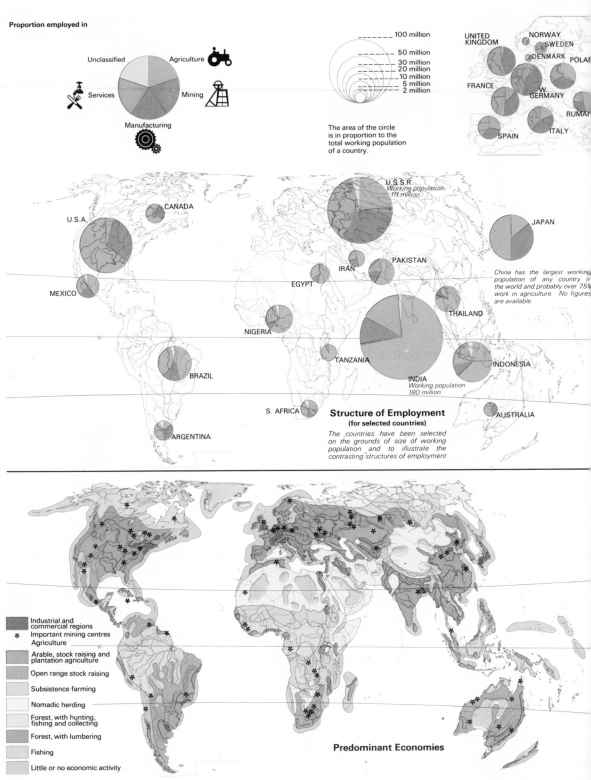

Proportion employed in

Unclassified | Agriculture
Services | Mining
Manufacturing

100 million
50 million
30 million
20 million
10 million
5 million
2 million

The area of the circle is in proportion to the total working population of a country.

UNITED KINGDOM | NORWAY | SWEDEN | DENMARK | POLAND
FRANCE | W. GERMANY | RUMANIA
SPAIN | ITALY

CANADA
U.S.A.
MEXICO
U.S.S.R.
Working population 111 million
JAPAN
IRAN | PAKISTAN
EGYPT
JAPAN
NIGERIA
THAILAND
TANZANIA
INDONESIA
BRAZIL
INDIA
Working population 180 million
S. AFRICA
ARGENTINA
AUSTRALIA

China has the largest working population of any country in the world and probably over 75% work in agriculture. No figures are available.

Structure of Employment
(for selected countries)

The countries have been selected on the grounds of size of working population and to illustrate the contrasting structures of employment

Industrial and commercial regions
* Important mining centres
Agriculture
Arable, stock raising and plantation agriculture
Open range stock raising
Subsistence farming
Nomadic herding
Forest, with hunting, fishing and collecting
Forest, with lumbering
Fishing
Little or no economic activity

Predominant Economies

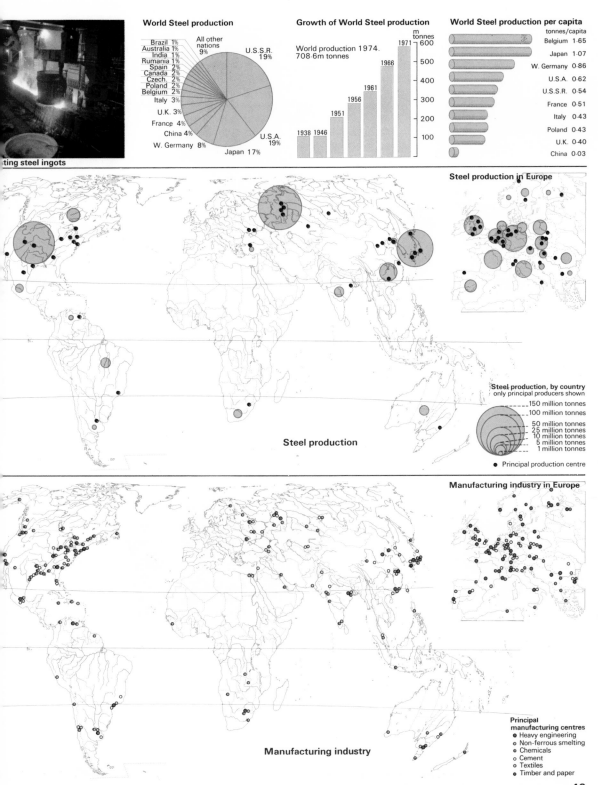

World Steel production

U.S.S.R. 19%
U.S.A. 19%
Japan 17%
W. Germany 8%
China 4%
France 4%
U.K. 3%
Italy 3%
Belgium 2%
Poland 2%
Czech. 2%
Canada 2%
Spain 2%
Rumania 1%
India 1%
Australia 1%
Brazil 1%
All other nations 9%

Growth of World Steel production

World production 1974.
708·6m tonnes

m tonnes
1938 1946 1951 1956 1961 1966 1971
600
500
400
300
200
100

World Steel production per capita

	tonnes/capita
Belgium	1·65
Japan	1·07
W. Germany	0·86
U.S.A.	0·62
U.S.S.R.	0·54
France	0·51
Italy	0·43
Poland	0·43
U.K.	0·40
China	0·03

ting steel ingots

Steel production in Europe

Steel production

Steel production, by country
only principal producers shown

150 million tonnes
100 million tonnes
50 million tonnes
25 million tonnes
10 million tonnes
5 million tonnes
1 million tonnes

• Principal production centre

Manufacturing industry in Europe

Manufacturing industry

Principal
manufacturing centres
• Heavy engineering
○ Non-ferrous smelting
• Chemicals
○ Cement
○ Textiles
• Timber and paper

43

Transport

Shipyards

Japan 17 609	
Sweden 2206	
West Germany 2151	
Spain 1428	
France 1349	
U.K. 1281	
Denmark 1125	
Italy 1028	
Norway 1012	
U.S.A. 801	
Yug. 774	
Neth. 723	

Shipbuilding
tonnage launched
in thousand gross
registered tons

● Principal shipbuilding centres

Aircraft Industry

In 1975 there were approximately 10 000 civil passenger airliners in service. This diagram shows where they were built.

U.S.A. 53%	U.S.S.R. 33%	U.K. 6% Netherlands 3% France 2%

Trade in Aircraft and Aircraft Engines
1973 *million U.S. $.*

	Exports			Imports	
	Aircraft.	Engines		Aircraft.	Engines
U.S.A.	4143	714	U.S.A.	563	218
U.K.	605	591	Canada	438	108
France	360	150	France	400	250
Canada	325	132	U.K.	389	393
W. Germ.	200		Australia	342	20
Neth.	192	89	W. Germ.	279	
Italy	137		Japan	236	107

Concorde and Boeing 747

● Principal aircraft manufacturing centres

Motor vehicles

Production 1973 thousand units	Exports 1973	Imports million U.S. $.
U.S.A. 12 638	6076	1005
Japan 7088	4899	193
W. Germany 3949	9107	996
France 3596	3779	1903
U.K. 2164	2701	1599
Italy 1960	1963	1263
Canada 1604	4814	5349
U.S.S.R. 1604	611	240
Belgium 938	2215	1457

Locomotive works

Railway vehicles

Exports 1973		Imports million U.S. $.	
U.S.A.	219·2	Yugoslavia	109·2
France	210·2	Brazil	65·8
Japan	186·3	S. Africa	48·4
W. Germany	157·7	W. Germany	47·4
Canada	76·1	U.S.A.	39·0
Yugoslavia	59·6	Belg.-Lux.	34·9
Italy	42·2	Netherlands	34·4
Spain	42·2	France	31·3
U.K.	38·6	Canada	30·0
Sweden	24·2	Argentina	25·7
Belg.-Lux.	22·0	Italy	22·9
Portugal	14·4	Sweden	19·4
Austria	11·8	S. Korea	18·8

Car assembly line

● Principal locomotive building centres

● Principal motor vehicle plants

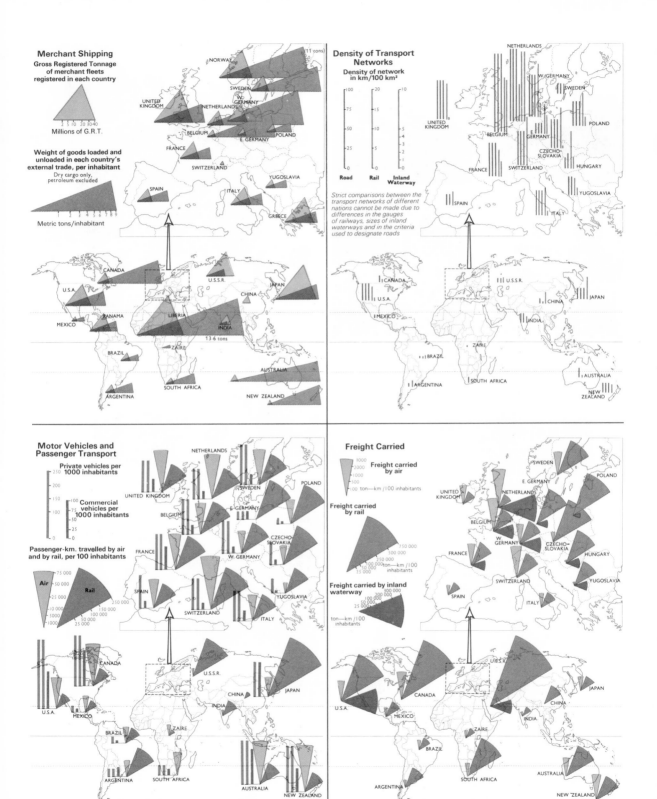

Merchant Shipping

Gross Registered Tonnage of merchant fleets registered in each country

2 5 10 20 30 40
Millions of G.R.T.

Weight of goods loaded and unloaded in each country's external trade, per inhabitant

Dry cargo only, petroleum excluded

1 2 3 4 5 6 7 8 9
Metric tons/inhabitant

NORWAY (11 tons)
SWEDEN
W. GERMANY
UNITED KINGDOM
NETHERLANDS
BELGIUM
E. GERMANY
POLAND
FRANCE
SWITZERLAND
YUGOSLAVIA
SPAIN
ITALY
GREECE

CANADA
U.S.S.R.
JAPAN
U.S.A.
CHINA
PANAMA
LIBERIA
MEXICO
INDIA
13·6 tons
BRAZIL
ZAIRE
AUSTRALIA
SOUTH AFRICA
ARGENTINA
NEW ZEALAND

Density of Transport Networks

Density of network in km/100 km²

Road	Rail	Inland Waterway
100	20	10
75	15	5
50	10	4
25	5	3
		2
		1

Strict comparisons between the transport networks of different nations cannot be made due to differences in the gauges of railways, sizes of inland waterways and in the criteria used to designate roads

NETHERLANDS
W. GERMANY
SWEDEN
UNITED KINGDOM
BELGIUM
E. GERMANY
POLAND
FRANCE
CZECHO-SLOVAKIA
HUNGARY
SWITZERLAND
SPAIN
ITALY
YUGOSLAVIA

CANADA
U.S.S.R.
JAPAN
U.S.A.
CHINA
MEXICO
INDIA
BRAZIL
ZAIRE
ARGENTINA
SOUTH AFRICA
AUSTRALIA
NEW ZEALAND

Motor Vehicles and Passenger Transport

Private vehicles per 1000 inhabitants

250
200
150
100
50
0

Commercial vehicles per 1000 inhabitants

100
75
50
25
0

Passenger-km. travelled by air and by rail, per 100 inhabitants

Air
75 000
50 000
25 000
10 000
5000
1000

Rail
250 000
150 000
100 000
50 000
25 000

NETHERLANDS
SWEDEN
POLAND
UNITED KINGDOM
BELGIUM
E. GERMANY
CZECHO-SLOVAKIA
FRANCE
W. GERMANY
SPAIN
YUGOSLAVIA
SWITZERLAND
ITALY

CANADA
U.S.S.R.
JAPAN
U.S.A.
CHINA
MEXICO
INDIA
BRAZIL
ZAIRE
ARGENTINA
SOUTH AFRICA
AUSTRALIA
NEW ZEALAND

Freight Carried

Freight carried by air

3000
2000
1000
500
100 ton—km/100 inhabitants

Freight carried by rail

750 000
500 000
100 000
50 000
25 000
ton—km/100 inhabitants

Freight carried by inland waterway

300 000
100 000
50 000
25 000
ton—km/100 inhabitants

SWEDEN
POLAND
E. GERMANY
NETHERLANDS
UNITED KINGDOM
BELGIUM
CZECHO-SLOVAKIA
W. GERMANY
HUNGARY
FRANCE
SWITZERLAND
YUGOSLAVIA
SPAIN
ITALY

U.S.S.R.
JAPAN
CANADA
CHINA
U.S.A.
MEXICO
INDIA
ZAIRE
BRAZIL
AUSTRALIA
SOUTH AFRICA
ARGENTINA
NEW ZEALAND

Trade

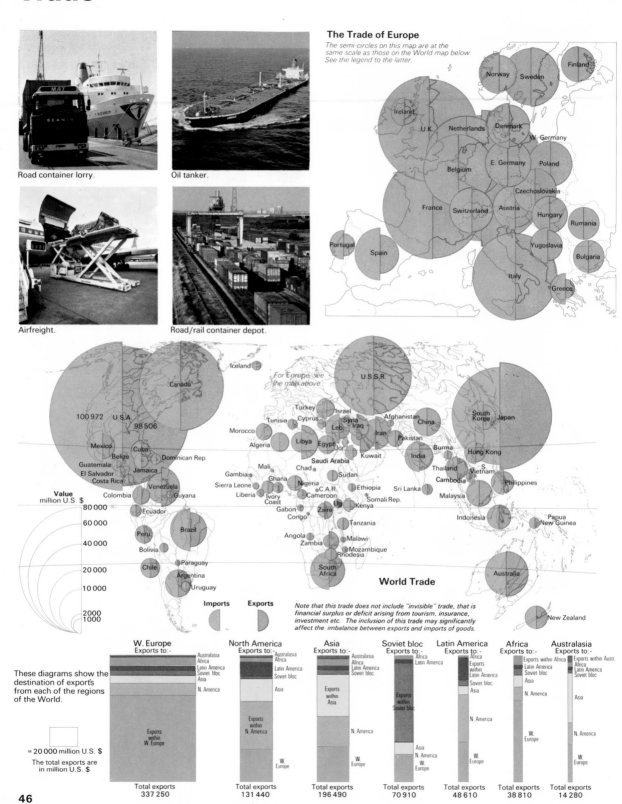

Road container lorry.

Oil tanker.

Airfreight.

Road/rail container depot.

The Trade of Europe

The semi-circles on this map are at the same scale as those on the World map below. See the legend to the latter.

Norway Sweden Finland
Ireland U.K. Netherlands Denmark W. Germany
Belgium E. Germany Poland
France Switzerland Austria Czechoslovakia
Portugal Spain Hungary Rumania
Italy Yugoslavia Bulgaria
Greece

Iceland For Europe see the map above U.S.S.R.
Canada
100 972 U.S.A. 98 506 Turkey Israel Afghanistan China South Korea Japan
Mexico Tunisia Cyprus Syria Iraq Iran Pakistan
Morocco Leb Kuwait Burma Hong Kong
Cuba Algeria Libya Egypt Jor. India Thailand S. Vietnam
Belize Dominican Rep. Saudi Arabia Cambodia
Guatemala Jamaica Mali Chad Sudan Sri Lanka Philippines
El Salvador Gambia Ghana Nigeria Ethiopia Malaysia
Costa Rica Sierra Leone C.A.R. Somali Rep.
Colombia Venezuela Guyana Liberia Ivory Coast Cameroon Indonesia Papua New Guinea
Ecuador Gabon Ug. Kenya
Congo Zaire Tanzania
Peru Brazil Angola Malawi
Bolivia Zambia Mozambique
Rhodesia Australia
Paraguay South Africa **World Trade**
Chile Argentina
Uruguay New Zealand

Value million U.S. $
80 000
60 000
40 000
20 000
10 000
2000
1000

Imports **Exports**

Note that this trade does not include "invisible" trade, that is financial surplus or deficit arising from tourism, insurance, investment etc. The inclusion of this trade may significantly affect the imbalance between exports and imports of goods.

These diagrams show the destination of exports from each of the regions of the World.

☐ = 20 000 million U.S. $
The total exports are in million U.S. $

W. Europe
Exports to:-
Australasia
Africa
Latin America
Soviet bloc
Asia
N. America
Exports within W. Europe
Total exports
337 250

North America
Exports to:-
Australasia
Africa
Latin America
Soviet bloc
Asia
Exports within N. America
W. Europe
Total exports
131 440

Asia
Exports to:-
Australasia
Africa
Latin America
Soviet bloc
Exports within Asia
N. America
W. Europe
Total exports
196 490

Soviet bloc
Exports to:-
Africa
Latin America
Exports within Soviet bloc
Asia
N. America
W. Europe
Total exports
70 910

Latin America
Exports to:-
Africa
Exports within Latin America
Soviet bloc
Asia
N. America
W. Europe
Total exports
48 610

Africa
Exports to:-
Exports within Africa
Soviet bloc
Asia
N. America
W. Europe
Total exports
38 810

Australasia
Exports to:-
Exports within Austr.
Africa
Latin America
Soviet bloc
Asia
N. America
W. Europe
Total exports
14 280

46

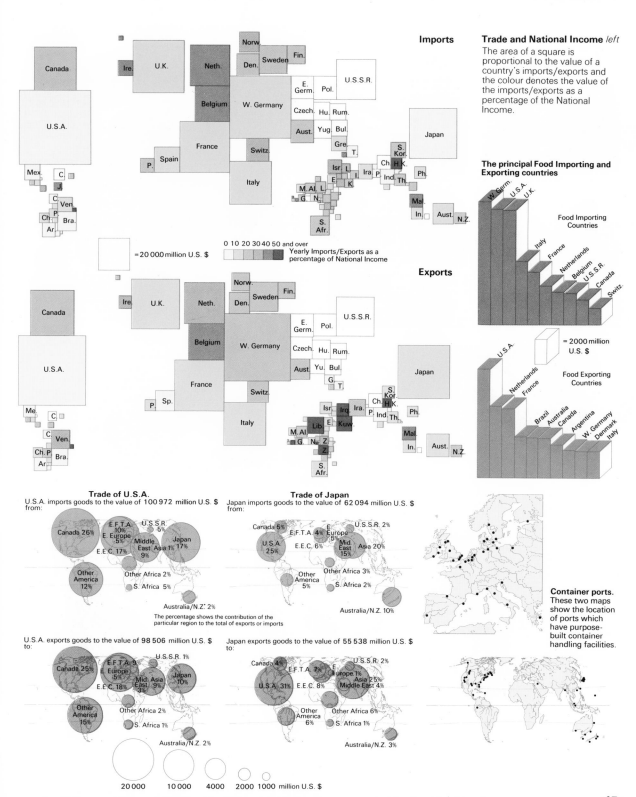

Imports

Trade and National Income *left*
The area of a square is proportional to the value of a country's imports/exports and the colour denotes the value of the imports/exports as a percentage of the National Income.

The principal Food Importing and Exporting countries

Food Importing Countries

= 20 000 million U.S. $

0 10 20 30 40 50 and over
Yearly Imports/Exports as a percentage of National Income

Exports

= 2000 million U.S. $

Food Exporting Countries

Trade of U.S.A.
U.S.A. imports goods to the value of 100 972 million U.S. $ from:

Canada 26%
E.F.T.A. 10%
E. Europe 5%
U.S.S.R. 5%
Middle East 9%
Asia 1%
Japan 17%
E.E.C. 17%
Other America 12%
Other Africa 2%
S. Africa 5%
Australia/N.Z. 2%

The percentage shows the contribution of the particular region to the total of exports or imports

Trade of Japan
Japan imports goods to the value of 62 094 million U.S. $ from:

Canada 5%
E.F.T.A. 4%
E. Europe 5%
U.S.S.R. 2%
U.S.A. 25%
E.E.C. 6%
Mid. East 15%
Asia 20%
Other America 5%
Other Africa 3%
S. Africa 2%
Australia/N.Z. 10%

U.S.A. exports goods to the value of 98 506 million U.S. $ to:

Canada 25%
E.F.T.A. 9%
E. Europe 5%
U.S.S.R. 1%
E.E.C. 18%
Mid East 3%
Asia 9%
Japan 10%
Other America 15%
Other Africa 2%
S. Africa 1%
Australia/N.Z. 2%

Japan exports goods to the value of 55 538 million U.S. $ to:

Canada 4%
E.F.T.A. 7%
E. Europe 1%
U.S.S.R. 2%
U.S.A. 31%
E.E.C. 8%
Middle East 4%
Asia 25%
Other America 6%
Other Africa 6%
S. Africa 1%
Australia/N.Z. 3%

Container ports.
These two maps show the location of ports which have purpose-built container handling facilities.

20 000   10 000   4000   2000 1000 million U.S. $

47

Wealth

The living standard of a few highly developed, urbanised, industrialised countries is a complete contrast to the conditions of the vast majority of economically undeveloped, agrarian states. It is this contrast which divides mankind into rich and poor, well fed and hungry. The developing world is still an overwhelmingly agricultural world: over 70% of all its people live off the land and yet the output from that land remains pitifully low. Many Africans, South Americans and Asians struggle with the soil but the bad years occur only too frequently and they seldom have anything left over to save. The need for foreign capital then arises.

National Income *see right*
The gap between developing and developed worlds is in fact widening eg. in 1938 the incomes for the United States and India were in the proportions of 1:15; now they are 1:35.

Islands *see map right*
a Antilles   h Mauritius
b Martinique   j Solomon
c Barbados   k New Hebrides
d Cape Verde   l Fiji
e Bahrein   m New Caledonia
f Comoro   n Tonga
g Reunion

Incomes per capita in U.S. dollars 1972

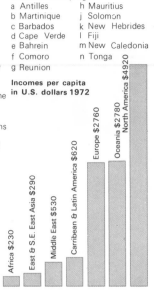

Africa $230
East & S.E. East Asia $290
Middle East $530
Carribean & Latin America $620
Europe $2760
Oceania $2780
North America $4920

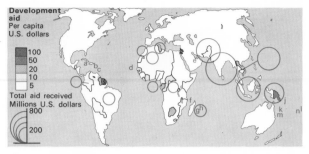

Development aid
Per capita
U.S. dollars

100
50
20
10
5

Total aid received
Millions U.S. dollars
800
200

Development aid
The provision of foreign aid, defined as assistance on concessional terms for promoting development, is today an accepted, though controversial aspect of the economic policies of most advanced countries towards less developed countries. Aid for development is based not merely on economic considerations but also on social, political and historical factors. The most important international committee set up after the war was that of the U.N.; practically all aid however has been given bi-laterally direct from an industrialised country to an under-developed country. Although aid increased during the 1950's the donated proportion of industrialised countries GNP has diminished from 0·5 to 0·4%. Less developed countries share of world trade also decreased and increased population invalidated any progress made.

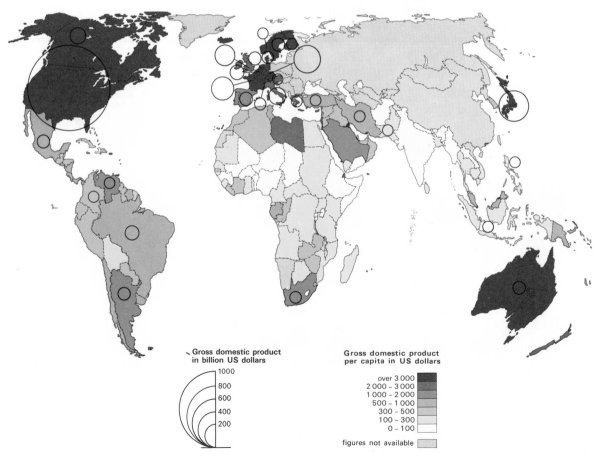

Gross domestic product in billion US dollars
1000
800
600
400
200

Gross domestic product per capita in US dollars
over 3 000
2 000 – 3 000
1 000 – 2 000
500 – 1 000
300 – 500
100 – 300
0 – 100

figures not available

GENERAL REFERENCE

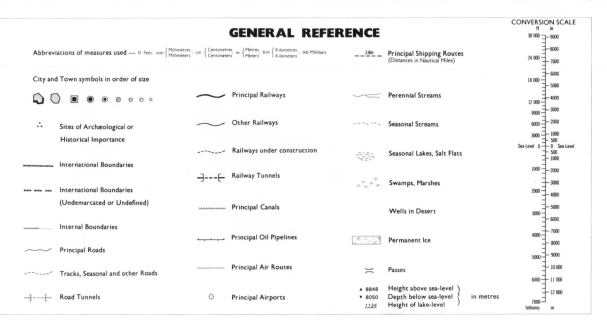

Abbreviations of measures used — ft Feet; mm {Millimetres / Millimeters}; cm {Centimetres / Centimeters}; m {Metres / Meters}; Km {Kilometres / Kilometers}; mb Millibars

City and Town symbols in order of size

∴ Sites of Archæological or Historical Importance

———————— International Boundaries

— — — — International Boundaries (Undemarcated or Undefined)

·············· Internal Boundaries

〜〜 Principal Roads

----- Tracks, Seasonal and other Roads

→---← Road Tunnels

〜〜 Principal Railways

〜〜 Other Railways

----- Railways under construction

→---← Railway Tunnels

⌂⌂⌂⌂ Principal Canals

—+—+— Principal Oil Pipelines

———— Principal Air Routes

✿ Principal Airports

----3386---- Principal Shipping Routes (Distances in Nautical Miles)

〜〜 Perennial Streams

----〜 Seasonal Streams

⸝⸍ Seasonal Lakes, Salt Flats

⁗ Swamps, Marshes

Wells in Desert

▦ Permanent Ice

⤨ Passes

▲ 8848 Height above sea-level }
▼ 8050 Depth below sea-level } in metres
1134 Height of lake-level }

CONVERSION SCALE

THE WORLD
Physical

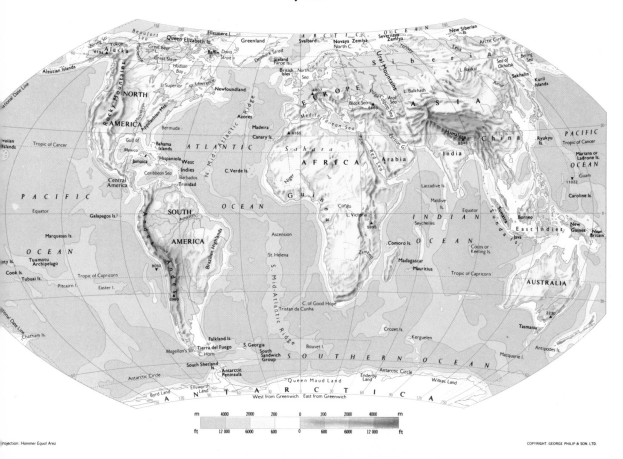

Projection: Hammer Equal Area

COPYRIGHT. GEORGE PHILIP & SON. LTD.

Projection : Hammer Equal Area

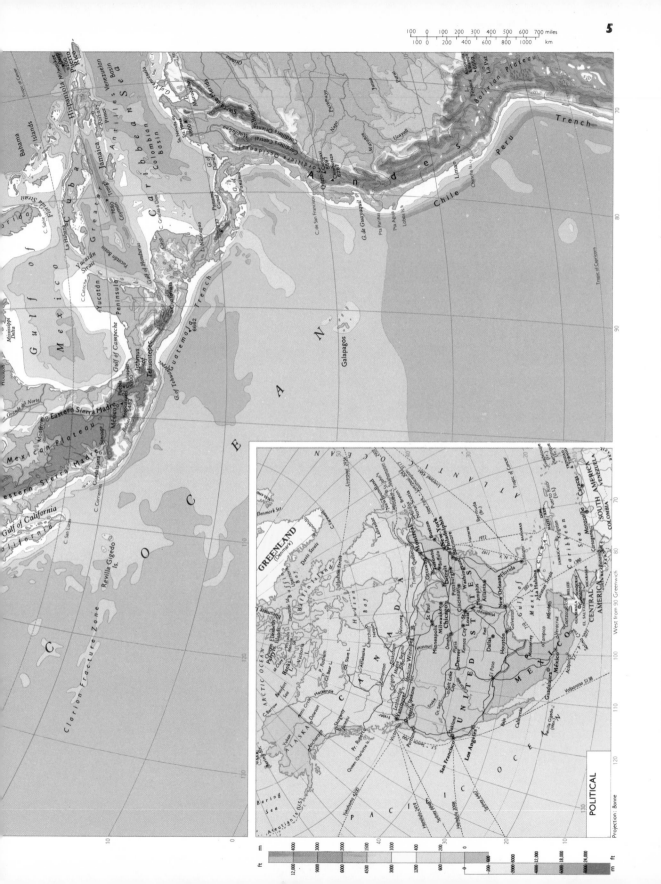

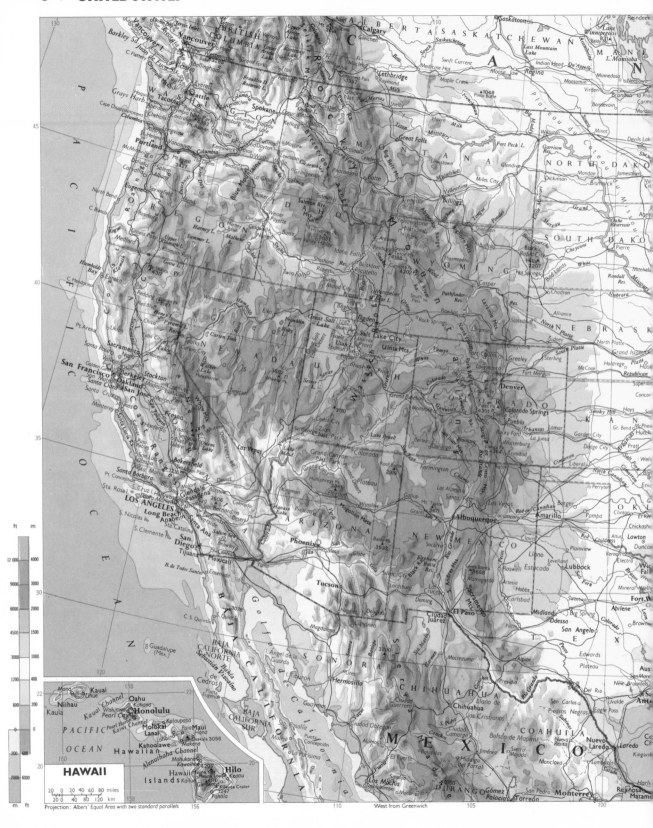

HAWAII

20 0 20 40 60 80 miles
40 80 120 km

Projection: Albers' Equal Area with two standard parallels

West from Greenwich

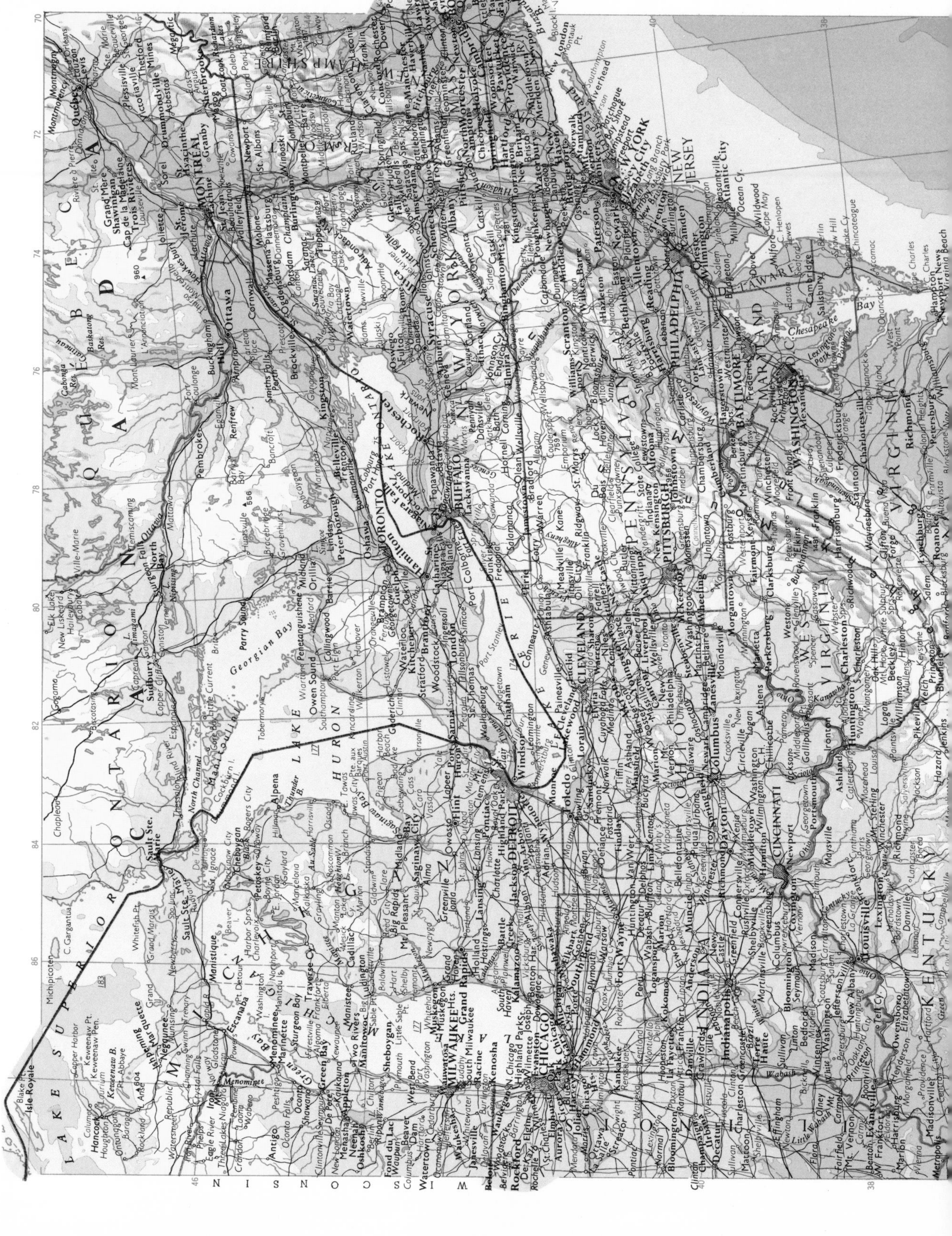
LAKE SUPERIOR
ONTARIO
QUEBEC
CANADA
MICHIGAN
LAKE HURON
Georgian Bay
LAKE ONTARIO
LAKE ERIE
NEW YORK
PENNSYLVANIA
OHIO
INDIANA
ILLINOIS
KENTUCKY
WEST VIRGINIA
VIRGINIA
MARYLAND
DELAWARE
NEW JERSEY
VERMONT
NEW HAMPSHIRE
MASSACHUSETTS
WISCONSIN
CHICAGO
DETROIT
CLEVELAND
BUFFALO
TORONTO
MONTREAL
BOSTON
NEW YORK
PHILADELPHIA
PITTSBURGH
BALTIMORE
WASHINGTON
CINCINNATI
MILWAUKEE
Ottawa
Quebec

50 0 50 100 miles
50 0 50 100 150 km

Continuation
Eastwards
On same scale

COPYRIGHT GEORGE PHILIP & SON, LTD

MAINE

NEW HAMPSHIRE

Bangor · Old Town · Waterville · Augusta · Portland · Saco · Biddeford · Portsmouth · Newburyport · Dover

VIRGINIA

NORTH CAROLINA

Raleigh · Durham · Greensboro · Winston-Salem · Charlotte · Wilmington · Fayetteville · Goldsboro · New Bern

TENNESSEE

Nashville · Knoxville · Chattanooga · Murfreesboro

SOUTH CAROLINA

Columbia · Charleston · Spartanburg · Greenville · Sumter · Florence

GEORGIA

Atlanta · Macon · Columbus · Savannah · Augusta · Albany · Valdosta

ALABAMA

Birmingham · Montgomery · Mobile · Tuscaloosa · Selma · Dothan

MISSISSIPPI

Meridian · Hattiesburg · Laurel · Biloxi

FLORIDA

Jacksonville · Orlando · Tampa · St. Petersburg · Miami · Ft. Lauderdale · West Palm Beach · Daytona Beach · Gainesville · Tallahassee · Pensacola · Panama City · Sarasota · Fort Myers

BAHAMAS

Great Abaco I. · Little Abaco I. · Grand Bahama I. · Freeport · Great Guana Cay

ATLANTIC OCEAN

GULF OF MEXICO

EVERGLADES NAT. PARK

West from Greenwich

Projection: Alber's Equal Area with two standard parallels

6000 4500 3000 1500 1200 600 400 200 0 m
ft 200 600 2000 6000 12,000

28 76 78 82 84 80 36 34 30 26

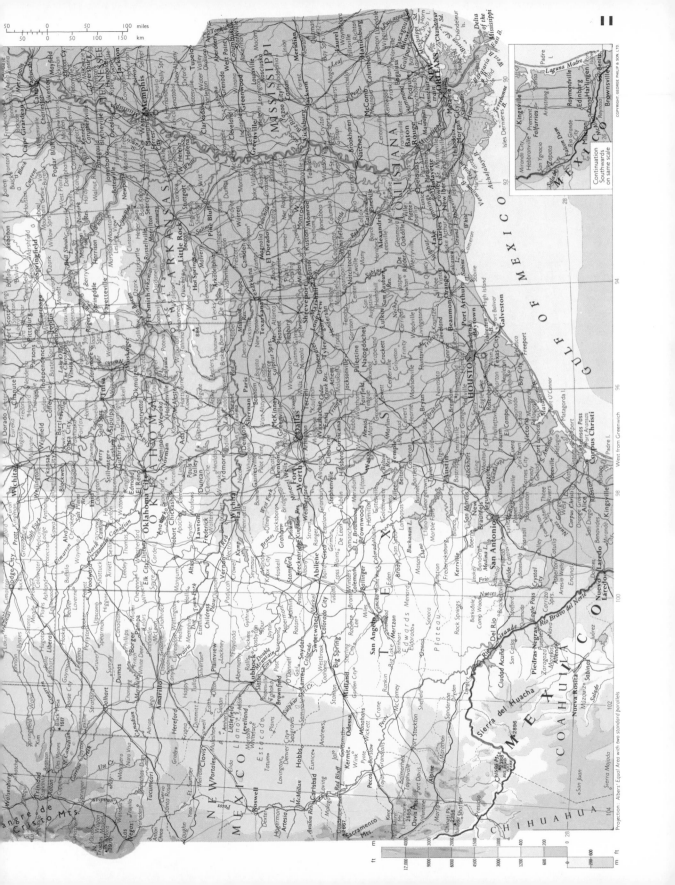

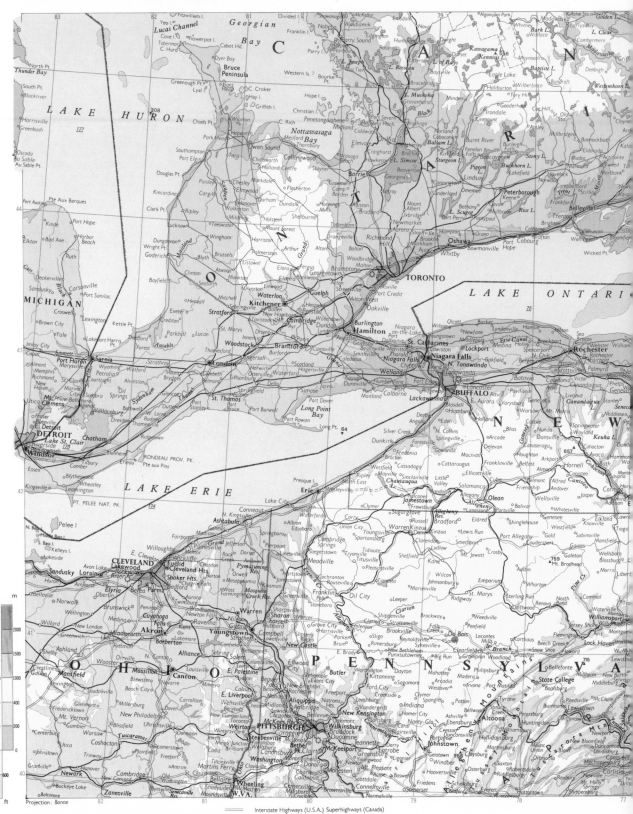

Projection: Bonne

══════ Interstate Highways (U.S.A.) Superhighways (Canada)
══════ Interstate Highways and Superhighways under Construction

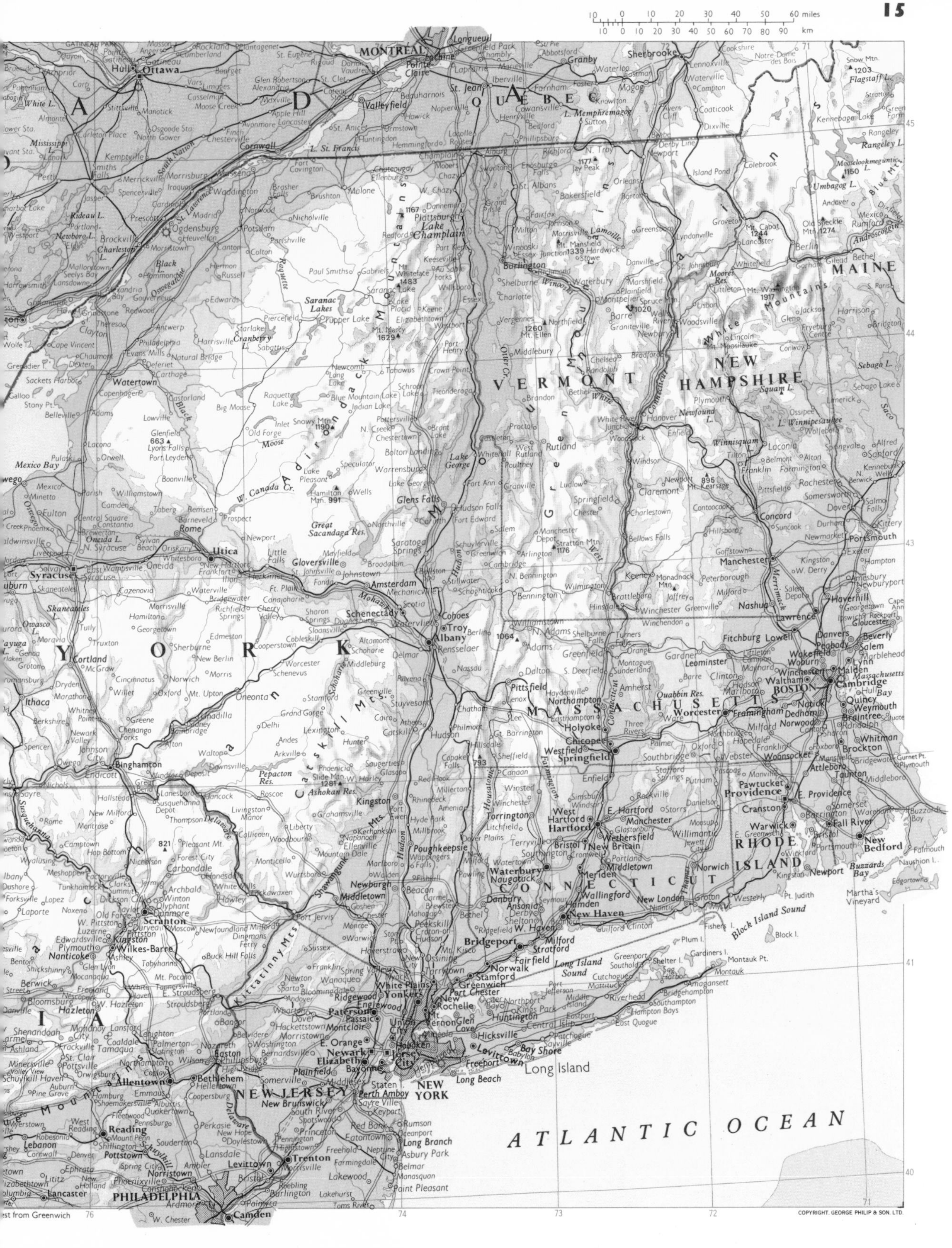

10 0 10 20 30 40 50 60 miles
10 0 10 20 30 40 50 60 70 80 90 km

MONTREAL

QUEBEC

MAINE

VERMONT

NEW HAMPSHIRE

Adirondack Mountains

Lake Champlain

Green Mountains

White Mountains

NEW YORK

MASSACHUSETTS

BOSTON

Cambridge

Worcester

Springfield

CONNECTICUT

RHODE ISLAND

Providence

Hartford

New Haven

Bridgeport

Stamford

Yonkers

NEW YORK

NEW JERSEY

Newark

Elizabeth

Jersey City

Trenton

PHILADELPHIA

Camden

Scranton

Wilkes-Barre

Allentown

Bethlehem

Reading

Lancaster

Binghamton

Ithaca

Syracuse

Utica

Rome

Watertown

Schenectady

Albany

Troy

Kingston

Poughkeepsie

Newburgh

Long Island

Long Island Sound

ATLANTIC OCEAN

Block Island Sound

Martha's Vineyard

Montauk Pt.

Ottawa

Hull

Cornwall

Burlington

Manchester

Concord

Portsmouth

Nashua

Lowell

Lawrence

Fall River

New Bedford

Newport

Buzzards Bay

East from Greenwich

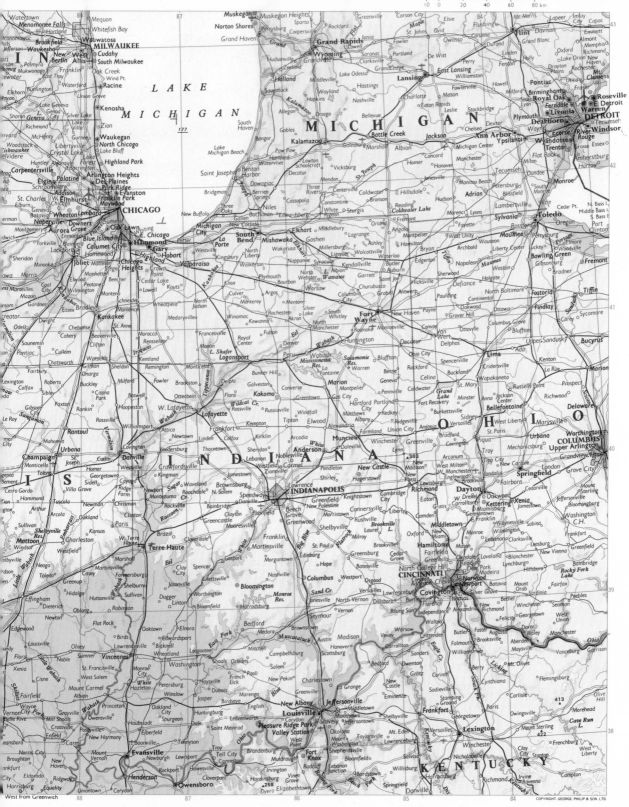

SEATTLE-PORTLAND
REGION
On same scale

PACIFIC OCEAN

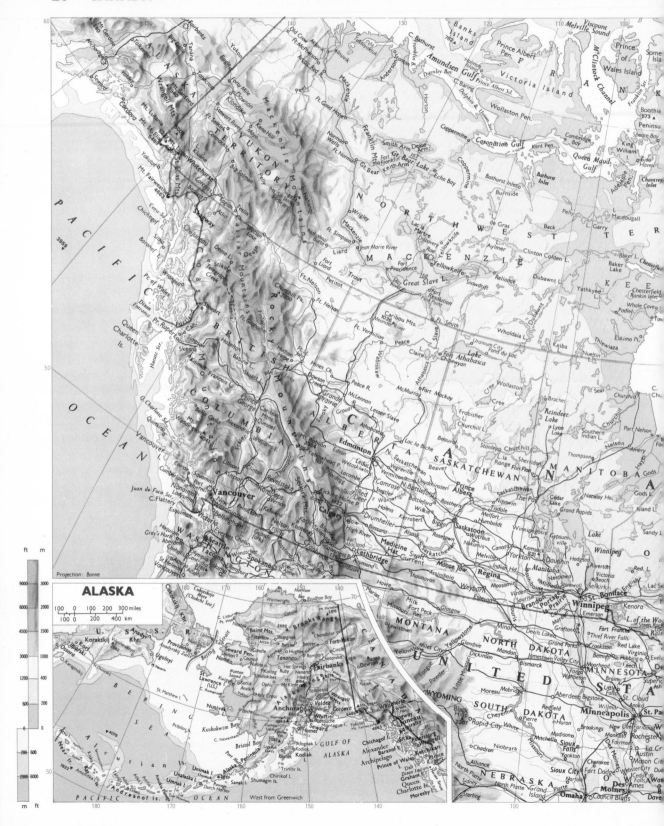

ALASKA

Projection: Bonne

100 0   100   200   300 miles
100 0   200   400 km

COPYRIGHT. GEORGE PHILIP & SON, LTD.

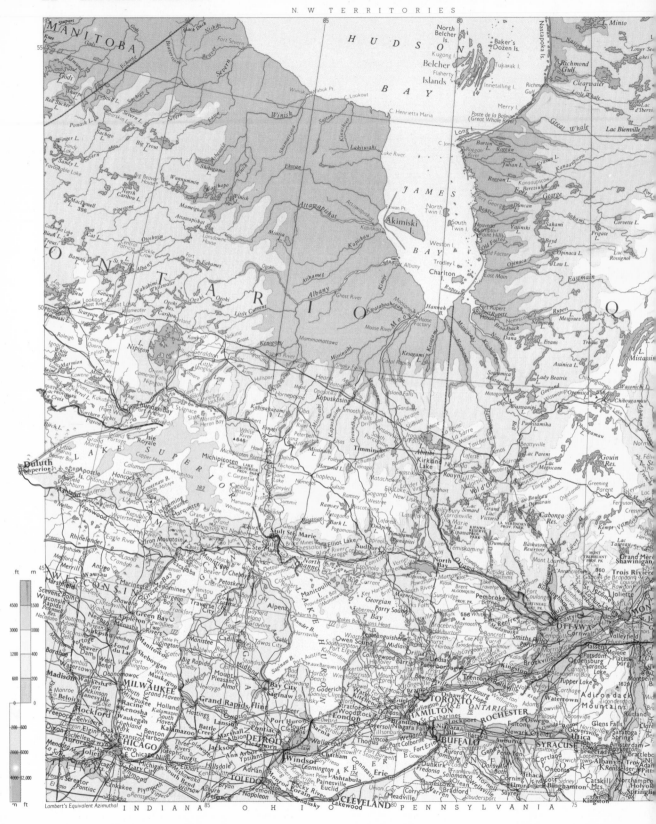

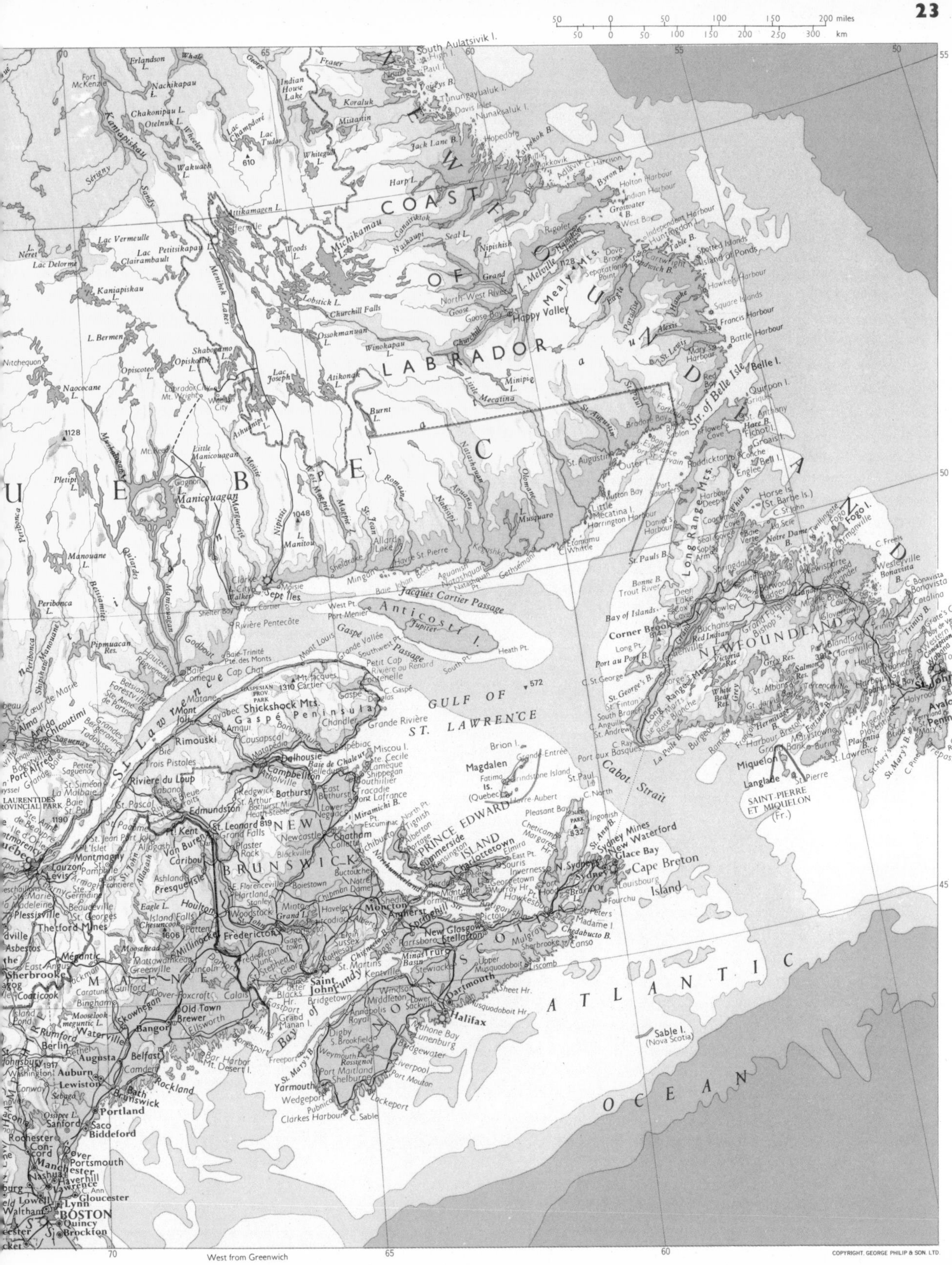

50 0 50 100 150 200 miles
50 0 50 100 150 200 250 300 km

QUEBEC

COAST OF LABRADOR

NEWFOUNDLAND

Str. of Belle Isle
Belle I.

Long Range Mts.

Corner Brook
Bay of Islands

Gander
Grand Falls

St. John's
Avalon Peninsula

Happy Valley
Goose Bay
Churchill Falls
Labrador City
Wabush

Michikamau L.
Mealy Mts.

Manicouagan
Sept Iles
Moisie

ANTICOSTI I.

GULF OF ST. LAWRENCE

Jacques Cartier Passage

Gaspé Peninsula
Shickshock Mts.
Gaspé

Rimouski
Rivière du Loup
Matane

NEW BRUNSWICK

Fredericton
Saint John
Moncton
Bathurst
Edmundston
Campbellton
Chatham
Newcastle

PRINCE EDWARD ISLAND
Charlottetown
Summerside

Magdalen Is.
(Quebec)

Cabot Strait

MIQUELON
Langlade
St. Pierre
SAINT-PIERRE ET MIQUELON (Fr.)

NOVA SCOTIA
Halifax
Truro
New Glasgow
Sydney
Glace Bay
Cape Breton Island
Louisbourg

Bay of Fundy
Yarmouth
Bridgetown
Digby
Lunenburg
Bridgewater
Liverpool
Shelburne

Sable I. (Nova Scotia)

ATLANTIC OCEAN

MAINE

Bangor
Augusta
Waterville
Lewiston
Auburn
Portland
Bath
Rockland
Biddeford
Saco
Sanford

BOSTON
Quincy
Brockton
Lynn
Gloucester
Lawrence
Lowell
Nashua
Manchester
Concord
Portsmouth
Rochester
Dover

Labrador Sea

70   West from Greenwich   65   60

COPYRIGHT. GEORGE PHILIP & SON. LTD.

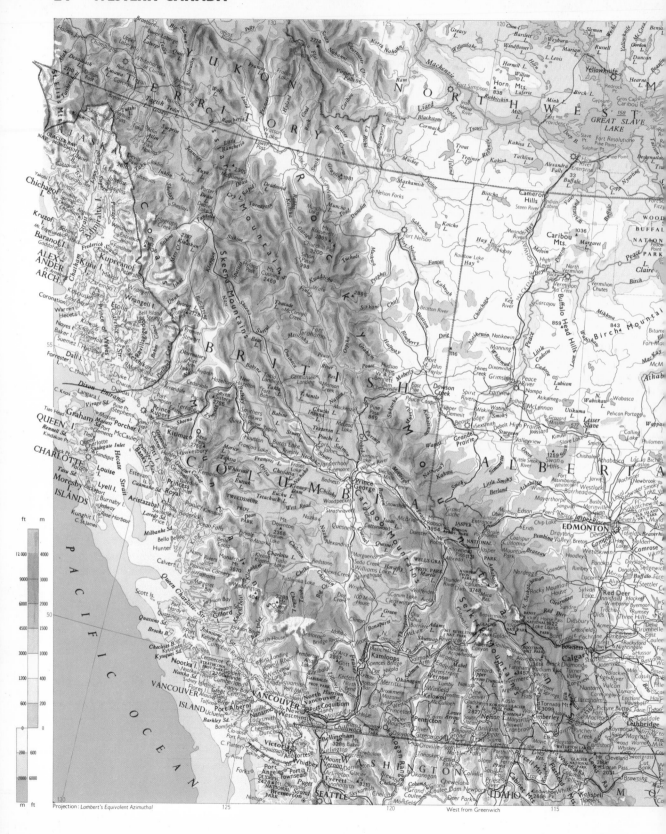

50 0 50 100 150 200 miles
50 0 50 100 150 200 250 300 km

MACKENZIE

TERRITORIES

KEEWATIN

HUDSON

BAY

SASKATCHEWAN

MANITOBA

ONTARIO

Lake Athabasca

Wollaston L.

Reindeer L.

Southern Indian L.

Churchill

Lac la Ronge

Flin Flon

The Pas

Cedar Lake

LAKE WINNIPEG

Lake Winnipegosis

Lake Manitoba

Prince Albert

NORTH Battleford

Saskatoon

Humboldt

Yorkton

Dauphin

Regina

Moose Jaw

Brandon

WINNIPEG

St. Boniface

Portage la Prairie

Swift Current

Medicine Hat

Cypress Hills

Kenora

Lake of the Woods

Rainy Lake

Duluth

NORTH DAKOTA

MINNESOTA

MONTANA

Minot

Williston

Devils Lake

Grand Forks

Bemidji

Hibbing

Grand Rapids

Fort Peck Lake

Garrison Reservoir

COPYRIGHT. GEORGE PHILIP & SON. LTD.

110   105   100   95

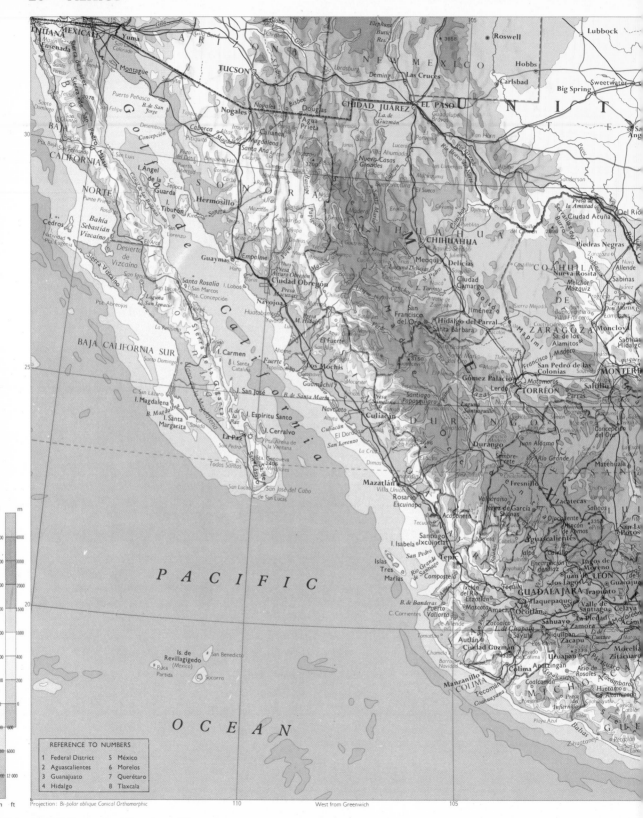

REFERENCE TO NUMBERS

1 Federal District   5 México
2 Aguascalientes   6 Morelos
3 Guanajuato   7 Querétaro
4 Hidalgo   8 Tlaxcala

Projection: Bi-polar oblique Conical Orthomorphic

West from Greenwich

50 0 50 100 150 200 miles
50 0 100 200 300 km

Wichita Falls · Denison · Paris · Bald · Hope
Sherman · Texarkana · ARKANSAS · Camden · Greenville
Denton · Greenville · Texarkana · El Dorado · MISSISSIPPI · Tuscaloosa · Opelika · Columbus · McRae
FORT WORTH · DALLAS · Marshall · Monroe · Vicksburg · Meridian · Montgomery · Phenix City · Americus · Cordele · Tifton
Ranger · Longview · Shreveport · Tallulah · Jackson · Troy · Albany · GEORGIA · Waycross
Cleburne · Corsicana · Tyler · ALABAMA · Dothan · Valdosta
D · Hillsboro · Palestine · Nacogdoches · Alexandria · Natchez · Hattiesburg · Laurel · FLORIDA · Tallahassee
Brownwood · Waco · Lufkin · Sabine · Baton Rouge · McComb · Bogalusa · Biloxi · MOBILE · Panama City · Apalachee Bay · Lake
Temple · Huntsville · Bryan · Beaumont · Lafayette · Hammond · Gulfport · Pensacola · C. San Blas · Suwannee
Austin · HOUSTON · Port Arthur · NEW ORLEANS · Breton Sound · Apalachee Bay · Clearwater
San Antonio · Rosenberg · Galveston · Atchafalaya Bay · Mississippi Delta · Terrebonne B.
Victoria · Corpus Christi

GULF OF

Alice · Kingsville · Laguna Madre
Laredo · Nuevo Laredo · Camargo · McAllen · Harlingen · Brownsville
Reynosa · Matamoros · Laguna Madre

MEXICO

Linares · Sierra de Tamaulipas · Soto la Marina
Ciudad Victoria · Ciudad Mante · Pta. Jerez
Ciudad Madero · Tampico · Laguna de Tamiahua
Ciudad Valles · Tantoyuca · Rio Rojo · Tuxpan
Poza Rica · Papantla · Nautla
Pachuca · Huauchinango · Tulancingo · Teziutlán
MEXICO · Jalapa · Veracruz
Orizaba · Córdoba · Alvarado
Tehuacán · Tlacotalpan · San Andrés Tuxtla
Cuernavaca · PUEBLA · Coatzacoalcos · Frontera · Ciudad del Carmen · Laguna de Términos
Acayucan · Villahermosa
Iguala · Chilpancingo · CHIAPAS · Cárdenas · TABASCO
Oaxaca · Minatitlán · CAMPECHE
OAXACA · Tuxtla Gutiérrez · San Cristóbal de las Casas · Comitán
Acapulco · Ixtepec · Tehuantepec · Salina Cruz · Golfo de Tehuantepec
Huixtla · Tapachula · GUATEMALA · HONDURAS · Tegucigalpa

Golfo de Campeche

Champotón · Campeche · Chenkan
Isla Desterrada · Isla Perez
Progreso · Motul · Tizimín · Puerto Morelos
Mérida · Izamal · Espita · Valladolid · Isla Cozumel
YUCATÁN · Chichén Itzá · Peto · B. de la Ascensión
Tekax · Vigía Chico · B. del Espíritu Santo
Hopelchén · QUINTANA ROO
Juárez · Bacalar · Chetumal
Belize City · BELIZE · Ambergris Cay · Turneffe Is.
Orange Walk · Islas de la Bahía · Roatán
Puerto Barrios · Puerto Cortés · La Ceiba
San Pedro Sula · El Progreso
GUATEMALA

CUBA

Canal de Yucatán
C. San Antonio · Pta. Catoche · C. Catoche · Río Lagartos

COPYRIGHT. GEORGE PHILIP & SON, LTD.

GULF OF MEXICO

M E X I C O

Isla Desterrada

Isla Pérez

Progreso
Motul
Mérida
Temax
YUCATÁN
Izamal
Tizimin
Valladolid
Isla Cozumel

Campeche

QUINTANA
ROO

CAMPECHE

Ciudad del Carmen
Laguna de Términos

Ambergris Cay

Belize City
Turneffe Is.
BELIZE

GUATEMALA
Huehuetenango
Cobán

Comitán

Golfo de Honduras
Islas de la Bahía
Roatán

Puerto Barrios
Puerto Cortés
La Ceiba

San Pedro Sula

HONDURAS

GUATEMALA
Jalapa
Zacapa
Chiquimula

Santa Ana
Suchitoto
Cojutepeque
Zacatecoluca

Tegucigalpa

Mosquitia
Laguna Caratasca
C. Falso
Puerto Cabo Gracias á Dios
C. Gracias á Dios

SAN SALVADOR
EL SALVADOR
Usulután
San Miguel

Esteli
Matagalpa

Cayos Miskitos
(Nicaragua)

Puerto Cabezas

Chinandega
León

NICARAGUA

I. de Providencia
(Colombia)

MANAGUA
Masaya
Granada
Diriamba
Lago de Nicaragua

Bluefields

I. de San Andrés
(Colombia)

Islas del Maíz
(Nicaragua, U.S.A.)

San Juan del Sur
Nicaragua
San Juan del Norte

Golfo de Papagayo

COSTA RICA
Alajuela
San José
Cartago
Limón

Puntarenas
Pen. de Nicoya

PANAMÁ
CANAL ZONE
(U.S.A.)
Colón

Archipiélago de las Mulatas

Golfo del Darién

David
Golfo de Chiriquí
Golfo de Panamá
Arch. de las Perlas

Pen. de Osa

CUBA

(Havana) LA HABANA
LA MARIANAO
Guanabacoa

Pinar del Río

Matanzas
Cárdenas
Colón
Santa Clara
Caibarién
Placetas
Morón

Cienfuegos

Ciego de Ávila

Trinidad
Sancti Spíritus
Camagüey

Nuevitas

Victoria de las Tunas

HOLGUÍN
Bayamo
Manzanillo

Cayman Islands
Little Cayman

Grand Cayman

Montego Bay

JAMAICA

KINGSTON
Spanish Town

MIAMI
Fort Myers
Boca Raton
Fort Lauderdale

Key West

Florida Bay

GREAT BAHAMA BANK

Nassau
New Providence

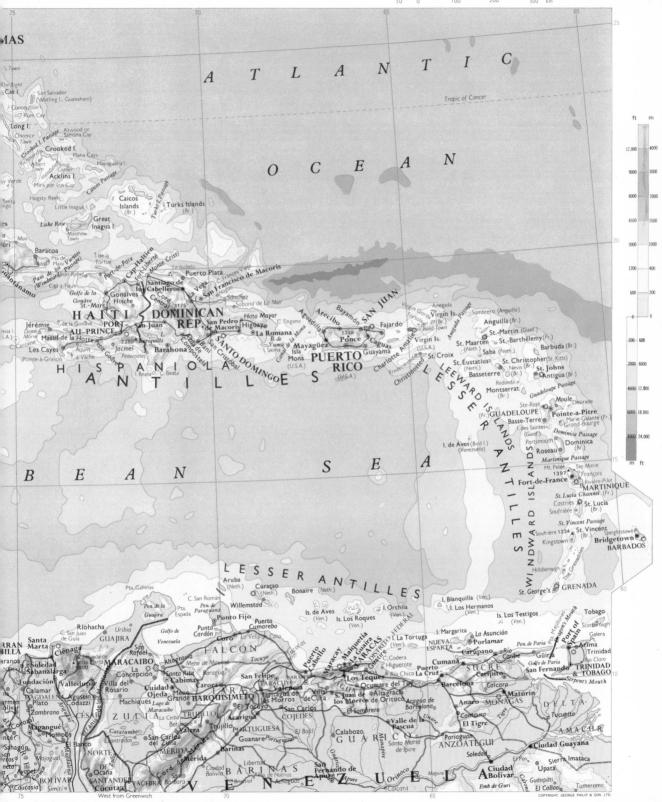

Projection : Sanson-Flamsteed's Sinusoidal

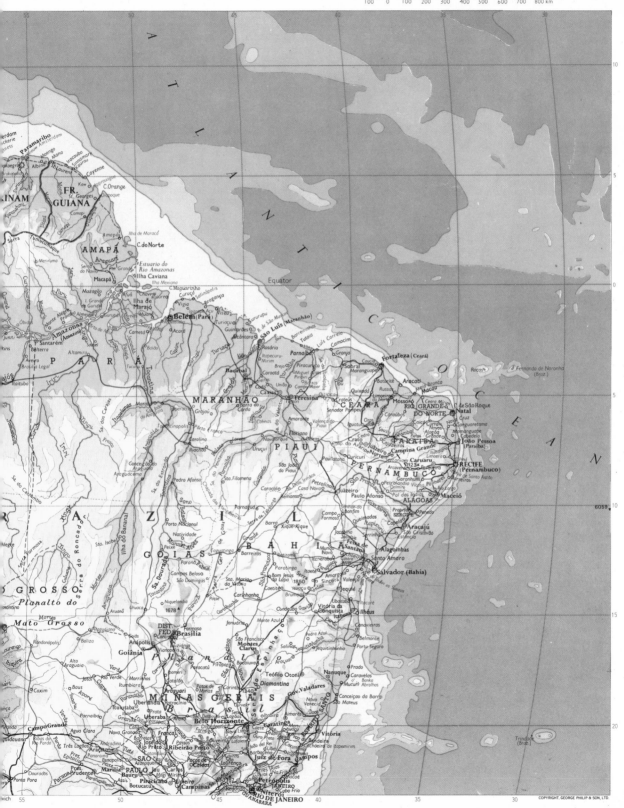

100   0   100   200   300   400   500 miles
100   0   100 200 300 400 500 600 700 800 km

ATLANTIC

Paramaribo
New Amsterdam
Amsterdam
Zeelandia
Mana
Iracoubo
Kaw
Coppename
Albina
Laurent
Cayenne
St. George
C. Orange
SINAM
FR.
GUIANA
C. Apaque

AMAPÁ
Araguari
Rio Grande
Macapá
C. do Norte
Ilha de Maracá
Ilha Caviana
Estuario do
Rio Amazonas
Ilha Mexiana

Equator

Ilha de
Marajó
C. Maguarinho
Curuçá
Salinópolis
Bragança
Vigia
Viseu
Guimarães
Belém (Pará)
Acará
Turiaçu
b. de São Marcos
São Luís (Maranhão)
Alcântara
Barreirinhas

PARÁ

Santarém
Rosária
Parnaíba
Luís Correia
Granja
Camocim
Tutóia

Bacabal
Coroatá
Caxias
União
Piracuruca
Piripiri
Fortaleza (Ceará)
Sobral
Maranguape
Baturité
Aracati
Macau
Quixadá
Russas
C. Branca
Rocas (Braz.)
Fernando de Noronha (Braz.)

MARANHÃO
Teresina
CEARÁ
Crateús
Mossoró
RIO
GRANDE
DO NORTE
Natal
C. de São Roque
Cruz

Floriano
PIAUÍ
Uruçuí
São João
do Piauí
Sta. Filomena
Paulistana
Serra Talhada
Cedro
Crato
Juazeiro do Norte
Campina Grande
Caruaru
PARAÍBA
João Pessoa
(Paraíba)
Cabedelo
RECIFE
(Pernambuco)

PERNAMBUCO
Petrolândia
Juàzeiro
Paulo Afonso
Caracol
Casa Nova
Remanso
Penedo
ALAGOAS
Maceió

B R A Z I L

Porto Nacional
Natividade
Peixe
Pedro Afonso
Barra
Xique-Xique
Campo
Formoso
Queimadas
Jacobina
Senhor do
Bonfim
SERGIPE
Aracaju
São Cristóvão
Estância
6059

GOIÁS
Barreiras
BAHIA
Feira de Santana
Santo Amaro
Alagoinhas
Castro Alves
Salvador (Bahia)

GROSSO
Planalto do
Mato Grosso
Bom Jesus
da Lapa
1850
Itaberaba
Valença
Jequié
DIST.
FED.
Brasília
Formosa
Vitória da
Conquista
Itabuna
Ilhéus

Goiânia
Anápolis
Niquelândia
1678
Januária
Monte Azul
Porto Seguro

P l a n a l t o
d e
Salinas
Prado
Caravelas
Abrolhos

Uberlândia
Uberaba
Araguari
MINAS GERAIS
Diamantina
Teófilo Otoni
Nanuque
Gov. Valadares
Conceição da Barra
São Mateus

Brasil
Belo Horizonte
Vitória

CampoGrande
SÃO
PAULO
Franca
Ribeirão Preto
Juiz de Fora
Campos
Trindade (Braz.)

Marília
Piracicaba
Limeira
Campinas
Petrópolis
RIO DE JANEIRO
Niterói
GUANABARA
Cabo Frio

ATLANTIC   OCEAN

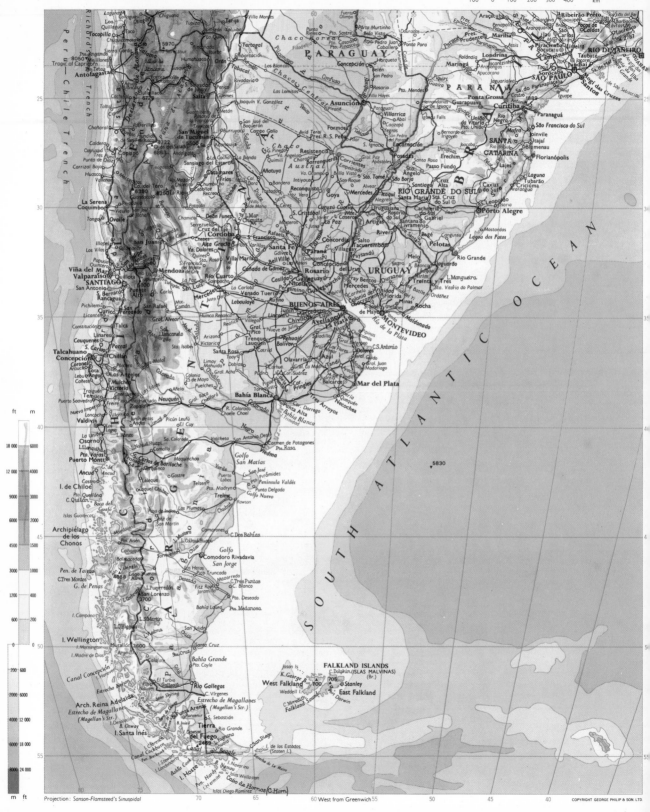

Projection: *Sanson-Flamsteed's Sinusoidal*

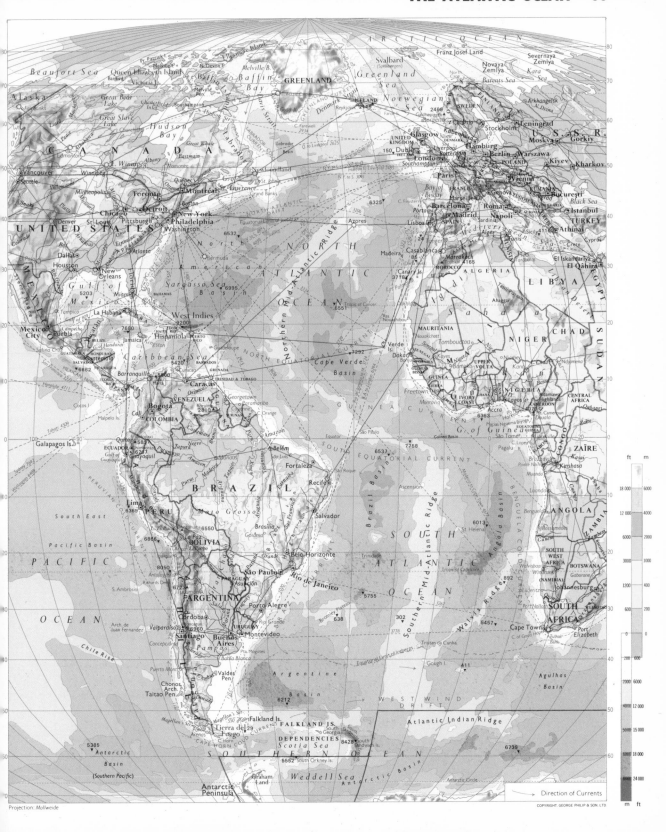

Projection: Mollweide

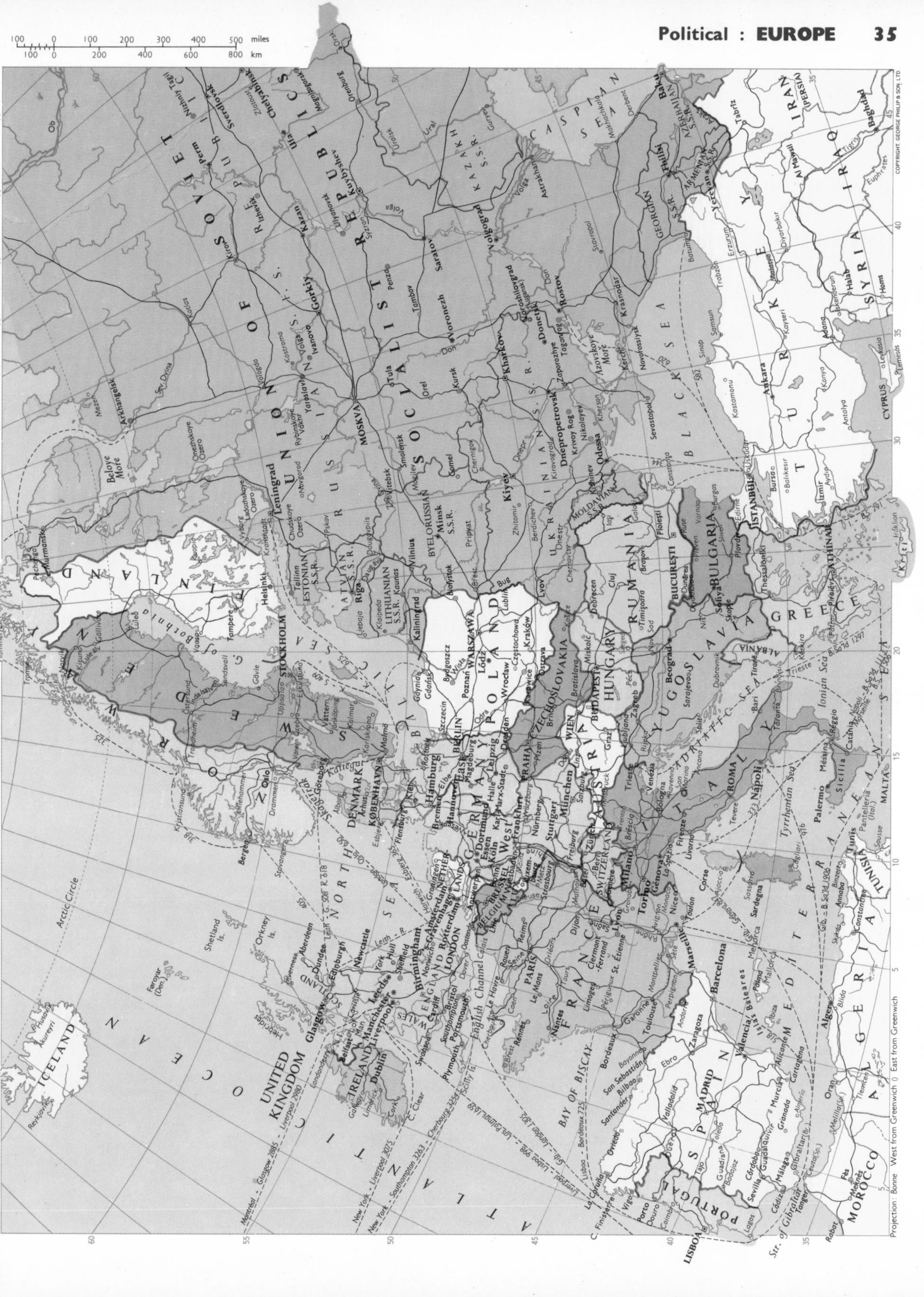
100 0 100 200 300 400 500 miles
100 0 200 400 600 800 km
UNION OF SOVIET SOCIALIST REPUBLICS
R. S. F. S. R.
RUSSIAN S. F. S. R.
MOSKVA
Leningrad
UKRAINIAN S. S. R.
BYELORUSSIAN S.S.R.
ESTONIAN S.S.R.
LATVIAN S.S.R.
LITHUANIAN S.S.R.
MOLDAVIAN S.S.R.
GEORGIAN S.S.R.
ARMENIAN S.S.R.
AZERBAIJAN S.S.R.
KAZAKH S.S.R.
FINLAND
Helsinki
SWEDEN
STOCKHOLM
NORWAY
Oslo
DENMARK
KØBENHAVN
UNITED KINGDOM
LONDON
IRELAND
Dublin
ICELAND
Reykjavik
NETHERLANDS
Amsterdam
BELGIUM
BRUSSEL
LUX.
FRANCE
PARIS
SWITZERLAND
Bern
GERMANY
West
BERLIN
POLAND
WARSZAWA
CZECHOSLOVAKIA
PRAHA
AUSTRIA
WIEN
HUNGARY
BUDAPEST
RUMANIA
BUCUREȘTI
BULGARIA
Sofiya
YUGOSLAVIA
Beograd
ALBANIA
Tiranë
GREECE
ATHINAI
ITALY
ROMA
SPAIN
MADRID
PORTUGAL
LISBOA
TURKEY
Ankara
ISTANBUL
SYRIA
IRAQ
Baghdad
IRAN (PERSIA)
CYPRUS
MALTA
MOROCCO
ALGERIA
TUNISIA
Tunis
ATLANTIC OCEAN
NORTH SEA
BALTIC SEA
BLACK SEA
CASPIAN SEA
MEDITERRANEAN SEA
BAY OF BISCAY
Adriatic Sea
Ionian Sea
Tyrrhenian Sea
English Channel
Gulf of Bothnia
Arctic Circle
Str. of Gibraltar
Projection: Bonne West from Greenwich 0 East from Greenwich
COPYRIGHT. GEORGE PHILIP & SON, LTD.

20 0 20 40 60 80 100 miles
20 0 20 40 60 80 100 120 140 160 km

Orkney Is.
N. Ronaldsay
Westray
Sanday
Stronsay
Hoy · Kirkwall
South Ronaldsay
Pentland Firth
Thurso
Wick

Shetland Is.
Unst
Yell
Foula · Mainland · Lerwick
Fair I.

ATLANTIC OCEAN

Pentland Firth
Thurso
Wick

St. Kilda

Stornoway
Lewis

Outer Hebrides
North Uist
Benbecula
South Uist
Barra

Harris
North Minch
Ullapool
Invergordon
Dingwall
Nairn
Elgin
Lossiemouth
Buckie
Banff
Fraserburgh
Peterhead

Rhum
Eigg
Coll
Tiree

Portree
Kyle
Lochalsh

N. West Highlands
Laig
Golspie
Moray Firth
Inverness
Ness
Kingussie
Ben Nevis 1343
Fort William
Ballachulish

SCOTLAND
Grampian Mts.
Ballater
Balmoral
Blair Atholl

Aberdeen
Stonehaven
Montrose
Forfar
Arbroath

Staffa
Iona
Mull
Oban

Colonsay

Firth of Lorn

Loch Lomond
Crieff
Perth
Dundee
Firth of Tay
Cupar
St. Andrews

Islay

Jura
Stirling
Alloa
Kirkcaldy
Leven
Dunfermline
Forth
Dunbar

Kintyre

Campbeltown

Helensburgh
Greenock
Dumbarton
Paisley
Glasgow
Edinburgh
Leith

Arran
Firth of Clyde
Ayr
Kilmarnock
Saltcoats
Irvine
Prestwick

Hamilton
Motherwell
Peebles
Galashiels
Selkirk
Jedburgh
Hawick
Moffat

NORTH SEA

Berwick-upon-Tweed

Cheviot Hills
Alnwick

Malin Hd.
Tory I.
Aran

Derryveagh Mts.
Letterkenny
Lifford

Londonderry
Coleraine
Portrush
Antrim Mts.
Ballymena
Bangor
Larne

NORTHERN IRELAND
Belfast
Lisburn

North Channel

Stranraer
Wigtown
Kirkcudbright
Mull of Galloway

Dumfries
Carlisle

Newcastle
Tynemouth
South Shields
Sunderland
Gateshead
Durham
Hartlepool

Donegal Bay
Bundoran
Sligo
Enniskillen
Omagh
Armagh
Monaghan
Clones
Newry
Dundalk

St. Bee's Hd.
Whitehaven
Cumbrian Mts.
978
Kendal
Windermere

Appleby
Darlington
Stockton
Middlesbrough
Whitby
Northallerton
N. York Moors
Scarborough

IRISH SEA
Isle of Man
Douglas

Barrow
Morecambe Bay
Lancaster
Ripon
York
Flamborough Hd.

Ballina
Castlebar
Westport
Connemara
Galway
Galway Bay

Roscommon
Longford
Mullingar
Athlone

Drogheda
Dublin (Baile Atha Cliath)
Dun Laoghaire
Bray

Blackpool
Preston
Southport
Bolton
Burnley
Blackburn
Halifax
Huddersfield
Bradford
Leeds
Wakefield
Barnsley
Keighley
Hull
Beverley
Spurn Hd.
Grimsby

Liverpool Bay
Holyhead
Anglesey
Beaumaris
Llandudno
Rhyl
Birkenhead
St. Helens
Salford
Manchester
Liverpool
Warrington
Rotherham
Sheffield
Chesterfield
Lincoln
Skegness

IRELAND

Tullamore
Kildare
Naas
Wicklow Mts.
Wicklow
Arklow

Denbigh
Ruthin
Chester
Crewe
Macclesfield
Mansfield
Stoke-on-Trent
Derby
Nottingham
Grantham
The Wash
Kings Lynn
Boston

Cardigan Bay
Caernarfon Bay
Caernarfon
Snowdon 1085
Pwllheli

Bala
Dolgellau (Dolgelley)
Welshpool
Montgomery
Shrewsbury
Stafford
Wolverhampton
Walsall
Leicester
Oakham
Peterborough
Huntingdon
The Fens
Norwich
Gt. Yarmouth
Lowestoft

W. Cambrian Mts. E.

Aberystwyth

Rhayader
Llandrindod Wells
Kidderminster
Birmingham
Coventry
Rugby
Northampton
Wellingborough
Bedford
Cambridge
Bury St. Edmunds
Ipswich

ENGLAND

Ennis
Limerick
Golden Vale
Tipperary
Thurles
Kilkenny
Carlow
Enniscorthy
New Ross
Wexford
Rosslare

Cardigan
Fishguard
St. David's Hd.

Hereford
Worcester
Leamington
Warwick
Stratford-on-Avon
Banbury
Wellingborough

Aylesbury
Hertford
St. Albans
Watford
Luton
Colchester
The Naze
Harwich

Tralee
Mallow
Fermoy
Dungarvan
Waterford

Haverfordwest
Pembroke
Milford Haven
Carmarthen
Llanelli
Swansea
Port Talbot

Merthyr Tydfil
Brecon
Monmouth
Gloucester
Cheltenham
Oxford
Reading
Slough
Windsor
London
Chelmsford
Southend
Thames
Chatham
Gillingham
Margate
Canterbury

Macgillycuddy's Reeks 1040
Killarney
Blarney
Cork
Bandon
Kinsale
Cobh
Cork Harbour
Youghal

Rhondda
Newport
Cardiff
Bristol
Bath
Trowbridge
Wells
Swindon
Chilterns
Aldershot
Guildford
Reigate
Maidstone
Ashford
Dover
Folkestone

C. Clear
Bantry

Bristol Channel
Lundy I.
Ilfracombe
Weston-super-Mare
Salisbury Plain
Wilton
Salisbury
Winchester
Southampton
South Downs
Lewes
Newhaven
Brighton
Worthing
Hastings
Eastbourne

Hartland Point
Barnstaple
Exmoor
Taunton
Yeovil
Dorchester
Poole
Isle of Wight
Newport
Bournemouth
Needles
Portsmouth
Chichester

Bude
Dartmoor
Exeter
Axminster

ENGLISH CHANNEL

Land's End
Scilly Is.
Penzance
Falmouth
Truro
Camborne
St. Austell
Plymouth
Devonport
Dartmouth
Torquay
Weymouth

Lizard
Start Pt.

Dieppe

West from Greenwich   East from Greenwich

Projection: Conical with two standard parallels

COPYRIGHT, GEORGE PHILIP & SON, LTD.

ft m
3000 1000
1800 600
1200 400
600 200
300 100
0 0
100 300
200 600
400 1200
m ft

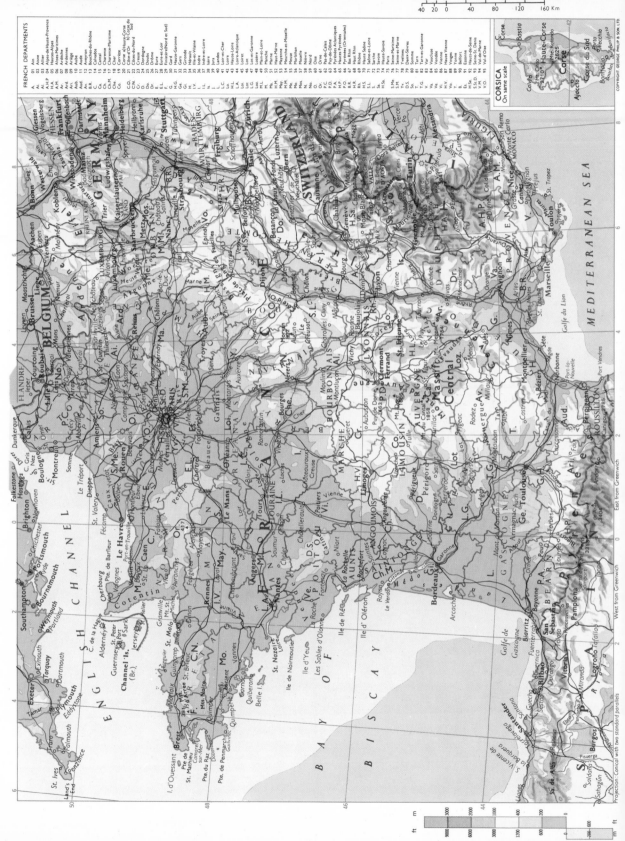

20 10 0   20   40   60   80   100 miles
40 20 0   40   80   120   160 Km

FRENCH DEPARTMENTS

01	Ain	Ai.
02	Aisne	Ai.
03	Allier	Al.
04	Alpes-de-Haute-Provence	A.H.P.
05	Hautes-Alpes	H.A.
06	Alpes-Maritimes	A.M.
07	Ardèche	Ard.
08	Ardennes	Ard.
09	Ariège	Ar.
10	Aube	Au.
11	Aude	Aud.
12	Aveyron	Av.
13	Bouches-du-Rhône	B.R.
14	Calvados	C.
15	Cantal	Can.
16	Charente	Ch.
17	Charente-Maritime	Ch.M.
18	Cher	Che.
19	Corrèze	Co.
20a	Corse a)Haute-Corse	C.C.
20b	b) Corse du Sud	
21	Côte-d'Or	C.O.
22	Côtes-du-Nord	C.N.
23	Creuse	Cr.
24	Dordogne	D.
25	Doubs	Do.
26	Drôme	Dr.
27	Eure	E.
28	Eure-et-Loir	E.L.
29	Finistère(Nord et Sud)	F.
30	Gard	G.
31	Haute-Garonne	H.G.
32	Gers	Ge.
33	Gironde	Gi.
34	Hérault	H.
35	Ille-et-Vilaine	I.V.
36	Indre	I.
37	Indre-et-Loire	I.L.
38	Isère	Is.
39	Jura	J.
40	Landes	L.
41	Loir-et-Cher	L.C.
42	Loire	Lo.
43	Haute-Loire	H.L.
44	Loire-Atlantique	L.A.
45	Loiret	Loi.
46	Lot	Lot
47	Lot-et-Garonne	L.G.
48	Lozère	Loz.
49	Maine-et-Loire	M.L.
50	Manche	Ma.
51	Marne	Mar.
52	Haute-Marne	H.M.
53	Mayenne	May.
54	Meurthe-et-Moselle	M.M.
55	Meuse	Me.
56	Morbihan	Mo.
57	Moselle	Mos.
58	Nièvre	Ni.
59	Nord	No.
60	Oise	O.
61	Orne	Or.
62	Pas-de-Calais	P.C.
63	Puy-de-Dôme	P.D.
64	Pyrénées-Atlantiques	P.A.
65	Hautes-Pyrénées	H.P.
66	Pyrénées(Orientales)	P.O.
67	Bas-Rhin	B.Rh.
68	Haut-Rhin	H.Rh.
69	Rhône	Rh.
70	Haute-Saône	H.Sa.
71	Saône-et-Loire	S.L.
72	Sarthe	Sa.
73	Savoie	Sav.
74	Haute-Savoie	H.Sa.
75	Paris	Pa.
76	Seine-Maritime	S.M.
77	Seine-et-Marne	S.M.
78	Yvelines	Y.
79	Deux-Sèvres	D.S.
80	Somme	So.
81	Tarn	T.
82	Tarn-et-Garonne	T.G.
83	Var	Va.
84	Vaucluse	V.
85	Vendée	Ve.
86	Vienne	Vi.
87	Haute-Vienne	H.V.
88	Vosges	Vo.
89	Yonne	Yo.
90	Belfort	B.
91	Essonne	Es.
92	Hauts-de-Seine	H.Se.
93	Seine-St. Denis	S.S.D.
94	Val-de-Marne	V.M.
95	Val-d'Oise	V.O.

CORSICA
On same scale

Corse
Haute-Corse
Corse du Sud

MEDITERRANEAN SEA

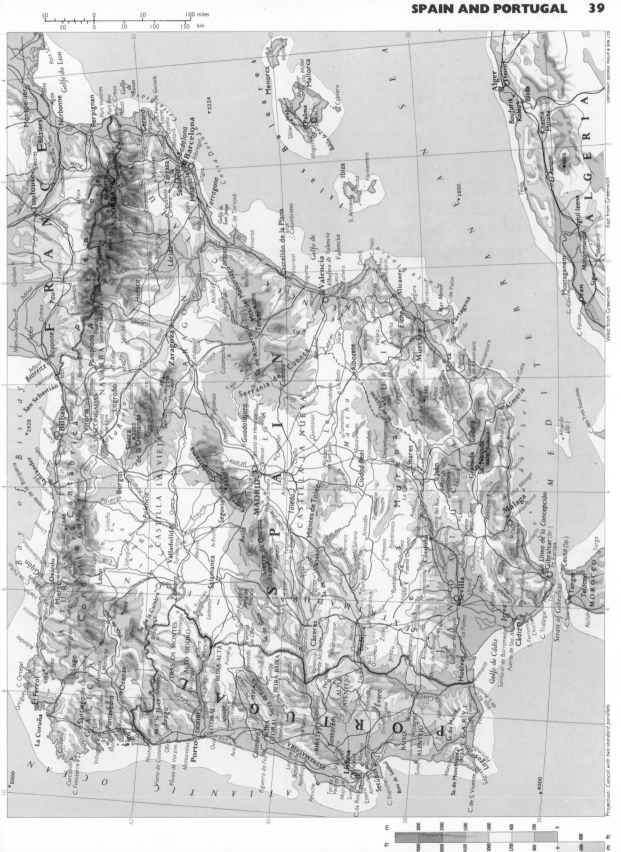

LIGURIAN SEA

TYRRHENIAN SEA

ADRIATIC

SARDEGNA (SARDINIA)

CORSE (CORSICA) (Fr.)

MALTA

S.E. EUROPE POLITICAL

Projection: Conical with two standard parallels

M E D I T E R R

50 | 0 | 50 | 100 miles
50 | 0 | 50 | 100 | 150 km

U.S.S.R.

R U M A N I A

Szentes · Békéscsaba · Mții 1848 · Abrud · T r a n s i l v a n i a · Carpații · Odorhei · Bîrlad · Kagul
Kiskőrös · Kiskunhalas · Mako · Crișul · Alb · Sighișoara · Sfântu Gheorghe · Tecuci · Ozero Sasyk · Kiliya
Kalocsa · Hódmezővásárhely · Alba-Iulia · Mediaș · Focșani · Izmail
Szekszárd · **Szeged** · Arad · Mureș · Brad · Sibiu · Brașov · Rîmnicu Sărat · **Galați** · Ozero
Pécs · Suborica · Sentat · Kikinda · Lugoj · Deva · Simeria · vf. Negoiu 2507 · Buzău · **Brăila** · Sulina
Mohács · Sombor · **Timișoara** · Bèsej · Caransebeș · Peleaga 2509 · Parîngul Mare 2518 · Turnu Roșu · Cîmpulung · **Ploiești** · Gura
Drava · Baja · Banat · Reșița · Tîrgu-Jiu · Rîmnicu Vîlcea · Tîrgoviște · Buzău · Portiței
Osijek · **Novi Sad** · Zrenjanin · V a l a h i a · Ialomița · Mamaia
Brod · Petrovaradin · Vršac · Mehadia · Pitești · **București** (Bucharest) · **Constanța**
Odžak · Brčko · Zemun · Pančevo · Bela Crkva · Porțile de Fier · Orșova · **Turnu-Severin** · Argeș · Oltenița · Călărași · Cernavodă
Bijeljina · **Beograd** (Belgrade) · Smederevo · Slatina · Giurgiu · Silistra · Mangalia
Tuzla · Požarevac · Craiova · Vedea · Tutrakan · Dobrich
J U G O S L A V I J A · Valjevo · Negotino · Bor · Caracal · Turnu Măgurele · Zimnicea · **Ruse** (Ruschuk) · Tolbuhin · Nos Kaliakra

Sarajevo · Han Pijesak · Titovo Užice · Čačak · Zaječar · Calafat · Lom · Oryahovo · Somovit · Svishtov · Razgrad · Türgovishte · Kolarovgrad (Shumen) · **Varna**

Konjic · Višegrad · Kragujevac · Kruševac · Niš · Vratsa · **Pleven** · Gorna Oryahovitsa · Tŭrnovo · **B L A C K**
Foča · 2522 Durmitor · Novi Pazar · Kuršumlija · Pirot · Dragoman · 2168 · S t a r a · P l a n i n a · Tetéven · Sliven · **Burgas** · **S E A**
Stolac · Pljevlja · Kosovska Mitrovica · Leskovac · Dragoman · **Sofiya** (Sofia) 2198 · **B U L G A R I A** · Karlovo · Kazanlŭk · Stara Zagora · Sliven · Poljanovgrad · Aytos
Nikšić · C R N A · G O R A · Priština · Vranje · Pernik · Radomir · Stanke Dimitrov (Dupnitsa) · Trajanova Vrata · Pazardzhik · Dimitrovgrad · Yambol · Aytos
Trebinje · **Titograd** (Podgorica) · Đakovica · Prizren · Skopje · Kumanovo · Kyustendil · Musala 2925 · **Plovdiv** · Khaskovo · Dimitrovgrad · Stikhovo
Cetinje · Skadarsko Jezero · Tetovo · Titov Veles · Kočani · Štip · Strumica · R h o d ó p i · P l a n i n a · **Edirne** · Istranca Dağları 1018 · **TURKEY** · Karadeniz
Ulcinj · Bar · Korab 2764 · Debar · Gostivar · Prilep · Crna · Momchilgrad · Arda · Smolyan · Dhidhimotikhon · Beykoz

A L B A N I A · Tirane · Shkumbin · Elbasan · Bitola (Monastir) · Dojran · Serrai · T H R Á K I · Kešan · Tekirdag · **Istanbul** · Üsküdar
Durrës · 2258 · Ohrid · Prespa · Florina · Drama · Philippi · Xánthi · Ergene · Marmara denizi · İmralı
Kep-i-Rodonit · Berat · Korçë · Kastoria · Véroia · **Thessaloníki** · 1127 Thásos · Alexandroúpolis · Enez · Saros Körfezi · Gelibolu · **Bursa**
Kep-i-Palit · Vlórë (Vlore) · Kozáni · Yiannitsá · Polígiros · Athos 2033 · Samothráki 1600 · Marmara denizi · Çanakkale · Bozcaada
Vijosë · G R E C E · Óros Ólimbos (Olympus) 2917 · Thermaïkós Kólpos · Ákra Platí · Limnos · Gökçeada · Ákra Piáka · Boğazı (Troy/Ilium) · Edremit · 2181
Bríndisi · Sazan · Smólikas 2637 · Píndos · Kalabáka · Trikkala · T H E S S A L I A · Áyios Evstrátios · Baba Burun · Ayvalık · **TURKEY** · A n a d o l u
Lecce · Íoánnina · **Lárisa** · 1575 · Skíros · Bergama · Akhisar
Str. of Otranto · Kérkyra (Corfu) · Kardhítsa · **Vólos** · Pagasitikós Kólpos · Ilíodhrómia · **Lésvos** · 968 · Menemen
Capo Sta. Maria di Leuca · Préveza · Fársala · Lamía · Vória Sporádhes · Turgutlu
Paxoí · Árta · Á i g a i o n · 1297 · **Izmir** (Smyrna) · 2157 · Alaşehir
Levkás (Sta. Maura) · S T E R E Á · E L L A S · Thermopílai · Évvoia · **Khíos** · Çeşme · Salihli
Ithaki · Agrínion 2510 · 1743 · Khalkís · Ákra Kafirévs · Sámos · Büyük Menderes · 2308
Kefallinía · Mesolóngion · Návpaktos 2457 · Thívai · Marathón · 1398 · Ákra Kafirévs · Aydın · Mstik
I O N I A N · Pátrai · Korinthiakós Kólpos · Mégara · **Athínai** (Athens) · Ándros · Sámos · Mísa 2294
S E A · Zákinthos · Erímanthos 2224 · Killini · Kórinthos · Mykínai · Píraiévs · Tínos · Mykónos · Ikaría · Pátmos · Kerme Körfezi
Zákinthos · Pírgos · **PELOPONNISOS** · Argos · Návplion · Idhra · Kíthnos · Ermoúpolis · Sýros · **Náxos** · Léros · Kos
Trípolis · Argolikós Kólpos · Sérifos · Páros · 1001 · K I K L Á D H E S · Kálimnos · D O D E K A N I S O S
Kiparissiakós Kólpos · Sífnos · Síkinos · Amorgós · Astipálaia · Tílos
Filiatró · Messíni · Kalámata · Milos · Thíra · **Ródhos** 4486
5121 · Spárti · Lakonikós Kólpos · **M E D I T E R R A N E A N S E A** · Kárpathos 1215
Ákra Taínaron · Ákra Maléa · **Kíthira** · Kásos
Andikíthira · K R I T I · Ákra Lithínon

East from Greenwich

COPYRIGHT. GEORGE PHILIP & SON. LTD.

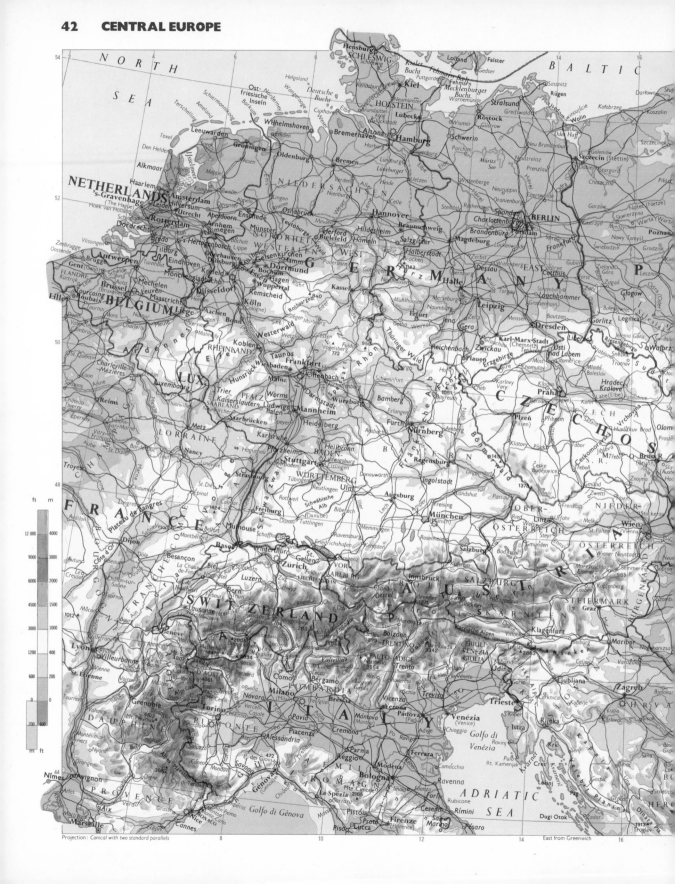

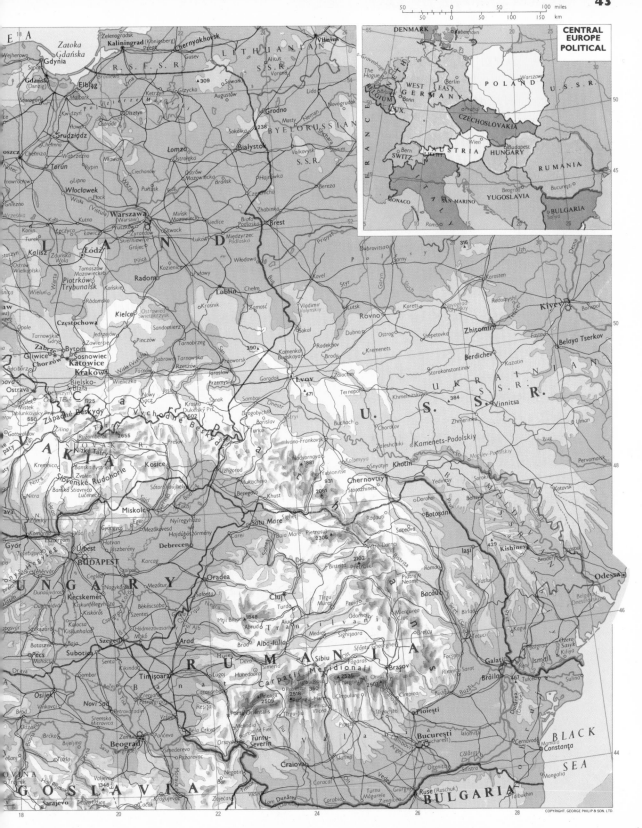

CENTRAL EUROPE POLITICAL

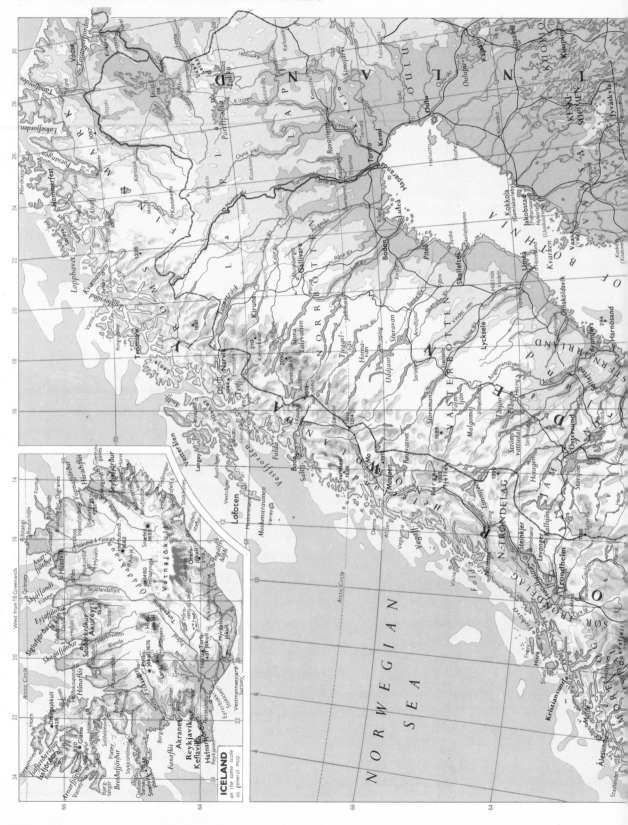

ICELAND
on the same scale
as general map

20 10 0   20   40   60   80   100 miles
40 20 0   40   80   120   160 km

FINLAND

HÄME
Tampere
Pori
Rauma
Uusikaupunki
Turku (Åbo)
HELSINKI (Helsingfors)
Hanko (Hangö)
Hämeenlinna
Lahti
Kotka

GULF OF FINLAND

Tallinn
Haapsalu
Hiiumaa (Dagö)
Saaremaa (Ösel)
Kingisepp

ESTONIAN S.S.R.

Rakvere
Valga
Viljandi

Pärnu

GULF OF RIGA
Rigas Jūras Līcis

Ruhnu

LATVIAN S.S.R.
Riga
Valmiera
Jelgava
Tukums

Ventspils
Liepāja
Klaipėda

LITHUANIAN S.S.R.
Kaunas
Vilnius
Panevėžys
Šiauliai

R.S.F.S.R.
Sovetsk
Chernyakhovsk
Kaliningrad
Baltiysk

POLAND

Gdynia
Gdańsk
Zatoka Gdańska
Elbląg
Grudziądz
Toruń
Bydgoszcz

Białystok
Grodno
Augustów
Łomża
Ostrołęka

BALTIC SEA

Gotland
Visby
Gotska Sandön
Fårö

Öland
Kalmar
Borgholm

Bornholm
Rønne

Szczecin (Stettin)

SWEDEN

STOCKHOLM
Uppsala
Västerås
Eskilstuna
Södertälje
Nynäshamn
Norrköping
Nyköping
Oxelösund
Linköping
Motala
Katrineholm
Örebro
Västervik
Oskarshamn
Nässjö
Jönköping
Växjö
Vimmerby
Ljungby
Kalmar
Karlskrona
Karlshamn
Kristianstad

GOTLAND
SMÅLAND
BLEKINGE
KRONOBERG

Falun
Borlänge
Mora
Gävle
Söderhamn
Hudiksvall
Bollnäs
Avesta
Hedemora
Ludvika
Sala
Köping

DALARNA
VÄRMLAND
VÄSTMANLAND
SÖDERMANLAND
KOPPARBERG

Karlstad
Arvika
Kristinehamn
Filipstad
Skövde
Mariestad
Lidköping
Vänern
Vänersborg
Trollhättan
Uddevalla
Göteborg
Borås
Alingsås
Ulricehamn
Mölndal

BOHUSLÄN
HALLAND
Varberg
Falkenberg
Halmstad
Ängelholm
Helsingborg
Landskrona
MALMÖ
Lund
Trelleborg
Ystad
Simrishamn

Vättern
Vänern

NORWAY
OSLO
Drammen
Kongsberg
Hønefoss
Gjøvik
Lillehammer
Hamar
Elverum
Kongsvinger
Halden
Sarpsborg
Fredrikstad
Moss
Skien
Larvik
Tønsberg
Horten
Sandefjord
Porsgrunn

OPPLAND
HEDMARK
BUSKERUD
AKERSHUS
ØSTFOLD
VESTFOLD
TELEMARK
AUST-AGDER
VEST-AGDER
ROGALAND

Arendal
Grimstad
Lillesand
Kristiansand
Mandal
Farsund
Flekkefjord
Egersund (Eigersund)
Sandnes
Stavanger
Kopervik
Haugesund

Bergen
Hardangerfjorden

DENMARK
København (Copenhagen)
Roskilde
Helsingør
Køge
Næstved
Slagelse
Korsør
Kalundborg
Holbæk
Nykøbing
Sjælland
Fyn
Odense
Svendborg
Nyborg
Bælt
Store Bælt
Lille Bælt

JYLLAND
Frederikshavn
Hjørring
Thisted
Limfjorden
Ålborg
Randers
Århus
Viborg
Silkeborg
Herning
Horsens
Vejle
Fredericia
Kolding
Esbjerg
Varde
Ringkøbing
Åbenrå
Sønderborg
Haderslev

Skagerrak
Kattegat
The Sound
Øresund

GERMANY
Hamburg
Lübeck
Kiel
Flensburg
Rostock
Schwerin
Wismar
Bremen
Bremerhaven
Wilhelmshaven
Oldenburg
Emden
Lüneburg
Neumünster
Elbe
Weser

NETHERLANDS
Groningen

Nordfriesische Inseln
Ostfriesische Inseln
Helgoland

East from Greenwich

Projection : Conical with two standard parallels

m ft
6000 4500 3000 1200 600 200 0
2000 1500 1000 400 200 0 m

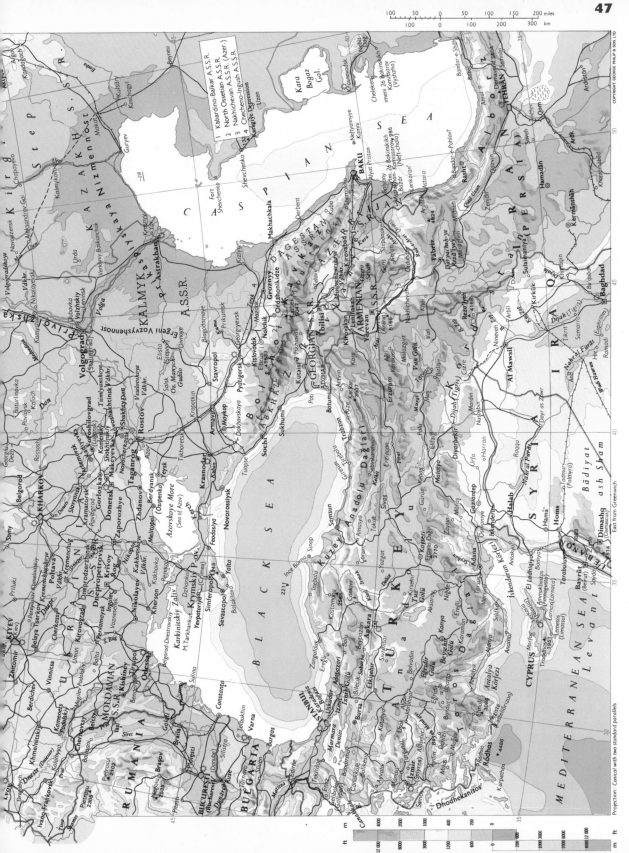

100 50 0 50 100 150 200 miles

100 0 100 200 300 km

1 Kabardino-Balkar A.S.S.R.
2 North Ossetian A.S.S.R. (Azer.)
3 Nakhichevan A.S.S.R. (Azer.)
4 Checheno-Ingush A.S.S.R.
5 Kargye Depression

Kara
Bogaz
Gol.

C A S P I A N   S E A

K i r g i z   S t e p.

K A Z A K H S K A Y A   Nizmennost

KALMYK   A.S.S.R.

Ergeni Vozvyshennost

VOLGOGRAD
(Stalingrad)

Astrakhan

A B K H A Z   B O L S H O Y

DAGESTAN

Makhachkala

Derbent

BAKU

A Z E R B A I J A N   S.S.R.

Grozny

Ordzhonikidze

GEORGIAN S.S.R.

Tbilisi

ARMENIAN
S.S.R.

Yerevan

Tabriz

E L B U R Z

TEHRAN

P E R S I A   (I R A N)

Hamadān

Kermānshāh

Baghdad

Al Mawsil

Mosul

I R A Q

KHARKOV

Rostov

Taganrog

Azovskoye More
(Sea of Azov)

Krasnodar

Novorossiysk

B L A C K   S E A

Sochi

Sukhumi

Batumi

Trabzon

Erzurum

Diyarbakir

S Y R I A   (?)

Halab

Homs

Hamā

Dimashq
(Damascus)

L E B A N O N

Bādiyat ash Sham

KIYEV
(Kiev)

U K R A I N E

Dnepropetrovsk

Donetsk

Zaporozhye

Kherson

Nikolayev

Odessa

MOLDAVIAN
S.S.R.

Krymskiy P-ov.

Simferopol

Sevastopol

Yalta

T U R K E Y

Ankara

Kayseri

Adana

İzmir
(Smyrna)

Bursa

İstanbul

Marmara
Denizi

C Y P R U S

M E D I T E R R A N E A N   S E A

L e v a n t

BUCUREŞTI
(Bucharest)

R U M A N I A

B U L G A R I A

Varna

Burgas

Constanţa

D o b r o g e a

Dhodhekanisos

Ródhos

Karpathos

ft 12 000 6000 3000 1200 600 0 200 900 m
m 4000 2000 1000 400 200 0 1000 3000 6000 12 000 ft

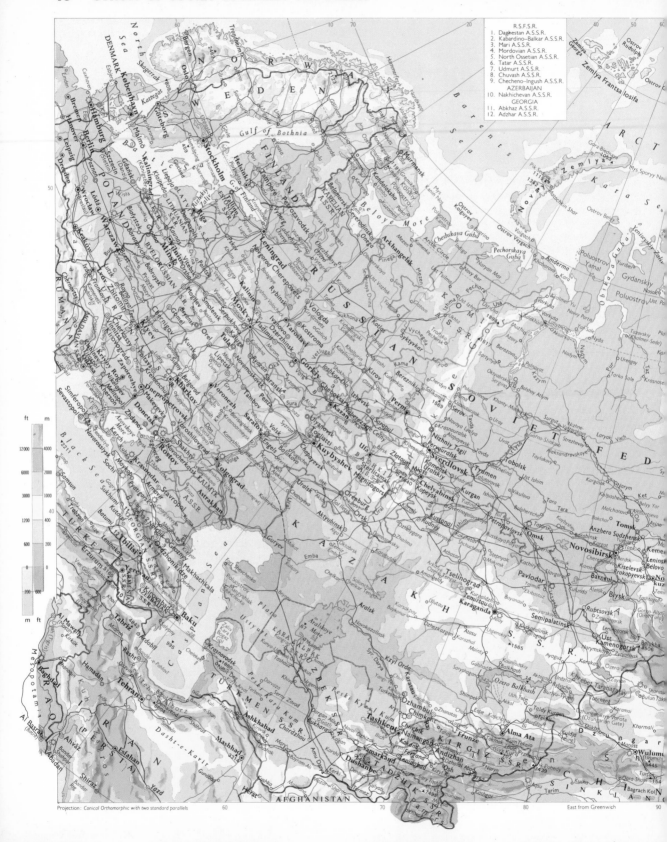

R.S.F.S.R.
1. Daghestan A.S.S.R.
2. Kabardino–Balkar A.S.S.R.
3. Mari A.S.S.R.
4. Mordovian A.S.S.R.
5. North Ossetian A.S.S.R.
6. Tatar A.S.S.R.
7. Udmurt A.S.S.R.
8. Chuvash A.S.S.R.
9. Checheno–Ingush A.S.S.R.
AZERBAIJAN
10. Nakhichevan A.S.S.R.
GEORGIA
11. Abkhaz A.S.S.R.
12. Adzhar A.S.S.R.

Projection: Conical Orthomorphic with two standard parallels

East from Greenwich

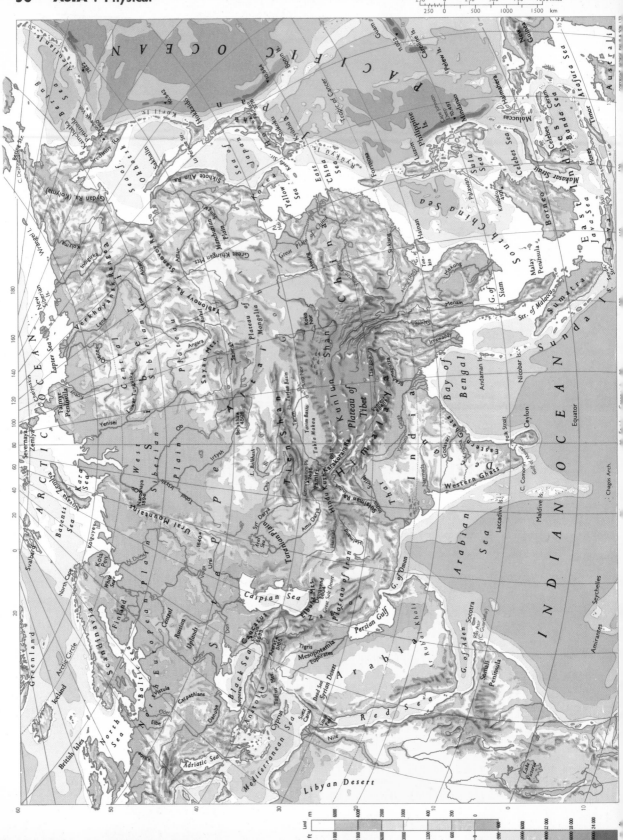

250 0 250 500 750 1000 miles
250 0   500   1000   1500 km

OCEAN

PACIFIC OCEAN

Aleutian Is.
Bering Sea
Kamchatskiy
Mys Chukotskiy
Petropavlovsk

Sea of Okhotsk
Sakhalin
Kuril Is.
Khabarovsk
Vladivostok

JAPAN
Sea of Japan
Hokkaido
Honshu
Tokyo
Yokohama
Osaka
Nagasaki
Shikoku
Kyushu
Ryukyu Is. (Nansei)

KOREA
SOUTH
Seoul
Pusan
Yellow Sea

Manchuria
Harbin
Changchun
Shenyang (Mukden)
Peiping
Tientsin
Tsingtao
Nanking
Wuhan
Shanghai
Hangchow
Foochow
Canton
HONG KONG
Macau
Hainan

INNER MONGOLIA
MONGOLIA
Ulaanbaatar (Ulan Bator)
Hovd

CHINESE REPUBLIC
C H I N A
Sian
Chengtu
Chungking
Kunming

SINKIANG-UIGUR CHINESE REPUBLIC
Wulumuchi (Urumchi)
Kashgar
Soche

TIBET
Lhasa

PHILIPPINES
Luzon
Manila
Mindoro
Samar
Leyte
Mindanao
Sulu Sea
Celebes Sea

New Guinea
Moluccas
Maluku
Halmahera
Ceram
Sulawesi
Borneo
Brunei
Sabah
Sarawak
Kuching
I N D O N E S I A
Sumatra
Jakarta
Ujung Pandang
Surabaja

MALAYSIA
Kuala Lumpur
Singapore
Selat Sunda

BURMA
Mandalay
Rangoon
Irrawaddy

THAILAND (SIAM)
Bangkok
G. of Siam

VIETNAM
Hanoi
Hue
HO CHI MINH (Saigon)
LAOS
Vientiane
CAMBODIA
Phnom Penh

Andaman Is. (India)
Nicobar Is. (India)
Bay of Bengal
South China Sea

SRI LANKA (CEYLON)
Colombo

I N D I A
Delhi
Agra
Kanpur
Lucknow
Allahabad
Varanasi
Calcutta
BANGLADESH
Dacca
Bombay
Hyderabad
Madras
Pondicherry
Calicut
Goa
Ahmadabad
Nagpur

NEPAL
Kathmandu
BHUTAN

KASHMIR
Lahore
PAKISTAN
Karachi
Quetta

AFGHANISTAN
Kabul
Kandahar
Herat

INDIAN OCEAN
Lakshadweep Is. (India)
Maldive Is. (India)
Seychelles
Amirantes
Equator

I R A N (PERSIA)
Tehran
Esfahan
Shiraz
Zahedan
Meshed
Bandar e Bushehr

IRAQ
Baghdad
Al Basrah
Tigris
Euphrates

TURKEY
Ankara
Istanbul
Izmir
Erzurum

Caspian Sea
Black Sea
Astrakhan
Baku
Tbilisi
Yerevan
Batumi

SAUDI ARABIA
Al Madinah (Medina)
Makkah (Mecca)
Riyadh

OMAN
U.A.E.
QATAR
Bahrain
Kuwait
Persian Gulf
G. of Oman
Muscat

YEMEN
SOUTH YEMEN
Aden
G. of Aden
Socotra (South Yemen)

S.S.R.
U.S.S.R.
Moskva (Moscow)
Leningrad
Murmansk
Arkhangelsk
Sverdlovsk
Chelyabinsk
Magnitogorsk
Omsk
Novosibirsk
Tomsk
Krasnoyarsk
Irkutsk
Yakutsk
Chita
Ulan Ude

Tashkent
Samarkand
Bukhara
Ashkhabad
Khiva
Alma Ata
Semipalatinsk

Ob
Lena
Yenisey
Aral Sea
Lake Balkash

ARCTIC OCEAN
Arctic Circle
Limit of Ice (Spring)
Barents Sea
Kara Sea
Novaya Zemlya
Severnaya Zemlya
Svalbard
Franz Josef Land

ICELAND
UNITED KINGDOM
London
Paris
Roma
EUROPE
Berlin
Wien
Warszawa
Beograd
Athinai
Thessaloniki
Mediterranean Sea
North Sea
Rhine
Danube

Red Sea
Nile
EGYPT
LIBYA
El Qâhira
El Iskandarîya
Aswân

SYRIA
Halab
Dimashq
LEBANON
Bayrût
ISRAEL
JORDAN
Jerusalem
Amman

A F R I C A
SUDAN
El Khartûm
El Obeid
ETHIOPIA
Addis Abeba
SOMALI REP
Mogadishu
KENYA
Nairobi
Mombasa
UGANDA
Lake Victoria
TANZANIA
Dar es Salaam
ZAMBIA
MALAWI
ZAIRE
RWANDA
BURUNDI

East from Greenwich

Projection: Bonne

1949–1967 Armistice lines between Israel and the Arab States.

MEDITERRANEAN SEA

LEBANON

SYRIA

Sūr (Tyre)

Qiryat Shemona

Under Israeli Occupation

BIRKET RAM

Nahariyya

Hagalil (Galilee)

'Akko (Acre)

Qiryat Yam

Qiryat Bialik

KEFAR NAHUM (CAPERNAUM)

HAIFA

Qiryat Ata

Yam Kinneret (Sea of Galilee)

Tiberias

Tirat Karmel

Nazareth

'ATLIT

MEGIDDO

Afula

QESARI (CAESAREA)

N. Hadera

Hadera

Shomeron (Samaria)

Netanya

Tulkarm

Nābulus

SHECHEM

JACOB'S WELL

SAMARIA

TEL ARSHAF

Herzliyya

Ramat HaSharon

SHILO

TEL AVIV

YAFO (Jaffa)

Ramat Gan

Petah Tiqwa

Bat Yam

Holon

Israeli Occupation

JORDAN

Rishon Le Zion

Lod (Lydda)

Ramla

Rehovot

Rām Allāh

El Arīhā (Jericho)

'AMMAN

Ashdod

TEL GEZER

JERUSALEM (Yerushalayim, Al Quds)

Hussein (Allenby) Bridge

Ashqelon

Qiryat Gat

Bayt Jālā

Bayt Lahm (Bethlehem)

QUMRAN

BURAK SULAYMAN (SOLOMON'S POOLS)

BET GUVRIN

TEL LAKHISH

Hebron

Gaza

Gaza Strip

Khān Yūnis

Be'er Sheva'

En Gedi

MESADA

EGYPT

DEAD SEA

Be'er Sheva'

Ha Negev

Dimona

Mizpe Ramon

Under EGYPT Occupation

PETRA

Continuation Southwards

Projection: Conical with two standard parallels

East from Greenwich

COPYRIGHT. GEORGE PHILIP & SON, LTD.

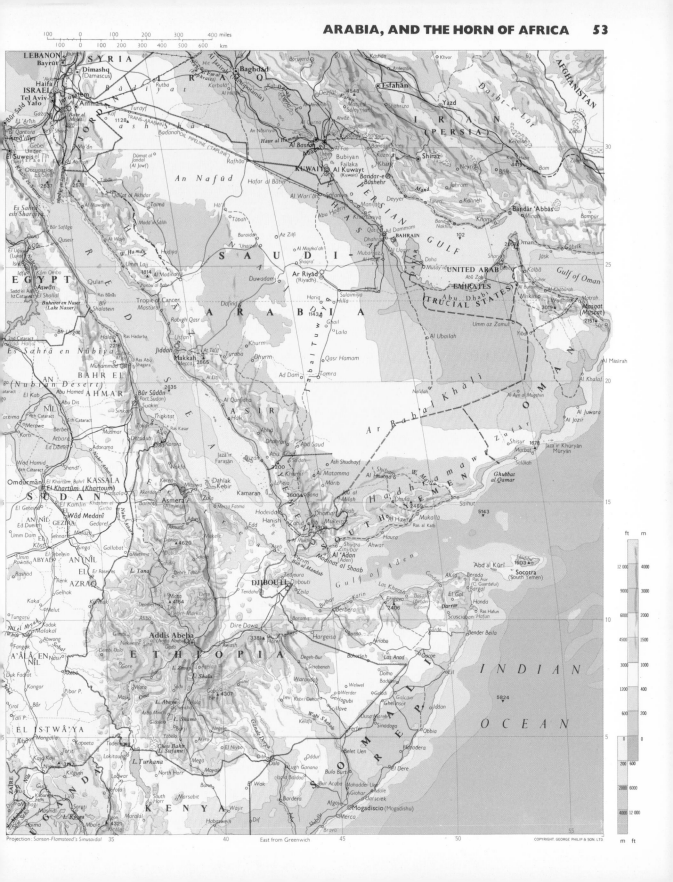

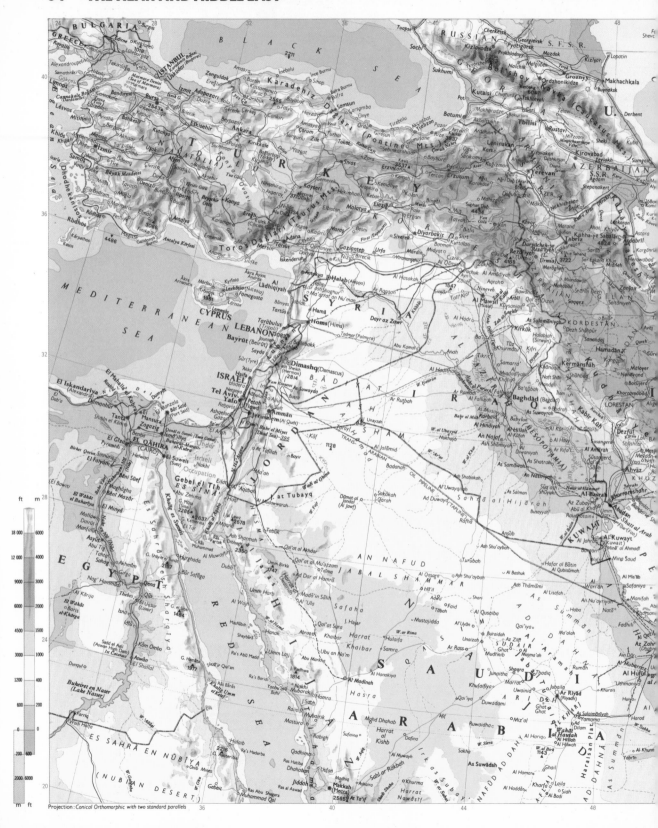

Projection: Conical Orthomorphic with two standard parallels

100   0   100   200   300 miles
100   0   100   200   300   400   500 km

KAZAKH S.S.R.
Plato Ustyurt
Aralskoye More
Muynak

U Z B E K S. S. R.
PESKI KYZYL KUM
KAZAKH S.S.R.
Turkestan
Chimkent
Lenger
Talass

Shevchenko
Kazakhskii Zaliv
Sartas
Kara Bogaz Gol
Krasnovodski Poluostrov
Krasnovodsk
Krasnovodski Zaliv
Poluostrov Cheleken
Ostrov Ogurchinski

T U R K M E N S. S. R.
KARA KUM
Nukus
Urgench
Turtkul
Khiva
Gizhduvan
Bukhara
Kogan
Karshi
Chardzhou
Kerki
Andkhui
Mary (Mery)
Bairam Ali
Iolotan
Tedzhen
Tashkepri
Serakhs
Ashkhabad
Mohammadabad
Dushak

Tashkent
Chirchik
Angren
Kokand
Namangan
Andizhan
Margelan
Fergana
Leninabad
Kanibadam
Osh
Kara Kul

TADZHIK S.S.R.
Dushanbe
Ordzhonikidzeabad
Kurgan-Tyube
Kulyab

CHINA
Kashgar (Shufu)
Yangi Hissar
Tien Shan
Pamir

A F G H A N I S T A N
Mazar-i-Sharif
BALKH
Maimana
Herat
BADGHIS
Band-i-Turkistan
BAMIAN
KABUL
Kabul
PESHAWAR
Rawalpindi
Jelalabad
Ghazni
Gardez
KANDAHAR
Kandahar
Girishk
Farah
Zaranj
Seistan
Dasht-i-Margo
Registan
CHAKHANSUR
HELMAND
URUZGAN
Quetta

P E R S I A (I R A N)
Mashhad (Meshed)
Neyshabur
Sabzevar
Torbat-e Heydariyeh
Torbat-e Jam
Khvaf
KHORASAN
DASHT-E KAVIR
(Great Salt Desert)
Birjand
Qayen
Ferdows
Tabas
Deyhuk
Yazd
Esfahan
Na'in
Ardakan
FARS
Shiraz
Kerman
KERMAN
Bam
Zahedan (Duzdab)
Mirjaveh
Nosratabad
BALUCHISTAN
Iranshahr
Bampur
Chah Bahar
Jask

PAKISTAN
KARACHI
Hyderabad
Larkana
Sukkur
Multan
BAHAWALPUR
Khairpur
Nawabshah

INDIA
GREAT INDIAN DESERT
Jamnagar
Porbandar
Dwarka
Gulf of Kutch
Rann of Kutch
KUTCH

QATAR
Doha
Al Wakrah
UNITED ARAB EMIRATES
(TRUCIAL STATES)
Abu Dhabi
DHAFRA
Al Wahat al Buraimi
Dubay
OMAN
Masqat (Muscat)
Sohar
Gulf of Oman
Ra's al Hadd
Tropic of Cancer

A R A B I A N S E A

PERSIAN GULF
BAHRAIN
Manama
Ras Masandam

CASPIAN SEA
MAZANDARAN
Kuhha-Ye Alborz
Damavand
SEMNAN
Semnan
Tehran
Qom
Kashan
ESFAHAN
Shahr Kord

East from Greenwich

SOUTH ASIA

U.S.S.R.

AFGHANISTAN

HERAT · GHOR · BADGHIS · FARYAB · SAMANGAN · BADAKHSHAN · TAKHAR · BAGLAN · PARWAN · KUNAR · PESHAWAR

HELMAND · KANDAHAR · ZABUL · GHAZNI · URUZGAN · WARDAK · LOGAR · NANGARHAR · PAKTYA · KATTAWAZ-URGUN

Herat · Kabul · Kandahar · Quetta · Peshawar · Rawalpindi · Islamabad · RAWALPINDI · Lahore · Amritsar

DASHT-I-MARGO · REGISTAN · Toba Kakar · Khojak Pass · Bolan Pass

JAMMU AND KASHMIR · Srinagar · HIMACHAL PRADESH · Simla · Dehra Dun · Hardwar

PUNJAB · Ludhiana · Ambala · Patiala · Chandigarh · Saharanpur · Karnal · Muzaffarnagar · Meerut

Lyallpur · Multan · Bahawalpur · BAHAWALPUR · Bikaner · HARYANA · DELHI · Moradabad · Rampur

KHAIRPUR · Sukkur · SIND · Karachi · Hyderabad · Thar Desert · Indian Desert · RAJASTHAN · Jodhpur · Jaipur · Ajmer · Alwar · Mathura · Agra · Aligarh

KARACHI · HYDERABAD · Mouths of the Indus

ARABIAN SEA

Tropic of Cancer

Rann of Kutch · GUJARAT · Bhuj · Ahmadabad · Rajkot · Jamnagar · Junagadh · Porbandar · Bhavnagar · Vadodara (Baroda) · Bharuch · Surat

Gulf of Kutch · Gulf of Cambay · Kathiawar

INDIA · MADHYA PRADESH · Indore · Ujjain · Bhopal · Nagpur · Gwalior · Jhansi

Daman · DADRA & NAGAR HAVELI · Nasik · Malegaon · Dhulia · Jalgaon · Akola · Amraoti · Wardha

BOMBAY · MAHARASHTRA · Poona (Pune) · Ahmadnagar · Aurangabad · Sholapur · Kolhapur · Satara

GOA · Panaji (Panjim) · Marmagao · Belgaum · Dharwar · Hubli · Bijapur · Gulbarga · Raichur

ANDHRA PRADESH · Hyderabad · Nizamabad · Warangal

Inset: Continuation Southwards on same scale

Dharwar · GOA · Hubli · Gadag · Bellary · KARNATAKA · Bangalore · Mysore · Mangalore · Kurnool · Guntakal

Madras · Vellore · Pondicherry · Cuddalore · TAMIL NADU · Salem · Coimbatore · Erode · Tiruchirappalli · Thanjavur · Nagappattinam

Calicut (Kozhikode) · Palghat · Trichur · Ernakulam · Mattancheri · Alleppey · Quilon · Trivandrum · Nagercoil · Cape Comorin

Madurai · Tirunelveli · Palk Strait · Adam's Bridge · Gulf of Mannar · Palk Bay

SRI LANKA (CEYLON) · Colombo · Kandy · Moratuwa · Mt. Lavinia · Galle · Trincomalee · Dondra Head

Malabar Coast · Coromandel Coast · Pulicat Lake

Legend

ft	m
18 000	6000
12 000	4000
9000	3000
6000	2000
4500	1500
3000	1000
1200	400
600	200
0	0
600	200

Continuation Southwards on same scale

Projection: Conical with two standard parallels

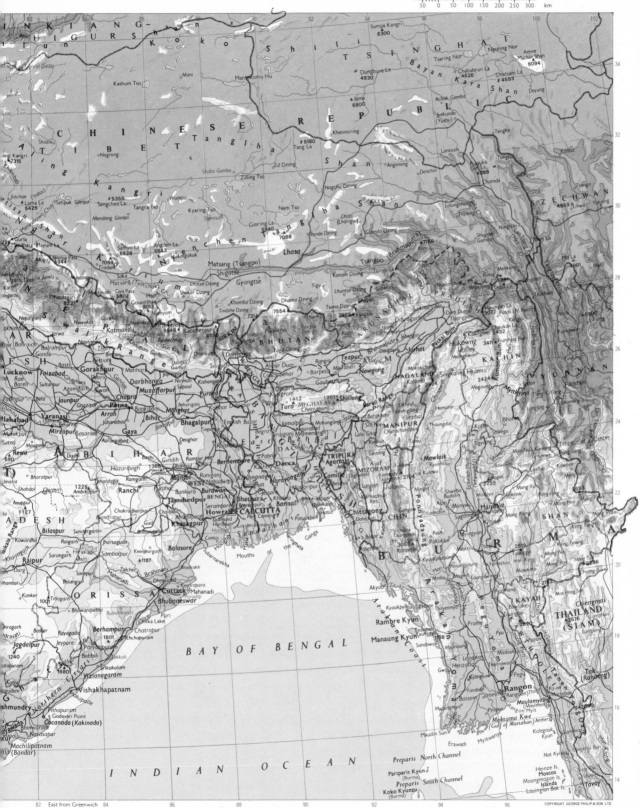

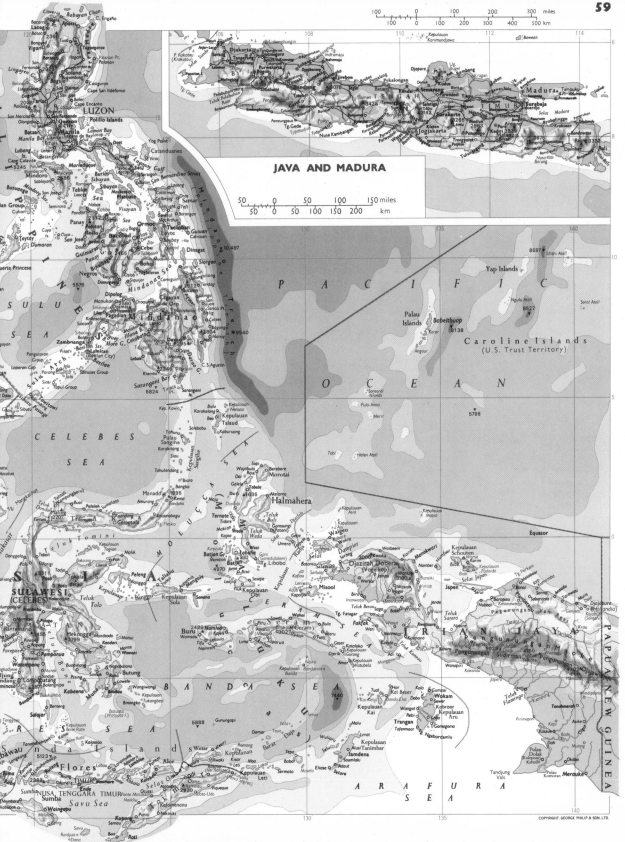

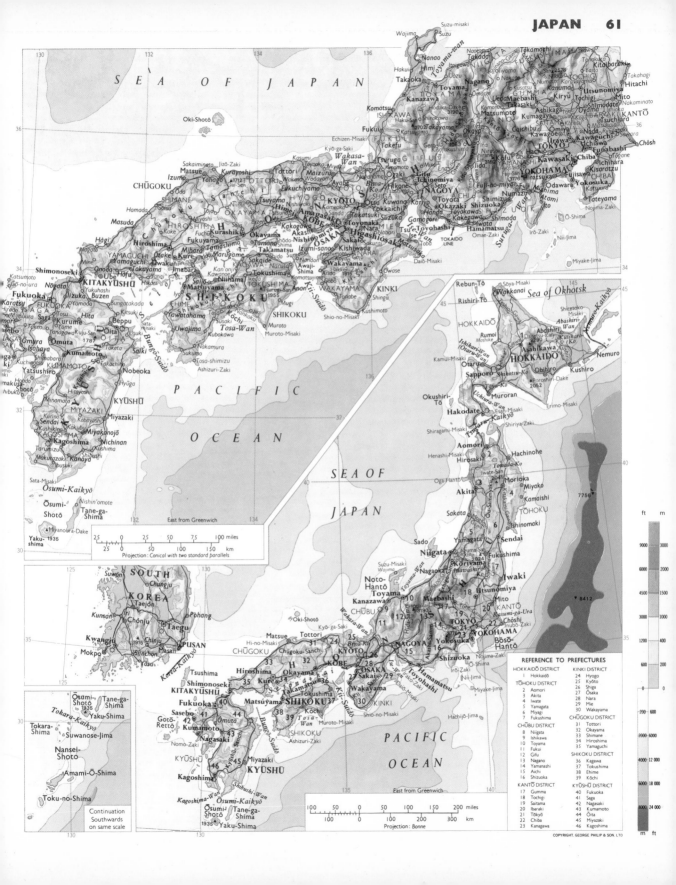

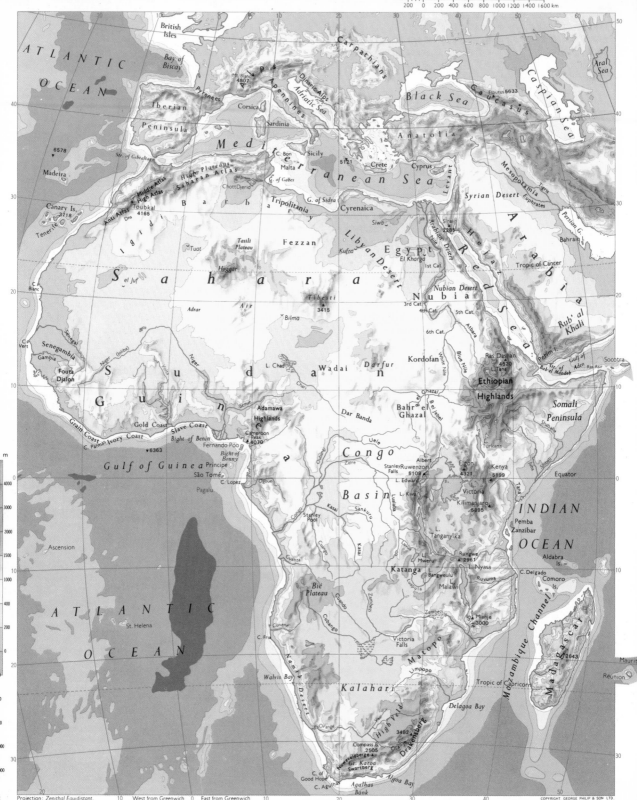

ATLANTIC

OCEAN

British
Isles

Bay of
Biscay

Carpathians

Black Sea

Caucasus 5633

Aral
Sea

Caspian Sea

Iberian
Peninsula

Pyrenees

Alps
Mt Blanc
4807

Apennines

Corsica

Dinaric Alps
Adriatic Sea

Anatolia

Mesopotamia

6578

Madeira

Str. of Gibraltar

High Plateaus
Saharan Atlas

Middle Atlas

High Atlas

Sardinia

C. Bon
Malta

Sicily

G. of Gabes

5121

Crete

Cyprus

Tigris

Euphrates

Mediterranean Sea

Levant

Syrian Desert

Persian G.

Bahrain

Canary Is.

Tenerife

Anti Atlas
Toubkal
4165

Drâa

B a r b a r y

Tripolitania

G. of Sidra

Cyrenaica

Siwa

Arabian Desert

Sinai
2285

Hejaz

Tropic of Cancer

Rub' al
Khali

Igidi

S e l Juf

S a h a r a

Tuat

Tasili
Plateau

Fezzan

Hoggar

Kufra

Libyan Desert

Egypt

El Kharga

1st Cat.

Nile

Red Sea

Arabia

C. A.
Blanc

Adrar

Aïr

Bilma

Tibesti
3415

Nubian Desert

3rd Cat

Nubia

4th Cat.

5th Cat.

6th Cat.

Atbara

Ras Dashan
4620

Perim I.

Str. of
Bab el Mandeb

Gulf of
Aden

Socotra

Ras Asir

C.
Vert

Senegambia

Gambia

Fouta
Djalon

Senegal

Niger

(Joliba)

Volta

Niger

S u d a n

L. Chad

Chari

Wadai

Darfur

Kordofan

White Nile

Blue Nile

L. Tana

Ethiopian
Highlands

Somali
Peninsula

G u i n e a

Grain Coast

C. Palmas

Gold Coast

Ivory Coast

Slave Coast

Benue

Adamawa
Highlands

Cameroon
Peak
4070

Bight of Benin

Bahr el
Ghazal

Dar Banda

Bahr el Ghazal

Ghazal

Bahr el Jebel

Shabelle

6363

Fernando Póo

Bight of
Bonny

Gulf of Guinea

Príncipe

São Tomé

Pagalu

C. Lopez

Ogowé

Ogooué

Uele

Zaïre

Congo

Stanley
Falls

Albert

Ruwenzori
5108

Elgon
4321

Kenya
5199

Equator

INDIAN

OCEAN

Ascension

ATLANTIC

OCEAN

St. Helena

Congo

Stanley
Pool

Kasai

Sankuru

Kassai

Cuango

Basin

Lualaba

L. Kivu

L. Edward

Victoria

Kilimanjaro
5895

Pemba

Zanzibar

Bié
Plateau

Cunene

Cubango

Zambezi

L.
Tanganyika

Katanga

Bangweulu

L.
Mweru

Rungwe
2961

L. Nyasa

Malawi

Ruvuma

C. Delgado

Comoro
Is.

Aldabra
Is.

Turkana

Loangwa

Mlanje
3000

Luapula

Victoria
Falls

Matopo

Limpopo

Zambezi

Mozambique Channel

Madagascar
2643

Mauritius

Réunion

Namib Desert

Walvis Bay

C. Frio

Kalahari

Tropic of Capricorn

Delagoa Bay

Algoa Bay

Orange

Highveld

Compass B.
2505

Nieuweveldberge

Gr. Karoo

Swartberg

3482

Drakensberg

C. of
Good Hope

C. Agulhas

Agulhas
Bank

ft   m

12 000   4000

9000   3000

6000   2000

4500   1500

3000   1000

1200   400

600   200

0   0

200   600

1000   3000

4000   12 000

6000   18 000

m   ft

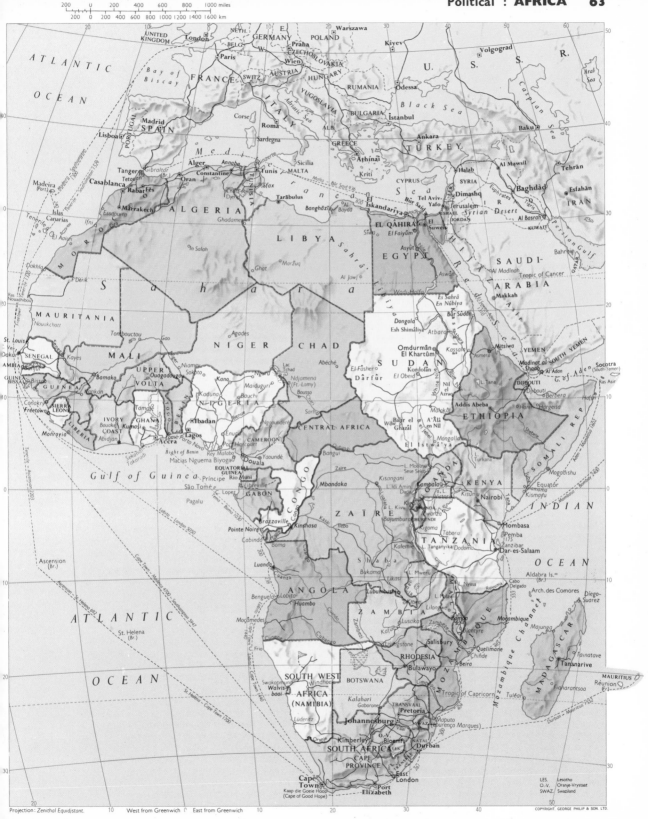

200   0   200   400   600   800   1000 miles
200   0   200   400   600 1000 1200 1400 1600 km

ATLANTIC OCEAN

UNITED KINGDOM   London   NETH.   E. GERMANY   POLAND   Warszawa

Paris   FRANCE   BELG.   W. GERMANY   Praha   CZECHOSLOVAKIA   Kiyev   U. S. S. R.   Volgograd

Bay of Biscay   SWITZ.   AUSTRIA   HUNGARY   RUMANIA   Odessa   Aral Sea

ITALY   YUGOSLAVIA   Black Sea   Caspian Sea

SPAIN   MADRID   Corse   Roma   BULGARIA   İstanbul   Baku

PORTUGAL   Lisboa   Sardegna   GREECE   Ankara   TURKEY   Al Mawsil   Tehrān

Madeira (Port.)   Tanger   Algér   Annaba   Tunis   Sicilia   MALTA   Athínai   Kriti   CYPRUS   SYRIA   Halab   Baghdād   Esfahān

Casablanca   Rabat Fès   TUNISIA   Mediterranean Sea   Tel Aviv-Yafo   Dimashq   IRAN

Marrakech   ALGERIA   Ghadames   LIBYA   EL QAHIRA   El Suweis   JORDAN   Al Basrah   KUWAIT

Islas Canarias   MOROCCO   EGYPT   SAUDI-ARABIA   Bahrain   QATAR

Dakhla   Sahara   Aswân   Al Madinah   Tropic of Cancer

MAURITANIA   Nouakchott   Es Sahrâ En Nûbiya   Bûr Sûdân   Makkah

SENEGAL   Tombouctou   Gao   NIGER   CHAD   SUDAN   Dongola   Atbara   YEMEN   SOUTH YEMEN   Socotra

GAMBIA   MALI   Niamey   Omdurmân El Khartûm   Asmera   DJIBOUTI

GUINEA BISSAU   Bamako   UPPER VOLTA   Ouagadougou   NIGERIA   Kano   Maiduguri   Dârfûr   El Fasher   El Obeid   ETHIOPIA   Addis Abeba   SOMALI REP.

SIERRA LEONE   Freetown   GUINEA   IVORY COAST   GHANA   Ibadan   Lagos   CENTRAL AFRICA   Bangui   Addis Abeba

LIBERIA   Monrovia   CAMEROON   Yaoundé   Douala   ZAÏRE   KENYA   Mogadishu

Gulf of Guinea   EQUATORIAL GUINEA   Libreville   GABON   CONGO   Brazzaville   Kinshasa   Nairobi   Mombasa   INDIAN OCEAN

São Tomé   Príncipe   ANGOLA   TANZANIA   Dodoma   Dar-es-Salaam   Zanzibar

Ascension (Br.)   Luanda   ZAÏRE   L. Tanganyika   Arch. des Comores   Diego-Suarez

ATLANTIC OCEAN   Benguela   Lobito   ZAMBIA   Lusaka   Blantyre   MOZAMBIQUE   MADAGASCAR   Tananarive   MAURITIUS   Réunion

St. Helena (Br.)   SOUTH WEST AFRICA (NAMIBIA)   Windhoek   BOTSWANA   RHODESIA   Salisbury   Bulawayo   Beira   Tropic of Capricorn

Kalahari   TRANSVAAL   Pretoria   Johannesburg   Maputo   Tuléar

Walvis baai   Lüderitz   Kimberley   Bloemfontein   SOUTH AFRICA   CAPE PROVINCE   Durban

Cape Town   Kaap die Goeie Hoop (Cape of Good Hope)   Port Elizabeth   East London

LES.   Lesotho
O.V.   Orange-Vrystaat
SWAZ.   Swaziland

ATLANTIC OCEAN

Projection: Zenithal Equidistant.   West from Greenwich   East from Greenwich   COPYRIGHT. GEORGE PHILIP & SON. LTD.

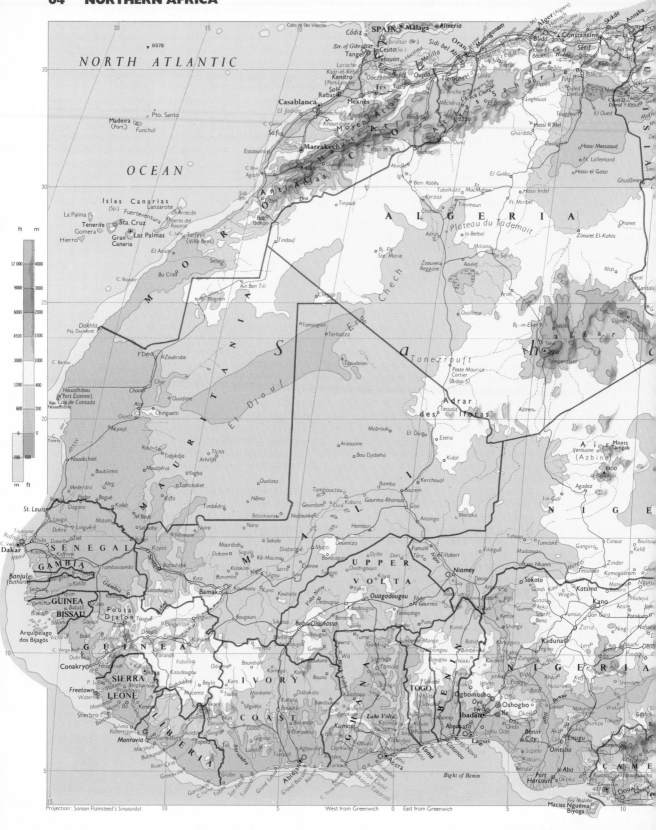

NORTH ATLANTIC

OCEAN

ALGERIA

MOROCCO

MAURITANIA

El Djouf

MALI

SENEGAL

GAMBIA

GUINEA

BISSAU

GUINEA

SIERRA

LEONE

LIBERIA

IVORY

COAST

GHANA

TOGO

BENIN

UPPER

VOLTA

NIGERIA

NIGE

CAME

Dakar

Bamako

Conakry

Freetown

Monrovia

Abidjan

Accra

Lagos

Niamey

Ouagadougou

Islas Canarias

Casablanca

Marrakech

SPAIN

Projection : Sanson Flamsteed's Sinusoidal

West from Greenwich   East from Greenwich

Bight of Benin

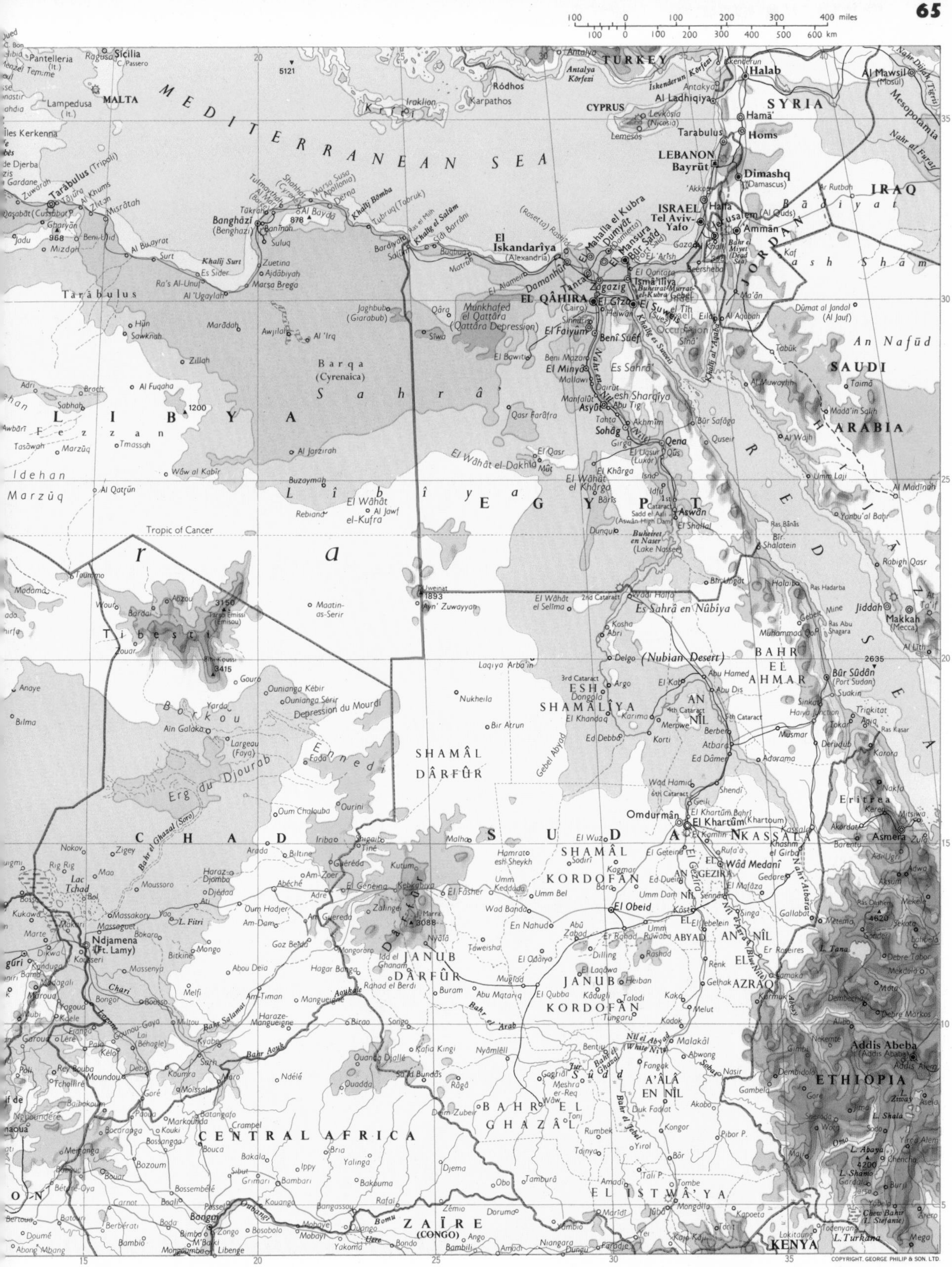

100   0   100   200   300   400 miles
100   0   100   200   300   400   500   600 km

TURKEY

MALTA

M E D I T E R R A N E A N   S E A

CYPRUS

SYRIA

Al Mawsil (Mosul)

Halab

Al Ladhiqiya
Hama
Homs
Tarabulus
LEBANON
Bayrut
Dimashq (Damascus)

IRAQ

Tarabulus (Tripoli)

Banghazi (Benghazi)

ISRAEL
Tel Aviv-Yafo
Jerusalem (Al Quds)
Amman
JORDAN

El Iskandariya (Alexandria)

El Qahira (Cairo)
El Gizira

SAUDI

ARABIA

Barqa (Cyrenaica)

L I B Y A

Munkhafed el Qattâra (Qattara Depression)

El Faiyum

Beni Suef

El Minya

E G Y P T

S a h r â

An Nafûd

Makkah (Mecca)

Tibesti

Tropic of Cancer

El Kharga

Aswan
Aswân High Dam

Buheiret en Naser
(Lake Nasser)

Es Sahrâ en Nûbiya

B A H R
E L
A H M A R

R   E   D

S   E   A

(Nubian Desert)

Bûr Sûdân (Port Sudan)
Suakin

C H A D

Lac Tchad

ESH
SHAMALIYA

AN
NIL

Omdurmân
El Khartûm (Khartoum)

KASSALA

Eritrea

Asmera

SHAMAL
DÂRFÛR

SHAMAL
KORDOFAN

El Obeid

AN
NIL
EL
GEZIRA

Wâd Medani

Gedaref

JANUB
DÂRFÛR

JANUB
KORDOFAN

ABYAD

AN NIL
EL
AZRAQ

Nyala

S U D A N

L. Tana

Addis Abeba (Addis Ababa)

ETHIOPIA

CENTRAL AFRICA

BAHR EL
GHAZÂL

White Nile

A'ÂLA
EN NIL

EL ISTWÂ'YA

Ndjamena (Ft. Lamy)

ZAÏRE
(CONGO)

KENYA

L. Turkana

COPYRIGHT GEORGE PHILIP & SON LTD

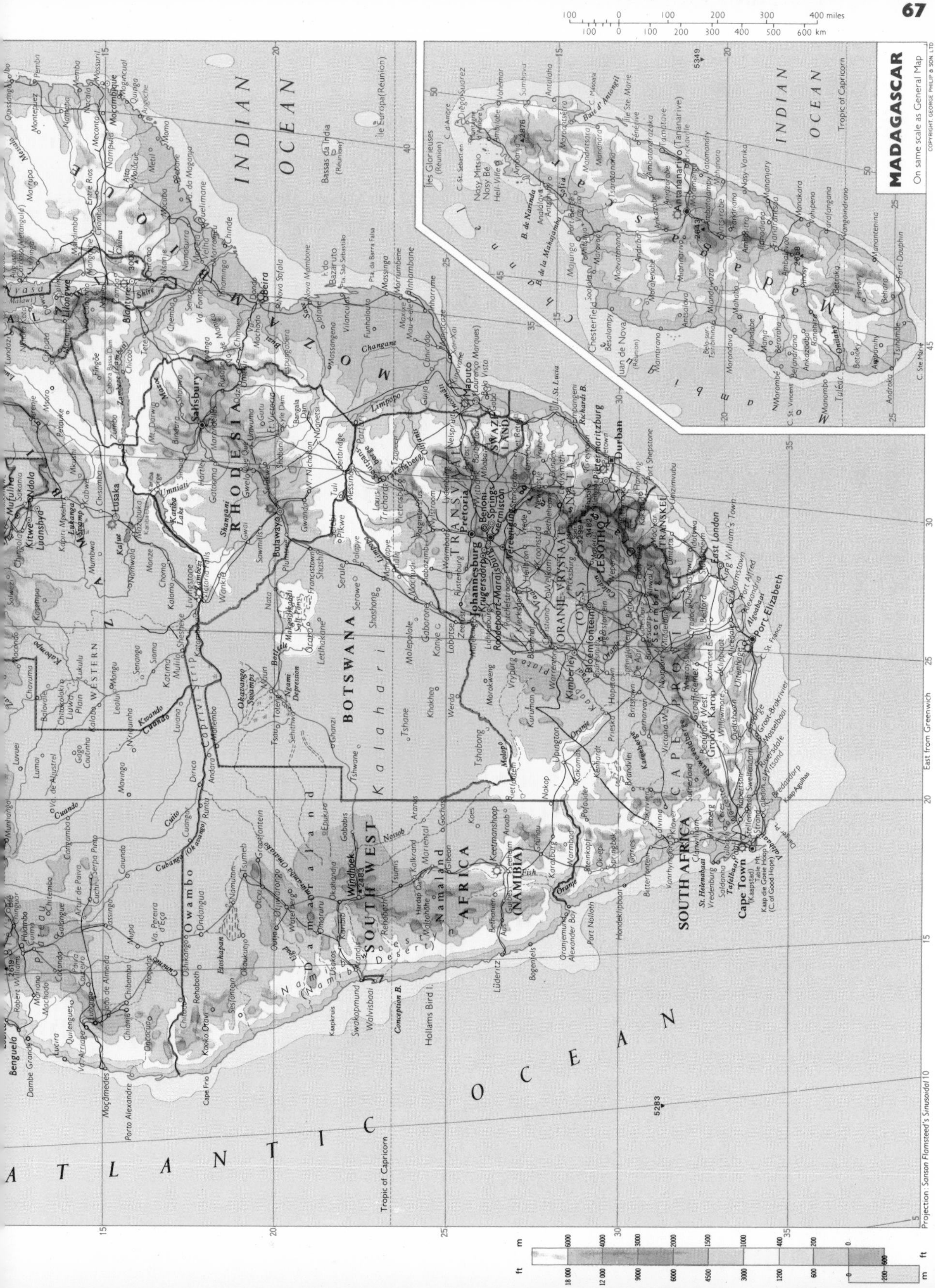

100 0 100 200 300 400 miles
100 0 100 200 300 400 500 600 km

MADAGASCAR
On same scale as General Map

COPYRIGHT GEORGE PHILIP & SON, LTD

INDIAN OCEAN

INDIAN OCEAN

ATLANTIC OCEAN

Tropic of Capricorn

East from Greenwich

Projection Sanson Flamsteed's Sinusoidal 10

RHODESIA

BOTSWANA

SOUTH WEST AFRICA
(NAMIBIA)

SOUTH AFRICA

TRANSVAAL

ORANJE VRYSTAAT (O.F.S.)

CAPE PROVINCE

LESOTHO

TRANSKEI

SWAZILAND

NATAL

Kalahari

Namaland

Damaraland

Kalahari Desert

Namib Desert (Namib)

Caprivi Strip

Cape Town
Durban
Johannesburg
Pretoria
Bloemfontein
Kimberley
Port Elizabeth
East London
Windhoek
Walvis Bay
Lüderitz
Salisbury
Bulawayo
Lusaka
Benguela
Maputo

Tropic of Capricorn

m ft
ft m

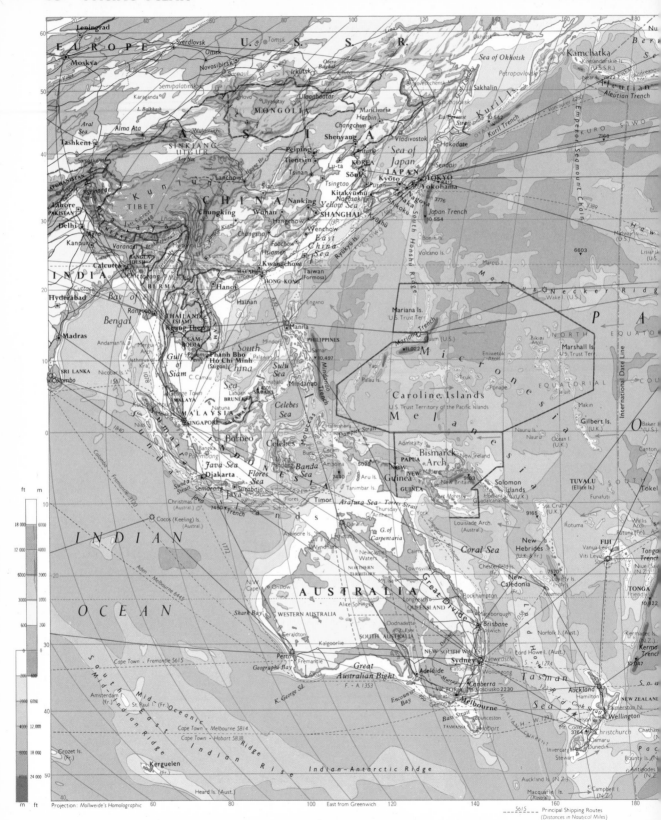

_____ 5615 Principal Shipping Routes
(Distances in Nautical Miles)

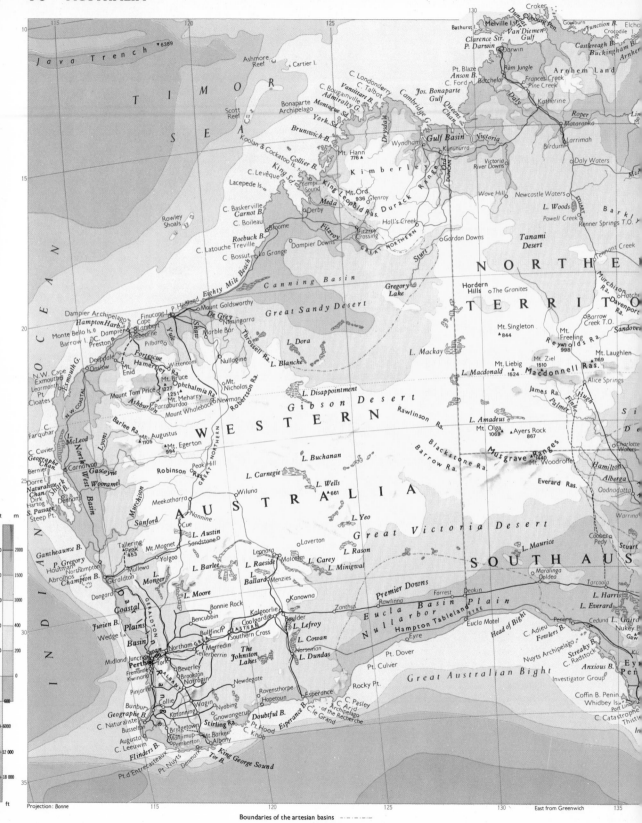

Boundaries of the artesian basins ------

Projection: Bonne

East from Greenwich

Scale bar:
100   0   100   200 miles
100   0   100   200   300   400 km

AUSTRALASIA
POLITICAL

QUEENSLAND

NEW SOUTH WALES

VICTORIA

TASMANIA

on same scale

COPYRIGHT. GEORGE PHILIP & SON. LTD.

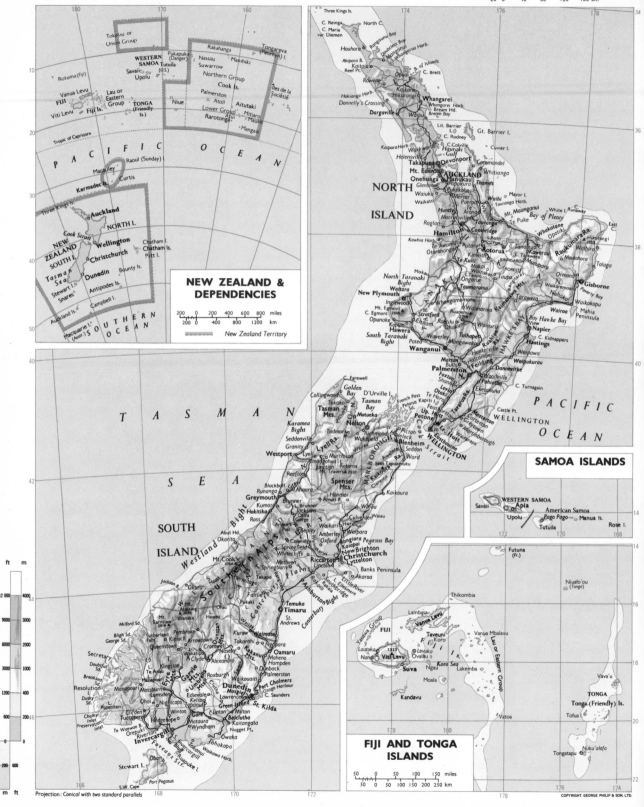

NEW ZEALAND & DEPENDENCIES

200   0   200   400   600   800 miles
200   0   400   800   1200 km

New Zealand Territory

SAMOA ISLANDS

WESTERN SAMOA
Savaii   Apia
Upolu   American Samoa Is.
  Pago Pago   Manua Is.
Tutuila   Rose I.

FIJI AND TONGA ISLANDS

50   0   50   100   150 miles
50   0   50   100   150   250 km

NORTH ISLAND

SOUTH ISLAND

TASMAN SEA

PACIFIC OCEAN

SOUTHERN OCEAN

Projection: Conical with two standard parallels

COPYRIGHT. GEORGE PHILIP & SON, LTD.

Index

The map page numbers are in bold type. An asterisk before the page number indicates that the place is on an inset map. The symbol ■ indicates country names and □ denotes administrative subdivision.

In some cases the same place occurs a number of times within the same country and also in other countries. In these cases the names are arranged in country order and for the names occurring within the same country only the administrative unit names are shown. For example:-

Rochester, Canada
Rochester, Minn.   U.S.A. does not appear in the index
Rochester, N.H.

The latitudes and longitudes are intended primarily as a guide to finding places in the atlas and in some cases are only approximate.

Alta.	Alberta	E.	East	N.	North	R.	River
Afghan.	Afghanistan	Fla.	Florida	N.B.	New Brunswick	R.I.	Rhode Island
Arch.	Archipelago	G.	Gulf, golfo	N.C.	North Carolina	Ra.	Range
Arg.	Argentina	Ga.	Georgia	N.D.	North Dakota	Reg.	Region
Ariz.	Arizona	Germ.	Germany	N.H.	New Hampshire	Rep.	Republic
Ark.	Arkansas	Gt.(er)	Great, Greater	N.J.	New Jersey	Res.	Reservoir
B.	Bay	Guat.	Guatemala	N.S.	Nova Scotia	S.	South
B.C.	British Columbia	Hd.	Head	N.W.T.	Northwest Territories	S. Afr.	South Africa
Bol.	Bolivia	I.(s)	Island (s)	N.Y.	New York	S.C.	South Carolina
C.	Cape	Ill.	Illinois	N.Z.	New Zealand	S.D.	South Dakota
C. Prov.	Cape Province	Ind.	Indiana	Nat. Pk.	National Park	Sa.	Sierra
Calif.	California	Kans.	Kansas	Neths.	Netherlands	Sask.	Saskatchewan
Chan.	Channel	Ky.	Kentucky	Nev.	Nevada	Sd.	Sound
Colo.	Colorado	L.	Lake	Nfld.	Newfoundland	Str.	Strait
Conn.	Connecticut	La.	Louisiana	Nic.	Nicaragua	Tenn.	Tennessee
Cont.	Continent	Man.	Manitoba	Ont.	Ontario	Tex.	Texas
Cord.	Cordillera	Mass.	Massachusetts	Ore.	Oregon	Urug.	Uruguay
Cr.	Creek	Me.	Maine	P.E.I.	Prince Edward Island	Va.	Virginia
Czech.	Czechoslovakia	Mex.	Mexico	Pa.	Pennsylvania	Vt.	Vermont
Del.	Delaware	Mich.	Michigan	Para.	Paraguay	W.	West
Des.	Desert	Minn.	Minnesota	Pen.	Peninsula	W.Va.	West Virginia
Dist.	District	Miss.	Missouri	Pt.	Point	Wash.	Washington
Dom. Rep.	Dominican Republic	Mt.(s)	Mountain (s)	Que.	Quebec	Wis.	Wisconsin

A

37	Aachen	50 47N	6 4 E
37	Aalst	50 56N	4 2 E
47	Aare, R	47 37N	8 13 E
64	Aba	5 10N	7 19 E
53	Aba Saud	17 15N	44 23N
52	Abadan	30 22N	48 20 E
52	Abasan	31 19N	34 21 E
60	Abashiri	44 0N	144 15 E
6	Abaya, L.	6 30N	37 50 E
38	Abbeville	50 6N	1 49 E
64	Abéché	13 50N	20 35 E
45	Abenra	55 4N	9 23 E
64	Abeokuta	7 3N	3 19 E
25	Aberdeen, Canada	52 20N	106 8w
36	Aberdeen, U.K.	57 9N	2 6w
11	Aberdeen, S.D.	45 30N	98 30w
*18	Aberdeen, Wash.	47 0N	123 58w
36	Aberystwyth	52 25N	4 6w
64	Abidjan	5 26N	3 58w
11	Abilene, Kansas	39 0N	96 16w
11	Abilene, Texas	32 22N	99 40w
22	Abitibi, L.	48 42N	79 45w
47	Abkhaz A.S.S.R. □	43 0N	41 0 E
45	Abo=Turku	60 27N	22 14 E
9	Absaroka Ra.	44 40N	110 0w
53	Abu Dhabi □	24 28N	54 36 E
54	Abu Kamal	34 30N	41 0 E
53	Abu Zabi	24 28N	54 36 E
60	Abukuma-Gawa	37 30N	140 30 E
26	Acámbaro	20 0N	100 40w
26	Acaponeta	22 30N	105 20w
27	Acapulco	16 51N	99 56w
27	Acatlán	18 10N	98 3w
17	Acayucán	17 59N	94 58w
64	Accra	5 35N	0 6w
49	Achinsk	56 49N	90 37 E
29	Acklin's I.	22 30N	74 0w
71	Acland, mt.	24 50s	148 20 E
32	Aconcagua, mt.	32 15s	70 30w
52	Acre=Akko	32 35s	35 4 E
30	Acre □	9 1s	71 0w
53	Ad Dam	20 33N	44 45 E
53	Ad Dammam	26 20N	50 5 E
17	Ada, Ohio	40 46N	83 49w
11	Ada, Okla.	34 50N	96 45w
66	Adamaoua, Massif de l-	7 20N	12 20 E
40	Adamello, mt.	46 10N	10 34 E
15	Adams	42 37N	73 7w
56	Adam's Bridge	9 15N	79 40 E
56	Adam's Peak	6 55N	80 45 E
54	Adana	37 0N	35 16 E

54	Adapazari	40 48N	30 25 E
53	Addis Abeba	9 2N	38 42 E
71	Adelaide	34 55s	138 32 E
53	Aden=Al'Adan	12 50N	45 0 E
53	Aden, G. of	13 0N	50 0 E
40	Adige, R.	45 9N	11 25 E
15	Adirondack Mts.	44 0N	74 15w
12	Admiralty Inlet	48 0N	122 40w
24	Admiralty I.,	57 50N	134 30w
64	Adrar des Iforas, reg.	19 40N	1 40 E
17	Adrian	41 54N	84 2w
40	Adriatic Sea	43 0N	16 0 E
53	Adwa	14 15N	38 52 E
47	Adzhar A.S.S.R. □	42 0N	42 0 E
41	Aegean Sea	38 0N	25 0 E
61	Aerht'ai Shan	46 40N	92 45 E
55	Afghanistan ■	33 0N	65 0 E
*20	Afognak, I.	58 15N	152 30w
52	'Afula	32 37N	35 17 E
54	Afyon	38 46N	30 33 E
64	Agadez	16 58N	7 59 E
64	Agadir	30 28N	9 35w
57	Agartala	23 50N	91 23 E
56	Agra	27 17N	77 58 E
54	Agri Dagi, mt.	39 50N	44 15 E
26	Agua Prieta	31 20N	109 32w
29	Aguadilla	18 27N	67 10w
26	Aguascalientes	22 0N	102 12w
52	Agur	31 42N	34 55 E
64	Ahaggar, plateau	23 0N	6 30 E
56	Ahmadabad	23 0N	72 40 E
56	Ahmadnagar	19 7N	74 46 E
28	Ahuachapán	13 54N	89 52w
54	Ahvaz	31 20N	48 40 E
53	Ahwar	13 48N	46 35 E
9	Aiken	33 34N	81 50w
38	Ain □	46 5N	5 20 E
64	Air, plateau	18 30N	8 0 E
38	Aisne, R.	49 26N	5 31 E
38	Aisne □	49 42N	3 40 E
*72	Aitutaki	18 52s	159 48w
38	Aix	43 32N	5 27 E
*38	Ajaccio	41 55N	8 40 E
56	Ajmer	26 28N	74 37 E
60	Akashi	34 45N	135 0 E
41	Akhelóös, R.	38 36N	21 14 E
22	Akimiski I.	52 50N	81 30w
60	Akita	39 45N	140 0 E
52	Akko	32 35N	35 4 E
56	Akola	20 42N	77 2 E
*44	Akranes	64 19N	22 6w
14	Akron	41 7N	81 31w
21	Akpatok I.	60 30N	68 0w
47	Aktyubinsk	50 10N	57 3 E
*44	Akureyri	65 40N	18 6w

57	Akyab	20 15N	92 45 E
53	Al'Adan	12 50N	45 0 E
54	Al Amarah	31 55N	47 15 E
54	Al'Aqabah	29 37N	35 0 E
52	Al Barah	31 55N	35 12 E
54	Al Basrah	0 30N	47 55 E
54	Al Buraimi	24 15N	55 43 E
54	Al Hadithan	34 0N	41 13 E
54	Al Hillah	32 30N	44 25 E
54	Al Jazirah, reg.	34 0N	43 0 E
53	Al Khalaf	20 31N	58 4 E
54	Al Kuwayt	29 20N	48 0 E
54	Al Ladhiqiyah	35 30N	38 45 E
53	Al Madinah	24 35N	39 52 E
54	Al Mawsil	36 15N	43 5 E
54	Al Qamishli	37 10N	41 10 E
53	Al Wari'ah	27 50N	47 30 E
54	Ala Dag, mt.	37 55N	35 13 E
61	Ala Shan	39 50N	103 30 E
9	Alabama, R.	31 8N	87 57w
9	Alabama □	31 0N	87 0w
31	Alagôas □	9 0s	36 0w
31	Alagoinhas	12 0s	38 20w
29	Alajuela	10 2N	84 8w
12	Alamogordo	32 59N	100 6w
13	Alamosa	37 30N	106 0w
45	Aland, I.	60 15N	20 0 E
61	Alashanchih	38 58N	105 14 E
*20	Alaska, G. of	58 0N	145 0w
*20	Alaska Pen.	56 0N	160 0w
*20	Alaska Ra.	62 50N	151 0w
*20	Alaska □	65 0N	150 0w
40	Alba	44 41N	8 1 E
40	Alba-Iulia	46 8s	23 39 E
39	Albacete	38 50N	2 0w
41	Albania ■	41 0N	20 0 E
71	Albany, Australia	35 1s	117 58 E
9	Albany, Ga.	31 40N	84 10w
15	Albany, N.Y.	42 40N	73 47w
12	Albany, Ore.	44 41N	123 0w
22	Albany, R.	52 17N	81 31w
39	Albarracín, Sa. de	40 25N	1 26w
9	Albemarle	35 27N	80 15w
70	Alberga, R.	26 50s	135 40 E
24	Alberni	49 16N	124 48w
11	Albert Lea	4 32s	93 20w
66	Albert Nile, R.	3 36N	32 2 E
66	Albertville=Kalemie	5 55s	29 9 E
13	Albuquerque	35 5N	106 47w
71	Albury	36 0s	146 50 E
39	Alcaraz, Sa. de	38 40N	2 20w
39	Alcobaça	39 32N	9 0w

39	Aldan, R.	63 28N	129 35 E
38	Alderney, I.	49 42N	2 12w
49	Aleksandrovsk-Sakhalinskiy	50 50N	142 20 E
*6	Alenuihaha Chan.	20 25N	156 0w
54	Aleppo=Halab	36 10N	37 15 E
11	Alert Bay	50 35N	126 55w
40	Alessándria	44 54N	8 37 E
44	Alesund	62 28N	6 12 E
*20	Aleutian Is.	52 0N	175 0w
24	Alexander Arch.	57 0N	135 0w
24	Alexandria Canada	47 11N	74 18w
17	Alexandria, Ind.	40 16N	85 41w
11	Alexandria, La.	31 20N	92 30w
8	Alexandria, Va.	38 47N	77 1w
65	Alexandria=El Iskandariya	31 0N	30 0 E
41	Alexandroúpolis	40 50N	25 54 E
39	Algarve □	37 15N	8 10w
39	Algeciras	36 9N	5 28w
64	Alger	36 42N	3 8 E
64	Algeria ■	35 10N	3 11 E
64	Algiers=Alger	36 42N	3 8 E
19	Alhambra	34 0N	118 10w
39	Alicante	38 23N	0 30w
11	Alice	27 47N	98 1w
70	Alice Springs	23 36s	133 53 E
48	Alida	49 25N	101 55w
56	Aligarh	27 55N	78 10 E
23	Alingsas	57 57N	12 36 E
14	Aliquippa	40 38N	80 18w
56	Alkmaar	52 37N	4 45 E
57	Allahabad	25 25N	81 58 E
14	Allegheny Mts.	38 0N	80 0w
8	Allegheny Res.	42 0N	78 56w
15	Allentown	40 36N	75 30w
*56	Alleppey	9 30N	76 28 E
10	Alliance, Nebr.	42 10N	102 50w
14	Alliance, Ohio	40 55N	81 6w
38	Allier, R.	46 58N	3 4 E
38	Allier □	46 25N	3 0 E
18	Alliston	44 9N	79 52w
23	Alma	48 33N	71 39w
43	Alma Ata	43 20N	76 50 E
39	Almadén	38 49N	4 52w
39	Almanzor, Pico de	40 15N	5 18w
39	Almanzora, R.	38 56N	8 54w
39	Almazán	41 30N	2 30w
37	Almelo	52 22N	6 42 E
39	Almería	36 52N	2 32w
18	Alpaugh	35 53N	119 29w
38	Alpes-de-Haute-Provence □	44 42N	6 20 E
38	Alpes-Maritimes □	43 55N	7 10 E
11	Alpine	30 35N	103 35w

Alps, mts. Baker Lake

Page	Place	Lat.	Long.
42	Alps, mts.	47 0N	8 0E
38	Alsace, reg.	48 15N	7 25E
61	Altai, mts=Aerht'ai Shan	46 40N	92 45E
61	Altanbulag	50 16N	106 30E
16	Alton	38 55N	90 5W
42	Altona	53 22N	9 56E
14	Altoona	40 32N	78 24W
61	Altyn Tagh	39 0N	90 0E
53	Alula	11 5N	50 45E
59	Alusi	7 35S	131 40E
27	Alvarado	18 40N	95 50W
56	Alwar	27 38N	76 34E
70	Amadeus, L.	24 54S	131 0E
21	Amadjuak L.	64 0N	72 50W
60	Amagasaki	34 42N	135 20E
60	Amakusa-Shoto	32 15N	130 10E
60	Amani-O-Shima	28 15N	129 20E
31	Amapá □	1 40N	52 0W
25	Amaranth	50 36N	98 43W
19	Amargosa Ra.	36 30N	116 45W
11	Amarillo	35 14N	107 45W
31	Amazon, R.= Amazonas, R.	0 5S	50 0W
31	Amazonas, R.	0 5S	50 0W
30	Amazonas □	4 20S	64 0W
52	Amazya	31 32N	34 54E
56	Ambala	30 23N	76 56E
30	Ambato	1 5S	78 42W
42	Amberg	49 25N	11 52E
27	Ambergris Cay	18 0N	88 0W
59	Ambon	3 35S	128 20E
14	Ambridge	40 36N	80 14W
48	Amderma	69 45N	61 30E
26	Ameca	20 30N	104 0W
37	Ameland, I.	53 27N	5 45E
27	Amecameca	19 10N	98 57W
9	Americus	32 0N	84 10W
37	Amersfoort	52 9N	5 23E
16	Ames	42 0N	93 40W
23	Amherst, Canada	45 48N	64 8W
15	Amherst, U.S.A.	42 23N	72 31W
22	Amherstburg	42 6N	83 6W
38	Amiens	49 54N	2 16E
51	Amirante Is.	6 0S	53 0E
54	Amman	32 0N	35 52E
52	Ammi'ad	32 55N	35 32E
61	Amne Machin Shan	34 25N	99 40E
22	Amos	48 35N	78 7W
23	Amqui	48 18N	67 34W
56	Amraoti	20 55N	77 45E
56	Amreli	21 35N	71 17E
56	Amritsar	31 35N	74 57E
37	Amsterdam, Netherlands	52 23N	4 54E
15	Amsterdam, U.S.A.	42 58N	74 10W
48	Amu Darya, R.	43 40N	59 1E
*20	Amukta, Passage	52 25N	172 0W
20	Amundsen G.	70 30N	12 30W
49	Amur, R.	52 56N	141 10E
72	Amuri Pass	42 31S	172 11E
53	An Nafud, reg.	28 15N	41 0E
54	An Najaf	32 3N	44 15E
58	An Nhan	13 53N	109 6E
52	Anabta	32 19N	35 7E
12	Anaconda	46 7N	113 0W
*18	Anacortes	48 30N	122 37W
54	Anadolu, reg.	38 0N	29 0E
49	Anadyr	64 35N	177 20E
49	Anadyr, R.	64 55N	176 5E
49	Anadyrskiy Zaliv	64 0N	180 0E
19	Anaheim	33 51N	117 57W
58	Anambas, Kepulauan	3 20N	106 30E
31	Anápolis	16 15S	48 50W
55	Anarak	33 25N	53 40E
54	Anatolia= Anadolu, reg.	38 0N	39 0E
18	Anchor Bay	38 47N	123 32W
*20	Anchorage	61 10N	149 50W
30	Ancohuma, mt.	16 0S	68 50W
40	Ancona	43 38N	13 30E
32	Ancud	42 0S	73 50W
39	Andalucia □	37 36N	4 30W
9	Andalusia	31 51N	86 30W
17	Anderson, Ind.	40 5N	85 40W
9	Anderson, S.C.	34 32N	82 40W
30	Andes, Cord. de los	20 0S	68 0W
56	Andhra Pradesh □	15 0N	80 0E
48	Andizhan	41 10N	72 0E
39	Andorra ■	42 30N	1 30E
*20	Andreanof Is.	51 0N	178 0W
40	Andria	41 13N	16 17E
28	Andros I., Bahamas	24 25N	78 0W
41	Ándros I., Greece	37 45N	24 42E
28	Andros Town	24 43N	77 47W
39	Andújar	38 3N	4 4W
39	Aneco, Pico de	42 38N	0 40E
49	Angara, R.	58 6N	93 0E
49	Angarsk	52 34N	103 54E
44	Angermanälven	62 48N	17 56E
38	Angers	47 28N	0 33W
67	Angola ■	12 30S	18 30E
38	Angoulême	45 39N	0 9E
29	Anguilla, I.	18 15N	63 5W
61	Anhwei □	31 50N	117 30E
61	Ankang	32 4N	109 27E
54	Ankara	40 0N	32 54E
61	Anking	30 34N	117 1E
17	Ann Arbor	42 17N	83 45W
64	Annaba	36 50N	7 55E
58	Annam= Trung Phan, reg.	15 0N	108 0E
8	Annapolas	39 0N	76 30W
23	Annapolis Royal	44 45N	65 31W
38	Annecy	45 55N	6 8E
9	Anniston	33 45N	85 50W
61	Anshan	41 3N	122 58E
61	Anshun	26 2N	105 57E
61	Ansi	40 21N	9 10E
70	Anson, B.	13 20S	129 30E
21	Ansonia	41 20N	73 5W
22	Ansonville	48 45N	80 41W
54	Antakya	36 14N	36 10E
54	Antalya	36 52N	30 45E
54	Antalya Körfezi	36 15N	31 30E
33	Antarctic Peninsula	67 0S	60 0W
2	Antarctica, cont.	90 0S	0 0
64	Anti Atlas, mts.	30 30N	6 30W
23	Anticosti I.	49 20N	62 40W
10	Antigo	45 8N	89 5W
28	Antigua	13 34N	90 41W
29	Antigua, I.	17 0N	61 50W
18	Antioch	38 1N	121 49W
*72	Antipodes, Is.	49 45S	178 40E
32	Antofogasta	23 50S	70 30W
36	Antrim, Mts. of	54 57N	6 8W
67	Antsirabe	19 55S	47 2E
61	Antung	40 10N	124 18E
37	Antwerpen	51 13N	4 25E
57	Anuppur	23 7N	81 51E
70	Anxious, B.	33 24S	134 45E
61	Anyang	36 7N	114 26E
48	Anzhero Sudzhensk	56 7N	86 0E
40	Anzio	41 28N	12 37E
60	Aomori	40 45N	140 45E
40	Aosta	45 43N	7 20E
26	Apatzinán	19 0N	102 20W
37	Apeldoorn	52 13N	5 57E
*72	Apia	13 50S	171 50W
27	Apizaco	19 26N	98 9W
10	Apostle Is.	47 0N	90 30W
15	Appalachian Mts.	38 0N	80 0W
40	Appennini, mts.	41 0N	15 0E
10	Appleton	44 17N	88 25W
53	'Aqaba, Khalij al	28 30N	34 45E
52	'Aqraba	32 9N	35 20E
53	Ar Rab'al Khali, reg.	21 0N	51 0E
53	Ar Riyad	24 41N	46 42E
31	Aracajú	10 55S	37 4W
31	Araçatuba	10 38N	74 9W
52	'Arad, Israel	31 15N	35 13E
43	Arad, Rumania	46 11N	21 20E
59	Arafura Sea	10 0S	135 0E
39	Aragón, R.	42 13N	1 44W
39	Aragón □	41 0N	1 0W
31	Araguaia, R.	5 21S	48 41W
57	Arakan Coast	19 0N	93 0E
57	Arakan Yoma, mts.	20 0N	94 30E
48	Aralsk	46 50N	61 20E
48	Aralskoye More	44 30N	60 0E
40	Aranci	41 0N	9 35E
54	Ararat, mt.=Agri Dagi, mt.	39 50N	44 15E
54	Arbil	36 15N	44 5E
18	Arbuckle	39 1N	122 3W
38	Arcachon	44 40N	1 10W
2	Arctic, reg.	90 0N	0 0
21	Arctic Bay	73 2N	85 11W
3	Arctic Ocean	85 0N	170 0E
20	Arctic Red River	67 27N	133 46W
54	Ardabril	38 15N	48 18E
38	Ardèche □	44 42N	4 16E
19	Arden	36 1N	115 14W
37	Ardennes, reg.	50 10N	5 45E
38	Ardennes □	49 40N	4 40E
55	Ardestan	33 20N	52 28E
11	Ardmore, Okla.	34 10N	97 5W
15	Ardmore, Pa.	40 1N	75 18W
29	Arecibo	18 29N	66 42W
45	Arendal	58 28N	8 46E
30	Arequipa	16 20S	71 30W
40	Arezzo	43 28N	11 50E
32	Argentina ■	35 0S	66 0W
19	Arguello, Pt.	34 35N	120 39W
45	Arhus	56 9N	10 13E
30	Arica	18 2S	70 20W
38	Ariège □	43 0N	1 30E
26	Ario de Rosales	19 12N	101 42W
30	Aripuana, R.	5 7S	60 24W
13	Arizona □	34 20N	111 30W
61	Arka Tagh	36 30N	90 0E
11	Arkansas, R.	33 48N	91 4W
11	Arkansas □	34 50N	93 40W
11	Arkansas City	37 4N	97 3W
17	Arlington Heights	42 5N	87 59W
36	Armagh	52 22N	6 40W
38	Armagnac, reg.	43 44N	0 10E
47	Armavir	45 2N	41 7E
30	Armenia	4 35N	75 45W
47	Armenian S.S.R. □	40 0N	41 0E
71	Armidale	30 36S	151 40E
24	Armstrong	50 25N	119 10W
37	Arnhem	51 58N	5 55E
70	Arnhem, B.	12 20S	136 10E
70	Arnhem Land	13 10S	135 0E
40	Arno, R.	43 41N	10 17E
22	Arnprior	45 26N	76 21W
57	Arrah	25 35N	84 32E
36	Arran, I.	55 34N	5 12W
38	Arras	50 17N	2 46E
27	Arriaga	21 55N	101 23W
19	Arroyo Grande	35 7N	120 34W
61	Arshan	46 59N	120 0E
47	Artemovsk	48 35N	37 55E
11	Artesia	32 55N	104 25W
72	Arthur's Pass	42 54S	171 35E
32	Artigas	30 20S	56 30W
38	Artois, reg.	50 20N	2 30E
29	Aruba, I.	12 30N	70' 0W
57	Arunachal Pradesh □	28 0N	95 0E
66	Arusha	3 20S	36 40E
23	Arvida	48 25N	71 11W
45	Arvika	59 40N	12 36E
19	Arvin	35 12N	118 50W
46	Arzamas	55 23N	43 50E
54	As Salt	32 2N	35 43E
54	As Samawah	31 15N	45 15E
54	As Sulamaniyah	35 35N	45 29E
52	As Zahiriya	31 27N	34 59E
60	Asahikawa	43 45N	142 30E
57	Asansol	23 40N	87 1E
23	Asbestos	45 46N	71 57W
15	Asbury Park	40 13N	74 1W
2	Ascension, I.	7 57S	14 22W
40	Ascoli Piceno	42 51N	13 34E
53	Aseb	13 0N	42 40E
72	Ashburton	43 53S	171 48E
52	Ashdod	31 48N	34 39E
9	Asheville	35 39N	82 30W
60	Ashikaga	36 28N	139 29E
60	Ashizuri-Zaki	32 35N	132 50E
48	Ashkabad	37 57N	58 23E
8	Ashland, Ky.	38 25N	82 40W
*9	Ashland, Me.	46 34N	68 26W
14	Ashland, Ohio	40 52N	82 19W
15	Ashland, Pa.	40 47N	76 21W
10	Ashland, Wis.	46 40N	90 52W
52	Ashqelon	31 42N	34 55E
14	Ashtabula	41 52N	80 48W
40	Asinara, G. dell'	41 0N	8 30E
40	Asinara, I.	41 5N	8 15E
53	Asir, Ras	11 55N	51 0E
53	Asir, reg.	18 40N	42 30E
52	Asira esh Shamaliya	32 18N	35 14E
53	Asmera	15 19N	38 55E
72	Aspiring, Mt.	44 23S	168 46E
57	Assam □	25 45N	92 30E
37	Assen	53 0N	6 35E
25	Assiniboia	49 38N	105 59W
40	Assisi	43 4N	12 36E
40	Asti	44 54N	8 11E
*18	Astoria	46 16N	123 50W
47	Astrakhan	46 25N	48 5E
39	Asturias □	43 15N	6 0W
32	Asunción	25 21S	57 30W
65	Aswân	24 4N	32 57E
65	Aswân High Dam= Sadd el Aali	24 5N	32 54E
65	Asyût	27 11N	31 4E
32	Atacama, Desierto de	24 0S	69 20W
59	Atapupu	9 0S	124 51E
18	Atascadero	35 29N	120 40W
65	Atbara	17 42N	33 59E
65	Atbara, Nahr	17 40N	33 56E
10	Atchison	39 40N	95 0W
24	Athabasca	54 4N	113 17W
25	Athabasca, L.	59 7N	110 0W
25	Athabasca, R.	58 40N	110 50W
23	Athens, Ga.	33 56N	83 24W
8	Athens, Ohio	39 52N	82 6W
41	Athens=Athínai	37 58N	23 43E
41	Athínai	37 58N	23 43E
36	Athlone	53 26N	7 57W
23	Atholville	47 59N	66 45W
58	Atjeh □	4 50N	96 0E
9	Atlanta	33 50N	84 24W
8	Atlantic City	39 25N	74 25W
33	Atlantic Ocean	0 0N	20 0W
64	Atlas Saharien, mts.	33 25N	1 20E
24	Atlin	59 35N	133 43W
22	Attawapiskat L.	52 18N	87 54W
22	Attawapiskat, R.	52 57N	82 18W
52	Attil	32 23N	35 4E
15	Attleboro	41 56N	71 17W
58	Attopeu	14 56N	106 50E
18	Atwater	37 21N	120 36W
38	Aube, R.	48 34N	3 43E
38	Aube □	48 15N	4 5E
9	Auburn, Ala.	32 37N	85 30W
18	Auburn, Calif.	38 54N	121 4W
17	Auburn, Ind.	41 22N	85 4W
*9	Auburn, Me.	44 6N	70 14W
8	Auburn, N.Y.	42 57N	76 39W
*18	Auburn, Wash.	47 18N	122 13W
72	Auckland	36 52S	174 46E
*72	Auckland, Is.	51 0S	166 0E
38	Aude □	43 5N	2 30E
71	Augathella	26 2S	146 29E
42	Augsburg	48 22N	10 54E
70	Augusta, Australia	34 22S	115 10E
40	Augusta, Italy	37 14N	15 12E
9	Augusta, Ga.	33 29N	81 59W
*9	Augusta, Me.	44 20N	69 46E
43	Augustów	53 51N	23 0E
70	Augustus, Mt.	24 14S	116 48E
56	Aurangabad	19 58N	75 43E
10	Aurora, Colo.	39 44N	104 55W
17	Aurora, Ill.	41 42N	88 20W
10	Austin, Minn.	43 37N	92 59W
11	Austin, Tex.	30 20N	97 45W
70	Austin, L.	27 40S	118 0E
70	Australia ■	25 0S	135 0E
71	Australian Alps	36 30S	148 8E
71	Australian Capital Territory □	35 15S	149 8E
42	Austria ■	47 20N	13 20E
26	Autlán	19 40N	104 30W
38	Auvergne, reg.	45 25N	2 30E
38	Auvergne, Mts. d'	45 30N	2 50E
19	Avalon	33 49N	118 16W
23	Avalon Pen.	47 30N	55 30W
19	Avawatz Mts.	35 35N	116 20W
39	Aveira	40 37N	8 38W
32	Avellaneda	34 41S	58 25W
29	Aves, I. de	15 42N	63 38W
38	Aveyron □	44 16N	2 40E
38	Avignon	43 57N	4 49E
39	Avila	40 39N	4 42W
60	Awaji-Shima	34 21N	134 51E
*44	Axarfjördur	66 15N	16 45W
60	Ayabe	35 18N	135 15E
30	Ayacucho	13 0S	74 0W
36	Aylesbury	51 48N	0 49W
36	Ayr	55 29N	4 28W
54	Az Zubayr	30 23N	47 43E
54	Azärbaijan □	36 45N	45 0E
64	Azbine=Aïr, plateau	18 0N	8 30E
47	Azerbaijan S.S.R. □	40 30N	47 30E
33	Azores, Is.	38 30N	28 0W
47	Azovskoye More	46 0N	36 0E
29	Azúa de Compostela	18 25N	108 0W
28	Azuero, Pen. de	7 30N	80 30W
32	Azul	36 45S	59 50W
60	Azuma-San	37 55N	140 7E
19	Azusa	34 8N	117 55W

B

Page	Place	Lat.	Long.
37	Baarn	52 12N	5 17E
53	Bab al Mandab, str.	12 35N	43 25E
55	Babol	36 40N	52 50E
54	Babylon	32 40N	44 30E
31	Bacabal	5 20S	56 45W
43	Bacau	46 35N	26 55E
59	Bacolod	10 50N	123 0E
42	Bad Ischl	17 44N	13 38E
10	Bad Lands	43 0N	102 10W
39	Badajoz	38 50N	6 59W
55	Badakhshan □	36 30N	71 0E
39	Badalona	41 26N	2 15E
42	Baden-Baden	48 51N	8 12E
55	Badghis □	35 5N	64 0E
54	Badiyat ash Sham, reg.	32 30N	39 0E
21	Baffin B.	73 0N	67 0W
21	Baffin I.	68 0N	77 0W
59	Baganga	7 36N	126 38E
32	Bagé	31 20S	54 15W
19	Bagdad	34 37N	115 52W
54	Baghdad	33 20N	44 30E
55	Baghin	30 12N	56 45E
55	Baghlan	36 12N	69 0E
23	Bagotville	48 21N	70 53W
59	Baguio	16 26N	120 34E
28	Bahamas ■	24 40N	74 0W
56	Bahawalpur	29 37N	71 40W
31	Bahia=Salvador	13 0S	38 30W
32	Bahía Blanca	38 5S	62 13W
52	Bahr el Miyet	31 30N	35 30E
53	Bahrain ■	26 0N	50 35E
23	Baie-Comeau	49 12N	68 10W
23	Baie-St-Paul	47 27N	70 30W
36	Baile Atha Cliath= Dublin	53 20N	6 18W
*20	Baird, Mts.	67 35N	161 30W
28	Baja California, pen.	28 0N	112 50E
20	Baker Lake	64 20N	96 10W

Bakers Dozen, Is. Bo

22 Bakers Dozen, Is. 57 30N 79 0W
19 Bakersfield 35 25N 119 0W
54 Bakhtiara □ 32 0N 49 0E
43 Bakony Hegyseg, mts. 47 10N 17 30E
47 Baku 40 25N 49 45E
54 Ba'labakk 34 0N 36 10E
58 Balabas Str. 7 53N 117 5E
46 Balakovo 52 4N 47 55E
57 Balasore 21 5N 87 3E
41 Balaton, L. 46 56N 17 55E
29 Balboa 9 0N 79 30W
32 Balcarce 38 0S 58 10W
25 Balcarres 50 48N 103 33W
72 Balclutha 46 15S 169 45E
39 Baleares, Islas 39 30N 3 0E
58 Bali, I. 8 20S 115 0E
54 Balikesir 39 35N 27 58E
58 Balikpapan 1 10S 116 55E
55 Balkh=Wazirabad 36 44N 66 47E
55 Balkh □ 36 44N 66 47E
48 Balkhash, Ozero 46 0N 74 50E
71 Ballarat 37 33S 143 50E
70 Ballard, L. 29 20S 120 10E
71 Balonne, R. 28 47S 147 56E
26 Balsas, R. 17 55N 102 10W
45 Baltic Sea 56 0N 18 0E
8 Baltimore 39 8N 76 37W
55 Baluchistan, reg. 27 30N 65 0E
64 Bamako 12 34N 7 55W
42 Bamberg 49 54W 10 53E
66 Bamenda 5 57N 10 11E
55 Bamian □ 35 0N 67 0E
55 Bampur 27 15N 60 21E
55 Banada Darya y Oman □ 25 30N 56 0E
43 Banat, reg. 45 45N 21 15E
23 Bancroft 45 3N 77 51W
55 Band-i-Turkistan, mts. 35 2N 64 0E
58 Banda Atjeh 5 35N 95 20E
59 Banda Sea 6 0S 130 0E
57 Bandar=Masulipatnam 16 12N 81 21E
55 Bandar Abbas 27 15N 56 15E
58 Bandar Seri Begawan 4 52N 115 0E
55 Bandar-e-Lengeh 26 35N 54 58E
54 Bandar-e-Pahlavi 37 30N 49 30E
55 Bandar-e Rig 29 30N 50 45E
55 Bandar-e Shah 37 0N 54 10E
54 Bandar-e Shahpur 30 30N 49 5E
31 Bandeira, Pico da 20 12S 42 10W
54 Bandirma 40 20N 28 0E
58 Bandjarmasin 3 20S 114 35E
*59 Bandung 6 36S 107 48E
28 Banes 21 0N 75 42W
24 Banff 51 10N 115 34W
25 Banff Nat. Pk. 51 15N 115 38W
67 Bangala Dam 21 7S 31 25E
56 Bangalore 12 59N 77 40E
65 Banghazi 32 11N 20 3E
58 Bangka, I. 2 0S 105 50E
58 Bangkok=Krung Thep 13 45N 100 35E
57 Bangladesh ■ 24 0N 90 0E
*9 Bangor 44 48N 68 42W
66 Bangui 4 23N 18 35E
66 Bangweulu, L. 11 0S 30 0E
29 Bani 18 16N 70 22W
52 Bani Na'im 31 31N 35 10E
65 Baninah 32 0N 20 12E
40 Banja Luka 44 49N 17 26E
64 Banjul 13 28N 16 40W
20 Banks, I. 73 30N 120 0W
72 Banks Peninsula 43 45S 173 15E
19 Banning 35 56N 116 52W
43 Banska Bystrica 48 46N 19 14E
59 Bantul 7 55S 110 19E
29 Baracoa 20 20N 74 30W
29 Barahona 18 13N 71 7W
24 Baranof 57 10N 134 56W
24 Baranof I. 57 0N 135 10W
46 Baranovichi 53 10N 27 0E
29 Barbados ■ 13 0N 59 30W
62 Barbary, reg. 30 0N 15 0E
14 Barberton 41 1N 81 36W
29 Barbuda, I. 17 30N 61 40W
71 Barcaldine 23 33S 145 13E
39 Barcelona 41 21N 2 10E
71 Barcoo, R. 25 30S 142 50E
56 Bareilly 28 22N 79 27E
48 Barents Sea 73 0N 39 0E
38 Barfleur, Pte. de 49 40N 1 17W
40 Bari 41 6N 16 52E
57 Barisal 22 50N 90 32E
58 Barito 3 32S 114 29E
70 Barkly Tableland 19 50S 138 40E
70 Barlee, L. 29 15S 119 0E
40 Barletta 41 20N 16 17E
48 Barnaul 53 20N 83 40E
37 Barneveld 43 16N 75 14W
71 Barney, mt 28 13S 152 32E
36 Barnsley 53 33N 1 29W
56 Baroda=Vadodara 22 20N 73 10E
65 Barqa, reg. 27 50N 22 45E
30 Barquisimeto 9 58N 69 13W
30 Barrancabermeja 7 0N 83 50W
30 Barranquilla 11 0N 74 50W
15 Barre 44 12N 72 30W
54 Barrhead 54 10N 114 30W
22 Barrie 44 25N 79 45W
15 Barrington 41 44N 71 18W
36 Barrow 54 8N 3 15W
70 Barrow, I. 20 45S 115 20E
19 Barstow 34 54N 117 1W
71 Bartle Frère, mt. 17 27S 145 50E
11 Bartlesville 36 50N 95 58W
71 Barwon, R. 30 0S 148 5E
38 Bas Rhin □ 48 40N 7 30E
42 Basel 47 35N 7 35E
61 Bashi Chan 21 15N 122 0E
46 Bashkir A.S.S.R. □ 54 0N 57 0E
59 Basilan City=Lamitan 6 40N 122 10E
*71 Bass Strait 40 0S 146 0E
24 Bassano 50 47N 112 28W
29 Basse-Terre 16 0N 61 40W
57 Bassein 19 26N 72 48E
29 Basseterre 17 17N 62 43W
*38 Bastia 42 10N 9 30E
52 Bat Yam 32 2N 34 44E
59 Bataan, pen. 14 40N 120 25E
28 Batabanò 22 40N 82 20W
59 Batangas 13 53N 121 9E
14 Batavia 43 0N 78 11W
36 Bath, England 51 22N 2 22W
*9 Bath, Me. 43 55N 69 49W
14 Bath, N.Y. 42 20N 77 19W
71 Bathurst, Australia 33 25S 149 31E
23 Bathurst, Canada 47 36N 65 39W
64 Bathurst, Gambia= Banjul 13 28N 16 40W
20 Bathurst, C. 70 30N 128 30W
20 Bathurst Inlet 66 50N 108 1W
70 Bathurst, I. 11 30S 130 10E
11 Batley 53 43N 1 38W
11 Baton Rouge 30 30N 91 5W
58 Battambang 13 7N 103 12E
25 Battle, R. 52 43N 108 15W
17 Battle Creek 42 20N 85 10W
25 Battleford 52 45N 108 15W
53 Batu, mt. 6 55N 39 45E
59 Batuan 9 15N 125 18E
47 Batumi 41 30N 41 30E
59 Baubau 5 25S 123 50E
31 Bauru 22 10S 49 0W
8 Bay City 43 35N 83 51W
15 Bay Shore 40 44N 73 15W
72 Bay View 39 25S 176 50E
28 Bayamo 20 20N 76 40W
29 Bayamon 18 24N 66 10W
42 Bayern □ 49 7N 11 30E
38 Bayeux 49 17N 0 42W
49 Baykal, Ozero 53 0N 108 0E
38 Bayonne, France 43 30N 1 28W
15 Bayonne, U.S.A. 40 41N 74 7W
42 Bayreuth 49 56N 11 35E
54 Bayrut 33 53N 35 31E
52 Bayt Jala 31 43N 35 11E
52 Bayt Lahm 31 43N 35 12E
11 Baytown 29 42N 94 57E
15 Beacon 41 30N 73 58W
16 Beardstown 40 1N 90 26W
10 Beatrice 40 20N 96 40W
23 Beattyville 48 52N 77 9W
67 Beaufort West 32 18S 22 36E
22 Beauhornois 45 19N 73 52W
19 Beaumont, Calif 33 56N 116 58W
11 Beaumont, Tex. 30 5N 94 8W
25 Beausejour 50 4N 96 31W
25 Beauval 55 9N 107 37W
10 Beaver Dam 42 28N 88 50W
14 Beaver Falls 40 46N 80 19W
24 Beaverlodge 55 13N 119 26W
*18 Beaverton 45 29N 122 48W
56 Beawar 26 3N 74 18E
64 Béchar 31 38N 2 18E
8 Beckley 37 50N 81 8W
36 Bedford.U.K. 52 8N 0 29W
17 Bedford, Ind. 38 52N 86 29W
14 Bedford, Ohio 41 23N 81 32W
17 Beech Grove 39 43N 86 3W
52 Be'er Sheva' 31 15N 34 48E
54 Behbehan 30 30N 50 15E
67 Beira 19 50S 34 52E
54 Beirut=Bayrut 33 53N 35 31E
67 Beitbridge 22 12S 30 0E
43 Békéscsaba 46 40N 21 10E
58 Belawan 3 33N 98 32E
46 Belaya, R. 56 0N 54 32E
47 Belaya Tserkov 49 45N 30 10E
22 Belcher Is. 56 20N 79 20W
31 Belém 1 27S 48 29W
36 Belfast, U.K. 54 35N 5 56W
*9 Belfast, U.S.A. 44 27N 69 1W
38 Belfort 47 38N 6 50E
38 Belfort □ 47 38N 6 52E
56 Belgaum 15 55N 74 35E
37 Belgium ■ 51 30N 5 0E
47 Belgorod 50 35N 36 35E
41 Belgrade=Beograd 44 50N 20 37E
58 Belitung, Pulau 3 10S 107 50E
27 Belize ■ 17 0N 88 0W
27 Belize City 17 25N 88 0W
24 Bella Coola 52 22N 126 45W
14 Bellaire 40 2N 80 45W
56 Bellary 15 10N 76 56E
23 Belle, I., Canada 51 57N 55 21W
38 Belle I., France 47 20N 3 10W
23 Belle Isle, Str. of 51 30N 56 30W
17 Bellefontaine 40 22N 83 46W
22 Belleville, Canada 44 5N 76 10W
16 Belleville, Ill. 38 30N 90 0W
14 Belleville, Pa. 40 30N 77 43W
24 Bellevue, Canada 49 35N 114 22W
*18 Bellevue, U.S.A. 47 37N 122 12W
21 Bellin 60 0N 70 0W
*18 Bellingham 48 45N 122 27W
42 Bellinzona 46 11N 9 1E
15 Belmar 40 11N 74 1W
27 Belmopan 17 2N 88 31W
31 Belo Horizonte 19 55S 43 56W
24 Beliot 42 35N 89 0W
46 Beloretsk 54 0N 58 0E
48 Belovo 54 30N 86 0E
46 Beloye More 66 0N 38 0E
47 Beltsy 47 48N 28 0E
48 Belukha, mt. 49 50N 86 50E
48 Belyy, Ostrov 73 30N 71 0E
10 Bemidji 47 30N 94 50W
36 Ben Nevis, mt. 56 48N 5 0W
57 Benares=Varanasi 25 22N 8 8E
12 Bend 44 2N 121 15W
53 Bender Beila 9 30N 50 48E
71 Bendigo 36 40S 144 15E
52 Bene Beraq 32 6N 34 29E
57 Bengal, B. of 19 0N 89 0E
65 Benghazi=Banghazi 32 11N 20 3E
25 Bengough 49 24N 105 8W
67 Benguela 12 37S 13 25E
65 Beni Suêf 29 5N 31 6E
18 Benicia 38 3N 122 9W
64 Benin ■ 8 0N 2 0E
64 Benin, Bight of 5 0N 3 0E
64 Benin City 6 20N 5 31E
67 Benoni 26 11S 28 18E
71 Bentinck, I. 17 3S 1 9 35E
17 Benton 38 0N 88 55W
17 Benton Harbor 42 10N 86 28W
64 Benue R. 7 48N 6 46E
41 Beograd 44 50N 20 37E
60 Beppu 33 15N 131 30E
53 Berbera 10 30N 45 2E
47 Berdichev 49 57N 28 38E
47 Berdyansk 46 45N 36 49E
14 Berea 41 22N 81 52W
59 Berebere 2 25N 128 45E
46 Berezniki 59 25N 56 5E
40 Bergamo 45 42N 9 40E
45 Bergen 60 23N 5 27E
37 Bergen-op-Zoom 51 30N 4 18E
38 Bergerac 44 51N 0 30E
57 Berhampore 24 2N 88 27E
57 Berhampur 19 15N 84 54E
*20 Bering Sea 58 0N 177 0W
*20 Bering Str. 66 0N 170 0W
18 Berkeley 38 0N 122 20W
42 Berlin, Germany 52 32N 13 24E
15 Berlin, U.S.A. 44 29N 71 10W
33 Bermuda, I. 32 45N 65 0W
42 Bern 46 57N 7 28E
42 Bernina, mt. 46 11N 9 55E
52 Beror Hayil 31 32N 34 34E
15 Berwick 41 3N 76 15W
36 Berwick on Tweed 55 57N 2 0W
38 Besançon 47 15N 6 0E
9 Bessemer 33 25N 87 0W
52 Bet She'an 32 30N 35 30E
52 Bet Shemesh 31 37N 34 59E
52 Bethany=Eizariya 31 47N 35 15E
*9 Bethel Park 44 25N 70 48W
52 Bethlehem, Israel= Bayt Lahm 31 43N 35 12E
15 Bethlehem, U.S.A. 40 39N 75 24W
16 Bettendrof 41 32N 90 30W
24 Beverly, Canada 53 34N 113 24W
15 Beverly, U.S.A. 42 33N 70 53W
19 Beverly Hills 34 4N 118 29W
37 Beverwijk 52 28N 4 38E
52 Bezet 33 4N 35 8E
38 Béziers 43 20N 3 12E
57 Bhagalpur 25 10S 87 0E
57 Bhamo 24 15N 97 15E
56 Bharat=India ■ 23 0N 77 30E
56 Bharuch 21 47N 73 0E
57 Bhatpara 22 50N 88 25E
56 Bhavnagar 21 45N 72 10E
56 Bhopal 23 20N 77 53E
57 Bhubaneswar 20 15N 85 50E
56 Bhusawal 21 1N 75 56E
57 Bhutan ■ 27 25N 89 50E
66 Biafra, B. of=Bonny, B. of. 3 30N 9 20E
43 Bialystok 53 10N 23 10E
38 Biarritz 43 29N 1 33W
23 Bic 48 20N 68 41W
9 Biddeford 43 30N 70 26W
67 Biè Plateau 12 0S 16 0E
42 Biel 47 8N 7 14E
43 Biele Karpaty, Mts. 49 5N 18 0E
42 Bielefeld 52 2N 8 31E
43 Bielsko-Biala 49 49N 19 2E
58 Biên Hoa 11 3N 106 53E
25 Bienfait 49 9N 102 49W
22 Bienville, L. 55 5N 72 40W
19 Big Bear City 34 16N 116 51W
15 Big Belts Mts. 46 50N 111 30W
8 Big Rapids 43 42N 85 27W
11 Big Spring 32 10N 101 25W
25 Biggar 52 4N 108 0W
12 Bighorn, R. 46 9N 107 28W
12 Bighorn Mts. 44 30N 107 20W
57 Bihar 25 12N 85 33E
57 Bihar □ 25 0N 86 0E
43 Bihor, Mt. 46 29N 22 47E
56 Bijapur 26 30N 82 7E
56 Bikaner 28 2N 73 18E
68 Bikini Atoll 12 0N 167 30E
57 Bilaspur 22 2N 82 15E
39 Bilbao 43 16N 2 56W
12 Billings 45 4N 108 29W
65 Bilma 18 50N 13 30E
11 Biloxi 30 30N 89 0W
59 Binalbagan 10 15N 123 0E
15 Binghamton 42 8N 75 54W
58 Binh Dinh=An Nhan 13 53N 109 6E
64 Binzert 37 15N 9 50E
25 Birch Hills 52 59N 105 25W
25 Birch River 52 23N 101 6W
70 Birdum 15 50S 133 0E
55 Birjand 32 57N 59 10E
36 Birkenhead 53 24N 3 2W
36 Birmingham, U.K. 52 30N 1 55W
9 Birmingham, Ala. 33 31N 86 50W
17 Birmingham, Mich. 42 33N 83 15W
49 Birobidzhan 48 48N 132 57E
25 Birtle 50 25N 101 3W
33 Biscay, Bay of 44 0N 4 0W
23 Bishop's Falls 49 1N 55 30W
64 Biskra 34 50N 5 52E
10 Bismarck 46 49N 100 49W
68 Bismark Arch 3 30S 148 30E
64 Bissau 11 45N 15 45W
43 Bistrita, R. 47 9N 24 35E
41 Bitola 42 5N 21 21E
12 Bitterroot Ra. 46 0N 114 20W
60 Biwa-Ko 35 15N 135 45E
48 Biysk 52 34N 85 15E
64 Bizerte=Binzert 37 15N 9 50E
10 Black Hills 44 0N 103 50W
11 Black Mesa, mt 36 57N 102 55W
47 Black Sea 43 0N 35 0E
24 Black Diamond 50 42N 114 14W
64 Black Volta, R. 8 43N 1 15W
71 Blackall 24 26S 145 27E
36 Blackburn 53 44N 2 30W
12 Blackfoot 43 13N 112 12W
36 Blackpool 5 48N 3 3W
23 Blacks Harb. 45 3N 66 49W
49 Blagoveshchensk 50 20N 127 30E
*18 Blaine 48 59N 122 44W
24 Blairmore 49 36N 114 26W
38 Blanc, Mt. 45 48N 6 50E
23 Blanc-Sablon 51 25N 57 7W
32 Blanca, B. 39 10S 61 30W
13 Blanca Pk. 37 35N 105 29W
71 Blanche, L. 29 15S 139 40E
37 Blankenberge 51 19N 3 8E
67 Blantyre 15 47S 35 0E
55 Blenheim 41 38S 174 5E
64 Blida 36 30N 2 49E
22 Blind River 46 10N 82 58W
15 Block Island Sd. 41 10N 71 45W
67 Bloemfontein 29 6S 26 14E
38 Blois 47 35N 1 20E
17 Bloomingburg 39 36N 83 24W
16 Bloomington, Ill. 40 25N 89 0W
17 Bloomington, Ind. 39 10N 86 30W
15 Bloomsburg 41 0N 76 27W
71 Blue Mts., Australia 33 40S 150 0E
14 Blue Mts., U.S.A. 45 15N 119 0W
17 Blue, R. 38 11N 86 19W
65 Blue Nile R.=Nil el Azraq, R. 15 38N 32 31E
9 Blue Ridge, mts. 36 30N 80 15W
8 Bluefield 37 18N 81 14W
28 Bluefields 12 0N 83 50W
77 Bluff 46 36S 168 20E
17 Bluffton 40 44N 85 11W
32 Blumenau 27 0S 49 0W
19 Blythe 33 37N 114 36W
64 Bo 7 55N 11 50W

Carlsbad, N. Mex. Columbus, Nebr.

11 Carlsbad, N.Mex. 32 20N 104 7W
25 Carlyle 49 38N 102 16W
25 Carmun 49 30N 98 0W
52 Carmel, Mt. 32 45N 35 3E
18 Carmel-by-the-Sea 36 33N 121 55W
17 Carmi 38 8N 88 11W
18 Carmichael 38 38N 121 19W
70 Carnarvon 24 50S 113 42E
*56 Carnatic, reg. 12 0N 79 0E
14 Carnegie 40 24N 80 6W
70 Carnegie, L. 26 5S 122 30E
70 Carnot, B. 17 20S 121 30E
69 Caroline I. 9 15N 150 3W
59 Caroline Is. 5 0N 140 0E
43 Carpathians, mts. 48 0N 24 0E
43 Carpatii Meridionali, mts. 45 30N 25 0E
71 Carpentaria, G.of 14 0S 139 0E
17 Carpentersville 42 7N 88 17W
19 Carpinteria 34 24N 119 31W
40 Carrara 44 5N 10 7E
16 Carroll 42 4N 94 52W
25 Carrot River 53 17N 103 35W
18 Carson City 39 12N 119 52W
30 Cartagena, Col. 10 25N 75 33W
39 Cartagena, Spain 37 38N 0 59W
30 Cartago, Colombia 4 45N 75 55W
28 Cartago, Costa Rica 9 50N 84 0W
11 Carthage 37 10N 94 20W
31 Caruaru 8 17S 35 58W
30 Carúpano 10 45N 63 15W
64 Casablanca 33 43N 7 24W
12 Cascade Ra. 44 0N 122 10W
39 Cascais 38 41N 9 25W
40 Caserta 41 5N 14 20E
19 Casmalia 34 47N 120 28W
12 Casper 42 52N 106 27W
47 Caspian Sea 43 0N 50 0E
24 Cassiar Mts. 60 20N 130 50W
40 Castellammare 38 2N 12 53E
39 Castellón de la Plana 39 58N 0 3W
*18 Castle Rock 46 17N 122 54W
24 Castlegar 49 19N 117 40W
71 Castlemaine 37 2S 144 12E
70 Castlereagh, B. 12 10S 135 10E
71 Castlereagh, R. 30 8S 142 21E
25 Castor 52 13N 111 53W
29 Castries 14 0N 60 50W
18 Castroville 36 46N 121 45W
29 Cat I. 24 30N 75 30W
39 Cataluna □ 41 40N 1 15E
32 Catamarca 28 30S 65 50W
40 Catánia 37 31N 15 4E
40 Catanzaro 38 54N 16 38E
70 Catastrophe, C. 34 59S 136 0E
27 Catoche, C. 21 40N 87 0W
15 Catskill Mts. 42 10N 74 30W
47 Caucasus Mts.= Bolshoi Kavkaz 42 30N 35 0E
23 Causapscal 48 22N 67 14W
59 Cavite 14 29N 120 55E
31 Caxias 5 0S 43 27W
32 Caxias do Sul 29 10S 51 10W
31 Cayenne 5 0N 52 18W
28 Cayman Is. 19 40N 79 50W
15 Cayuga L. 42 45N 76 45W
31 Ceará=Fortaleza 3 35S 38 35W
31 Ceará □ 5 0S 40 0W
59 Cebu 10 30N 124 0E
59 Cebu, I. 10 15N 123 40E
25 Cedar L. 53 20N 100 10W
16 Cedar, R. 41 17N 91 22W
16 Cedar Falls, Iowa 42 32N 92 27W
28 Cedar Falls, Wash. 47 25N 121 47W
40 Cefalù 38 3N 14 1E
26 Celaya 20 31N 100 37W
59 Celebes=Sulawesi □ 2 0S 120 0E
59 Celebes Sea 3 0N 122 0E
17 Celina 40 33N 84 34W
16 Centerville 40 43N 92 52W
30 Central, Cord. 5 0N 75 0W
66 Central African Empire ■ 7 0N 21 0E
15 Central Islip 40 47N 73 12W
34 Central Russian Uplands 54 0N 35 0E
50 Central Siberian Plateau 60 0N 110 0E
16 Centralia, Ill. 38 31N 89 8W
*18 Centralia, Wash. 46 43N 122 58W
59 Ceram Sea 2 30S 128 30E
40 Cerignola 41 17N 15 53E
40 Cesena 44 8N 12 15E
42 Ceskomoravska Vrchovina, mts. 49 20N 15 30E
71 Cessnock 32 50S 151 21E
64 Ceuta 35 52N 5 18W
38 Cevennes, reg. 44 0N 3 30E
*56 Ceylon= Sri Lanka ■ 7 0N 81 0E
65 Chad ■ 15 0N 19 0E
55 Chagai Hills 29 30N 64 0E
55 Chakhansur 32 11N 62 2E
38 Châlon 46 47N 4 51E
38 Chambéry 45 34N 5 55E
66 Chambeshi R. 11 21S 30 37E
23 Chambord 48 26N 72 4W
61 Chamdo 31 21N 97 2E
38 Chamonix 45 55N 6 51E
17 Champaign 40 8N 88 14W
70 Champion, B. 8 44S 114 36E
15 Champlain, L. 4 30N 73 20W
56 Chanda 19 57N 79 25E
56 Chandigarh 30 30N 76 58E
61 Changchih 36 11N 113 8E
61 Changchow, Fukien 24 31N 117 40E
61 Changchow, Kiangsu 31 47N 119 57E
61 Changchun 43 53N 125 19E
61 Changhua 24 6N 120 31E
61 Changkiakow 40 50N 114 53E
61 Changpai Shan 41 0N 128 0E
61 Changsha 28 10N 113 0E
61 Changteh 36 6N 114 21E
38 Channel Is., U.K. 49 30N 2 40W
19 Channel Is., U.S.A. 34 0N 120 0W
58 Chanthaburi 12 37N 102 9E
11 Chanute 37 45N 85 25W
58 Chao Phraya, R. 13 32N 100 36E
61 Chaochow 23 43N 116 35W
26 Chapala, L.de 20 10N 103 20W
46 Chapayevsk 52 58N 49 41E
57 Chapra 25 48N 84 50E
25 Chard 55 50N 110 55W
48 Chardzhou 39 6N 63 34E
38 Charente □ 45 40N 0 10E
38 Charente-Maritime □ 45 30N 0 45W
65 Chari, R. 12 58N 14 31E
55 Charikar 35 2N 69 11E
16 Chariton 41 1N 93 19W
16 Chariton, R. 39 19N 92 57W
37 Charleroi 50 24N 4 27E
10 Charles City 43 2N 92 41W
17 Charleston, Ill. 39 30N 88 10W
9 Charleston, S.C. 32 48N 79 58W
8 Charleston, W.Va. 38 24N 81 36W
17 Charlestown 38 27N 85 40W
71 Charleville 26 24S 146 15E
38 Charleville-Mézières 49 46N 4 43E
17 Charlotte, Mich. 42 36N 84 50W
9 Charlotte N.C. 35 3N 80 50W
29 Charlotte Amalie 18 22N 64 56W
42 Charlottenburg 59 54N 12 17E
8 Charlottesville 38 1N 78 30W
23 Charlottetown 46 19N 63 3W
23 Charny 46 3N 71 15W
71 Charters Towers 20 5S 146 13E
38 Chartres 48 29N 1 30E
*20 Chatanika 65 7N 147 31W
38 Châteaubriant 47 43N 1 23W
38 Châteauroux 46 50N 1 40E
24 Chatham, B.C. 57 31N 134 55W
23 Chatham, N.B. 47 2N 65 28W
22 Chatham, Ont. 42 24N 82 11W
*72 Chatham Is. 43 0S 177 10W
24 Chatham Str. 57 30N 134 45W
9 Chattahoochee, R. 30 52N 84 57W
9 Chattanooga 35 2N 85 18W
46 Cheboksary 56 9N 47 15E
8 Cheboygan 45 38N 84 29W
47 Checheno-Ingush A.S.S.R. □ 44 12N 45 17E
*18 Chehalis 46 40N 122 58W
61 Cheju Do 33 20N 126 30E
61 Chekiang □ 29 0N 120 0E
36 Chelmsford 51 44N 0 28E
36 Cheltenham 51 54N 2 4W
48 Chelyabinsk 55 10N 61 24E
24 Chemainus 48 54N 123 41W
46 Chemikovsk 54 58N 55 57E
42 Chemnitz= Karl-Marx-Stadt 50 50N 12 55E
61 Chengchow 34 48N 113 39E
61 Chengteh 40 58N 117 53E
61 Chengtu 30 39N 104 4E
61 Chenyuan 27 5N 108 16E
10 Chequamegon B. 46 40N 90 30W
38 Cher, R. 47 21N 0 29E
38 Cher □ 47 5N 2 30E
38 Cherbourg 49 39N 1 39W
49 Cheremkhovo 53 9N 103 5E
46 Cherepovets 59 8N 37 54E
47 Cherkassy 49 26N 32 4E
46 Chernigov 51 30N 31 18E
47 Chernovtsy 48 18N 25 56E
11 Cherokee, L.o' the 36 50N 95 12W
57 Cherrapunji 25 17N 91 47E
49 Cherskogo, Khrebet 66 0N 140 0E
8 Chesapeake 'B. 38 0N 76 12W
46 Cheshskaya Guba 66 50N 46 0E
36 Chester, England 53 12N 2 53W
16 Chester, Ill. 37 55N 89 49W
8 Chester, Pa. 39 50N 75 23W
9 Chester, S.C. 34 44N 81 13W
36 Chesterfield 53 14N 1 26W
20 Chesterfield Inlet 63 30N 91 0W
71 Chesterfield Is. 19 52S 158 15E
17 Cheviot 39 11N 84 35W
*36 Cheviot Hills 55 28N 2 8W
10 Cheyenne 41 8N 104 50W
10 Cheyenne, R. 44 40N 101 15W
61 Chiai 23 29N 120 27E
40 Chiávari 44 19N 9 19E
60 Chiba 35 36N 140 7E
22 Chibougamau 49 55N 74 22W
17 Chicago 41 45N 87 40W
17 Chicago Heights 41 29N 87 37W
24 Chichagof I. 57 45N 136 10W
27 Chichén Itzá 20 40N 88 32W
11 Chickasha 35 0N 98 0W
30 Chiclayo 6 42S 79 50W
18 Chico 39 45N 121 54W
15 Chicopee 42 6N 72 37W
23 Chicoutimi 48 28N 71 5W
21 Chidley, C. 60 30N 64 15W
57 Chiengmai 18 55N 98 55E
61 Chihfeng 42 10N 118 56E
26 Chihuahua 28 40N 106 3W
32 Chile ■ 35 0S 71 15W
32 Chillán 36 40S 72 10W
16 Chillicothe, Mo. 39 48N 93 33W
8 Chillicothe, Ohio 39 53N 82 58W
24 Chilliwack 49 10N 121 57W
32 Chiloé, I.de 42 50S 73 45W
27 Chilpancingo 17 30N 99 40W
61 Chilung 25 3N 121 45E
67 Chilwa, L. 15 15E 35 40E
30 Chimborazo, mt. 1 20S 78 55W
30 Chimbote 9 0S 78 35W
48 Chimkent 42 18N 69 36E
57 Chin □ 22 0N 93 0E
61 China ■ 25 40N 99 20E
28 Chinandega 12 30N 87 0W
61 Chinchow 41 10N 121 2E
57 Chindwin, R. 21 26N 95 15E
61 Chinkiang 32 2N 119 29E
19 Chino 34 1N 117 42W
25 Chinook 51 27N 110 56W
61 Chinwangtao 40 0N 119 31E
40 Chióggia 45 13N 12 15E
67 Chipata 13 38S 32 28E
10 Chippewa, R. 44 23N 92 1W
10 Chippewa Falls 44 55N 92 1W
28 Chiquimula 14 51N 89 37W
48 Chirchik 41 29N 69 35E
28 Chiriqui, G.de 8 0N 82 10W
11 Chisos Mts. 29 20N 103 15W
46 Chistopol 55 21N 50 37E
49 Chita 6 11N 72 28W
56 Chitral 35 50N 71 56E
57 Chittagong 22 19N 91 55E
32 Chivilcoy 35 0S 60 0W
67 Choma 16 48S 26 59E
61 Chonju 35 50N 127 4E
32 Chonos, Arch.de los 45 0S 75 0W
43 Chorzów 50 18N 19 0E
60 Choshi 35 45N 140 45E
18 Chowchilla 37 7N 120 16W
61 Choybalsan 48 2N 114 32E
72 Christchurch 43 33S 172 47W
29 Christiansted 17 45N 64 42W
69 Christmas I. 1 58N 157 27W
61 Chuanchow 24 57N 118 31E
32 Chubut, R. 43 20S 65 5W
61 Chuchow 43 20S 65 5W
46 Chudskoye Ozero 58 0N 27 45E
*20 Chugiak 61 25N 149 30W
60 Chugoku □ 35 0N 132 30E
60 Chugoku-Sanchi 34 58N 132 57E
49 Chukotskiy Khrebet 68 0N 175 0E
49 Chukotskoye More 69 0N 171 0W
19 Chula Vista 32 39N 117 5W
61 Chungking 29 30N 106 30E
61 Chungtien 28 0N 99 30E
25 Churchill 58 47N 94 11W
25 Churchill, C. 58 46N 93 12W
25 Churchill, R. 58 47N 94 12W
24 Churchill Pk. 58 10N 125 10W
46 Chuvash A.S.S.R. □ 55 30N 47 0E
8 Cicero 41 48N 87 48W
28 Ciego de Avila 21 50N 78 50W
28 Cienfuegos 22 10N 80 30W
19 Cima 35 14N 115 30W
17 Cincinnati 39 6N 84 11W
*38 Cinto, Mt. 42 24N 8 54E
*20 Circle 65 50N 144 4W
27 Citlaltepetl, mt. 19 0N 97 20W
26 Ciudad Acuña 29 20N 101 10W
30 Ciudad Bolivar 8 5N 63 30W
26 Ciudad Camargo 27 41N 105 10W
27 Ciudad del Carmen 18 20N 97 50W
30 Ciudad Guayana 8 16N 62 40W
26 Ciudad Guzmán 19 41N 103 29W
27 Ciudad Ixtepec 16 40N 95 10W
26 Ciudad Juárez 31 40N 106 28W
27 Ciudad Madero 22 19N 97 50W
27 Ciudad Mante 22 50N 99 0W
26 Ciudad Obregón 27 28N 109 59W
39 Ciudad Real 28 59N 3 55W
39 Ciudad Rodrigo 40 35N 6 32W
27 Ciudad Victoria 23 41N 99 9W
40 Civitavécchia 42 6N 11 46E
14 Clairton 40 18N 79 53W
24 Clarence Str., Alaska 55 25N 132 0W
70 Clarence, Str., Australia 12 0S 131 0E
15 Claremont 43 23N 72 20W
24 Claresholm 50 2N 113 35W
8 Clarksburg 39 18N 80 21W
11 Clarksdale 34 12N 90 33W
12 Clarkston 46 28N 117 2W
9 Clarksville 36 32N 87 20W
36 Clear, C. 51 26N 9 30W
16 Clear Lake City 43 8N 93 23W
9 Clearwater 27 58N 82 45W
22 Clearwater L. 56 10N 75 0W
12 Clearwater Mts. 40 20N 115 30W
11 Cleburne 32 18N 97 25W
38 Clermont Ferrand 45 46N 3 4E
14 Cleveland Ohio 41 30N 81 41W
9 Cleveland, Tenn. 35 9N 84 52W
14 Cleveland Heights 41 30N 81 34W
9 Clifton Forge 37 49N 79 51W
24 Clinton, B.C. 51 6N 121 36W
22 Clinton, Ont. 43 37N 81 32W
17 Clinton, Ind. 39 40N 87 24W
16 Clinton, Iowa 41 50N 90 18W
15 Clinton, Mass. 42 25N 71 41W
71 Cloncurry 20 40S 140 28E
12 Cloud Pk. 44 30N 107 10W
18 Cloverdale 38 48N 123 1W
18 Clovis, Calif. 36 49N 119 42W
11 Clovis, N.Mex. 34 24N 103 12W
43 Cluj 46 47N 23 38E
72 Clutha, R. 46 20S 169 49E
36 Clyde, Firth of 55 20N 5 0W
36 Clyde, R. 55 56N 4 29W
19 Coachella 33 41N 116 10W
24 Coaldale 49 43N 112 37W
24 Coast Mts. 52 0N 126 0W
12 Coast Ra. 41 0N 123 0W
70 Coastal Plains Basin 30 10S 115 30E
28 Coatepec, Guat. 14 46N 91 55W
27 Coatepec, Mex. 19 27N 96 58W
23 Coaticook 45 8N 71 48W
27 Coatzacoalcos 18 7N 94 35W
22 Cobalt 47 24N 79 41W
28 Cobán 15 30N 90 21W
71 Cobar 31 27S 145 48E
36 Cobh 51 50N 8 18W
22 Cobourg 43 58N 78 10W
70 Cobourg Pen. 11 20S 132 15E
57 Cocanada 16 55N 82 20E
30 Cochabamba 17 15S 66 20W
58 Cochin China= Nam-Phan, reg. 10 30N 106 0E
24 Cochrane, Alta 51 11N 114 28W
22 Cochrane, Ont. 49 4N 81 1W
28 Coco, R. 15. 0N 83 8W
68 Cocos Is. 12 12S 96 54E
7 Cod, C. 42 8N 70 10W
12 Coeur d'Alene 47 45N 116 51W
11 Coffeyville 37 0N 95 40W
71 Coffs Harbour 30 16S 153 5E
15 Cohoes 42 46N 73 42W
*56 Coimbatore 11 2N 76 59E
39 Coimbra 40 15N 8 27W
28 Cojutepegue 13 41N 88 54W
36 Colchester 51 54N 0 55E
25 Cold Lake 54 27N 110 10W
17 Coldwater 41 57N 85 0W
36 Coleraine 55 8N 6 40E
26 Colima 19 10N 103 40W
26 Colima, Nevado de 19 33N 103 38W
70 Collier, B. 16 0S 124 0E
22 Collingwood 44 30N 80 20W
16 Collinsville 38 41N 89 59W
38 Colmar 48 5N 7 20E
37 Cologne=Köln 50 56N 9 58E
30 Colombia ■ 3 45N 73 0W
*56 Colombo 6 56N 79 58E
28 Colón, Cuba 22 42N 80 54W
28 Colón, Panama 9 20N 80 0W
32 Colorado, R., Arg. 39 50S 62 8W
11 Colorado, R., U.S.A. 28 36N 95 59W
10 Colorado □ 40 0N 104 0W
13 Colorado Aqueduct 34 0N 115 20W
13 Colorado Plat. 36 40N 110 30W
10 Colorado Springs 38 55N 104 50W
19 Colton 34 4N 117 20W
16 Columbia, Mo. 38 58N 92 20W
15 Columbia, Pa. 40 2N 76 30W
9 Columbia, S.C. 34 01 81 0W
9 Columbia, Tenn. 35 40N 87 0W
*18 Columbia, R. 46 15N 124 5W
12 Columbia Plat. 47 30N 118 30W
9 Columbus, Ga. 32 30N 84 58W
17 Columbus, Ind. 39 14N 85 55W
11 Columbus, Miss. 33 30N 88 26W
10 Columbus, Nebr. 41 30N 97 25W

Columbus, Ohio

Dolbeau

17	Columbus, Ohio	39 57N	83 1W
16	Columbus Junc.	41 17N	91 22W
*20	Colville, R.	70 25N	150 30W
57	Comilla	23 22N	91 18E
*40	Comino, I.	36 0N	14 22E
27	Comitán	16 18N	92 9W
48	Communizma Pic	38 57N	72 1E
40	Como	45 48N	9 5E
40	Como, L.di	46 5N	9 17E
32	Comodoro Rivadavia	45 50S	69 40W
*56	Comorin, C.	8 3N	77 40E
24	Comox	49 41N	124 56W
26	Compostela	21 15N	104 53W
19	Compton	33 54N	118 13W
64	Conakry	9 29N	13 49W
38	Concarneau	47 52N	3 56W
32	Concepción, Chile	36 50S	73 0W
32	Concepción, Para.	23 30S	57 20W
19	Concepcion, Pt.	34 27N	120 27W
26	Concepción del Oro.	24 40N	101 30W
32	Concepción del Uruguay	32 35S	58 20W
26	Conchos, R.	29 32N	104 25W
18	Concord, Calif.	37 59N	122 2W
15	Concord, N.H.	43 5N	71 30W
9	Concord, N.C.	35 28N	80 35W
32	Concordia, Arg.	31 20S	58 2W
10	Concordia, U.S.A.	39 35N	97 40W
71	Condamine, R.	26 56S	149 10E
66	Congo, R.=Zaïre, R.	6 4S	12 24E
66	Congo ■	1 0S	15 0E
66	Congo=Zaïre ■	3 0S	22 0E
62	Congo Basin	0 0	20 0E
22	Coniston	46 29N	80 51W
14	Conneaut	41 57N	80 34W
15	Connecticut □	41 45N	72 45W
15	Connecticut, R.	41 17N	72 21W
14	Connellsville	40 1N	79 35W
36	Connemara, dist.	53 29N	9 45W
17	Connorsville	39 40N	85 10W
15	Conshohocken	40 5N	75 18W
25	Consort	52 1N	110 46W
63	Constanţa	44 11N	28 39E
64	Constantine	36 25N	6 43E
57	Cooch-Behar	26 20N	89 27E
*20	Cook, Inlet	60 30N	152 0W
*72	Cook, Is.	20 0S	158 0W
72	Cook, Mt.	43 36S	170 9E
72	Cook Strait	41 15S	174 29E
9	Cookeville	36 12N	85 30W
71	Cooktown	15 30S	145 16E
70	Coolgardie	30 55S	121 8E
9	Cooper R.	32 50N	79 56W
71	Cooper Creek	28 0S	139 0E
12	Coos Bay	43 26N	124 7W
71	Cootamundra	34 36S	148 1E
45	Copenhagen= København	55 41N	12 34E
32	Copiapó	27 15S	70 20E
*20	Copper Center	61 58N	145 19W
22	Copper Cliff	46 28N	81 4W
24	Copper Mountain	49 19N	120 32W
20	Coppermine, R.	67 49N	115 4W
32	Coquimbo	30 0S	71 20W
21	Coral Harbour	64 8N	83 10W
68	Coral Sea	15 0S	150 0E
71	Coral Sea Basin	13 0S	147 0E
71	Coral Sea Islands Territory □	20 0S	155 0E
8	Corbin	37 0N	84 3W
18	Corcoran	36 6N	119 33W
32	Córdoba, Arg.	31 25S	64 10W
27	Córdoba, Mex.	18 53N	96 56W
39	Córdoba, Spain	37 50N	4 50W
32	Cordoba, Sa.de	31 10S	64 25W
*20	Cordova	60 29N	145 52W
41	Corfu=Kérkira, I.	39 40N	19 42E
36	Cork	51 54N	8 30W
23	Corner Brook	48 57N	57 57W
14	Corning	42 9N	77 4W
22	Cornwall	45 5N	74 45W
56	Coromandel Coast	13 30N	80 30E
19	Corona	33 52N	117 34W
19	Coronado	32 45N	117 9W
28	Coronado, B.de	9 0N	83 40W
20	Coronation G.	68 0N	114 0W
11	Corpus Christi	27 50N	97 28W
38	Corrèze □	45 20N	1 50E
32	Corrientes	27 30S	58 50W
28	Corrientes, C.	21 43N	84 30W
*38	Corse, C.	43 1N	9 25E
*38	Corse, I.	42 0N	9 0E
*38	Corse du Sud □	41 50N	9 0E
11	Corsicana	32 5N	96 30W
15	Cortland	42 36N	76 11W
30	Corumbá	19 1S	57 39W
12	Corvallis	44 36N	123 15W
27	Cosamaloapán	18 23N	95 50W
40	Cosenza	39 17N	16 14E
14	Coshocton	40 16N	81 51W
19	Costa Mesa	33 39N	117 55W
28	Costa Rica ■	10 10N	84 0W
59	Cotabato	7 8N	124 13E
10	Coteau du Missouri, Plat.du	47 0N	101 0W
38	Côte-d'Or □	47 30N	4 50E
38	Côtes-du-Nord □	48 28N	2 50W
64	Cotonou	6 20N	2 25E
32	Cotopaxi, mt.	0 30S	78 30W
36	Cotswold Hills	51 42N	2 10W
42	Cottbus	51 44N	14 20E
10	Council Bluffs	41 20N	95 50W
24	Courtenay	49 41N	124 58W
36	Coventry	52 25N	1 31W
19	Covina	34 5N	117 53W
17	Covington	39 4N	84 30W
70	Cowan, L.	33 40S	147 25E
71	Cowra	33 49S	148 42E
57	Cox's Bazar	21 25N	92 3E
24	Craig	55 29N	133 9W
43	Craiova	44 21N	23 48E
25	Cranberry Portage	54 36N	101 22W
24	Cranbrook	49 30N	115 55W
15	Cranston	41 47N	71 26W
17	Crawfordsville	40 2N	86 54W
12	Crazy Mts.	46 14N	110 30W
38	Crécy	48 50N	2 53E
25	Cree L.	57 30N	106 30W
40	Cremona	45 8N	10 2E
40	Cres, I.	44 58N	14 25E
24	Creston, Canada	49 6N	116 31W
16	Creston, U.S.A.	41 4N	94 22W
39	Creus, C.	42 20N	3 19E
38	Creuse, R.	47 0N	0 34E
38	Creuse □	46 55N	0 40E
36	Crewe	53 6N	2 28W
32	Criciúma	28 40S	49 23W
47	Crimea= Krymskiy Poluostrov	45 0N	34 0E
70	Croker, I.	11 12N	132 32S
25	Cromarty	58 5N	94 10W
29	Crooked I.	22 50N	74 10W
11	Crowley	30 15N	92 20W
17	Crown Point	41 25N	87 22W
24	Crowsnest Pass	49 39N	114 45W
32	Cruz Alta	28 38S	53 38W
32	Cruz del Eje	30 44S	64 49W
17	Crystal Lake	42 14N	88 19W
67	Cuando, R.	18 27S	23 32E
28	Cuba ■	21 30N	80 0W
67	Cubango, R.	18 50S	22 25E
30	Cúcuta	7 54N	72 31W
17	Cudahy	42 57N	87 52W
*56	Cuddalore	11 45N	79 46E
30	Cuenca, Ecuador	2 53S	78 59W
39	Cuenca, Spain	40 4N	2 8W
39	Cuenca, Serrania de	40 27N	1 57W
27	Cuernavaca	18 55N	99 15W
31	Cuiabá	15 35S	56 5W
67	Cuito, R.	18 1S	20 48E
26	Culiacán	24 48N	107 24W
30	Cumaná	10 30N	64 5W
24	Cumberland, Canada	49 37N	124 59W
8	Cumberland, U.S.A.	39 40N	78 47W
9	Cumberland, R.	37 9N	88 25W
21	Cumberland Pen.	67 0N	65 0W
9	Cumberland Plat.	36 0N	84 30W
67	Cunene, R.	17 20S	11 50E
40	Cúneo	44 23N	7 31E
71	Cunnamulla	28 2S	145 38E
29	Curaçao, I.	12 10N	69 0W
32	Curicó	34 55S	71 20W
32	Curitiba	25 20S	49 10W
57	Cuttack	20 25N	85 57E
14	Cuyahoga Falls	41 8N	81 29W
30	Cuzco	13 32S	72 0W
30	Cuzco, mt.	20 0S	66 50W
17	Cynthiana	38 23N	84 18W
25	Cypress Hills	49 40N	109 30W
54	Cyprus ■	35 0N	33 0E
65	Cyrenaica=Barqa, reg.	27 50N	22 45E
43	Czechoslovakia ■	49 0N	17 0E
43	Czestochowa	50 49N	19 7E

D

58	Da-Nang	16 4N	108 13E
53	Dabat	12 58N	37 48E
57	Dacca	23 43N	90 26E
56	Dadra & Nagar Haveli □	20 5N	73 0E
47	Dagestan A.S.S.R. □	42 30N	47 0E
19	Daggett	34 52N	116 53W
46	Dagö, I.=Hiiumaa, I.	58 50N	22 45E
59	Dagupan	16 3N	120 33E
53	Dahlak Kebir, I.	15 50N	40 10E
64	Dahomey=Benin ■	8 0N	2 0E
60	Daisetsu-Zan	43 40N	142 53E
64	Dakar	14 34N	17 29W
64	Dakhla	25 0N	13 30W
45	Dalälven, R.	60 38N	17 27E
61	Dalandzadgad	43 37N	104 17E
71	Dalby	27 10S	151 17E
23	Dalhousie	48 4N	66 23W
52	Daliyat el Karmel	32 41N	35 3E
24	Dall I.	54 50N	132 55W
11	Dallas	32 50N	96 50W
41	Dalmacija, dist.	43 20N	17 0E
71	Dalrymple, mt.	21 1S	148 39E
9	Dalton	34 45N	85 0W
70	Daly, R.	13 45S	130 50E
70	Daly Waters	16 15S	133 24E
56	Daman	20 25N	72 57E
65	Damanhûr	31 0N	30 30E
54	Damascus=Dimashq	33 30N	36 18E
43	Dâmbovita, R.	44 14N	26 13E
65	Damietta=Dumyât	31 24N	31 48E
70	Dampier	20 40S	116 30E
59	Dampier, Selat	0 40S	131 0E
15	Danbury	41 23N	73 27W
42	Danube=Dunarea, R.	45 20N	29 40E
15	Danvers	42 34N	70 56W
17	Danville, Ill.	40 10N	87 40E
17	Danville, Ky.	37 39N	84 46W
9	Danville, Va.	36 40N	79 20E
43	Danzig=Gdańsk	54 22N	18 40E
57	Darbhanga	26 15N	86 3E
54	Dardanelles= Cannakale Bogazi, str.	40 0N	26 20E
66	Dar-es-Salaam	6 50S	39 12E
65	Dârfûr □	12 35N	25 0E
72	Dargaville	35 57S	173 52E
28	Darién, G.de	9 0N	77 0W
57	Darjeeling	27 3N	88 18E
71	Darling, R.	34 7S	141 55E
70	Darling Range	32 30S	116 0E
36	Darlington	54 33N	3 33W
42	Darmstadt	49 51N	8 40E
36	Dartmoor	50 36N	4 0W
23	Dartmouth, Canada	44 40N	63 30W
36	Dartmouth, U.K.	50 21N	3 35W
70	Darwin	12 20S	130 50E
55	Daryacheh-i-Namakzar, L.	33 0N	60 45E
55	Daryacheh-ye Namak, L.	34 45N	51 36E
54	Daryacheh-ye Reza'iyeh, L.	37 40N	45 30E
55	Daryacheh-ye-Sistan, L.	31 0N	61 0E
55	Dash-e Kavir, des.	34 30N	55 0E
55	Dasht-e Lut, des.	31 30N	58 0E
55	Dasht-i-Margo, des.	30 40N	62 30E
46	Daugava, R.	57 0N	24 0E
46	Daugavpils	55 53N	26 32E
25	Dauphin	51 15N	100 5W
*56	Davangere	14 25N	75 50E
59	Davao	7 0N	125 40E
18	Davenport, Calif.	37 1N	122 12W
16	Davenport, Iowa	41 32N	90 42W
28	David	8 30N	82 30W
18	Davis	38 33N	121 44W
11	Davis Mts.	30 42N	104 15W
21	Davis Str.	66 30N	59 0W
17	Davison	43 2N	83 31W
42	Davos	46 48N	9 40E
20	Dawson	64 10N	139 30W
24	Dawson Creek	55 46N	120 14W
52	Dayr al-Ghusun	32 21N	35 4E
54	Dayr az Zawr	35 20N	40 5E
17	Dayton	39 45N	84 10W
9	Daytona Beach	29 14N	81 0W
67	De Aar	30 39S	24 0E
70	De Grey, R.	20 12S	119 11E
16	De Soto	38 8N	90 33W
52	Dead Sea=Bahr el Miyet	31 30N	35 0E
17	Dearborn	42 18N	83 10W
24	Dease Lake	58 27N	130 2W
19	Death Valley	36 0N	116 40W
25	Debden	53 31N	106 53W
53	Debre Markos	10 20N	37 40E
43	Debrecen	47 33N	21 42E
9	Decatur, Ala.	34 35N	87 0W
8	Decatur, Ill.	39 50N	89 32W
16	Decatur, Ind.	40 50N	84 56W
56	Deccan, reg.	14 0N	77 0E
15	Dedham	42 15N	71 10W
23	Deer Lake	49 10N	57 26W
17	Deer Park	39 13N	84 24W
17	Defiance	41 17N	84 22W
55	Deh Bid	30 39N	53 11E
56	Dehra Dun	30 20N	78 4E
19	Del Mar	32 58N	117 16W
11	Del Rio	29 15N	100 50W
19	Delano	35 48N	119 13W
17	Delaware	40 18N	83 4W
8	Delaware □	39 0N	75 40W
37	Delft	52 1N	4 22E
37	Delfzijl	53 20N	6 55E
56	Delhi	28 38N	77 17E
26	Delicias	28 10N	105 30W
17	Delphos	40 50N	84 20W
39	Demanda, Sierra de la	42 15N	3 0W
53	Dembecha	10 32N	37 30E
13	Deming, N.Mex.	32 10N	107 50W
*18	Deming, Wash.	48 49N	122 13W
37	Den Helder	52 57N	4 45E
37	Den Oever	52 56N	5 2E
18	Denair	37 32N	120 47W
11	Denison	33 50N	96 40W
54	Denizli	37 42N	29 2E
45	Denmark ■	34 59S	117 18E
11	Denton	33 12N	97 10W
70	D'Entrecasteaux, Pt.	34 50S	115 57E
10	Denver	39 45N	105 0W
56	Deolali	19 50N	73 50E
56	Dera Ghazi Khan	30 5N	70 43E
56	Dera Ismail Khan	31 50N	70 50E
47	Derbent	42 5N	48 15E
70	Derby, Australia	17 18S	123 40E
36	Derby, U.K.	52 55N	1 28W
15	Derby, U.S.A.	42 41N	78 58W
65	Derudub	17 31N	36 7E
16	Des Moines	41 35N	93 37W
16	Des Moines, R.	40 22N	91 26W
17	Des Plaines	42 2N	87 54W
53	Dese	11 5N	39 40E
32	Deseado, R.	40 0S	69 0W
42	Dessau	51 49N	12 15E
8	Detroit	42 20N	83 5W
10	Detroit Lakes	46 50N	95 50W
37	Deurne	51 12N	4 24E
42	Deutsche Bucht	54 30N	7 30E
38	Deux-Sèvres □	46 35N	0 20W
37	Deventer	52 15N	6 10E
10	Devils Lake	48 5N	98 50W
24	Devon	53 22N	113 44W
21	Devon I.	75 0N	86 0W
*71	Devonport, Australia	41 12S	146 28E
72	Devonport, N.Z.	36 49S	174 49E
54	Dezful	32 20N	48 30E
49	Dezhneva, Mys	66 6N	169 45W
53	Dhahran	26 9N	50 10E
53	Dhamar	14 46N	44 23E
56	Dharwar	15 29N	75 5E
41	Dhodhekanisos, Is.	36 35N	27 0E
56	Dhulia	20 58N	74 50E
18	Diablo Ra.	36 45N	121 20W
31	Diamantina	18 5S	43 40W
71	Diamantina, R.	24 0S	141 0E
57	Diamond Harbour	22 11N	88 14E
10	Dickinson	46 50N	102 40W
24	Didsbury	51 40N	114 8W
25	Diefenbaker, L.	51 7N	106 38W
67	Diégo-Suarez	12 25S	49 20E
38	Dieppe	49 54N	1 4E
23	Digby	44 37N	65 40W
54	Dijlah, Nahr	31 0N	47 25E
38	Dijon	47 20N	5 0E
18	Dikson	73 40N	80 5E
65	Dikwa	12 4N	13 30E
59	Dili	8 39S	125 34E
54	Dimashq	33 30N	36 18E
41	Dimitrovgrad	42 5N	25 35E
40	Dinara Planina	44 0N	17 30E
38	Dinard	48 38N	2 6W
18	Dinuba	36 32N	119 23W
59	Dipolog	8 40N	123 30E
53	Dire Dawa	9 35N	41 45E
28	Diriamba	11 51N	86 19W
70	Dirk Hartog, I.	25 58S	113 1E
70	Disappointment, L.	23 20S	122 40E
20	Discovery	63 0N	113 50W
8	District of Columbia □	38 55N	77 0W
56	Diu	20 45N	70 58E
18	Dixon, Calif.	38 27N	121 49W
16	Dixon, Ill.	41 50N	89 29W
24	Dixon Entrance	54 30N	132 0W
54	Diyarbakir	37 55N	40 18E
59	Djajapura	2 28S	140 38E
59	Djakarta	6 9S	106 49E
58	Djambi=Telanaipura	1 38S	103 30E
58	Djambi □	1 38S	103 30E
58	Djawa, I.	7 0S	110 0E
59	Djazirah Doberai, mts.	1 25S	133 0E
59	Djember	8 11S	113 41E
65	Djerba, I. de	33 56N	11 0E
53	Djibouti ■	11 30N	42 15E
54	Djilar, Nahr	31 0N	42 25E
59	Djombang	7 32S	112 12E
65	Djourab, Erg du	17 0N	18 0E
47	Dnepr, R.	46 30N	32 18E
47	Dneprodzerzhinsk	48 32N	34 30E
47	Dnepropetrovsk	48 30N	35 0E
47	Dnestr, R.	46 18N	30 17E
47	Dnieper, R.=Dnepr, R.	46 30N	32 18E
47	Dniester, R.= Dnestr, R.	46 18N	30 17E
59	Dobo	5 45S	134 15E
43	Dobruja, reg.	44 30N	28 30E
11	Dodge City	37 42N	100 0W
66	Dodoma	6 8S	35 45E
37	Doetinchen	51 59N	6 18E
53	Doha	25 15N	50 58E
23	Dolbeau	48 53N	72 14W

Dolo Ferganda

53 Dolo 45 25N 12 4E
40 Dolomiti, mts. 46 30N 11 40E
20 Dolphin & Union Str. 69 5N 114 45W
29 Dominica, I. 15 20N 61 20W
29 Dominican Rep. ■ 19 0N 70 30W
53 Domo 7 50N 47 10E
47 Don, R. 47 4N 39 18E
42 Donau, R. 45 20N 29 40E
36 Doncaster 53 31N 1 9W
56 Dondra Hd. 5 55N 80 40E
36 Donegal B. 54 30N 8 35W
47 Donetsk 48 0N 37 45E
65 Dongola 19 9N 30 22E
23 Donnacona 46 41N 71 41W
14 Donora 40 11N 79 52W
70 Dora, L. 22 0S 123 0E
38 Dordogne, R. 45 2N 0 35W
38 Dordogne □ 45 5N 0 40E
37 Dordrecht 51 48N 4 39E
38 Dore, Mt. 45 32N 2 50E
22 Dorion 45 23N 74 1W
61 Döröö Nuur 48 0N 93 0E
37 Dorsten 51 40N 6 55E
37 Dortmund 51 32N 7 28E
9 Dothan 31 10N 85 25W
38 Douai 50 21N 3 4E
66 Douala 4 0N 9 45E
38 Douanenez 48 6N 4 21W
38 Doubs, R. 46 54N 5 2E
38 Doubs □ 47 8N 5 40E
70 Doubtful, B. 34 55S 173 26E
36 Douglas, I.of M. 54 9N 4 29W
24 Douglas, Alaska 58 16N 134 26W
13 Douglas, Arizona 31 21N 109 30W
39 Douro, R. 41 8N 8 40W
36 Dover, U.K. 51 7N 1 19E
8 Dover, Del. 39 10N 75 31W
15 Dover, N.H. 43 12N 70 56W
15 Dover, N.J. 40 53N 74 34W
44 Dovrefjell, mts. 62 15N 9 33E
17 Dowagiac 41 59N 86 6W
17 Downers Grove 41 8N 88 1W
18 Doyle 40 2N 120 5W
67 Drakensberg, mts. 31 0S 25 0E
45 Drammen 59 44N 10 15E
43 Drava, R. 45 33N 18 55E
24 Drayton Valley 53 13N 114 59W
38 Drenthe □ 52 52N 6 40E
42 Dresden 51 2N 13 45E
41 Drin, R. 41 17N 20 2E
41 Drina, R. 44 53N 19 21E
36 Drogheda 53 45N 6 20W
38 Drôme □ 44 38N 5 15E
24 Drumheller 51 25N 112 40W
71 Drummond Range 23 45S 147 10E
22 Drummondville 45 55N 72 25W
25 Dryden 49 47N 92 50W
70 Drysdale, R. 13 59S 126 51E
16 Du Quoin 38 1N 89 14W
25 Dubawnt L. 63 0N 102 0W
53 Dubayy □ 24 10N 55 20E
71 Dubbo 32 11S 148 35E
36 Dublin, Eire 53 20N 6 18W
9 Dublin, U.S.A. 32 30N 83 0W
41 Dubrovnik 42 39N 18 6E
16 Dubuque 42 30N 90 41W
25 Duck Lake 52 49N 106 14W
39 Duero=Douro, R. 41 8N 8 40W
40 Dugi Otok, I. 44 0N 15 0E
37 Duisburg 51 27N 6 42E
10 Duluth 46 48N 92 10W
57 Dum Dum 22 39N 88 26E
58 Dumai 1 35N 101 20E
36 Dumbarton 55 58N 4 35W
36 Dumfries 55 4N 3 37W
65 Dumyât 31 24N 31 48E
42 Dunarea, R. 45 20N 29 40E
43 Dunaújváros 47 0N 18 57E
24 Duncan, Canada 48 47N 123 42W
11 Duncan, U.S.A. 34 25N 98 0W
36 Dundalk 53 55N 6 45W
22 Dundas 43 16N 79 58W
36 Dundee 56 29N 3 0W
72 Dunedin 45 50S 170 33E
36 Dunfermline 56 5N 3 28W
38 Dunkerque 51 2N 2 20E
14 Dunkirk 42 29N 79 20W
15 Dunmore 41 25N 75 38W
14 Duquesne 40 21N 79 51W
38 Durance, R. 43 55N 4 44E
26 Durango 24 3N 104 39W
11 Durant 34 0N 96 25W
32 Durazno 33 25N 56 38W
67 Durban 29 49S 31 1E
22 Durham, Canada 44 10N 80 49W
36 Durham, U.K. 54 47N 1 34W
9 Durham, U.S.A. 36 0N 78 55W
41 Durmitor, mt. 43 18N 19 0E
41 Durrës 41 19N 19 28E
72 D'Urville, I. 40 50S 173 55E
48 Dushanbe 38 40N 68 50E
20 Dutch Harbor 53 53N 166 32W
53 Duwadami 24 35N 44 15E
46 Dvinskaya Guba 65 0N 39 0E
11 Dyersburg 36 2N 89 20W
46 Dzerzhinsk 56 15N 43 15E
48 Dzhambul 43 10N 71 0E
49 Dzhugdzur, Khrebet 57 30N 138 0E
48 Dzhungarskiye Vorota 45 0N 82 0E
61 Dzungaria, reg. 44 10N 88 0E
48 Dzungarian Gate= Dzhungarskiye Vorota 45 0N 82 0E

E

19 Earlimart 35 53N 119 16W
***20** East, C. 51 21N 179 29W
23 East Angus 45 29N 71 40W
57 East Bengal, reg. 23 0N 90 0E
17 East Chicago 41 38N 87 37W
61 East China Sea 30 5N 126 0E
17 East Clarence Canyon Res. 39 30N 91 45W
32 East Falkland, I. 51 30S 58 30W
42 East Germany ■ 52 0N 12 30E
15 East Hartford 41 46N 72 39W
17 East Lansing 42 44N 84 29W
14 East Liverpool 40 39N 80 35W
67 East London 33 0S 27 55E
19 East Los Angeles 34 1N 118 9W
16 East Moline 41 31N 90 25W
15 East Orange 40 46N 74 13W
14 East Palestine 40 50N 80 33W
16 East Peoria 40 40N 89 34W
15 East Providence 41 49N 71 23W
16 East St.Louis 38 36N 90 10W
49 East Siberian Sea 73 0N 160 0E
36 Eastbourne 50 46N 0 18E
2 Easter I. 27 0S 109 0W
69 Easter Is. 27 0S 109 0W
***56** Eastern Ghats, mts. 15 0N 80 0E
58 Eastern Malaysia □ 5 0N 115 0E
22 Eastmain, R. 52 27N 72 26W
15 Easton, Pa. 40 42N 75 12W
***18** Easton, Wash. 47 14N 121 11W
22 Eastview 45 27N 75 40W
17 Eaton 39 45N 84 38W
15 Eatontown 40 18N 74 7W
10 Eau Claire 34 5N 81 2W
40 Éboli 40 39N 15 2E
39 Ebro, R. 40 43N 0 54E
60 Echigo-Sammyaku 37 50N 139 50E
20 Echo Bay 46 29N 84 4W
17 Ecorse 42 15N 83 9W
30 Ecuador ■ 2 0S 78 0W
37 Edam 53 21N 5 3E
37 Ede 52 4N 5 40E
***11** Edinburg 26 22N 98 10W
36 Edinburgh 55 57N 3 12W
54 Edirne 41 40N 26 45E
***18** Edmonds 47 48N 122 22W
24 Edmonton 53 30N 113 30W
23 Edmundston 47 23N 68 20W
24 Edson 53 35N 116 26W
66 Edward, L.=Idi Amin Dada, L. 0 25S 29 30E
19 Edwards 34 54N 117 53W
17 Edwardsburg 41 48N 86 5W
16 Edwardsville 38 49N 89 58W
17 Effingham 39 7N 88 33W
40 Égadi, Isole 37 55N 12 10E
70 Egerton, Mt. 24 42S 117 44E
72 Egmont, Mt. 39 17S 174 5E
65 Egypt ■ 28 0N 31 0E
42 Eifel, mts. 50 10N 6 45E
70 Eighty Mile Beach 19 30S 120 40E
53 Eil 8 0N 49 50E
37 Eindhoven 51 26N 5 30E
52 EizAriya 31 47N 35 15E
65 El Alamein 30 48N 28 58E
52 El Ariha 31 52N 35 27E
19 El Cajon 32 49N 117 0W
19 El Centro 32 48N 115 34W
11 El Dorado, Ark. 33 13N 92 40W
11 El Dorado, Kans. 37 55N 96 56W
65 El Faiyûm 29 19N 30 50E
65 El Fâsher 13 33N 25 26E
39 El Ferrol 43 29N 3 14W
26 El Fuerte 26 30N 108 40W
65 El Gezira 14 0N 33 0E
65 El Giza 30 0N 31 10E
65 El Iskandarîya 31 0N 30 0E
65 El Khârga, El Wâhât 25 30N 30 33E
65 El Khartûm 15 31N 32 35E
65 El Mahalla el Kubra 31 0N 31 0E
65 El Mansura 31 0N 31 19E
65 El Minya 28 7N 30 33E
19 El Monte 34 4N 118 2W
65 El Obeid 13 8N 30 10E
13 El Paso 31 50N 106 30W
18 El Paso Robles 35 38N 120 41W
65 El Qâhira 30 3N 31 15E
11 El Reno 35 30N 98 0W
19 El Rio 34 14N 119 10W
28 El Salvador ■ 13 50N 89 0W
65 El Suweis 29 58N 32 31E
65 El Uqsur 25 41N 32 38E
***52** Elat 29 30N 34 56E
54 Elazig 38 37N 39 22E
40 Elba, I. 42 48N 10 15E
42 Elbe, R. 53 50N 9 0E
13 Elbert, Mt. 39 12N 106 36W
43 Elblag 54 10N 19 25E
39 Elche 38 15N 0 42W
25 Eldorado 59 33N 108 30W
66 Eldoret 0 30N 35 17E
28 Eleuthera, I. 25 0N 76 20W
17 Elgin 42 2N 88 17W
66 Elila, R. 2 45S 25 53E
67 Elisabethville= Lubumbashi 11 32S 27 38E
71 Elisabeth, Australia 34 45S 138 39E
15 Elizabeth, U.S.A. 40 37N 74 12W
9 Elizabeth City 36 18N 76 16W
9 Elizabethton 36 20N 82 13W
17 Elizabethtown 37 42N 85 52W
22 Elk Lake 47 44N 80 20W
25 Elk Point 53 54N 110 54W
17 Elkhart 41 42N 85 55W
8 Elkins 38 53N 79 53W
13 Elko 40 40N 115 50W
68 Ellice Is.=Tuvalu 8 0S 176 0E
22 Elliot Lake 46 23N 82 39W
57 Ellore=Eluru 16 48N 81 8E
***9** Ellsworth 44 33N 68 26W
14 Ellwood City 40 50N 80 17W
***18** Elma 47 0N 123 25W
17 Elmhurst 41 52N 87 58W
8 Elmira 42 8N 76 49W
25 Elrose 51 12N 108 2W
57 Eluru 16 48N 81 8E
17 Elwood 40 17N 85 50W
14 Elyria 41 22N 82 8W
25 Embarras Portage 58 27N 111 28W
42 Emden 53 22N 7 12E
52 'Emeq Yizre'el, reg. 32 27N 35 12E
71 Emerald 23 30S 148 11E
25 Emerson 49 0N 97 12W
65 Emi Koussi 20 0N 18 55E
37 Emmen 52 48N 6 57E
16 Emmetsburg 43 7N 94 41W
26 Empalme 28 1N 110 49W
10 Emporia 36 41N 77 32W
42 Ems, R. 51 9N 9 26E
52 'En Kerem 31 47N 35 6E
32 Encarnación 27 15S 56 0W
19 Encinitas 33 3N 117 17W
71 Endeavour Str. 10 45S 142 0E
24 Enderby 50 40N 119 20E
15 Endicott 42 6N 76 3W
46 Engels 51 28N 46 6E
36 England □ 53 0N 2 0W
10 Englewood, Colo. 39 40N 105 0W
15 Englewood, N.J. 40 54N 73 59W
11 Enid 36 26N 97 52W
64 Ennedi 17 15N 22 0E
37 Enschede 52 13N 6 53E
26 Ensenada 31 50N 116 50W
66 Entebbe 0 4N 32 28E
32 Entre Ríos, reg. 30 30S 58 30W
64 Enugu 6 30N 7 30E
40 Eólie o Lípari, Isole 38 30N 14 50E
54 Ephesus 38 0N 27 30E
38 Epinal 48 19N 6 27E
66 Equatorial Guinea ■ 3 0N 10 0W
64 Er Rif, mts. 35 1N 4 1W
65 Er Roseires 11 55N 34 30E
57 Erawadi Myit, R. 15 50N 95 6E
54 Eregli 41 15N 31 30E
42 Erfurt 50 58N 11 2E
41 Ergene, R. 41 1N 26 22E
61 Erhlien 43 48N 111 59E
14 Erie 42 10N 80 7W
22 Erie, L. 42 30N 82 0W
60 Erimo-Misaki 41 50N 143 15E
53 Eritrea, reg. 14 0N 41 0E
37 Ermelo 52 53N 5 35E
***56** Ernakulam 9 59N 76 19E
***56** Erode 11 24N 77 45E
42 Erzgebirge, mts. 50 25N 13 0E
54 Erzurum 39 57N 41 15E
65 Es Sinâ', pen. 29 0N 34 0E
45 Esbjerg 55 29N 8 29E
8 Escanaba 45 44N 87 5W
37 Esch 49 32N 6 0E
37 Eschweiler 50 49N 6 14E
19 Escondido 33 7N 117 5W
28 Escuintla 14 20N 90 48W
55 Esfahan 33 0N 53 0E
45 Eskilstuna 59 22N 16 32E
25 Eskimo Point 61 10N 94 15W
54 Eskisehir 39 50N 30 35E
30 Esmeraldas 1 0N 79 40W
22 Espanola 46 15N 81 46W
70 Esperance 33 45S 121 55E
70 Esperance, B. 33 48S 121 55E
31 Espinhaco, Sa. do 17 30S 43 30W
31 Espírito Santo □ 20 23S 40 18W
64 Essaouira 31 32N 9 42W
37 Essen 51 28N 6 59E
30 Essequibo, R. 6 50N 58 30W
19 Essex 34 44N 115 14W
38 Essonne □ 48 30N 2 20E
11 Estacado, Llano 33 30N 102 40W
28 Estelí 13 9N 86 22W
25 Estevan 49 8N 102 59W
25 Eston 51 8N 108 40W
46 Estonian S.S.R. □ 58 30N 25 30E
39 Estrela, Sa.de 40 10N 7 45W
39 Estremadura □ 39 0N 9 0W
56 Etawah 26 48N 79 6E
25 Ethelbert 51 31N 100 23W
53 Ethopia ■ 8 0N 40 0E
40 Etna, mt. 37 45N 15 0E
70 Eucla Basin Plain 31 19S 126 9E
14 Euclid 41 32N 81 31W
11 Eufaula, L. 35 15N 95 28W
12 Eugene 44 0N 123 8W
54 Euphrates, R.= Nahr al Furat, R. 31 0N 47 25E
38 Eure □ 49 6N 1 0E
38 Eure-et-Loir □ 48 22N 1 30E
12 Eureka 40 50N 124 0W
39 Europa, Picos de 43 10N 5 0W
39 Europa, Pt. 36 3N 5 21W
37 Europoort 51 57N 4 10E
17 Evanston 42 0N 87 40W
17 Evansville 38 0N 87 35W
70 Everard, L. 31 30S 135 0E
57 Everest, Mt. 28 5N 86 58E
18 Everett 48 0N 122 10W
9 Everglades Nat.Park 26 0N 80 30W
39 Evora 38 33N 7 57W
41 Evvoia, I. 38 30N 24 0E
16 Excelsior Springs 39 20N 94 13W
36 Exe, R. 50 37N 3 25W
36 Exeter, U.K. 50 43N 3 31W
18 Exeter, U.S.A. 36 18N 119 9W
36 Exmoor 51 10N 3 55W
71 Expedition Range 24 30S 149 12E
66 Eyasi, L. 3 30S 35 0E
71 Eyre, L. 29 0S 137 0E
72 Eyre, Mts. 45 25S 168 25E
70 Eyre, Pen. 33 30S 137 17E

F

49 Faddeyevskiy, Ostrov 76 0N 150 0E
45 Fagersta 60 1N 15 46E
***20** Fairbanks 64 59N 147 40W
17 Fairborn 39 49N 84 2W
10 Fairbury 40 5N 97 5W
9 Fairfield, Ala. 33 30N 87 0W
18 Fairfield, Calif. 38 15N 122 3W
15 Fairfield, Conn. 41 9N 73 15W
17 Fairfield, Ill. 38 23N 88 22W
17 Fairfield, Ohio 39 20N 84 33W
18 Fairmead 37 5N 120 12W
8 Fairmont 38 29N 80 9W
24 Fairmont Hot Springs 50 19N 115 52W
24 Fairview 56 4N 118 23W
55 Faizabad, Afghan. 37 7N 70 33E
57 Faizabad, India 26 45N 82 10E
29 Fajardo 18 20N 65 39W
59 Fakfak 3 0S 132 15E
36 Falkirk 56 0N 3 47W
32 Falkland Is. 51 30S 59 0W
33 Falkland Is.Dependency 57 0S 40 0W
45 Falköping 58 12N 13 33E
14 Fall River 41 45N 71 5W
19 Fallbrook 33 23N 117 15W
36 Falmouth 50 9N 5 5W
45 Falun 60 32N 15 39E
54 Famagusta 35 8N 33 55E
24 Fanshaw 57 13N 133 30W
55 Farah 32 20N 61 21E
55 Farah, R. 31 30N 61 30E
33 Farewell, C. 59 40N 43 40W
10 Fargo 47 0N 97 0W
10 Faribault 44 15N 93 19W
55 Farrashband 28 57N 52 5E
14 Farrell 41 13N 80 30W
55 Fars □ 29 30N 55 0E
55 Faryab □ 36 0N 65 0E
56 Fatehgarh 27 25N 79 35E
57 Fatehpur 28 0N 75 4E
61 Fatshan 23 0N 113 4E
11 Fayetteville, Ark. 36 0N 94 5W
9 Fayetteville, N.C. 35 0N 78 0W
38 Fécamp 49 45N 0 22E
42 Fehmarn Baelt, str. 54 35N 11 20E
31 Feira de Santana 12 20S 39 0W
47 Feodosiya 45 2N 35 28E
53 Ferfer 5 18N 45 20E
48 Ferganda 40 23N 71 46E

Golden Herat

10 Golden 39 42N 105 30W
12 Golden Gate 37 54N 122 30W
9 Goldsboro 35 24N 77 59W
46 Gomel 52 28N 31 0E
64 Gomera, Is. 28 10N 17 5W
26 Gómez Palacio 25 40N 104 40W
55 Gonabad 34 15N 58 45E
29 Gonâves 19 20N 72 50W
29 Gonâve, G. de 19 29N 72 42W
53 Gonder 12 23N 37 30E
18 Gonzales 36 3lN 121 32W
67 Good Hope, C.of= Goeie Hoop, Kaap die 34 24S 18 30E
71 Goondiwindi 28 30S 150 21E
23 Goose Bay 53 15N 60 20W
57 Gorakhpur 26 47N 83 32E
72 Gore 46 5S 168 58E
65 Goré 7 59N 16 49E
55 Gorgan 36 55N 54 30E
46 Gorkiy 56 20N 44 0E
46 Gorkovskoye Vdkhr. 57 2N 43 4E
42 Görlitz 51 10N 14 59E
47 Gorlovka 48 25N 37 58E
59 Gorontalo 0 35N 123 13E
42 Gorzów 52 43N 15 15E
18 Goshen, Calif. 36 21N 119 25W
17 Goshen, Ind. 41 35N 85 50W
45 Götaland, reg. 58 0N 14 0E
45 Göteborg 57 43N 11 59E
42 Gotha 50 56N 10 42E
45 Gotland, I. 57 15N 18 30E
42 Göttingen 51 31N 9 55E
43 Gottwaldov 49 14N 17 40E
37 Gouda 52 lN 4 42E
33 Gough I. 40 10S 4 45W
31 Governador Valadares 18 15S 41 57W
32 Goya 29 10S 59 10W
40 Gozo, I. 36 0N 14 13E
71 Grafton, Australia 29 35S 152 0E
10 Grafton, U.S.A. 48 30N 97 25W
24 Graham I. 53 40N 132 30W
48 Graham, Ostrov 81 30N 62 30E
36 Grampian Highlands 56 50N 4 0W
64 Gran Canaria, I. 27 55N 15 35W
32 Gran Chaco, reg. 25 0S 61 0W
40 Gran Paradiso, mt. 45 32N 7 16E
40 Gran Sasso, mt. 42 25N 13 30E
28 Granada, Nic. 11 58N 86 0W
39 Granada, Spain 37 10N 3 35W
22 Granby 45 25N 72 45W
17 Grand, R. 43 4N 86 15W
29 Grand Bahama I. 26 40N 78 30W
23 Grand Bank 47 6N 55 46W
13 Grand Canyon 36 15N 112 20W
12 Grand Coulee Dam 48 0N 118 50W
23 Grand Falls, N.B. 47 2N 67 46W
23 Grand Falls, Nfld. 48 56N 55 40W
24 Grand Forks, Canada 49 20N 118 20W
10 Grand Forks, U.S.A. 48 0N 97 3W
17 Grand Haven 43 4N 86 13W
10 Grand Island 46 30N 86 40W
22 Grand' Mère 46 36N 72 40W
25 Grand Rapids, Canada 53 10N 99 18W
17 Grand Rapids, Mich. 42 57N 85 40W
10 Grand Rapids, Minn. 47 19N 93 29W
42 Grand St.Bernard, Col du 45 50N 7 10E
32 Grande, B. 50 30S 68 20W
28 Grande, R. 25 57N 97 11W
24 Grande Prairie 55 15N 118 50W
16 Grandview 38 53N 94 32W
17 Grandview Heights 40 1N 83 3W
17 Grandville 42 54N 85 46W
16 Granite City 38 45N 90 3W
12 Granite Pk. 45 8N 109 52W
36 Grantham 52 55N 0 39W
12 Grants Pass 42 30N 123 22W
18 Grass Valley 39 13N 121 4W
25 Gravelbourg 49 53N 106 33W
22 Gravenhurst 44 52N 79 20W
42 Graz 47 4N 15 27E
28 Great Abaco I. 26 15N 77 10W
71 Great Australian Basin 26 0S 140 0E
70 Great Australian Bight 33 30S 130 0E
28 Great Bahama I. 23 15N 78 0W
29 Great Bahama Bank 23 0N 78 0W
72 Great Barrier, I. 37 12S 175 25E
71 Great Barrier Reef 19 0S 149 0E
12 Great Basin 40 0N 116 30W
20 Great Bear L. 65 0N 120 0W
10 Great Bend 38 25N 98 55W
24 Great Central 49 19N 124 59W
71 Great Divide, mts. 23 0S 146 0E
28 Great Exuma I. 23 30N 75 50W
12 Great Falls 47 27N 111 12W
29 Great Inagua I. 21 0N 73 20W
56 Great Indian Desert 28 25N 72 0E
67 Great Namaqualand= Groot Namakwaland □ 26 0S 18 0E
66 Great Ruaha, R. 7 56S 37 52E
12 Great Salt L. 41 0N 112 30W
55 Great Salt Desert= Dasht-e Kavir, des. 34 30N 55 0E
12 Great Salt Lake Des. 40 20N 113 50W
55 Great Sand Desert= Dasht-e Lut,des. 31 30N 58 0E
70 Great Sandy Desert 21 0S 124 0E
24 Great Slave L. 61 30N 114 20W
70 Great Victoria Desert 29 30S 126 30E
61 Great Wall of China 38 30N 109 30E
22 Great Whale R. 55 17N 77 45W
36 Great Yarmouth 52 40N 1 45E
29 Greater Antilles, Is. 17 40N 74 0W
58 Greater Sunda Is. 2 30S 110 0E
39 Gredos, Sierra de 40 20N 5 0W
41 Greece ■ 40 0N 23 0E
10 Greeley 40 30N 104 40W
8 Green, B. 45 0N 87 30W
8 Green Bay 44 30N 88 0W
15 Green Mts. 43 45N 72 45W
17 Greencastle 39 38N 56 52W
18 Greenfield, Calif. 36 19N 121 15W
17 Greenfield, Ind., 39 47N 85 46W
15 Greenfield, Mass. 42 36N 72 36W
17 Greenfield, Ohio 39 21N 83 23W
17 Greenhills 39 18N 84 30W
33 Greenland ■ 66 0N 45 0W
33 Greenland Sea 73 0N 10 0W
36 Greenock 55 57N 4 46W
9 Greensboro 36 7N 79 46W
14 Greensburg, Pa. 40 18N 79 33W
17 Greensburg, Tenn. 39 20N 85 29W
17 Greenup 39 15N 88 10W
9 Greenville, Ala. 31 50N 86 37E
18 Greenville, Calif. 40 8N 120 57W
16 Greenville, Ill. 38 53N 89 25W
*9 Greenville, Me. 45 28N 69 35W
11 Greenville, Miss. 33 25N 91 0W
9 Greenville, N.C. 35 37N 77 26W
17 Greenville, Ohio 40 6N 84 38W
14 Greenville, Pa. 41 24N 80 23W
11 Greenville, Tex. 33 5N 96 5W
15 Greenwich 41 1N 73 38W
17 Greenwood, Ind. 39 37N 86 7W
11 Greenwood, Miss. 33 30N 90 4W
9 Greenwood, S.C. 34 13N 82 3W
70 Gregory, L. 20 10S 127 30E
71 Gregory Range 19 0S 143 10E
29 Grenada ■ 12 10N 61 40W
25 Grenfell 50 25N 102 56W
38 Grenoble 45 12N 5 42E
71 Grey Range 27 0S 143 30E
72 Greymouth 42 29S 171 13E
18 Gridley 39 22N 121 42W
36 Grimsby 53 35N 0 5W
16 Grinnell 41 45N 92 43W
67 Griqualand West, reg. 28 40S 23 30E
38 Gris Nez, C. 50 50N 1 35E
46 Grodno 53 42N 23 52E
37 Groningen 53 15N 6 35E
67 Groot Karoo, reg. 32 30S 23 0E
71 Groot Eylandt 14 0S 136 50E
42 Gross Glockner Pass 47 5N 12 40E
15 Groton 41 19N 72 12W
19 Grover City 35 7N 120 37W
49 Groznyy 43 20N 45 45E
43 Grudziadz 53 30N 18 47E
26 Guadalajara, Mexico 20 40N 103 20W
39 Guadalajara, Spain 40 37N 3 12W
68 Guadalcanal 10 0S 100 0E
39 Guadalquivir, R. 36 45N 6 25W
19 Guadalupe 34 58N 120 34W
39 Guadalupe, Sa.de 39 28N 5 30W
39 Guadarrama, Sa.de 41 0N 4 0W
29 Guadeloupe ■ 16 20N 61 40W
39 Guadiana, R., Port. 37 14N 7 22W
39 Guadiana, R., Spain 37 56N 3 15W
39 Guadix 37 18N 3 11W
32 Gualeguay 33 10S 59 20W
32 Gualeguaychu 33 3S 58 31W
3 Guam, I. 13 27N 144 45E
26 Guamúchil 25 25N 108 3W
31 Guanabara □ 23 0S 43 25W
28 Guanabacoa 23 8N 82 18W
28 Guanajay 22 56N 82 42W
26 Guanajuato 20 40N 101 20W
28 Guane 22 10N 84 0W
29 Guantánamo 20 10N 75 20W
30 Guaporé,R. 11 55S 65 4W
32 Guarapuava 25 20S 51 30W
28 Guatemala ■ 14 40N 90 30W
28 Guatemala 14 40N 90 30W
29 Guayama 17 59N 66 7W
30 Guayquil 2 15S 79 52W
30 Guayaquil, G.de 3 10S 81 0W
26 Guaymas 27 50N 111 0W
22 Guelph 43 35N 80 20W
38 Guernsey, I. 49 19N 104 45W
36 Guildford 51 14N 0 34W
64 Guinea ■ 10 20N 10 0W
62 Guinea, reg. 9 0N 5 0E
64 Guinea-Bissau ■ 11 45N 15 45W
28 Güines 22 50N 82 0W
59 Guivan 11 5N 125 55E
56 Gujarat □ 23 20N 71 0E
56 Gujranwala 32 10N 74 12E
56 Gulbarga 17 20N 76 50E
70 Gulf Basin 15 20S 129 0E
11 Gulfport 30 28N 89 3W
25 Gulf Lake 50 6N 108 29W
56 Guna 24 40N 77 19E
57 Guntur 16 23N 80 30E
47 Guryev 47 5N 52 0E
11 Guthrie 33 55N 97 30W
16 Guttenburg 42 47N 91 6W
30 Guyana ■ 5 0N 59 0W
56 Gwalior 26 12N 78 10E
67 Gwelo 19 28S 29 45E
33 Gwelo, R. 18 45S 28 36E
48 Gydanskiy Poluostrov 70 0N 78 0E
71 Gympie 26 11S 152 38E
43 Györ 47 41N 17 40E
25 Gypsumville 51 46N 98 38W

H

60 Hachinohe 40 30N 141 29E
60 Hachiöji 33 3N 139 55E
52 Hadar Ramatayim 32 9N 34 54E
52 Hadera 32 27N 34 55E
53 Hadhramawt, reg. 15 30N 49 30E
54 Haft Gel 31 30N 49 32E
52 Hagalil, reg. 32 53N 35 18E
37 Hagen 51 21N 7 29E
8 Hagerstown 39 39N 77 46W
60 Hagi 34 30N 131 30E
38 Hague, C.de la 49 43N 1 57W
52 Haifa 32 46N 35 0E
61 Haikow 20 0N 110 20E
61 Haliar 49 12N 119 37E
22 Haileybury 47 27N 79 39W
37 Hainaut □ 50 30N 4 0E
24 Haines Junction 60 45N 137 30W
61 Haiphong 20 55N 105 42E
29 Haiti ■ 19 0N 72 30W
65 Haiya Junction 18 20N 36 40E
60 Hakodate 41 45N 140 44E
60 Haku-San 36 9N 136 46E
54 Halab 36 10N 37 15E
42 Halberstadt 51 53N 11 2E
45 Halden 59 7N 11 23E
52 Halhul 31 35N 35 7E
23 Halifax, Canada 44 38N 63 35W
36 Halifax, U.K. 53 43N 1 5lW
71 Halifax Bay 18 50S 147 0E
55 Halil, R. 27 40N 58 30E
21 Hall Lake 68 41N 82 17W
37 Halle, Belgium 50 44N 4 13E
42 Halle, E.Germany 51 29N 12 0E
70 Hall's Creek 18 20S 128 0E
59 Halmahera, I. 0 40N 128 0E
45 Halmstad 56 37N 12 56E
54 Hama 33 5N 36 40E
54 Hamadan 34 52N 48 32E
60 Hamamatsu 34 45N 137 45E
45 Hamar 60 48N 11 7E
42 Hamburg 53 32N 9 59E
15 Hamden 42 12N 74 60W
45 Hämeenlinna 61 3N 24 26E
42 Hameln 52 7N 9 24E
70 Hamersley Ra. 22 0S 117 45E
71 Hamilton, Australia 37 37S 142 0E
*29 Hamilton, Bermuda 32 15N 64 45W
22 Hamilton, Canada 43 20N 79 50W
72 Hamilton, N.Z. 37 47S 175 19E
17 Hamilton, Ind. 41 36N 87 30W
17 Hamilton, Ohio 39 26N 84 30W
70 Hamilton, R. 23 30S 139 47E
23 Hamilton Inlet 54 0N 57 30W
25 Hamlota 50 11N 100 36W
37 Hamm 51 40N 7 58E
44 Hammerfest 70 39N 23 41E
17 Hammond 41 40N 87 30W
8 Hampton 37 47N 76 18W
55 Hamun Hélmand, L. 31 15N 61 15E
61 Hanchung 33 10N 107 2E
8 Hancock 47 10N 88 35W
53 Handa 10 37N 51 2E
*52 Hanegev, reg. 30 50N 35 0E
24 Haney 49 20N 122 40W
18 Hanford 36 20N 119 39W
61 Hangchow 30 17N 120 1E
61 Hangchow Wan 30 30N 121 30E
24 Hanna 51 38N 111 54W
16 Hannibal 39 42N 91 22W
42 Hannover 52 23N 9 43E
61 Hanoi 21 5N 150 40E
22 Hanover 44 9N 81 2W
44 Haparanda 65 52N 24 8E
23 Happy Valley 53 15N 61 8W
*52 Har Ramon, mt. 30 27N 34 42E
52 Har Yehuda, reg. 31 35N 34 57E
53 Harad 24 15N 49 0E
61 Harbin 45 46N 126 51E
23 Harbour Breton 47 29N 55 48W
23 Harbour Grace 47 40N 53 22W
45 Hardangerfjorden 60 15N 6 0E
67 Hardap Dam 24 32S 17 50E
24 Hardisty 52 40N 111 18W
56 Hardwar 29 58N 78 16E
52 Hare Meron, mt. 32 59N 35 24E
53 Harer 9 20N 42 8E
53 Hargeisa 9 30N 44 2E
*11 Harlingen 53 11N 5 25E
44 Härnösand 62 38N 18 5E
70 Harris, L. 31 10S 135 10E
17 Harrisburg, Ill. 37 42N 88 30W
14 Harrisburg, Pa. 40 18N 76 52W
*20 Harrison, B. 70 30N 151 30W
8 Harrisonburg 38 28N 78 52W
16 Harrisonville 38 39N 94 21W
22 Harriston 43 54N 80 53W
17 Harrodsburg 37 46N 84 51W
16 Harry S.Truman Res. 38 18N 93 25W
15 Hartford, Conn. 41 46N 72 41W
17 Hartford, Mich. 42 12N 86 10W
17 Hartford City 40 27N 85 22W
56 Haryana □ 29 0N 76 10E
42 Harz, mts. 51 40N 10 40E
53 Hasa, reg. 26 0N 49 0E
56 Hashefela, reg. 31 30N 34 43E
37 Hasselt 50 56N 5 21E
36 Hastings, U.K. 50 51N 0 36E
72 Hastings, N.Z. 39 39S 176 52E
10 Hastings, U.S.A. 44 41N 92 51W
61 Hatgal 50 40N 100 0E
9 Hatteras, C. 35 10N 75 30W
11 Hattiesburg 31 20N 89 20W
45 Haugesund 59 23N 5 13E
64 Haut Atlas, mts. 32 0N 7 0W
38 Haut-Rhin □ 48 0N 7 15E
*38 Haute-Corse □ 42 17N 9 0E
38 Haute-Garonne □ 43 28N 1 30E
38 Haute-Loire □ 45 5N 3 50E
38 Haute-Marne □ 48 10N 5 20E
38 Haute-Saône □ 47 45N 6 10E
38 Haute-Savoie □ 46 0N 6 20E
38 Haute-Vienne □ 45 50N 1 10E
23 Hauterive 49 12N 68 16W
38 Hautes-Alpes □ 44 42N 6 20E
38 Hautes-Pyrénées □ 43 0N 0 10E
38 Hauts-de-Seine □ 48 52N 2 15E
28 Havana=La Habana 23 8N 82 22W
22 Havelock 45 17N 78 38W
15 Haverhill 42 47N 71 5W
12 Havre 48 40N 109 34W
*6 Hawaii, I. □ 20 0N 155 0W
*6 Hawaiian Is. 20 30N 156 0W
72 Hawera 39 35S 174 19E
72 Hawke, B. 39 45S 176 35E
22 Hawkesbury 45 35N 74 40W
71 Hay 34 30S 144 51E
24 Hay River 60 50N 115 50W
*20 Hayes, mt. 63 37N 146 43W
25 Hayes, R. 57 3N 92 12W
10 Hays 38 55N 99 25W
18 Hayward 37 40N 122 5W
8 Hazard 37 18N 83 10W
24 Hazelton 55 20N 127 42W
15 Hazleton 40 58N 76 0W
52 Hazor 33 2N 35 2E
55 Hazrat 37 14N 68 47E
18 Healdsburg 38 37N 122 52W
*20 Healy 63 30N 149 0W
22 Hearst 49 40N 83 41W
19 Heber 32 44N 115 32W
52 Hebron 31 32N 35 6E
24 Hecate Str. 53 20N 131 0W
37 Heemstede 52 19N 4 37E
37 Heerenveen 52 57N 5 55E
37 Heerlen 50 55N 6 0E
42 Heidelberg 49 23N 8 41E
42 Heilbronn 49 8N 9 13E
61 Heilungkiang □ 47 30N 129 0E
11 Helena 46 40N 112 0W
19 Helendale 34 45N 117 18W
72 Helensville 36 41S 174 29E
44 Helgeland, reg. 66 20N 13 30E
42 Helgoland, I. 54 10N 7 51E
37 Hellendoorn 52 24N 6 27E
37 Helmond 51 29N 5 41E
55 Helmand, R. 31 42N 61 45E
55 Helmand □ 34 0N 67 0E
45 Helsingborg 56 3N 12 42E
45 Helsingor 56 2N 12 35E
45 Helsinki 60 15N 25 3E
19 Hemet 33 45N 116 58W
39 Henares, R. 40 24N 3 30W
17 Henderson, Ky. 37 50N 87 35W
19 Henderson, Nev 36 2N 114 59W
9 Henderson, N.C. 36 18N 78 23W
37 Hengelo 52 15N 6 48E
61 Hengyang 26 57N 112 28E
25 Henribourg 53 25N 105 38W
57 Henzada 17 38N 95 35E
55 Herat 34 20N 62 7E

Herault Jiddah

38	Herault □	43 34N	3 15E
25	Herbert	50 26N	107 13W
36	Hereford	52 4N	2 42W
42	Herford	52 7N	8 40E
18	Herlong	40 9N	120 8W
54	Hermon, mt.=Sheikh, J. ash, mt.	33 26N	35 51E
26	Hermosillo	29 10N	111 0W
43	Hernád, R.	47 56N	21 8E
37	Herne	51 33N	7 12E
45	Herning	56 8N	9 0E
16	Herrin	37 48N	89 2W
37	Herstal	50 40N	5 38E
71	Hervey Bay	25 0S	153 0E
52	Herzliyya	32 10N	34 50E
19	Hesperia	34 25N	117 18W
10	Hibbing	47 30N	93 0W
9	Hickory	35 46N	81 17W
15	Hicksville	40 46N	73 32W
60	Hida-Sammyaku	36 30N	137 40E
26	Hidalgo del Parral	26 10N	104 50W
64	Hierro	27 57N	17 56E
60	Higashiosaka	34 39N	135 35E
24	High Level	58 32N	117 5W
9	High Point	35 37N	79 58W
24	High Prairie	55 26N	116 29W
24	High River	50 35N	113 52W
17	Highland	41 33N	87 27W
17	Highland Park, Ill.	42 10N	87 50W
8	Highland Park, Mich.	42 25N	83 6W
29	Higüay	18 37N	68 42W
46	Hiiumaa	58 50N	22 45E
53	Hijaz, reg.	26 0N	37 30E
72	Hikurangi, mt.	37 55S	178 4E
42	Hildesheim	52 9N	9 55E
17	Hillsboro, Ohio	39 12N	83 37W
*18	Hillsboro, Oreg.	45 31N	122 59W
*6	Hilo	19 44N	155 5W
37	Hilversum	52 14N	5 10E
56	Himachal Pradesh □	31 30N	77 0E
57	Himalaya, mts.	29 0N	84 0E
60	Himejji	34 50N	134 40E
54	Hims=Homs	34 40N	36 45E
29	Hinche	19 9N	72 1W
55	Hindukush, mts.	36 0N	71 0E
24	Hines Creek	56 15N	118 36W
57	Hirakud Dam	21 32N	83 45E
60	Hiratsuka	35 40N	139 36E
60	Hirosaki	40 34N	140 28E
60	Hiroshima	34 30N	132 30E
29	Hispaniola, I.	19 0N	71 0W
60	Hitachi	36 40N	140 35E
45	Hjorring	57 29N	9 59E
*71	Hobart, Australia	42 50S	147 21E
17	Hobart, U.S.A.	41 32N	87 15W
11	Hobbs	32 40N	103 3W
37	Hoboken, Belgium	51 11N	4 21E
15	Hoboken, U.S.A.	40 45N	74 3W
53	Hodeida	14 50N	43 0E
52	Hodiyya	31 40N	33 48E
43	Hódmerzövasarhely	46 28N	20 22E
37	Hoek van Holland	52 0N	4 7W
61	Hofei	31 45N	116 36E
61	Hokang	47 36N	130 28E
60	Hokkaido, I.	43 30N	143 0E
28	Holguin	20 50N	76 20W
17	Holland	42 47N	86 7W
59	Hollandia=Djajapura	2 28N	140 38E
18	Hollister	36 51N	121 24W
52	Holon	32 2N	34 47E
36	Holyhead	53 18N	4 38W
15	Holyoke	42 12N	72 37W
*20	Homer	59 40N	151 35W
17	Homewood	41 44N	87 44W
54	Homs	34 40N	36 45E
61	Honan □	33 50N	113 15E
28	Honduras ■	14 40N	86 30W
18	Honey L.	40 16N	120 19W
38	Honfleur	49 25N	0 10E
61	Hong Kong ■	22 11N	114 14E
*6	Honolulu	21 19N	157 52W
60	Honshu, I.	36 0N	138 0E
37	Hoogeveen	52 44N	6 30E
37	Hoogezand	53 11N	6 45E
24	Hoonah	58 7N	135 26W
17	Hoopeston	40 28N	87 40W
37	Hoorn	52 38N	5 4E
19	Hoover Dam	36 0N	114 45W
24	Hope, Canada	49 23N	121 26W
19	Hope, U.S.A.	33 45N	113 40W
28	Hope Town	26 30N	76 30W
61	Hopei □	39 25N	116 45E
50	Hopetown	29 34S	24 3E
8	Hopkinsville	36 52N	87 26W
18	Hopland	38 58N	123 7W
*18	Hoquiam	47 0N	123 55W
55	Hormoz	27 35N	55 0E
55	Hormuz, Str.of	26 30N	56 30E
32	Horn, C.=Hornos, C.de	55 50S	67 30W
14	Hornell	42 19N	77 40W
32	Hornos, C.de	55 50S	67 30W
45	Horsens	55 52N	9 51E
45	Horten	59 25N	10 32E
39	Hospitalet	41 21N	2 6E
32	Hoste, I.	55 0S	69 0W
11	Hot Springs, Ark.	34 30N	93 0W
10	Hot Springs, S.Dak.	43 25N	103 30W
61	Hotien	37 6N	79 59E
*9	Houlton	46 5N	68 0W
11	Houma	29 35N	90 50W
15	Housatonic, R.	41 10N	73 7W
15	Houston	29 50N	95 20W
61	Hovd	48 2N	91 37E
57	Howrah	22 37N	88 27E
42	Hradec Králové	50 15N	15 50E
61	Hsiamen	24 25N	118 4E
61	Hsinchu	24 55N	121 0E
30	Huacho	11 10S	77 35W
30	Huancayo	12 5S	75 0W
30	Huánuco	9 55S	76 15W
30	Huaraz	9 30S	77 32W
30	Huascarán, mt.	9 0S	77 30W
27	Huauchinango	20 11N	98 3W
56	Hubli	15 22N	75 15E
36	Huddersfield	53 38N	1 49W
25	Hudson, Canada	50 5N	92 10W
15	Hudson, U.S.A.	42 15N	73 47W
15	Hudson, R.	40 42N	74 2W
21	Hudson B.	60 0N	86 0W
21	Hudson Str.	62 0N	70 0W
25	Hudson Bay	52 51N	102 23W
58	Hué	16 30N	107 35E
28	Huehuetenango	15 20N	91 28W
39	Huelva	37 18N	6 57W
39	Huesca	42 8N	0 25W
71	Hughenden	20 52S	144 10E
61	Huhehot	40 52N	111 36E
27	Huixtla	15 9N	92 28W
53	Hula	6 33N	38 30E
22	Hull, Canada	45 20N	75 40W
36	Hull, U.K.	53 45N	0 20W
36	Humber, R.	53 40N	0 10W
25	Humboldt	52 12N	105 7W
12	Humboldt, R.	40 2N	118 31W
71	Hume, L.	36 0S	147 0E
18	Humphreys, Mt.	37 17N	118 40W
61	Hunan □	27 30N	111 30E
43	Hunedoara	45 40N	22 50E
43	Hungary ■	47 20N	19 20E
34	Hungary, Plain of	47 0N	20 0E
61	Hungtze Hu	33 20N	118 35E
42	Hunsrück, mts.	50 0N	7 30E
22	Huntingdon	45 5N	74 10W
17	Huntington, Ind.	40 53N	85 30W
15	Huntington, N.Y.	40 51N	73 25W
19	Huntington Beach	33 39N	118 0W
72	Huntly	37 34S	175 11E
22	Huntsville, Canada	45 20N	79 13W
9	Huntsville, U.S.A.	34 45N	86 35W
*71	Huonville	43 0S	147 5E
61	Hupei □	31 5N	113 5E
10	Huron	44 30N	98 20W
22	Huron, L.	45 0N	83 0W
44	Húsavik	66 3N	17 13W
45	Huskvarna	57 47N	14 15E
11	Hutchinson	38 3N	97 59W
40	Hvar, I.	43 10N	16 45E
61	Hwainan	32 44N	117 1E
61	Hwang Ho	37 10N	117 30E
61	Hwangshih	30 27N	115 0E
56	Hyderabad, India	17 10N	78 29E
56	Hyderabad, Pakistan	25 23N	68 36E

I

43	Ialomita, R.	44 42N	27 51E
43	Iasi	47 10N	27 40E
64	Ibadan	7 22N	3 58E
30	Ibagué	4 27N	73 14W
34	Iberian Peninsula	40 0N	5 0W
22	Iberville	45 18N	73 14W
39	Ibiza, I.	39 0N	1 30E
30	Icá	14 0S	75 30W
44	Iceland ■	65 0N	19 0W
60	Ichihara	35 31N	140 5E
60	Ichinomiya	35 20N	136 50E
12	Idaho □	44 10N	114 0W
12	Idaho Falls	43 30N	112 10W
41	Idhi Oros, mt.	35 15N	24 45E
66	Idi Amin Dada, L.	0 25S	29 30E
37	Ieper	50 51N	2 53E
64	Ife	7 30N	4 31E
48	Igarka	67 30N	87 20E
52	Ignace	49 25N	91 40W
27	Iguala	18 20N	99 40W
37	IJmuiden	52 28N	4 35E
37	IJessel, R.	51 54N	4 38E
37	IJesselmeer, L.	52 45N	5 20E
38	Ile de France, reg.	49 0N	2 20E
31	Ilheus	15 0S	39 10W
*20	Iliamna, L.	59 45N	154 54W
38	Ille-et-Vilaine □	48 10N	1 30W
16	Illinois, R.	38 58N	90 27W
10	Illinois □	40 15N	89 30W
59	Iloilo	10 45N	122 33E
60	Imabari	34 4N	133 0E
46	Imandra, Ozero	67 45N	33 0E
25	Imperial	51 21N	105 26W
19	Imperial Beach	32 35N	117 8W
19	Imperial Valley	32 50N	115 30W
57	Imphal	24 15N	94 0E
52	Imwas	31 51N	34 59E
64	In Salah	27 12N	2 28E
72	Inangahua Junction	41 52S	171 59E
44	Inari, L.	69 0N	28 0E
61	Inchon	37 32N	126 45E
57	Indaw	24 15N	96 5E
18	Independence, Calif.	36 48N	118 12W
16	Independence, Iowa	42 28N	91 54W
11	Independence, Kans.	37 13N	95 43W
11	Independence, Mo.	39 4N	94 27W
56	India ■	23 0N	77 30E
25	Indian Head	50 32N	103 31W
68	Indian Ocean	5 0S	75 0E
14	Indiana	40 37N	79 9W
17	Indiana □	40 0N	86 0W
17	Indianapolis	39 42N	86 10W
16	Indianola	41 22N	93 34W
49	Indigirka, R.	70 48N	148 54E
19	Indio	33 43N	116 13W
58	Indonesia ■	5 0S	115 0E
56	Indore	22 42N	75 53E
38	Indre □	47 12N	1 39E
38	Indre-et-Loire □	47 12N	0 40E
56	Indus, R.	24 20N	67 47E
22	Ingersoll	43 2N	80 53W
72	Inglewood, N.Z.	39 9S	174 14E
19	Inglewood, U.S.A.	33 58N	118 27W
42	Ingolstadt	48 45N	11 26W
46	Ingulek	47 43N	33 14E
67	Inhambane	23 54S	35 30E
61	Ining	43 57N	81 20E
42	Inn, R.	48 35N	13 28E
36	Inner Hebrides, Is.	57 20N	6 40W
61	Inner Mongolia □	44 50N	117 40E
24	Innisfail	52 2N	113 57W
42	Innsbruck	47 16N	11 23E
21	Inoucdjouac	58 27N	78 6W
43	Inowraclaw	52 50N	18 20E
46	Inta	66 2N	60 8E
42	Interlaken	46 41N	7 50E
20	Inuvik	68 25N	133 30W
72	Invercargill	46 24S	168 24E
36	Inverness	57 29N	4 12W
41	Ionian Sea	38 40N	20 0E
16	Iowa, R.	41 10N	91 2W
10	Iowa □	42 18N	93 30W
16	Iowa City	41 40N	91 35W
16	Iowa Falls	42 51N	93 16W
61	Ipin	28 58N	104 45E
58	Ipoh	4 36N	101 4E
71	Ipswich, Australia	27 38S	152 37E
36	Ipswich, U.K.	52 4N	1 9E
30	Iquique	20 19S	70 5W
30	Iquitos	3 45S	73 10W
41	Iráklion	35 20N	25 12E
55	Iran ■	33 0N	53 0E
50	Iran, Plateau of	31 0N	57 0E
26	Irapuato	20 40N	101 40W
54	Iraq ■	33 0N	44 0E
36	Ireland ■	53 0N	8 0W
59	Irian Jaya □	5 0S	138 0E
36	Irish Sea	54 0N	145 12E
49	Irkutsk	52 10N	104 20E
8	Ironton	38 35N	82 40W
10	Ironwood	46 30N	90 10W
22	Iroquois Falls	48 46N	80 41W
57	Irrawaddy, R.=Erawadi Myit, R.	15 50N	95 6E
48	Irtysh, R.	61 4N	68 52E
39	Irún	43 20N	1 52W
*44	Isafjördur	66 10N	23 15W
40	Ischia	40 45N	13 51E
60	Ise	34 29N	136 41E
38	Isère, R.	44 59N	4 51E
38	Isère □	45 15N	5 40E
60	Ise-Wan	34 45N	136 45E
60	Ishikari-Wan	43 25N	141 1E
8	Ishpeming	46 30N	87 40W
54	Iskenderun	36 32N	36 10E
19	Isla Vista	34 25N	119 53W
56	Islamabad	33 42N	73 10E
65	Ismâ'iliya	30 37N	32 18E
54	Isparta	37 47N	30 30E
52	Israel ■	32 0N	34 50E
48	Issyk Kul	42 30N	77 30E
54	Istanbul	41 0N	29 0E
40	Istra, dist.	55 55N	36 50E
32	Itajai	27 0S	48 45W
40	Italy ■	42 0N	13 0E
15	Ithaca	42 25N	76 30W
25	Ituna	51 10N	103 30W
18	Ivanhoe	36 23N	119 13W
47	Ivano-Frankovsk	49 0N	24 40E
46	Ivanovo	57 0N	40 59E
64	Ivory Coast ■	7 30N	5 0E
40	Ivrea	45 30N	7 52E
21	Ivujivic	62 24N	77 55W
60	Iwaki	37 3N	140 55E
60	Iwakuni	34 15N	132 8E
60	Iwate-San	40 39N	140 18E
64	Iwo	7 38N	4 11E
27	Izamel	20 56N	89 1W
37	Izegem	50 55N	3 12E
46	Izhevsk	56 51N	53 14E
54	Izmir	38 25N	27 9E
54	Izmit	40 45N	29 50E
27	Izúcar de Matamoros	18 2N	98 17W

J

53	Jabal Tuwayq, mts.	25 30N	46 0E
52	Jabaliya	31 32N	34 27E
56	Jabalpur	23 9N	79 58E
17	Jackson, Mich.	42 18N	84 25W
11	Jackson, Miss.	32 20N	90 11W
9	Jackson, Tenn.	35 40N	88 50W
18	Jacksonville, Calif.	47 48N	120 25W
9	Jacksonville, Fla.	30 15N	81 38W
16	Jacksonville, Ill.	39 42N	90 15W
56	Jacobabad	28 20N	68 29E
23	Jacques Cartier Passage	49 50N	62 30W
19	Jacumba	32 37N	116 11W
39	Jaén	5 25S	78 40W
52	Jaffa=Tel Aviv Yafo	32 3N	34 46E
*56	Jaffna	9 45N	80 2E
57	Jagdalpur	19 3N	82 6E
28	Jagüey Grande	22 35N	81 7W
55	Jahrom	28 30N	53 31E
56	Jaipur	26 54N	72 52E
44	Jakobstad	63 40N	22 42E
55	Jalalabad	34 30N	70 29E
19	Jalama	34 28N	120 30W
28	Jalapa, Guat.	14 45N	89 59W
27	Jalapa, Mex.	19 30N	96 50W
56	Jalgaon	21 3N	76 35E
56	Jalna	19 48N	75 57E
39	Jalón, R.	41 47N	1 4W
28	Jamaica ■	18 10N	77 30W
52	Jamma'in	32 8N	35 12E
10	James, R.	42 52N	97 18W
22	James B.	53 30N	80 30W
14	Jamestown, N.Y.	42 5N	79 15W
10	Jamestown, N.D.	47 0N	98 30W
56	Jammu & Kashmir □	32 46N	75 57E
56	Jamnagar	22 30N	70 0E
57	Jamshedpur	22 44N	86 20E
2	Jan Mayen, I.	71 0N	11 0W
55	Jandaq	34 3N	54 22E
16	Janesville	42 39N	89 1W
60	Japan ■	36 0N	136 0E
60	Japan, Sea of	40 0N	135 0E
59	Japen, I.	1 50S	136 0E
30	Japura, R.	3 8S	64 46W
69	Jarvis I.	0 15S	159 55W
55	Jask	25 38N	57 45E
24	Jasper, Canada	52 53N	119 5W
17	Jasper, U.S.A.	38 24N	86 56W
24	Jasper Nat.Pk.	52 55N	118 10W
24	Jasper Place	53 33N	113 25W
57	Jaunpur	25 46N	82 44E
58	Java, I.=Djawa, I.	7 0S	110 0E
58	Java Sea	4 35S	107 15E
58	Java Trench	10 0S	110 0E
29	Javellanos	22 59N	99 41W
19	Jean	35 25N	115 20W
14	Jeannette	40 20N	79 35W
65	Jebel, Bahr el.R.	9 48N	30 11E
16	Jefferson City, Mo.	38 34N	92 10W
10	Jefferson City, Tenn.	36 8N	83 30W
17	Jeffersonville	38 17N	85 44W
42	Jelenia Góra	50 50N	15 45E
46	Jelgava	56 41N	22 49E
42	Jena	50 56N	11 33E
52	Jenin	32 28N	35 18E
16	Jennings, Ill.	38 44N	90 17W
11	Jennings, La.	30 10N	92 45W
29	Jérémie	18 40N	74 10W
39	Jerez, Andalucia	36 41N	6 8W
39	Jerez, Extremadura	38 20N	6 45W
26	Jerez de Garcia Salinas	22 39N	103 0W
52	Jericho=El Ariha	31 52N	35 27E
38	Jersey, I.	49 13N	2 7W
15	Jersey City	40 41N	74 8W
16	Jerseyville	39 7N	90 22W
52	Jerusalem	31 47N	35 10E
71	Jervis, B.	35 8S	150 46E
58	Jesselton=Kota Kinabalu	6 0N	116 12E
57	Jessore	23 10N	89 10E
56	Jhang Maghiana	31 15N	72 15E
56	Jhansi	25 30N	78 36E
57	Jharsaguda	21 51N	84 1E
56	Jhelum, R.	31 12N	72 8E
53	Jiddah	21 29N	39 16E

Jifna Koh-i-Baba, mts.

52 Jifna 31 58N 35 13E
53 Jima 7 40N 36 55E
26 Jiménez 27 10N 105 0W
66 Jinja 0 25N 33 12E
26 Jiquilpan 19 57N 102 42W
31 João Pessoa 7 10S 35 0W
56 Jodhpur 26 23N 73 2E
59 Jogjakarta 7 49S 110 22E
67 Johannesburg 26 10S 28 8E
15 Johnson City, N.Y. 42 7N 75 57W
9 Johnson City, Tenn. 36 18N 82 21W
24 Johnsons Crossing 60 29N 133 18W
66 Johnston Falls 10 31S 28 45E
15 Johnstown, N.Y. 43 0N 74 22W
14 Johnstown, Penn. 40 20N 78 56W
58 Johor Baharu 1 28N 103 46E
32 Joinville 26 15S 48 55W
17 Joliet 41 32N 88 5W
22 Joliette 46 3N 73 24W
11 Jonesboro 35 50N 90 45W
45 Jönköping 57 45N 14 15E
11 Joplin 37 0N 94 25W
54 Jordan ■ 31 0N 36 0E
52 Jordan, R. 31 46N 35 33E
57 Jorhat 26 45N 94 20E
64 Jos 9 53N 8 51E
70 Josph Bonaparte Gulf 14 0S 29 0E
45 Jotunheimen, mts 61 30N 9 0E
55 Jouzjan □ 36 0N 66 0E
28 Jovellanos 22 40N 81 10W
26 Juan Aldama 24 20N 103 23W
*18 Juan de Fuca, Str. 48 15N 124 0W
31 Juàzeiro 9 30S 40 30W
31 Juàzeiro do Norte 7 10S 39 18W
65 Jûbâ 4 57N 31 35E
39 Júcar, R. 39 9N 0 8W
27 Juchitán 16 27N 95 5W
52 Judaea=Har Yehuda, reg. 31 35N 34 57E
28 Juigalpa 12 6N 85 26W
31 Juiz de Fora 21 43S 43 19W
30 Juliaca 15 25S 70 10W
56 Jullundur 31 20N 75 40E
37 Jumet 50 27N 4 25E
57 Jumna, R.=Yamuna, R. 25 25N 81 50E
56 Junagadh 21 30N 70 30E
70 Junction, B. 11 52S 133 55E
10 Junction City 39 4N 96 55W
32 Jundiai 23 11S 46 52W
24 Juneau 58 26N 134 30W
32 Junin 34 33S 60 57W
65 Jur, R. 9 18N 29 36W
38 Jura, mts. 46 35N 6 5E
38 Jura □ 46 47N 5 45E
70 Jurien, B. 30 17S 115 0E
30 Juruá, R. 2 37S 65 44W
61 Jyekundo 32 50N 96 50E
45 Jylland, reg. 56 25N 9 30E
44 Jyväskylä 62 12N 25 47E

K

67 Kaapstad=Cape Town 33 55S 18 22E
66 Kabalo 6 0S 27 0E
47 Kabardino-Balkar A.S.S.R. □ 43 30N 43 30E
66 Kabarega Falls 2 15N 31 38E
67 Kabompo, R. 13 30S 24 14E
55 Kabul 34 28N 69 18E
57 Kachin □ 26 0N 97 0E
54 Kackar, mt. 40 45N 41 30E
47 Kadiyevka 48 35N 38 30E
64 Kaduna 10 30N 7 21E
67 Kafue, R. 15 56S 28 55E
60 Kagoshima 31 36N 130 40E
*6 Kahana 21 34N 157 52W
55 Kahnuj 27 55N 57 40E
*6 Kahoolawe 20 33N 156 37W
61 Kaifeng 34 49N 114 30E
72 Kaikohe 35 25S 173 49E
*6 Kailua 21 24N 157 44W
72 Kaimanawa Mts. 39 15S 175 56E
64 Kainji Dam 10 1N 4 40E
42 Kaiserslautern 49 30N 7 43E
*6 Kaiwi Chan. 21 15N 157 30W
44 Kajaani 64 15N 27 43E
22 Kakabeka Falls 48 24N 89 37W
47 Kakhovskoye Vdkhr. 47 5N 34 16E
57 Kakinada=Cocanada 16 5N 82 20E
60 Kakogawa 34 46N 134 51E
67 Kalahari Desert 24 0S 22 0E
17 Kalamazoo 42 20N 85 35W
56 Kalat 29 8N 66 31E
*6 Kalaupapa 21 11N 156 59W
66 Kalemie 5 55S 29 9E
70 Kalgoorie 30 40S 121 22E
58 Kalimantan □ 0 30N 114 0E
46 Kalinin 56 55N 35 55E
46 Kaliningrad 54 42N 20 32E
12 Kalispell 48 20N 114 22W
43 Kalisz 51 45N 18 8E
45 Kalmar 56 39N 16 22E
47 Kalmyk A.S.S.R. □ 46 5N 46 1E
46 Kaluga 54 35N 36 10E
46 Kama, R. 55 45N 52 0E
60 Kamaisha 39 20N 142 0E
53 Kamaran, I. 15 28N 42 35E
49 Kamchatka, Poluostrov 57 0N 160 0E
47 Kamenets Podolsky 48 40N 26 30E
47 Kamensk Shakhtinskiy 48 23N 40 20E
48 Kamensk Uralskiy 56 25N 62 45E
66 Kamina 8 45S 25 0E
24 Kamloops 50 40N 120 20W
66 Kampala 0 20N 32 30E
37 Kampen 52 33N 5 53E
58 Kampot 10 36N 104 10E
46 Kamskoye Vdkhr. 58 0N 56 0E
66 Kananga 5 55S 22 18E
*18 Kanaskat 47 19N 121 55W
60 Kanazawa 36 30N 136 38E
57 Kanchenjunga, mt. 27 50N 88 10E
61 Kanchow 25 58N 114 55E
55 Kandahar 31 32N 65 30E
46 Kandalaksha 67 9N 32 30E
46 Kandalakshskiy Zaliv 66 0N 35 0E
*72 Kandavu, I. 19 3S 178 13E
*56 Kandy 7 18N 80 43E
71 Kangaroo, I. 35 45S 137 0E
46 Kanin, Poluostrov 68 0N 45 0E
46 Kanin Nos.Mys 68 45S 43 20E
17 Kankakee 41 7N 87 52W
17 Kankakee, R. 41 23N 88 16W
9 Kannapolis 35 32N 80 37W
64 Kano 12 2N 8 30E
60 Kanoya 31 25N 130 50E
56 Kanpur 26 35N 80 20E
16 Kansas City, Kans. 39 0N 94 40W
16 Kansas City, Mo. 39 3N 94 30W
10 Kansas □ 38 45N 98 15W
61 Kansu □ 35 30N 104 30E
60 Kanto-Sanchi 35 59N 138 43E
60 Kanto □ 36 25N 140 30E
61 Kaohsiung 22 35N 120 16E
67 Kapiri Mposhi 13 59S 28 43E
55 Kapisa □ 34 45N 69 30E
22 Kapuskasing 49 25N 82 26W
47 Kara Bogaz Gol. 41 0N 53 30E
48 Kara Kalpak A.S.S.R. □ 43 0N 60 0E
48 Kara Kum, Peski 39 30N 60 0E
48 Kara Sea 75 0N 70 0E
56 Karachi 24 53N 67 0E
54 Karadeniz Bogazi, Str. 41 10N 29 5E
54 Karadeniz Daglari, mts. 41 30N 35 0E
56 Karakoram, mts. 35 20N 76 0E
72 Karamea Bight 41 22S 171 40E
60 Karatsu 33 30N 130 0E
40 Karawanken, mts. 46 30N 14 40E
66 Karema 6 49S 30 24E
67 Kariba 16 28S 28 36E
67 Kariba Dam 16 28S 28 36E
67 Kariba L. 16 40S 28 25E
65 Karima 18 32N 31 48E
58 Karimata, Selat 2 0S 108 20E
47 Karkinitskiy Zaliv 45 36N 32 35E
42 Karl-Marx-Stadt 50 50N 12 55E
42 Karlovy Vary 50 13N 12 51E
45 Karlshamn 56 10N 14 51E
45 Karlskoga 59 22N 14 33E
45 Karlskrona 56 10N 15 35E
42 Karlsruhe 49 3N 8 23E
45 Karlstad 59 24N 13 35E
56 Karnal 29 42N 77 2E
57 Karnaphuli Res. 22 40N 92 20E
42 Karnische Alpen, mts. 46 36N 13 0E
66 Karonga 9 57S 33 55E
41 Kárpathos, I. 35 37N 27 10E
54 Kars 40 40N 43 5E
48 Karsakpay 47 49N 66 41E
66 Kasai, R. 3 2S 16 57E
55 Kashan 34 5N 51 30E
61 Kashgar 39 46N 75 52E
65 Kassalâ 15 23N 36 26E
42 Kassel 51 19N 9 32E
59 Kassue 6 58S 139 21E
41 Kastoria 40 30N 21 19E
56 Kasur 31 5N 74 25E
59 Kataloka 3 54S 131 27E
70 Katanning 33 40S 117 33E
70 Katherine 14 27S 132 20E
57 Katmandu 27 45N 85 12E
43 Katowice 50 17N 19 5E
45 Katrineholm 59 9N 16 12E
64 Katsina 7 10N 9 20E
55 Kattawaz-Urgun □ 32 48N 68 23E
45 Kattegat, str. 57 0N 11 20E
37 Katwijk-aan-Zee 52 12N 4 24E
*6 Kauai I. 19 30N 155 30W
*6 Kauai Chan. 21 45N 158 50W
*6 Kaula I. 21 45N 160 30W
46 Kaunas 54 54N 23 54E
60 Kawagoe 36 0N 139 30E
60 Kawaguchi 35 52N 138 45E
*6 Kawaihae 20 2N 155 50W
60 Kawasaki 35 35N 138 42E
57 Kawthoolei □ 18 0N 97 30E
57 Kayah □ 19 15N 97 15E
54 Kayseri 38 45N 35 30E
48 Kazakh S.S.R. □ 49 0N 50 0E
46 Kazan 55 48N 49 3E
55 Kazerun 29 38N 51 40E
*6 Keaau 19 37N 155 2W
10 Kearney 40 45N 99 3W
44 Kebnekaise, mt. 67 52N 18 36E
43 Kecskemét 46 57N 19 35E
61 Keelung=Chilung 25 3N 121 45E
19 Keene, Calif. 35 13N 118 33W
15 Keene, N.H. 42 56N 72 17W
25 Keewatin 49 46N 94 34W
20 Keewatin □ 63 20N 94 40W
41 Kefallinía, I. 38 28N 20 30E
52 Kefar Nahum 32 54N 35 32E
52 Kefar Sava 32 11N 34 54E
44 Keflavík 64 2N 22 35W
36 Keighley 53 52N 1 54W
54 Kelkit Cayi, R. 40 46N 36 32E
24 Kelowna 49 54N 119 29W
*18 Kelso 46 9N 122 54W
25 Kelvington 52 10N 103 32W
48 Kemerovo 55 20N 85 50E
44 Kemi 65 44N 24 34E
22 Kemptville 45 1N 75 38W
17 Kendallville 41 27N 85 16W
59 Kendari 3 50S 122 30E
*20 Kendi 60 20N 151 0W
64 Kenitra 34 15N 6 40W
12 Kennewick 46 11N 119 2W
20 Keno Hill 63 55N 135 18W
25 Kenora 49 50N 94 35W
17 Kenosha 42 33N 87 48W
14 Kent, Ohio 41 9N 81 22W
*18 Kent, Oregon. 47 23N 122 14W
17 Kenton 40 39N 83 36W
8 Kentucky, R. 38 41N 85 11W
8 Kentucky □ 37 30N 85 15W
23 Kentville 45 6N 64 29W
66 Kenya ■ 2 20N 38 0E
66 Kenya, mt. 0 10S 37 18E
16 Keokuk 40 24N 91 24W
*56 Kerala □ 11 0N 76 15E
55 Keray 26 15N 57 30E
47 Kerch 45 20N 36 20E
68 Kerguelen, I. 48 30S 69 40E
41 Kérkira 39 38N 19 50E
41 Kékira, I. 39 40N 19 42E
37 Kerkrade 50 53N 6 4E
*72 Kermadec, Is. 31 8S 175 16W
55 Kerman, Iran 30 15N 57 1E
18 Kerman, U.S.A. 36 43N 120 4W
54 Kermanshah 34 23N 47 0E
25 Kerrobert 51 55N 109 8W
61 Kerulen, R. 48 0N 114 0E
24 Ketchikan 55 21N 131 35W
17 Kettering 39 41N 84 10W
18 Kettleman City 36 6N 119 58W
16 Kewanee 41 14N 89 56W
28 Key West 24 40N 82 0W
15 Keyport 40 26N 74 12W
49 Khabarovsk 48 20N 135 0E
56 Khairpur 27 32N 68 49E
55 Khalj-e-Fars □ 28 20N 51 45E
41 Khalkís 38 27N 23 42E
52 Khan Yunis 31 21N 34 18E
55 Khanabad 36 45N 69 5E
54 Khanaqin 34 23N 45 25E
57 Kharagpur 22 20N 87 25E
54 Kharg.I. 29 15N 50 28E
47 Kharkov 49 58N 36 20E
53 Kharsaniya 27 10N 49 10E
65 Khartoum=El Khartûm 15 31N 32 35E
55 Khash 28 15N 61 5E
49 Khatanga 72 0N 102 20E
54 Khavar □ 37 20N 46 0E
47 Kherson 46 35N 32 35E
41 Khíos, I. 38 27N 26 9E
47 Khmelnitskiy 49 23N 27 0E
55 Khojak Pass 30 54N 66 29E
55 Khorasan □ 34 0N 58 0E
58 Khorat=Nakhon Ratchasima 14 59N 102 12E
54 Khorromshahr 30 29N 48 15E
61 Khotan=Hotien 37 6N 79 59E
57 Khulna □ 22 45N 89 34E
54 Khuzestan □ 31 0N 50 0E
55 Khvaf 34 33N 60 8E
55 Khvor 33 45N 55 0E
54 Khvoy 38 35N 45 0E
55 Khyber Pass 34 10N 71 8E
61 Kiamusze 46 45N 130 30E
61 Kian 27 1N 114 58E
61 Kiangsi □ 27 20N 115 40E
61 Kiangsu □ 33 0N 119 50E
66 Kibombo 3 57S 25 53E
24 Kicking Horse Pass 51 27N 116 25W
42 Kiel 54 16N 10 8E
43 Kielce 50 58N 20 42E
42 Kieler Bucht 54 30N 10 30E
47 Kiev=Kiyev 50 28N 30 29E
66 Kigoma-Ujiji 4 50S 26 47E
60 Kii-Sanchi 33 40N 135 0E
60 Kii-Suido 33 40N 135 0E
41 Kikládhes, Is. 37 20N 24 30E
*6 Kilauea Crater 19 24N 155 17W
66 Kilimanjaro, Mt. 3 7S 37 20E
25 Killarney, Canada. 49 11N 99 40W
36 Killarney, Eire 52 2N 9 30W
36 Kilmarnock 55 36N 4 30W
24 Kimberley, Canada 49 41N 115 59W
67 Kimberley, S.Africa 28 43S 24 46E
70 Kimberley, reg. 16 20S 127 0E
46 Kimry 56 55N 37 15E
58 Kinabalu, mt. 6 0N 116 0E
36 Kincardine 56 56N 2 28W
25 Kindersley 51 28N 109 10W
46 Kineshma 57 30N 42 5E
*71 King, I. 39 40S 144 0E
18 King City 36 13N 121 8W
21 King George Is. 57 20N 78 25W
71 Kingaroy 26 32S 151 51E
19 Kingman 35 12N 114 4W
18 Kings Canyon Nat.Park 36 48N 118 30W
36 King's Lynn 52 45N 0 25E
15 Kings Park 40 53N 73 16W
12 King's Pk. 40 46N 110 27W
18 Kingsbury 36 31N 119 33W
22 Kingston, Canada 44 20N 76 30W
28 Kingston, Jamaica 18 0N 76 50W
15 Kingston, N.Y. 41 55N 74 0W
15 Kingston, Pa. 41 16N 75 54W
29 Kingstown 13 10N 61 10W
22 Kingsville 27 30N 97 53W
61 Kingtehchen 29 8N 117 21E
22 Kinkardine 44 12N 81 36W
60 Kinki 33 30N 136 0E
52 Kinneret 32 44N 35 34E
66 Kinshasa 4 20S 15 15E
9 Kinston 35 18N 77 35W
49 Kirensk 57 50N 107 55E
48 Kirgiz S.S.R. □ 42 0N 75 0E
47 Kirgiziya Steppe 50 0N 55 0E
54 Kirikkale 39 50N 33 31E
61 Kirin 43 51N 126 33E
36 Kirkcaldy 56 7N 3 10W
22 Kirkland Lake 48 15N 80 0W
16 Kirksville 40 12N 92 35W
54 Kirkuk 35 30N 44 21E
16 Kirkwood 38 35N 90 24W
46 Kirov 58 35N 49 40E
47 Kirovabad 40 45N 46 10E
47 Kirovakan 41 0N 44 0E
47 Kirovograd 48 35N 32 20E
44 Kiruna 67 52N 20 15E
59 Kiruru 3 55S 134 55E
60 Kiryu 36 25N 139 20E
66 Kisangani 0 41N 25 11E
48 Kiselevsk 54 5N 86 6E
47 Kishinev 47 0N 28 50E
60 Kishiwada 34 50N 135 25E
60 Kiso-Gawa 35 20N 137 0E
60 Kiso-Sammyaku 35 43N 137 50E
66 Kisumu 0 3S 34 45E
60 Kitaibaraki 36 50N 140 45E
60 Kitakami-Gawa 39 30N 141 15E
60 Kitakyushu 33 50N 130 50E
66 Kitale 1 0N 35 12E
22 Kitchener 43 30N 80 30W
66 Kitega 3 30S 29 58E
24 Kitimat 53 55N 129 0W
67 Kitwe 12 54S 28 7E
66 Kivu, L. 1 48S 29 0E
47 Kiyev 50 28N 30 29E
47 Kiyevskoye Vdkhr 50 35N 30 29E
46 Kizel 59 0N 57 0E
42 Kladno 50 10N 14 7E
42 Klagenfurt 46 38N 14 20E
46 Klaipeda 55 43N 21 10E
12 Klamath Falls 42 40N 121 50W
12 Klamath Mts. 41 20N 123 0W
24 Klawak 55 35N 133 0W
67 Klerksdorp 26 51S 26 38E
37 Kleve 51 46N 6 10E
20 Klondike 64 0N 139 40W
49 Klyuchevsk, Mt. 55 50N 160 30E
37 Knokke 51 20N 3 17E
16 Knoxville, Iowa 41 19N 93 6W
9 Knoxville, Tenn. 35 58N 83 57W
21 Koartok 61 2N 69 37W
60 Kobe 34 45N 135 10E
45 Kobenhavn 55 41N 12 34E
42 Koblenz 50 21N 7 36E
60 Kochi 33 30N 133 35E
*20 Kodiak 57 48N 152 23W
*20 Kodiak, I. 57 30N 152 45W
60 Kofu 35 40N 138 30E
56 Kohat 33 40N 71 29E
55 Koh-i-Baba, mts. 34 30N 67 0E

Kohima **Linz**

57	Kohima	25 35N	94 10E
48	Kokand	41 0N	71 10E
61	Kokiu	23 30N	103 0E
44	Kokkola	63 50N	23 8E
61	Koko Nor	37 0N	100 0E
17	Kokomo	40 30N	86 6W
***56**	Kolar	13 12N	78 15E
***56**	Kolar Goldfields	12 58N	78 16E
41	Kolarovgrad	43 27N	26 42E
45	Kolding	55 30N	9 29E
56	Kolhapur	16 43N	74 15E
37	Köln	50 56N	9 58E
46	Kolomna	55 8N	38 45E
46	Kolskiy Poluostrov	67 30N	38 0E
66	Kolwezi	10 40S	25 25E
49	Kolyma, R.	64 40N	153 0E
46	Komi A.S.S.R. □	64 0N	55 0E
58	Kompong Cham	11 54N	105 30E
58	Kompong Som	11 3N	103 41E
49	Komsomolets, Ostrov	80 30N	95 0E
49	Komsomolsk	50 30N	157 0E
46	Königsberg= Kaliningrad	54 42N	20 32E
54	Konya	37 52N	32 35E
48	Kopeysk	54 55N	61 31E
45	Köping	59 31N	16 0E
41	Körab, mt.	41 44N	20 40E
40	Korcula, I.	42 57N	17 8E
54	Kordestan, reg.	37 30N	42 0E
54	Kordestan □	36 0N	47 0E
61	Korea B.	39 0N	124 0E
61	Korea Str.	34 0N	129 30E
41	Korinthiakós Kólpos	38 16N	22 30E
41	Kórinthos	37 56N	22 55E
60	Koriyama	37 25N	140 20E
***72**	Koro Sea	18 0S	180 0E
45	Korsor	55 20N	11 9E
37	Kortrijk	50 50N	3 17E
49	Koryakskiy Khrebet	61 0N	171 0E
71	Kosciusko, Mt.	36 27S	148 16E
43	Kosice	48 42N	21 15E
65	Kôstı	13 8N	32 43E
46	Kostroma	57 50N	41 58E
42	Koszalin	54 10N	16 10E
56	Kota	25 14N	75 49E
58	Kota Baharu	6 7N	102 14E
58	Kota Kinabalu	6 0N	116 12E
58	Kotabaru	3 20S	116 20E
45	Kotka	60 28N	26 58E
45	Kotlas	61 15N	47 0E
56	Kotri	25 22N	68 22E
49	Kotuy, R.	71 55N	102 5E
66	Kouilou	4 10S	12 5E
66	Kousseri	12 0N	14 55E
46	Kovrov	56 25N	41 25E
61	Kowloon	22 20N	114 15E
***20**	Koyukuk, R.	64 56N	157 30W
***56**	Kozhikode=Calicut	11 16N	75 48E
58	Kra, Kho Khot, pen.	10 15N	99 30E
41	Kragujevac	44 2N	20 56E
43	Kraków	50 4N	19 57E
41	Kraljevo	43 44N	20 41E
47	Kramatorsk	48 50N	37 30E
47	Krasnodar	45 5N	38 50E
46	Krasnoturinsk	59 39N	60 1E
47	Krasnovodsk	40 0N	52 52E
49	Krasnoyarsk	56 8N	93 0E
37	Krefeld	51 20N	6 22E
47	Kremenchug	49 5N	33 25E
47	Kremenchugskoye Vdkhr.	49 30N	34 25E
57	Krishnanagar	23 24N	88 33E
45	Kristiansand	58 9N	8 1E
45	Kristianstad	56 2N	14 9E
44	Kristiansund	63 7N	7 45E
45	Kristinehamn	59 18N	14 13E
41	Kriti, I.	35 15N	25 0E
47	Krivoy Rog	47 51N	33 20E
40	Krk, I.	45 5N	14 36E
46	Kronshtadt	60 5N	29 35E
67	Krugersdorp	26 5S	27 46E
58	Krung Thep	13 45N	100 35E
24	Kruzof I.	57 10N	135 40W
47	Krymskiy Poluostrov	45 0N	34 0E
58	Kuala Lumpur	3 9N	101 41E
58	Kualakapuas	2 55S	114 20E
61	Kucha	41 50N	82 30E
54	Kudha-ye Zagros, mts.	33 45N	47 0E
55	Kuhak	27 12N	63 10E
55	Kuh-e Aliju, mt.	31 30N	51 41E
55	Kuh-e Binalud, mts.	36 50N	59 0E
55	Kuh-e Dinar, mts.	30 48N	51 40E
55	Kuh-e Hazaran, mt.	29 35N	57 20E
55	Kuh-e Taftan, mt.	28 40N	61 0E
55	Kuhha-ye Bashakerd, mts.	26 45N	59 0E
24	Kuiu I.	57 45N	134 10W
60	Kumagaya	36 8N	139 23E
60	Kumamoto	32 45N	130 45E
64	Kumasi	6 41N	1 38W
66	Kumba	4 36N	9 24E
55	Kunar □	35 0N	71 0E
55	Kunduz	36 50N	68 50E
46	Kungur	57 20N	56 40E
61	Kunlun Shan	36 0N	86 30E
61	Kunming	25 11N	102 37E
44	Kuopio	62 53N	27 35E
59	Kupang	10 19S	123 39E
24	Kupreanof I.	56 50N	133 30W
60	Kurashiki	34 40N	133 50E
60	Kure	34 14N	132 32E
48	Kurgan	55 30N	65 0E
49	Kurilskiye Ostrova	45 0N	150 0E
56	Kurnool	15 45N	78 0E
46	Kursk	51 42N	36 11E
60	Kurume	33 15N	130 30E
60	Kushiro	43 0N	144 30E
***20**	Kuskokwim, B.	59 45N	162 25W
***20**	Kuskokwim, R.	60 17N	162 27W
48	Kustanai	53 20N	63 45E
54	Kutahya	39 25N	29 59E
47	Kutaisi	42 19N	42 40E
58	Kutaradja= Banda Atjeh	5 35N	95 20E
56	Kutch, G.of	22 50N	69 15E
56	Kutch, Rann of	24 0N	70 0E
53	Kuwait ■	29 30N	47 30E
46	Kuybyshev	53 10N	50 15E
46	Kuybyshevskoye Vdkhr.	55 2N	49 30E
67	Kwando, R.	18 27S	23 32E
61	Kwangchow	23 10N	113 10E
61	Kwangju	35 10N	126 45E
61	Kwangsi-Chuang □	23 30N	108 55E
61	Kwangtung □	23 35N	114 0E
61	Kweichow □	26 40N	107 0E
61	Kweilin	25 16N	110 15E
61	Kweiyang	26 30N	106 35E
***20**	Kwiguk	62 45N	164 28W
70	Kwinana	32 15S	115 47E
66	Kyoga, L.	1 35N	33 0E
60	Kyoto	35 0N	135 45E
60	Kyushu, I.	32 30N	131 0E
48	Kyzyl Kum, Peski	42 0N	65 0E
48	Kzyl Orda	44 50N	65 10E

L

40	L'Aquila	42 21N	13 24E
39	La Alcarria, reg.	40 25N	2 0W
26	La Barca	20 20N	102 40W
28	La Ceiba	15 40N	86 50W
39	La Coruña	43 20N	8 25W
10	La Crosse	43 48N	91 13W
8	La Fayette	40 22N	86 52W
9	La Grange	33 4N	85 0W
28	La Habana	23 8N	82 22W
39	La Línea de la Concepción	36 15N	5 23W
25	La Loche	56 29N	109 26W
37	La Louvière	50 27N	4 10E
23	La Malbaie	47 39N	70 9W
39	La Mancha, reg.	39 10N	2 54W
19	La Mesa	32 48N	117 5W
29	Le Moule	16 20N	61 22W
30	La Oroya	11 35S	75 52W
24	La Palma, I.	28 45N	17 50W
30	La Paz, Bolivia	16 20S	68 10W
26	La Paz, Mexico	24 10N	110 40W
23	La Pérade	46 38N	72 10W
26	La Piedad	20 20N	102 1W
32	La Plata	35 0S	57 55W
17	La Porte	41 40N	86 40W
16	La Porte City	42 19N	92 12W
32	La Rioja	29 20S	67 0W
39	La Rioja, reg.	29 30S	67 0W
38	La Rochelle	46 10N	1 9W
28	La Romana	18 27N	68 57W
16	La Salle	41 20N	89 6W
22	La Sarre	48 48N	79 12W
18	La Selva Beach	36 55N	121 51W
32	La Serena	29 55S	71 10W
40	La Spézia	44 8N	9 50E
22	La Tuque	47 26N	72 47W
22	La Vega	19 20N	70 30W
23	Labrador, reg.	54 0N	62 0W
23	Labrador City	52 57N	66 55W
59	Labuha	0 30S	127 30E
24	Lac la Biche	54 46N	111 58W
51	Laccadive Is.= Lakshadweep Is.	10 0N	72 30E
***18**	Lacey	47 7N	122 49W
22	Lachine	45 30N	73 40W
22	Lachute	45 38N	74 20W
8	Lackawanna	42 49N	78 50W
24	Lacombe	52 28N	113 44W
15	Laconia	43 31N	71 29W
46	Ladozhskoye Ozero	61 15N	30 30E
24	Ladysmith	48 59N	123 49W
68	Lae	6 48N	146 53E
17	Lafayette, Ind.	40 25N	86 53W
11	Lafayette, La.	30 18N	92 0W
45	Lagen, R.	59 3N	10 5E
55	Laghman □	35 0N	70 15E
64	Lagos, Nigeria	6 25N	3 27E
39	Lagos, Portugal	37 5N	8 41W
26	Lagos de Moreno	21 21N	101 55W
19	Laguna Beach	33 33N	117 51W
***6**	Lahaina	20 52N	156 41W
56	Lahore	31 32N	74 22E
45	Lahti	60 59N	25 45E
32	Lajes	27 48S	50 20W
11	Lake Charles	30 10N	93 10W
17	Lake Forest	42 15N	87 50W
15	Lake Placid	44 17N	73 59W
9	Lake Worth	26 36N	80 3W
22	Lakefield	44 25N	78 16W
9	Lakeland	28 0N	82 0W
19	Lakeside	32 52N	116 55W
19	Lakewood, Calif.	33 50N	118 8W
15	Lakewood, N.J.	40 6N	74 13W
14	Lakewood, Ohio	41 28N	81 50W
***18**	Lakewood, Wash.	48 9N	122 12W
51	Lakshadweep, Is.	10 0N	72 30E
19	Lama Linda	34 4N	117 17W
10	Lamar	38 9N	102 35W
11	Lamesa	32 45N	101 57E
66	Lambaréné	0 20S	10 12E
59	Lamitan	6 40N	122 10E
19	Lamont	35 15N	118 55W
40	Lampedusa, I.	35 36N	12 40E
6	Lanai I.	20 50N	156 55W
19	Lancaster, Calif.	34 42N	118 8W
14	Lancaster, N.Y.	42 54N	78 40W
15	Lancaster, Pa.	40 2N	76 19W
21	Lancaster Sd.	74 0N	84 0W
61	Lanchow	36 4N	103 44E
42	Landeck	47 9N	10 34E
38	Landes, reg.	44 20N	1 0W
38	Landes □	43 57N	0 48W
56	Landi Kotal	34 7N	71 6E
45	Landskrona	56 55N	12 57E
23	Langlade	46 55N	56 20W
38	Langres, Plateau de	47 45N	5 20E
38	Languedoc, reg.	43 58N	3 22E
15	Lansdale	40 15N	75 17W
17	Lansing	42 47N	84 32W
64	Lanzarote, I.	29 0N	13 40W
59	Laoag	18 7N	120 34E
58	Laos ■	17 45N	105 0E
44	Lappland, reg.	68 7N	24 0E
49	Laptev Sea	76 0N	125 0E
40	L'Aquila	42 21N	13 24E
12	Laramie	41 15N	105 29W
10	Laramie Mts.	42 0N	105 30W
22	Larder Lake	48 5N	79 43W
11	Laredo	27 34N	99 29W
41	Lárisa	39 38N	22 28E
56	Larkana	27 32N	68 2E
13	Las Cruces	32 25N	106 50W
64	Las Palmas	28 10N	15 28W
19	Las Vegas, Nev.	36 10N	115 5W
13	Las Vegas, N.Mex.	35 35N	105 10W
57	Lashio	23 0N	98 0E
30	Latacunga	0 50S	78 35W
22	Latchford	47 20N	79 50W
14	Latrobe	40 19N	79 23W
52	Latrun	31 50N	34 58E
46	Latvian S.S.R. □	56 45N	24 30E
***72**	Lau(Eastern) Group, Is.	18 0S	179 0W
42	Lauchhammer	51 30N	13 47E
70	Laughlen, Mt.	23 23S	134 23E
***71**	Launceston	41 24S	147 8E
11	Laurel	31 50N	89 0W
42	Lausanne	46 32N	6 38E
59	Laut, Pulau	3 40S	116 10E
23	Lauzon	46 48N	71 4W
52	Lavi	32 47N	35 25E
17	Lawrence, Ind.	39 50N	86 2W
10	Lawrence, Kans.	38 58N	95 14W
15	Lawrence, Mass.	42 42N	71 9W
17	Lawrenceburg	39 6N	84 51W
17	Lawrenceville	38 44N	87 41W
11	Lawton	34 33N	98 25W
40	Lazio □	42 0N	12 30E
38	Le Creusot	46 50N	4 24E
38	Le Havre	49 30N	0 5E
38	Le Mans	48 0N	0 10E
10	Le Mars	43 0N	96 0W
38	Le Puy	45 3N	3 52E
38	Le Tréport	50 3N	1 20E
10	Lead	44 20N	103 40W
25	Leader	50 53N	109 33W
22	Leamington	42 10N	82 30W
14	Leavenworth	39 25N	95 0W
16	Leawood	37 3N	94 31W
54	Lebanon ■	34 0N	36 0E
17	Lebanon, Ind.	40 3N	86 28W
15	Lebanon, Pa.	40 20N	76 25W
16	Lebanon, Mo.	37 41N	92 40W
17	Lebanon, Ohio	39 26N	84 13W
12	Lebanon, Oreg.	44 31N	122 57W
41	Lecce	40 20N	18 10E
42	Lech, R.	48 44N	10 56E
24	Leduc	53 16N	113 33W
36	Leeds	53 48N	1 34W
16	Lee's Summit	38 55N	94 23W
37	Leeuwarden	53 15N	5 48E
70	Leeuwin, C.	34 20S	115 9E
29	Leeward Is.	16 30N	63 30W
40	Leghorn=Livorno	43 32N	10 18E
42	Legnica	51 12N	16 10E
36	Leicester	52 40N	1 10W
37	Leiden	52 9N	4 30E
37	Leie, R.	51 3N	3 43E
71	Leigh Creek	30 28S	138 24E
42	Leipzig	51 20N	12 23E
36	Leith	55 59N	3 12W
37	Lek, R.	52 0N	6 0E
42	Léman, L.	46 26N	6 30E
16	Lemay	38 32N	90 17W
19	Lemon Grove	32 44N	117 2W
49	Lena, R.	72 25N	126 40E
48	Leninabad	40 10N	69 40E
47	Leninakan	41 0N	42 50E
46	Leningrad	59 55N	30 20E
48	Leninsk Kuznetskiy	55 10N	86 10E
38	Lens	50 26N	2 50E
49	Lensk	60 48N	114 55E
19	Lenwood	34 53N	117 7W
15	Leominster	42 32N	71 45W
26	León, Mexico	21 7N	101 30W
28	León, Nicaragua	12 20N	86 51W
39	León, Spain	42 38N	5 34W
66	Léopold II.L= Mai-Ndombe, L.	2 0S	18 0E
66	Léopoldville=Kinshasa	4 20S	15 15E
39	Lerida	41 37N	0 39E
38	Les Sables d'Olonne	46 30N	1 45W
67	Lesotho ■	29 40S	28 0E
29	Lesser Antilles, Is.	12 30N	61 0W
24	Lesser Slave L.	55 25N	115 25W
59	Lesser Sunda Is.	7 30S	117 0E
***18**	Lester	47 12N	121 29W
25	Lestock	51 25N	104 0W
41	Lésvos, I.	39 0N	26 20E
24	Lethbridge	49 45N	112 45W
19	Leucadia	33 4N	117 18W
37	Leuven	50 52N	4 42E
40	Levante, Riviera di, reg.	44 10N	9 37E
37	Leverkusen	51 2N	6 50E
23	Lévis	46 48N	71 9W
15	Levittown, N.Y.	40 41N	73 31W
15	Levittown, Pa.	40 9N	74 50W
54	Levkôsia	35 11N	33 21E
36	Lewis, I.	58 10N	6 40W
12	Lewis Ra.	48 30N	113 15W
17	Lewisburg	39 51N	84 33W
23	Lewisporte	49 15N	55 3W
12	Lewiston, Idaho	46 25N	117 1W
***9**	Lewiston, Maine	44 6N	70 13W
14	Lewistown	40 36N	77 31W
17	Lexington, Ky.	38 6N	84 30W
10	Lexington, Nebr.	40 48N	99 45W
59	Leyte, I.	11 0N	125 0E
61	Lhasa	29 50N	91 3E
61	Liaoning □	41 40N	122 30E
61	Liaotung Wan	40 0N	120 45E
61	Liaoyang	41 15N	123 10E
61	Liaoyuan	42 59N	125 8E
41	Liard, R.	61 51N	121 18W
64	Liberia ■	10 40N	85 30W
16	Liberty	39 15N	94 25W
17	Libertyville	42 17N	87 57W
66	Libreville	0 25N	9 26E
65	Libya ■	28 30N	17 30E
45	Lidköping	58 31N	13 14E
42	Liechtenstein ■	47 10N	9 35E
46	Liepaja	56 31N	21 1E
40	Liguria □	44 30N	8 50E
40	Ligurian Sea	43 20N	9 0E
71	Lihou Reef & Cays	17 25S	151 40E
66	Likasi	10 55S	26 48E
38	Lille	50 38N	3 3E
38	Lille Bælt, Str.	55 30N	9 45E
45	Lillehammer	61 8N	10 30E
67	Lilongwe	14 0S	33 48E
30	Lima, Peru	12 0S	77 0W
17	Lima, U.S.A.	40 42N	84 5W
37	Limburg □	51 20N	5 55E
36	Limerick	52 40N	8 38W
41	Limnos, I.	39 50N	25 5E
38	Limoges	45 50N	1 15E
28	Limón	10 0N	83 2W
35	Limousin, reg.	46 0N	1 0E
67	Limpopo, R.	25 15S	33 30E
27	Linares, Mexico	24 50N	99 40W
39	Linares, Spain	38 10N	3 40W
36	Lincoln, U.K.	53 14N	0 32W
18	Lincoln, Calif.	38 54N	121 17W
16	Lincoln, Ill.	40 9N	89 22W
***9**	Lincoln, Me.	45 22N	68 30W
10	Lincoln, Nebr.	40 50N	96 42W
23	Lindsay, Canada	44 21N	78 44W
18	Lindsay, U.S.A.	36 12N	119 5W
45	Linköping	58 28N	15 36E
42	Linz	48 18N	14 18E

Map	Place	Lat.	Long.
46	Lipetsk	52 45N	39 35E
37	Lippe,R.	51 39N	6 11E
37	Lippstadt	51 40N	8 19E
39	Lisboa	38 42N	9 10W
39	Lisbon=Lisboa	38 42N	9 10W
*20	Lisburne, C.	68 52N	166 14W
71	Lismore	28 44S	153 21E
22	Listowel	44 44N	80 58W
16	Litchfield	39 11N	89 39W
71	Lithgow	33 25S	150 8E
46	Lithuanian S.S.R. □	55 30N	24 0E
72	Little Barrier I.	36 12S	175 8E
12	Little Belt Mts.	46 50N	111 0W
22	Little Current	45 58N	81 56W
13	Little Colorado, R.	36 11N	111 48W
10	Little Missouri, R.	47 30N	102 25W
11	Little Rock	34 41N	92 10W
17	Little Wabash, R.	37 54N	88 5W
61	Liuchow	24 10N	109 10E
18	Livermore	37 41N	121 46W
23	Liverpool, Canada	44 5N	64 41W
36	Liverpool, U.K.	53 25N	3 0W
36	Liverpool B.	70 0N	128 0W
18	Livingston, Calif.	37 23N	120 43W
12	Livingston, Mont.	45 40N	110 40W
67	Livingstone	17 56S	25 45E
17	Livonia	42 25N	83 23W
40	Livorno	43 32N	10 18E
36	Lizard Pt.	49 57N	5 11W
40	Ljubljana	46 4N	14 33E
36	Llandudno	53 19N	3 51W
30	Llanos, reg.	3 25N	71 35W
25	Lloydminster	53 17N	110 0W
32	Llullaillaco, mt.	39 29N	2 53E
67	Lobito	12 18S	13 35E
42	Locarno	46 10N	8 47E
14	Lock Haven	41 8N	77 27W
23	Lockeport	43 42N	65 7W
17	Lockport, Ill.	41 36N	88 3W
14	Lockport, N.Y.	43 12N	78 42W
52	Lod	31 57N	34 54E
18	Lodi	38 8N	121 16W
43	Lódź	51 45N	19 27E
44	Lofoten, Is.	68 20N	14 0E
12	Logan	41 44N	111 50W
20	Logan, Mt.	60 40N	140 0W
17	Logansport	40 40N	86 20W
55	Logar □	33 50N	69 0E
65	Logone, R.	12 6N	15 2E
39	Logroño	42 28N	2 32W
38	Loir, R.	47 33N	0 32W
38	Loire, R.	47 16N	2 11W
38	Loire □	45 40N	4 5E
38	Loire-Atlantique □	47 25N	1 40W
38	Loiret □	47 58N	2 10E
38	Loir-et-Cher □	47 40N	1 20E
37	Lokeren	51 6N	3 59E
66	Lomami, R.	0 46N	24 16E
17	Lombard	41 53N	88 1W
40	Lombardia □	45 35N	9 45E
58	Lombok, I.	8 35S	116 20E
64	Lomé	6 9N	1 20E
66	Lomela, R.	0 14S	20 42E
36	Lomond, L.	58 8N	4 38W
19	Lompoc	34 35N	120 27W
43	Lomza	53 10N	22 2E
22	London, Canada	43 0N	81 15W
36	London, U.K.	51 30N	0 5W
36	Londonderry	55 0N	7 20W
32	Londrina	23 0S	51 10W
19	Long Beach, Calif.	33 46N	118 12W
15	Long Beach, N.Y.	40 35N	73 41W
15	Long Branch	40 18N	74 0W
29	Long I., Bahamas	23 20N	75 10W
15	Long I.U.S.A.	40 50N	73 20W
15	Long Island Sd.	41 5N	72 58W
23	Long Range Mts.	50 0N	57 0W
71	Longreach	23 28S	144 14E
12	Longs Pk.	40 20N	105 50W
11	Longview, Tex.	32 30N	94 45W
*18	Longview, Wash.	46 9N	122 58W
61	Lop Nor	40 20N	90 15E
44	Lopphavet, sea	70 12N	22 30E
14	Lorain	41 20N	82 5W
39	Lorca	37 41N	1 42W
54	Lorestan □	33 30N	48 30E
38	Lorient	47 45N	3 23W
27	Linares, Mexico	24 50N	99 40W
39	Linares, Spain	38 10N	3 40W
36	Lincoln, U.K.	53 14N	0 32W
18	Lincoln, Calif.	38 54N	121 17W
16	Lincoln, Ill.	40 9N	89 22W
*9	Lincoln, Me.	45 22N	68 30W
10	Lincoln, Nebr.	40 50N	96 42W
64	Lindi	10 0S	39 35E
23	Lindsay, Canada	44 21N	78 44W
18	Lindsay, U.S.A.	36 12N	119 5W
45	Linköping	58 28N	15 36E
61	Linsia	35 50N	103 0E
17	Linton	39 2N	87 10W
42	Linz	48 18N	14 18E
40	Lipari, I.	38 40N	15 0E
38	Lorraine	49 0N	6 0E
13	Los Alamos	35 57N	106 17W
18	Los Altos	37 23N	122 6W
19	Los Angeles	34 0N	118 10W
19	Los Angeles Aqueduct	35 22N	118 5W
18	Los Banos	37 4N	120 51W
18	Los Gatos	37 14N	121 59W
26	Los Mochis	25 45N	109 5W
38	Lot, R.	44 18N	0 20E
38	Lot □	44 39N	1 40E
32	Lota	37 5S	73 10W
66	Lotagipi Swamp	4 55N	35 0E
38	Lot-et-Garonne □	44 22N	0 30E
67	Louis Trichardt	23 0S	29 55E
23	Louisburg	45 55N	59 58W
22	Louisville	46 15N	72 57W
68	Louisiade Arch.	11 0S	153 0E
11	Louisiana □	30 50N	92 0W
17	Louisville, Ky.	38 15N	85 45W
14	Louisville, Ohio	40 50N	81 16W
39	Loulé	37 9N	8 0W
38	Lourdes	43 6N	0 3W
67	Lourenço Marques =Maputo	25 58S	32 32E
17	Loveland	39 16N	84 16W
15	Lowell	42 38N	71 19W
72	Lower Hutt	41 10S	174 55E
10	Lower Red.L.	48 0N	94 50W
15	Lowville	43 47N	75 29W
68	Loyalty Is.	21 0S	167 30E
61	Loyang	34 40N	112 28E
14	Lozère □	44 28N	3 34E
66	Lualaba, R.	0 26N	25 20E
66	Luanda	8 58S	13 9E
61	Luang Prabang	19 45N	102 10E
67	Luangwa, R.	15 40N	30 25E
67	Luanshya	13 3S	28 28E
66	Luapula, R.	9 26S	28 33E
52	Lubban	32 9N	35 14E
11	Lubbock	33 40N	102 0W
8	Lübeck	53 52N	10 41E
43	Lublin	51 12N	22 38E
67	Lubumbashi	11 32S	27 28E
40	Lucca	43 50N	10 30E
61	Luchow	29 2N	105 10E
57	Lucknow	26 50N	81 0E
37	Lüdenscheid	51 13N	7 37E
67	Luderitz	26 41S	15 8E
56	Ludhiana	30 57N	75 56E
8	Ludington	43 58N	86 27W
19	Ludlow	34 43N	116 10W
42	Ludwigsburg	48 53N	9 11E
42	Ludwigshafen	49 27N	8 27E
66	Lufira, R.	8 16S	26 27E
11	Lufkin	31 25N	94 40W
46	Luga	58 40N	29 55E
42	Lugano	46 0N	8 57E
47	Lugansk= Voroshilovgrad	48 38N	39 15E
39	Lugo	43 2N	7 35W
67	Lukanga Swamp	14 30S	27 40E
66	Lukenie, R.	2 44S	18 9E
44	Lule älv	65 35N	22 3E
44	Lulea	65 35N	22 10E
66	Lulonga, R.	0 43N	18 23E
66	Lulua, R.	5 2S	21 7E
66	Luluabourg=Kananga	5 55S	22 18E
72	Lumsden	45 44S	168 27E
45	Lund	55 42N	13 11E
23	Lunenburg	44 30N	64 30W
42	Lüneburger Heide, dist.	53 0N	10 0E
38	Luneville	48 36N	6 30E
67	Lusaka	15 28S	28 16E
61	Lu-ta	58 37N	28 40E
36	Luton	51 53N	0 24W
37	Luxembourg ■	50 0N	6 0E
37	Luxembourg	49 37N	6 9E
65	Luxor=El Uqsur	25 41N	32 38E
42	Luzern	47 3N	8 18E
59	Luzon, I.	16 30N	121 30E
47	Lvov	49 40N	24 0E
49	Lyakhovskiye Ostrova	73 0N	142 0E
56	Lyallpur	31 30N	73 5E
44	Lycksele	64 38N	18 40E
52	Lydda=Lod	31 57N	34 54E
8	Lynchburg	37 23N	79 10W
15	Lynn	42 28N	70 57W
25	Lynn Lake	56 30N	101 40W
*18	Lynnwood	47 49N	122 19W
38	Lyon	45 46N	4 50E
70	Lyons, R.	25 2S	115 9E
15	Lyons Falls	43 37N	75 22W
46	Lysva	58 7N	57 47N
72	Lyttelton	43 35S	172 44E

M

Map	Place	Lat.	Long.
54	Ma'an	30 12N	35 44E
37	Maas, R.	51 49N	5 1E
37	Maastricht	50 50N	5 40E
31	Macapá	0 0N	51 10W
70	McArthur, R.	15 54S	136 40E
61	Macau □	5 0S	36 40W
25	McClintock	57 45N	94 15W
16	M'Clintock	60 31N	134 33W
20	M'Clintock Chan.	71 0N	103 0W
11	McComb	31 20N	90 30W
10	McCook	40 15N	100 35W
70	Macdonald, L.	23 30S	129 0E
70	Macdonnell Ranges	23 40S	133 0E
31	Maceió	9 40S	35 41W
71	Macfarlane, L.	31 55S	136 42E
25	Macgregor	49 58N	98 46W
66	Machakos	1 30E	37 15E
30	Machala	3 10S	79 50W
71	Machattie, L.	24 50S	139 48E
57	Machilipatnam	16 12N	81 12E
66	Macias Nguema Biyoga, I.	3 30N	8 42E
71	Macintyre, R.,	28 38S	150 47E
71	Mackay	43 58N	113 37W
70	Mackay, L.	22 40S	128 35E
14	McKees Rocks	40 28N	80 10W
14	McKeesport	40 21N	79 50W
20	Mackenzie, R., Canada	69 15N	134 8W
66	Mackenzie, R., U.S.A.	36 10N	88 31W
20	Mackenzie □	65 0N	115 0W
20	Mackenzie Mts.	64 0N	128 0W
*20	McKinley, Mt.	63 10N	151 30W
24	McLennan	55 42N	116 50W
12	McMinnville	45 16N	123 11W
25	McMorran	51 19N	108 42W
25	McMurray	56 45N	111 27W
16	Macomb	40 27N	90 40W
38	Mâcon, France	46 19N	4 50E
9	Macon, U.S.A.	33 7N	88 31W
10	McPherson	38 25N	97 40W
*72	Macquarie, I.	54 29S	158 58E
71	Macquarie, R.	30 7S	147 24E
71	Macquarie Harbour	42 18S	145 25E
*67	Madagascar ■	20 0S	47 0E
68	Madang	5 0S	145 46E
17	Madeira	39 11N	84 22W
30	Madeira, R.	3 22S	58 45W
64	Madeira Is.	32 50N	17 0W
18	Madera	37 0N	120 1W
56	Madhya Pradesh □	21 50N	81 0E
53	Madinat al Shaab	12 50N	45 0E
17	Madison, Ind.	38 44N	85 23W
10	Madison, S.D.	44 0N	97 8W
16	Madison, Wis.	43 5N	89 22W
8	Madisonville	37 42N	87 30W
59	Madjene	3 27S	118 57E
*56	Madras	13 8N	80 19E
*11	Madre, Laguna	26 30N	90 20W
26	Madre, Sa.	16 0N	93 0W
28	Madre del Sur, Sa.	17 30N	100 0W
28	Madre Occidental, Sa.	27 0N	107 0W
28	Madre Oriental, Sa.	25 0N	100 0W
39	Madrid	40 25N	3 45W
59	Madura, I.	7 0S	113 20E
*56	Madurai	9 55N	78 10E
60	Maebashi	36 23N	139 4E
29	Maestra, Sa.	20 15N	77 0W
39	Maestrazgo, Mts.del	40 20N	0 20W
25	Mafeking, Canada	52 41N	101 6W
67	Mafeking, S.Africa	25 50S	25 38E
66	Mafia, I.	7 45S	39 50E
49	Magadan	59 30N	151 0E
32	Magallanes, Estrecho de	52 30S	75 0W
42	Magdeburg	52 8N	11 36E
23	Magdalen Is.	47 30N	61 45W
26	Magdalena	30 50N	112 0W
32	Magellan's Str.= Magallanes, Estr.de	52 30S	75 0W
40	Maggiore, L.	46 0N	8 35E
52	Maghar	32 54N	35 24E
46	Magnitogorsk	53 20N	59 0E
23	Magog	45 18N	72 9W
24	Magrath	49 25N	112 52W
54	Mahabad	36 50N	45 45E
54	Mahallat	33 55N	50 30E
57	Mahanadi, R.	20 0N	86 25E
15	Mahanoy City	40 49N	76 8W
56	Maharashtra □	19 30N	75 30E
72	Mahia Peninsula	39 9S	177 55E
23	Mahone Bay	44 27N	64 23W
*6	Mahukona	20 9N	155 56W
66	Mai-Ndombe, L.	2 0S	18 0E
55	Maimana	35 53N	64 38E
42	Main, R.	50 0N	8 18E
38	Main-et-Loire □	47 31N	0 30W
*9	Maine □	45 20N	69 0W
42	Mainz	50 0N	8 17E
30	Maiquetia	10 36N	66 57W
71	Maitland	32 44S	151 36E
28	Maiz, Is.del	12 15N	83 4W
60	Maizuru	35 25N	135 22E
67	Majunga □	17 0S	46 0E
58	Makasar, Selat	5 10S	119 20E
41	Makedonija □	41 53N	21 40E
*6	Makena	20 39N	156 27W
47	Makeyevka	48 0N	38 0E
67	Makgadikgadi Salt Pans	20 40S	25 45E
47	Makhachkala	42 58N	47 30E
66	Makindu	2 7S	37 40E
53	Makkah	21 27N	39 49E
56	Makran Coast Ra.	25 40N	64 0E
57	Maktama Kwe, G.	15 40N	96 30E
*56	Malabar Coast	11 0N	75 0E
58	Malacca, Str.of	3 0N	101 0E
39	Maladetta, mts.	42 40N	0 30E
39	Málaga	36 43N	4 32W
65	Malakâl	9 33N	31 50E
59	Malang	7 59S	112 35E
66	Malanje	9 50S	17 22E
22	Malartic	48 9N	78 9W
54	Malatya	38 25N	38 20E
67	Malawi ■	13 0S	34 0E
67	Malawi, L.= Nyasa, L.	12 30S	34 30E
58	Malaya □	4 0N	102 0E
58	Malaysia ■	5 0N	110 0E
15	Malden	42 26N	71 4W
50	Maldive Is.	2 0N	73 0E
56	Malegaon	20 30N	74 30E
64	Mali ■	15 0N	10 0W
36	Malin Hd.	55 18N	7 16W
66	Malindi	3 12S	40 5E
59	Malita	6 19N	125 39E
39	Mallorca, I.	39 30N	3 0E
37	Malmédy	80 25N	6 2E
45	Malmö	55 33N	13 8E
15	Malone	44 51N	74 17W
*40	Malta ■	35 50N	14 30E
59	Maluka	3 0S	128 0E
36	Man, Isle of □	54 15N	4 30W
*6	Mana	22 2N	159 46W
59	Manado	1 40N	124 45E
28	Managua	12 0N	86 20W
30	Manaus	3 0S	60 0W
38	Manche □	49 10N	1 20W
36	Manchester, U.K.	53 30N	2 15W
15	Manchester, Conn.	41 47N	72 31W
16	Manchester, Iowa	42 29N	91 27W
8	Manchester, Ky.	37 10N	83 45W
15	Manchester, N.H.	42 59N	71 28W
61	Manchouli	49 46N	117 24E
50	Manchurian Plain	47 0N	124 0E
57	Mandalay=Mandale	22 0N	96 10E
57	Mandale	22 0N	96 10E
10	Mandan	46 50N	101 0W
40	Manfredónia, G.di	41 30N	16 10E
*56	Mangalore	12 55N	74 47E
58	Manggar	2 50S	108 10E
56	Mangla Dam	33 32N	73 50E
23	Manicouagan, R.	49 11N	68 13W
23	Manicouagan L.	51 5N	68 40W
59	Manila	14 40N	121 3E
57	Manipur □	24 30N	94 0E
54	Manisa	38 38N	27 30E
8	Manistee	44 15N	86 20W
8	Manistique	45 59N	86 18W
25	Manitoba, L.	50 40N	98 30W
25	Manitoba □	55 30N	97 0W
22	Manitoulin, I.	45 40N	82 30W
25	Manitou	49 15N	98 32W
10	Manitowoc	44 8N	87 40W
30	Manizales	5 5N	75 32W
10	Mankato	44 8N	93 59W
*56	Mannar, G.of	8 30N	79 0E
42	Mannheim	49 28N	8 29E
24	Manning	56 55N	117 37W
59	Manokwari	0 54N	134 0E
21	Mansel I.	62 0N	79 50W
14	Mansfield	40 45N	82 30W
30	Manta	1 0S	80 40W
16	Manteca	37 48N	121 13W
31	Mantiqueira, Sa.da	22 0S	44 0W
40	Mántova	45 10N	10 47E
40	Mantua=Mántova	45 10N	10 47E
72	Manukau	37 1S	174 55E
66	Manyara, L.	3 40S	35 50E
28	Manzanillo, Cuba	20 20N	77 10W
26	Manzanillo, Mexico	19 0N	104 20W
25	Maple Creek	49 55N	128 5W
*18	Maple Valley	47 25N	122 3W
10	Maplewood	38 33N	90 18W
67	Maputo	25 58S	32 32E
32	Mar, Sa.do	25 0S	48 0W
32	Mar Del Plata	38 0S	57 30W
30	Maracaibo	10 40N	71 37W
30	Maracaibo, L.de	9 20N	71 30W
30	Maracay	10 20N	67 35W
31	Marajó, I.de	1 0S	49 30W
31	Maranhão=São Luís	2 39S	44 15W
31	Maranhão □	5 0S	46 0W
71	Maranoa, R.	27 50S	148 37E
30	Marañón, R.	4 30N	73 35W
54	Maras	37 36N	36 53E
41	Marathón, Greece	38 11N	23 58E
53	Marbat	17 0N	54 45E
39	Marbella	36 30N	4 57W

Marblehead **Morava, R. Yugoslavia**

15 Marblehead 42 30N 70 51W
37 Marche-en-Famenne 50 14N 5 19E
40 Maremma, reg. 42 30N 11 30E
30 Margarita, I.de 11 0N 64 0W
46 Mari A.S.S.R. □ 56 30N 48 0E
68 Mariana Is. 17 0N 145 0E
28 Marianao 23 8N 82 42W
40 Maribor 46 36N 15 40E
21 Maricourt 61 35N 72 0W
29 Marie Galante, I. 16 0N 61 20W
9 Marietta, Ga. 34 0N 84 30W
8 Marietta, Ohio 39 27N 81 27W
31 Marilia 22 0S 50 0W
18 Marina 36 41N 121 48W
10 Marinette 45 4N 87 40W
32 Maringá 23 35S 51 50W
16 Marion, Ill. 37 44N 88 56W
17 Marion, Ind. 40 35N 85 40W
16 Marion, Iowa 42 2N 91 36W
17 Marion, Ohio 40 38N 83 8W
9 Marion, S.C. 34 11N 79 22W
9 Marion, Vn. 36 51N 81 29W
41 Maritsa, R. 41 40N 26 45E
55 Marjan 32 5N 68 20E
15 Marlboro 42 21N 71 33W
54 Marmara, Sea of= Marmara Denizi 40 45N 28 15E
54 Marmara Denizi 40 45N 28 15E
54 Marmaris 36 50N 28 14E
40 Marmolada, mt. 46 25N 11 55E
22 Marmora 44 28N 77 41W
38 Marne, R. 48 49N 2 24E
38 Marne □ 49 0N 4 10E
69 Marquesas Is. 9 30S 140 0W
8 Marquette 46 30N 87 21W
64 Marrakech 31 40N 8 0W
66 Marsabit 2 18N 38 0E
40 Marsala 37 48N 12 25E
38 Marseille 43 18N 5 23E
11 Marshall, Ark. 35 58N 92 40W
17 Marshall, Ill. 39 23N 87 42W
17 Marshall, Mich. 42 16N 84 58W
16 Marshall, Mo. 39 7N 93 12W
68 Marshall Is. 9 0N 171 0E
16 Marshalltown 42 0N 93 0E
57 Martaban, G. of= Maktama Kwe G. 15 40N 96 30E
58 Martapura 3 22S 114 56E
15 Martha's Vineyard 41 25N 70 35W
18 Martinez 37 55N 121 55W
*29 Martinique ■ 14 40N 61 0W
14 Martins Ferry 40 6N 80 44W
8 Martinsburg 39 30N 77 57W
17 Martinsville, Ill. 39 20N 87 53W
17 Martinsville, Ind. 39 26N 86 25W
9 Martinsville, Va. 36 41N 79 52W
72 Marton 40 4S 175 23E
71 Mary Kathleen 20 35S 139 48E
71 Maryborough 25 31S 152 37E
8 Maryland □ 39 10N 76 40W
18 Marysville, Calif. 39 9N 121 35W
*18 Marysville, Wash. 48 3N 122 11W
23 Marystown 47 10N 55 9W
16 Maryville, Mo. 40 21N 94 52W
9 Maryville, Ten. 35 50N 84 0W
61 Masan 35 15N 128 30E
28 Masaya 12 0N 86 7W
58 Masbate, I. 12 20N 123 30E
67 Maseru 29 18S 27 30E
55 Mashhad 36 20N 59 35E
66 Masindi 1 40N 31 43E
54 Masjed Soleyman 31 55N 49 25E
16 Mason City 43 9N 93 12W
53 Masqat 23 37N 58 35E
15 Massachusetts □ 42 25N 72 0W
15 Massachusetts B. 42 20N 70 50W
15 Massena 44 56N 74 54W
38 Massif Central, mts. 45 30N 2 21E
14 Massillon 40 48N 81 32W
72 Masterton 40 56S 175 39E
53 Mastura 23 7N 38 52E
57 Masulipatnam 16 12N 81 12E
59 Mataboor 1 41S 138 3E
22 Matachewan 47 56N 80 39W
66 Matadi 5 52S 13 31E
28 Matagalpa 13 10N 85 40W
27 Matamoros 25 50N 97 30W
23 Matane 48 51N 67 32W
28 Matanzas 23 0N 81 40W
58 Mataram 8 41S 116 10E
26 Matehuala 23 40N 100 50W
56 Mathura 27 30N 77 48E
31 Mato Grosso, Planalto do 15 0N 54 0W
31 Mato Grosso □ 14 0S 55 0W
53 Matrah 23 38N 58 34E
60 Matsue 35 25N 133 10E
60 Matsumoto 36 15N 138 0E
60 Matsusaka 34 35N 136 25E
60 Matsuyama 33 45N 132 45E
*56 Mattancheri 9 50N 76 15E
22 Mattawa 46 20N 78 45W
42 Matterhorn, mt. 45 58N 7 39E
17 Mattoon 39 29N 88 22W
58 Matua 2 58S 110 52E
30 Maturín 9 45N 63 11W
*6 Maui I. 20 45N 156 20E
57 Maulamyaing 16 30N 97 38E
17 Maumee 41 34N 83 39W
59 Maumere 8 38S 122 13E
*6 Mauna Kea, mt. 19 50N 155 28W
*6 Mauna Loa, mt. 19 50N 155 28W
64 Mauritania ■ 20 50N 10 0W
3 Mauritius, I. 20 0S 57 0E
57 Mawlaik 23 38N 94 24E
28 May Pen 17 58N 77 15W
29 Mayagüez 18 12N 67 9W
27 Mayapán 20 38N 89 27W
38 Mayenne 48 20N 0 38W
38 Mayenne □ 48 10N 0 40W
24 Mayerthorpe 53 57N 115 8W
47 Maykop 44 35N 40 25E
20 Mayo 63 36N 135 54W
17 Maysville 38 39N 83 46W
17 Maywood 41 53N 87 51W
55 Mazan Deran □ 36 30N 53 30E
55 Mazar-i-Sharif 36 41N 67 0E
28 Mazatenango 14 35N 91 30W
26 Mazatlán 23 10N 106 30W
67 Mbabane 26 18S 31 6E
66 Mbale 1 8N 34 12E
66 Mbeya 8 54S 33 29E
19 Mead, L. 36 10N 114 10W
25 Meadow Lake 54 8N 108 26W
14 Meadville 41 38N 80 9W
24 Meander River 59 2N 117 42W
53 Mecca, Saudi Arab.= Makkah 21 27N 39 49E
19 Mecca, U.S.A. 33 35N 116 4W
15 Mechanville 42 54N 73 42W
37 Mechelen 51 2N 4 29E
42 Mecklenburger Bucht 54 20N 11 40E
58 Medan 3 40N 98 38W
30 Medellín 6 15N 75 35W
12 Medford 42 20N 122 52W
12 Medicine Bow Ra. 41 10N 106 25W
25 Medicine Hat 50 0N 110 45W
39 Medina 24 35N 39 52E
70 Meekatharra 26 32S 118 29E
56 Meerut 29 1N 77 50E
23 Mégantic 45 36N 70 56W
57 Meghalaya □ 25 30N 91 0E
57 Meiktila 21 0N 96 0E
64 Meknes 33 57N 5 39W
58 Mekong, R. 10 33N 105 24E
58 Melaka 2 15N 102 3E
68 Melanesia, Is. 4 0S 155 0E
71 Melbourne 37 40S 145 0E
26 Melchor Múzquiz 27 50N 101 40W
25 Melfort 52 52N 104 37W
64 Melilla 35 21N 2 57W
47 Melitopol 46 50N 35 22E
42 Melk 48 13N 15 20E
32 Melo 32 20S 54 10W
25 Melville 51 0N 102 50W
70 Melville I. 11 30S 131 0E
23 Melville, L. 59 30N 53 40W
21 Melville, Pen. 68 0N 84 0W
46 Memel=Klaipeda 55 43N 21 10W
11 Memphis 35 7N 90 0W
10 Menasha 44 13N 88 27W
18 Mendota, Calif. 36 45N 120 23W
16 Mendota, Ill. 41 33N 89 7W
32 Mendoza 32 50S 68 52W
37 Menen 50 47N 3 7E
18 Menlo Park 37 28N 122 15W
8 Menominee 45 9N 87 39W
17 Menomonee Falls 43 11N 88 7W
39 Menorca, I. 40 0N 4 0E
58 Mentawai, Kepulauan 2 0S 99 0E
70 Menzies 29 40S 120 58E
52 Me'ona 33 1N 35 15E
26 Meoqui 28 17N 105 29W
40 Merano 46 40N 11 10E
59 Merauke 8 29S 140 24E
33 Merca 1 48N 44 50E
18 Merced 37 25N 120 30W
32 Mercedes, Buenos Aires 34 40S 59 30W
32 Mercedes, San Luis 33 5S 65 21W
32 Mercedes, Urug. 33 12S 58 0W
72 Mercer 37 16S 175 5E
58 Mergui 12 30N 98 35E
58 Mergui Arch. 11 30N 97 30E
27 Mérida, Mexico 20 50N 89 40W
30 Mérida, Venezuela 8 36N 71 8W
15 Meriden 41 33N 72 47W
11 Meridian 31 55N 97 37W
37 Merksem 51 16N 4 25E
70 Merredin 31 28S 118 18E
15 Merrimack, R. 42 49N 70 49W
24 Merritt 50 7N 120 47W
36 Mersey, R. 53 25N 3 0W
36 Merthyr Tydfil 51 45N 3 23W
13 Mesa 33 20N 111 56W
52 Mesada 31 20N 35 19E
55 Meshed=Mashhad 36 20N 59 35E
54 Mesopotamia, reg.= Al Jazirah, reg. 33 30N 44 0E
40 Messina, Italy 38 10N 15 32E
67 Messina, S.Afr. 22 20S 30 12E
52 Messina, Str.di 38 5N 15 35E
41 Messiniakós Kólpos 36 45N 22 5E
24 Metchosin 48 22N 123 32W
38 Metz 49 8N 6 10E
38 Meurthe-et-Moselle □ 48 52N 6 0E
37 Meuse, R. 51 49N 5 1E
38 Meuse □ 49 8N 5 25E
26 Mexicali 32 40N 115 30W
26 Mexico ■ 20 0N 100 0W
16 Mexico 39 10N 91 53W
27 Mexico, G.of 25 0N 90 0W
15 Mexico B. 43 31N 76 17W
26 Mexico City 19 24N 99 9W
46 Mezen 65 50N 44 20E
9 Miami 25 52N 80 15W
9 Miami Beach 25 49N 80 6W
17 Miamisburg 39 38N 84 17W
54 Mianeh 37 30N 47 40E
61 Miaoli 24 33N 120 42E
46 Miass 24 59N 60 6E
8 Michigan, L. 44 0N 8 0W
8 Michigan □ 44 40N 85 40W
17 Michigan City 41 42N 86 56W
23 Michikamau L. 54 0N 64 0W
22 Michipicoten I. 47 45N 85 45W
46 Michurinsk 52 58N 40 27E
68 Micronesia, Is. 17 0N 160 0E
52 Midbar Yehuda, reg. 31 30N 35 18E
37 Middleburg 51 30N 3 37E
38 Middlesborough 54 35N 1 14W
15 Middlesex 40 29N 74 27W
15 Middletown, Conn. 41 37N 72 40W
15 Middletown, N.Y. 41 28N 74 28W
8 Middletown, Ohio 39 29N 84 25W
15 Middletown, Pa. 40 12N 76 44W
17 Middletown, Wis. 39 29N 84 25W
22 Midland, Canada 44 45N 79 53W
19 Midland, Calif. 33 52N 114 48W
8 Midland, Mich. 43 37N 84 14W
11 Midland, Texas 32 0N 102 3W
68 Midway I. 28 13N 177 22W
39 Mieres 43 18N 5 48W
52 Migdal 32 51N 35 30E
30 Milagro 2 30S 65 59W
40 Milan=Milano 45 28N 9 10E
40 Milano 45 28N 9 10E
36 Mildura 34 8S 142 7E
71 Miles 26 37S 150 10E
15 Milford, Conn. 41 13N 73 4W
8 Milford, Del. 38 52N 75 27W
15 Milford, Mass. 42 8N 71 32W
36 Milford Haven 51 43N 5 2W
18 Mill Valley 37 54N 122 32W
*9 Millinocket 45 45N 68 45W
8 Millville 39 22N 74 0W
21 Milne Inlet 72 30N 80 0W
17 Milwaukee 43 9N 87 58W
*18 Milwaukie 45 27N 122 38W
32 Minas 34 20S 55 15W
31 Minas Gerais □ 18 50S 46 0W
27 Minatitlán 17 58N 94 35W
59 Mindanao, I. 8 0N 125 0E
59 Mindanao Sea 8 50N 123 0E
59 Mindanao Trench 8 0N 128 0E
59 Mindoro, I. 13 0N 121 0E
39 Minho, R. 41 52N 8 51W
39 Minho □ 41 40N 8 30W
10 Minneapolis 44 58N 93 20W
25 Minnedosa 50 15N 99 50W
10 Minnesota □ 46 60N 94 0W
10 Minot 48 10N 101 15W
46 Minsk 53 52N 27 30E
23 Minto 46 5N 66 5W
23 Miquelon 47 6N 56 23W
58 Miri 4 18N 114 0E
57 Mirzapur 25 10N 82 45E
17 Mishawaka 41 40N 86 8W
28 Miskitos, Cayos 14 26N 82 50W
43 Miskolc 48 7N 20 50E
*11 Mission 26 15N 98 30W
24 Mission City 49 8N 122 18W
11 Mississipi, R. 29 0N 89 15W
11 Mississipi □ 33 0N 90 0W
12 Missoula 47 0N 114 0W
16 Missouri, R. 38 50N 90 8W
10 Missouri □ 38 25N 92 30W
22 Mistassini, L. 48 52N 72 12W
12 Mitchell 41 58N 98 0W
9 Mitchell, Mt. 35 40N 82 20W
71 Mitchell, R. 15 12S 141 35E
60 Mito 36 20N 140 30E
53 Mitsiwa 15 35N 39 25E
66 Mitumba, Chaîne des 10 0S 26 20E
60 Miyako 39 40N 141 75E
60 Miyakonojo 31 32N 131 5E
60 Miyazaki 32 0N 131 30E
57 Mizoram □ 23 0N 92 45E
16 Moberly 39 25N 92 25W
9 Mobile 30 41N 88 3W
9 Mobile B. 30 30N 88 0W
66 Mobutu Sese Seko, L. 1 40N 31 0E
67 Moçâmbique 15 3S 40 42E
67 Moçâmedes 15 10S 12 9E
40 Módena 44 39N 10 55E
18 Modesto 37 43N 121 0W
40 Módica 36 51N 14 47E
53 Mogadiscio 2 1N 45 20E
32 Mogi das Cruzes 23 31S 46 11W
46 Mogilev 53 54N 30 21E
13 Mogollon Mesa, mts. 33 25N 108 40W
15 Mohawk, R. 42 47N 73 42W
19 Mojave 35 3N 118 10W
19 Mojave Des. 35 0N 117 0W
61 Mokpo 34 48N 126 22E
37 Mol 51 11N 5 6E
47 Moldavian S.S.R. □ 47 0N 29 0E
40 Molfetta 41 12N 16 36E
16 Moline 41 30N 90 30W
30 Mollendo 17 0S 72 0W
45 Mölndal 57 39N 12 1E
*6 Molokai I. 21 8N 157 0W
59 Molucca Sea 4 0S 124 0E
59 Moluccas=Maluka □ 3 0S 128 0E
66 Mombasa 4 2S 39 43E
29 Mona, I. 18 5N 67 54W
38 Monaco ■ 43 36N 7 23E
15 Monadnock Mt. 42 52N 72 7W
39 Moncayo, mt. 41 48N 1 50W
37 Mönchengladbach 51 12N 6 23E
26 Monclova 26 50N 101 30W
23 Moncton 46 7N 64 51W
39 Mondego, R. 40 9N 8 52W
40 Mondoví 44 23N 7 56E
14 Monessen 40 9N 79 53W
65 Mongalla 5 8N 31 55E
70 Monger, L. 29 0S 117 15E
57 Monghyr 25 23N 86 29E
61 Mongolia ■ 47 0N 103 0E
58 Mongolia, Plateau of 45 0N 103 0E
25 Monk 47 7N 69 59W
16 Monmouth 40 55N 90 39W
19 Monolith 35 7N 118 22W
40 Monópoli 40 57N 17 18E
11 Monroe, La. 32 32N 92 4W
17 Monroe, Mich. 41 55N 83 26W
9 Monroe, N.Car. 35 2N 80 37W
*18 Monroe, Wash. 47 51N 121 58W
64 Monrovia, Liberia 6 18N 10 47W
13 Monrovia, U.S.A. 34 7N 118 1W
37 Mons 50 27N 3 58E
23 Mont-Joli 48 35N 68 11W
22 Mont Laurier 46 35N 75 30W
23 Montague 46 10N 62 39W
30 Montaña, reg. 9 0S 73 0W
12 Montana □ 47 0N 110 0W
38 Montauban 44 0N 1 21E
15 Montauk Pt. 41 4N 71 52W
38 Montbéliard 47 31N 6 48E
15 Montclair 40 49N 74 13W
38 Monte Carlo 43 46N 7 23E
22 Montebelle 45 40N 74 55W
19 Montecito 34 26N 119 39W
28 Montego Bay 18 30N 78 0W
38 Montélimar 44 33N 4 45E
27 Montemorolos 25 11N 99 42W
18 Monterey 36 35N 121 57W
18 Monterey B. 36 45N 121 55W
30 Monteria 8 46N 75 53W
26 Monterrey 25 40N 100 30W
31 Montes Claros 16 30S 43 50W
*18 Montesano 46 59N 123 36W
32 Montevideo 34 50S 56 11W
9 Montgomery 32 24N 86 20W
17 Monticello 40 45N 86 46W
38 Montluçon 46 22N 2 36E
23 Montmagny 46 58N 70 34W
23 Montmorency 46 53N 71 11W
8 Montpelier 44 15N 72 38W
38 Montpellier 43 37N 3 52E
22 Montréal 45 31N 73 34W
38 Montreuil 50 27N 1 45E
42 Montreux 46 26N 6 55E
13 Montrose 38 30N 107 52W
29 Montserrat, I. 16 40N 62 10W
39 Monzón 41 52N 0 10E
71 Moonie, R. 29 19S 148 43E
70 Moore, L. 29 30S 117 30E
10 Moorhead 47 0N 97 0W
19 Moorpark 34 17N 118 53W
22 Moose, R. 51 20N 80 24W
25 Moose Jaw 50 30N 105 30W
*9 Moosehead L. 45 40N 69 40W
25 Moosomin 50 8N 101 40W
22 Moosonee 51 25N 80 51W
56 Moradabad 28 50N 78 50E
*56 Moratuaw 6 45N 79 55E
42 Morava, R, Czech. 48 10N 16 59E
41 Morava, R, Yugoslavia 44 43N 21 3E

Moravian Heights, mts. Noordoost-Polder

34 Moravian Heights, mts. 49 30N 15 40E
36 Moray Firth 57 50N 3 30W
38 Morbihan □ 47 55N 3 0W
25 Morden 49 11N 98 6W
46 Mordovian A.S.S.R. □ 54 20N 44 30E
36 Morecambe B. 54 7N 3 0W
71 Moree 29 28S 149 48E
26 Morelia 19 40N 101 11W
39 Morena Sa. 38 20N 4 0W
13 Morenci 33 7N 109 20W
71 Moreton I. 27 10S 153 10E
11 Morgan City 29 40N 91 15W
18 Morgan Hill 37 8N 121 39W
8 Morgantown 39 39N 75 58W
60 Morioka 39 45N 141 8E
71 Mornington I. 16 30S 139 30E
26 Moroleon 20 8N 101 32W
28 Morón 22 0N 78 30W
25 Morris, Canada 49 21N 97 22W
17 Morris, U.S.A. 41 22N 88 26W
22 Morrisburg 44 54N 75 11W
15 Morristown, N.J. 40 48N 74 29W
9 Morristown, Tenn. 36 18N 83 20W
64 Morocco ■ 32 0N 5 50W
59 Morotai, I. 2 10N 128 30E
18 Morro Bay 35 22N 120 51W
38 Morvan, mt. 47 5N 4 0E
12 Moscow 46 45N 116 59W
46 Moscow=Moskva 55 45N 37 35E
42 Mosel, R. 50 22N 7 36E
38 Moselle □ 48 59N 6 35E
72 Mosgiel 45 53S 170 21E
66 Moshi 3 22S 37 18E
46 Moskva 55 45N 37 35E
28 Mosquitos, G.de los 9 15N 81 10W
45 Moss 59 27N 10 40E
25 Mossbank 49 56N 105 58W
67 Mosselbaai 34 11S 22 8E
71 Mossman 16 21S 145 15E
64 Mostaganem 35 51N 0 7E
54 Mosul=Al Mawsil 36 20N 43 5E
45 Motala 58 32N 15 1E
36 Motherwell 55 48N 4 0W
39 Motril 36 44N 3 37W
72 Motueka 41 7S 173 1E
27 Motul 21 0N 89 20W
57 Moulmein=Maulamyaing 16 30N 97 40E
14 Moundsville 39 55N 80 44W
17 Mount Carmel, Ill. 38 25N 87 46W
15 Mount Carmel, Pa. 40 48N 76 25W
17 Mount Clemens 42 36N 82 53W
22 Mount Forest 43 59N 80 43W
71 Mount Isa 20 42S 139 26E
70 Mount Magnet 28 2S 117 47E
16 Mount Pleasant, Iowa 40 58N 91 33W
8 Mount Pleasant, Mich. 43 38N 84 46W
17 Mount Sterling 38 4N 83 56W
70 Mount Tom Price 22 50S 117 40E
17 Mount Vernon, Ill. 38 19N 88 55W
17 Mount Vernon, Ind. 37 56N 87 54W
15 Mount Vernon, N.Y. 40 57N 73 49W
14 Mount Vernon, Ohio 40 23N 82 29W
*18 Mount Vernon, Wash. 48 25N 122 20W
23 Mount Wright 52 40N 67 30W
24 Mountain Park 52 55N 117 16W
13 Mountain View 37 26N 122 5W
36 Mourne Mts. 54 10N 6 0W
37 Mouscron 50 45N 3 12E
53 Moyale 3 30N 39 0E
64 Moyen Atlas, mts. 33 0N 5 0W
67 Mozambique ■ 15 3S 40 42E
*67 Mozambique Channel 19 0S 43 50E
66 Mpanda 6 23S 31 40E
67 Mpika 11 51S 31 25E
58 Mauraenim 3 40S 103 50E
58 Mauratewe 0 50S 115 0E
71 Mudgee 32 32S 149 31E
67 Mufulira 12 32S 28 15E
53 Mukalla 14 33N 49 2E
55 Mukur 32 50N 67 50E
28 Mulatas, Arch.de las 6 51N 78 31W
23 Mulgrave 45 38N 61 31W
39 Mulhacen, mt. 37 4N 3 20W
37 Mülheim 51 26N 6 53W
38 Mulhouse 47 44N 7 20E
58 Müller, Pegunungan 0 30N 113 30E
70 Mullewa 28 29S 115 30E
56 Multan 30 15N 71 30E
42 München 48 8N 11 33E
17 Muncie 40 10N 85 20W
67 Munhango, R. 11 20S 19 50E
42 Munich=München 48 8N 11 33E
42 Münster 51 58N 7 37E
44 Muonioälv 67 48N 23 25E
70 Murchison, R. 26 1S 117 6E
39 Murcia 38 2N 1 10W
43 Mures, R. 46 15N 20 13E
9 Murfreesboro 35 30N 86 21W
59 Muris 2 23S 140 40E
46 Murmansk 68 57N 33 10E
46 Murom 55 35N 42 3E
60 Muroran 42 25N 141 0E
16 Murphysboro 37 46N 89 20W
12 Murray 40 41N 111 58W
71 Murray, R. 35 22S 139 22E
71 Murray Bridge 35 6S 139 14E
71 Murrumbidgee, R. 34 30S 143 30E
71 Murwillumbah 28 18S 153 27E
41 Musala, mt. 42 13N 23 37E
53 Musay'id 24 59N 51 32E
53 Muscat=Masqat 23 37N 58 35E
16 Muscatine 41 25N 91 5W
70 Musgrave Ranges 26 0S 132 0E
17 Muskegon 43 15N 86 17W
17 Muskegon Heights 43 12N 86 12W
11 Muskogee 35 50N 95 25W
71 Muswellbrook 32 16S 150 56E
61 Mutankiang 44 35N 129 30E
56 Muzaffarnagar 29 26N 77 40E
57 Muzaffarpur 26 7N 85 32E
61 Muztagh, mt. 36 30N 87 22E
66 Mwanza 2 30S 32 58E
66 Mweru, L. 9 0S 29 0E
55 Mýcenae 37 44N 22 45E
57 Myingyan 21 30N 95 30E
57 Myitkyina 25 30N 97 26E
*56 Mysore 12 17N 76 41E

N

52 Na'an 31 53N 34 52E
52 Nabulus 32 14N 35 15E
67 Nacala 14 32S 40 34E
11 Nacogdoches 31 33N 95 30W
56 Nadiad 22 41N 72 56E
48 Nadym 63 35N 72 42E
59 Naga 13 38N 123 15E
57 Nagaland □ 26 0N 94 30E
60 Nagano 36 40N 138 10E
60 Nagaoka 37 30N 138 50E
*56 Nagappattinam 10 46N 79 51E
60 Nagasaki 32 47N 129 50E
*56 Nagercoil 8 12N 77 33E
60 Nagoya 35 10N 136 50E
56 Nagpur 21 8N 79 10E
52 Nahariyya 33 1N 35 5E
54 Nahavand 34 10N 48 30E
25 Naicam 52 25N 104 30W
66 Nairobi 1 17S 36 48E
66 Naivasha 0 40S 36 30E
55 Najafabad 32 40N 51 15E
53 Najd, reg. 26 30N 42 0E
47 Nakhichevan A.S.S.R. □ 39 14N 45 24E
49 Nakhodka 43 10N 132 45E
58 Nakhon Ratchasima 14 59N 102 12E
22 Nakina 50 10N 86 42W
45 Naksov 54 50N 11 8E
66 Nakuru 0 15S 35 5E
47 Nalchik 43 30N 43 33E
61 Nam Dinh 20 25N 106 5E
58 Nam-Phan, reg. 10 30N 106 0E
61 Nam Tso 30 40N 90 30E
48 Namangan 41 30N 71 30E
71 Nambour 26 38S 152 49E
61 Namcha Barwa, mt. 29 30N 95 10E
67 Namib Desert 22 30S 15 0W
67 Namibia= South-West Africa ■ 23 0S 17 0E
59 Namlea 3 10S 127 5E
12 Nampa 43 40N 116 40W
37 Namur 50 27N 4 52E
61 Nan Shan 38 0N 98 0E
24 Nanaimo 49 10N 124 0W
61 Nanchang 28 34N 115 48E
61 Nanchung 30 47N 105 59E
38 Nancy 48 42N 6 12E
56 Nanda Devi, mt. 30 30N 80 30E
56 Nander 19 10N 77 20E
38 Nanga Parbat, mt. 35 10N 74 35E
55 Nangarhar □ 34 20N 70 0E
61 Nanking 32 10N 118 50E
61 Nanning 22 50S 108 5E
61 Nanping 25 45N 118 5E
*60 Nansei-Shoto 29 0N 129 0E
38 Nantes 47 12N 1 33W
15 Nanticoke 41 12N 76 0W
24 Nanton 50 22N 113 47W
31 Nanuque 17 50S 40 21W
61 Nanyang 33 4N 112 55E
39 Nao,C. 38 44N 0 14E
18 Napa 38 18N 122 17W
22 Napanee 44 15N 76 57W
17 Naperville 41 47N 88 9W
40 Naples=Nápoli 40 50N 14 5E
17 Napoleon 41 23N 84 8W
40 Nápoli 40 50N 14 5E
60 Nara 34 40N 135 49E
57 Narayanganj 23 31N 90 33E
38 Narbonne 43 11N 3 0E
56 Narmada, R. 21 35N 72 35E
46 Narodnaya, mt. 65 5N 60 0E
71 Narrabri 30 19S 149 46E
71 Narrandera 34 42S 146 31E
70 Narrogin 32 58S 117 14E
46 Narva 59 10N 28 5E
44 Narvik 68 28N 17 26E
15 Nashua 42 50N 71 25W
9 Nashville 36 12N 86 46W
56 Nasik 20 2N 73 50E
56 Nasirabad 26 15N 74 45E
28 Nassau 25 0N 77 30W
65 Nasser, Buheiret en 23 0N 32 30E
65 Nasser, L.= Nasser, Buheiret en 23 0N 32 30E
45 Nässjö 57 39N 14 42E
31 Natal 5 47S 35 13W
67 Natal □ 28 30S 30 30E
11 Natchez 31 35N 91 25W
15 Natick 42 17N 71 21W
19 National City 32 45N 117 7W
66 Natron, L. 2 20S 36 0E
39 Navarra □ 42 40N 1 40W
29 Navassa I. 18 30N 75 0W
26 Navojoa 27 0N 109 30W
26 Navolato 24 47N 107 42W
41 Návpaktos 38 23N 21 42E
56 Nawabshah 26 15N 68 25E
41 Náxos, I. 37 8N 25 35E
55 Nay Band 27 20N 52 40E
52 Nazareth 32 42N 35 17E
26 Nazas, R. 25 20N 104 4W
66 N'djamena 12 4N 15 8E
66 N'Djolé 0 10S 10 45E
67 Ndola 13 0S 28 34E
36 Neagh, L. 54 35N 6 25W
*20 Near Is. 53 0N 172 0W
10 Nebraska □ 41 30N 100 0W
10 Nebraska City 40 40N 95 52W
46 Nébrodi, Monti 37 55N 14 35E
42 Neckar, R. 49 31N 8 26E
32 Necochea 38 30S 58 50W
10 Neenah 44 10N 88 30W
25 Neepawa 50 14N 99 28W
8 Negaunee 46 30N 87 36W
31 Negre, Pta. 18 40N 120 50E
32 Negro, R., Arg. 41 2S 62 47W
31 Negro, R., Brazil 3 0S 60 0W
59 Negros, I. 10 0N 123 0E
61 Neikiang 29 35N 105 10E
30 Neiva 2 56N 75 18W
53 Nekemte 9 4N 36 30E
24 Nelson, Canada 49 30N 117 20W
72 Nelson, N.Z. 41 18S 173 16E
25 Nelson, R. 57 4N 92 30W
25 Nelson House 55 50N 99 0W
46 Neman, R. 55 18N 21 23E
60 Nemuro 43 20N 145 35E
60 Nemuro-Kaikyo, Str. 43 30N 145 30E
*20 Nenana 63 34N 149 7W
11 Neosho, R. 35 48N 95 18W
57 Nepal ■ 28 0N 84 30E
15 Neptune City 40 12N 74 3W
52 Nes Ziyyona 31 56N 34 48W
36 Ness, L. 57 15N 4 30W
52 Netanya 32 20N 34 51E
37 Nethe, R. 51 10N 4 22E
37 Netherlands ■ 52 0N 5 30E
42 Neuchâtel 47 0N 6 55E
42 Neuchâtel, L.de 46 53N 6 50E
32 Neuquén 38 0S 68 0E
37 Neuss 51 12N 6 39E
16 Nevada 37 51N 94 22W
39 Nevada, Sa., Spain 37 3N 3 15W
18 Nevada, Sa., U.S.A. 39 0N 120 30W
12 Nevada □ 39 20N 117 0W
30 Nevada de Sta. Marta, Sa. 10 55N 73 50W
38 Nevers 47 0N 3 9E
29 Nevis, I. 17 0N 62 30W
17 New Albany 38 20N 85 50W
30 New Amsterdam 6 15N 57 30W
15 New Bedford 41 40N 70 52W
17 New Berlin 42 58N 88 7W
9 New Bern 35 8N 77 3W
11 New Braunfels 29 43N 98 9W
72 New Brighton 43 29S 172 43E
15 New Britain 41 41N 72 47W
68 New Britain, I. 6 0S 151 0E
15 New Brunswick 40 29N 74 27W
23 New Brunswick □ 46 50N 66 30W
68 New Caledonia 21 0S 165 0E
17 New Castle, Ind. 39 55N 85 23W
14 New Castle, Penn. 41 0N 80 20W
71 New England Ra. 29 30S 152 0E
23 New Glasgow 45 35N 62 39W
15 New Hampshire □ 43 40N 71 40W
16 New Hampton 43 3N 92 19W
15 New Haven 41 20N 72 54W
68 New Hebrides, Is. 15 0S 168 0E
11 New Iberia 30 2N 91 54W
68 New Ireland 3 0S 151 30E
15 New Jersey □ 39 50N 74 10W
14 New Kensington 40 36N 79 43W
22 New Liskeard 47 30N 79 40W
15 New London 41 23N 72 8W
13 New Mexico □ 34 30N 106 0W
*71 New Norfolk 42 46S 147 3E
11 New Orleans 30 0N 90 5W
14 New Philadelphia 40 30N 81 17W
72 New Plymouth 39 4S 174 5E
28 New Providence I. 25 0N 77 30W
15 New Rochelle 40 58N 73 52W
71 New South Wales □ 33 0S 146 0E
23 New Waterford 46 15N 60 5W
24 New Westminster 49 10N 122 52W
15 New York 40 43N 74 1W
15 New York □ 42 40N 76 0W
72 New Zealand ■ 40 0S 176 0E
15 Newark, N.J. 40 41N 74 12W
14 Newark, N.Y. 43 3N 77 6W
14 Newark, Ohio 40 5N 82 30W
19 Newberry Springs 34 51N 116 40W
15 Newburgh 41 30N 74 1W
71 Newcastle, Australia 32 52S 157 49E
23 Newcastle, Canada 47 0N 65 34W
67 Newcastle, S.Afr. 27 45S 29 58E
18 Newcastle, U.S.A. 38 53N 121 8W
36 Newcastle upon Tyne 54 59N 1 37W
*20 Newenham C. 58 37N 162 12W
23 Newfoundland, I. 49 0N 56 0W
23 Newfoundland □ 54 0N 58 0W
19 Newhall 34 23N 118 31W
18 Newman 37 19N 121 1W
36 Newport, I.of W. 50 43N 1 18W
36 Newport, Gwent 51 34N 2 59W
17 Newport, Ky. 39 6N 84 29W
15 Newport, R.I. 41 30N 71 19W
15 Newport, Vt. 44 57N 72 12W
19 Newport Beach 33 40N 117 58W
8 Newport News 37 2N 76 54W
36 Newry 54 10N 6 20W
16 Newton, Iowa 41 42N 93 3W
11 Newton, Kans. 38 2N 97 30W
8 Newton, Mass. 42 21N 71 10W
55 Neyshabur 36 10N 58 20E
47 Nezhin 57 5N 31 55E
66 Ngaoundéré 7 15N 13 35E
49 Ngawi 7 24S 111 26E
58 Nha Trang 12 16N 109 10E
22 Niagara Falls, Canada 43 7N 79 5W
14 Niagara Falls, U.S.A. 43 5N 79 0W
64 Niamey 13 27N 2 6E
58 Nias, I., 1 0N 97 40E
28 Nicaragua ■ 11 40N 85 30W
28 Nicaragua, L.de 12 50N 85 30W
40 Nicastro 39 0N 16 18E
38 Nice 43 42N 7 14E
22 Nicolet 46 13N 72 37W
54 Nicosia=Levkôsia 35 10N 33 25E
38 Niévre □ 47 10N 5 40E
64 Niger ■ 16 0N 8 0E
64 Niger, R. 5 33N 6 33E
64 Nigeria ■ 8 30N 8 0E
60 Niigata 37 58N 139 0E
60 Niihama 33 55N 133 10E
*6 Niihau I. 21 55N 160 10W
54 Nijmegen 51 50N 5 52E
47 Nikolayev 46 58N 32 7E
49 Nikolayevsk-na-Amur 53 40N 140 50E
47 Nikopol 47 35N 34 25E
65 Nîl, Nahr en 30 10N 31 6E
65 Nîl el Abyad, R. 15 38N 32 31E
65 Nîl el Azraq, R. 15 38N 32 31E
19 Niland 33 14N 115 31W
65 Nile R.= Nîl, Nahr en 30 10N 31 6E
17 Niles 41 50N 86 15W
38 Nîmes 43 50N 4 23E
54 Nineveh 36 25N 43 10E
61 Ningpo 29 50N 121 30E
61 Ningsia-Hui □ 37 20N 106 0E
61 Ningteh 26 45N 120 0E
10 Niobrara, R. 42 30N 103 0W
25 Nipawin 53 22N 104 0W
22 Nipigon 48 59N 88 21W
22 Nipigon, L. 49 40N 88 30W
22 Nipissing L. 46 20N 79 40W
19 Nipton 35 28N 115 20W
41 Nis 43 19N 21 58E
60 Nishinomiya 34 45N 135 20E
31 Niterói 22 52S 43 0W
*72 Niue, I. 19 2S 169 54W
56 Nizamabad 18 45N 78 7E
49 Nizhne Kolymsk 68 40N 160 55E
49 Nizhneudinsk 55 0N 99 20E
46 Nizhniy Tagil 57 45N 60 0E
49 Nizhnyaya Tunguska 65 48N 88 4E
43 Nizké Tatry, mts. 48 55N 20 0E
66 Nkhata Bay 11 33S 34 16E
60 Nobeoka 32 36N 131 41E
17 Noblesville 40 3N 86 1W
13 Nogales 31 36N 94 29W
*20 Nome 64 30N 165 30W
37 Noord Beveland, I. 51 45N 3 50E
37 Noord Brabant □ 51 40N 5 0E
37 Noordoost-Polder 52 45N 5 45E

Palma **Potsdam**

Map	Place	Lat.	Long.
39	Palma	39 33N	2 39E
28	Palma Soriano	20 15N	76 0W
19	Palmdale	34 35N	118 7W
*20	Palmer	61 36N	149 7W
72	Palmerston North	40 21S	175 39E
40	Palmi	38 21N	15 51E
30	Palmira	3 32N	76 16W
18	Palo Alto	37 25N	122 8W
19	Palos Verdes	33 45N	118 26W
48	Pamirs, mts.	37 40N	73 0E
9	Pamlico Sd.	35 20N	76 0W
11	Pampa	35 35N	100 58W
32	Pampas, reg.	34 0S	64 0W
39	Pamplona	42 48N	1 38W
28	Panamá ■	9 0N	80 0W
28	Panamá	8 48N	79 25W
28•	Panama Canal	9 10N	79 56W
9	Panama City	30 10N	85 41W
28	Panama, G.de	8 4N	79 20W
59	Panay, I.	11 0N	122 30E
58	Pankalpinang	2 0S	106 0E
40	Patelleria, I.	36 52N	12 0E
61	Paoki	34 25N	107 15E
61	Paoting	38 50N	115 30E
61	Paotow	40 45N	110 0E
28	Papagayo, G.de	10 4N	85 50W
27	Papantla	20 45N	97 5W
68	Papua New Guinea ■	8 0S	145 0E
31	Pará=Belém	1 27S	48 29W
31	Pará □	3 20S	52 0W
18	Paradise, Calif.	39 46N	121 37W
19	Paradise, Nev.	36 9N	115 10W
32	Paraguay ■	23 0S	57 0W
32	Paraguay, R.	27 18S	58 38W
31	Paraiba=João Pessoa	7 10S	35 0W
31	Paraiba □	23 0S	58 0W
31	Paramaribo	5 50N	55 10W
32	Paraná	12 30S	47 40W
32	Paraná, R.	12 30S	48 14W
32	Paraná □	24 0S	51 0W
32	Paranaguá	25 30S	48 30W
56	Parbhani	19 8N	76 52E
52	Pardes Hanna	32 28N	34 57E
42	Pardubice	50 3N	15 45E
30	Parecis, Sa.dos	14 8S	57 10W
22	Parent	47 55N	74 37W
43	Paringul-Mare, mt.	45 20N	23 37E
38	Paris, France	48 52N	2 20E
17	Paris, Ill.	39 36N	87 42W
17	Paris, Ky.	38 13N	84 14W
9	Paris, Tenn.	36 20N	88 20W
11	Paris, Tex.	33 40N	95 30W
38	Paris □	48 52N	2 20E
12	Park Ra.	40 0N	106 30W
17	Park Ridge	42 1N	87 50W
19	Parker	34 9N	114 17W
19	Parker Dam	34 13N	114 5W
8	Parkersburg	39 18N	81 31W
71	Parkes	33 9S	148 11E
*18	Parkland	47 9N	122 26W
24	Parksville	50 15N	113 40W
40	Parma, Italy	44 50N	10 20E
14	Parma, U.S.A.	41 22N	81 43W
31	Parnaíba	2 54S	41 47W
31	Parnaíba, R.	3 0S	41 50W
46	Pärnu	58 24N	24 32E
71	Paroo, R.	31 28S	143 32E
71	Paroo Channel	30 50S	143 35E
26	Parras	25 30N	102 30W
23	Parrsboro	45 24N	64 20W
2	Parry Is.	77 0N	110 0W
22	Parry Sound	45 20N	80 0W
11	Parsons	37 20N	95 10W
55	Parwan □	35 0N	69 0E
19	Pasadena, Calif.	34 5N	118 0W
11	Pasadena, Tex.	29 45N	95 14W
11	Pascagoula	30 30N	88 30W
12	Pasco	46 10N	119 0W
38	Pas-de-Calais □	50 30N	2 20E
15	Passaic	40 51N	74 8W
40	Passero, C.	36 42E	15 8E
32	Passo Fundo	28 10S	52 30W
30	Pasto	1 13N	77 17W
34	Patagonia, reg.	45 0S	69 0W
72	Patea	39 45S	174 30E
15	Paterson	40 55N	74 10W
56	Pathankot	32 18N	75 45E
56	Patiala	30 32N	76 26E
57	Patkai Bum, mts.	27 0N	95 30E
57	Patna	25 35N	85 18E
32	Patos, Lagoa dos	31 20S	51 0E
41	Pátrai	38 14N	21 47E
18	Patterson	37 28N	121 7W
16	Pattonsburg	40 3N	94 8W
38	Pau	43 19N	0 25W
26	Pátzcuaro	19 30N	101 40W
31	Paulo Afonso	9 21S	38 15W
40	Pavia	45 10N	9 10E
48	Pavlodar	52 33N	77 0E
15	Pawtucket	41 51N	71 22W
21	Payne=Bellin	60 1N	70 1W
32	Paysandú	32 19S	58 8W
15	Peabody	42 32N	70 55W
25	Peace, R.	59 0N	111 25W
25	Peace River	56 14N	117 17W
24	Peace River Res.	56 0N	124 0W
*6	Pearl City	21 21N	158 0W
*6	Pearl Harbour	21 20N	158 0W
18	Pebble Beach	36 34N	121 57W
46	Pechenga	69 30N	31 25E
46	Pechora	65 14N	57 18E
46	Pechora, R.	68 14N	54 10E
46	Pechorskaya Guba	69 50N	54 55E
11	Pecos, R.	29 42N	101 22W
43	Pécs	46 5N	18 15E
15	Peekskill	41 17N	73 55W
72	Pegasus, Bay	43 20S	173 10E
57	Pegu	17 20N	96 29E
57	Pegu Yoma, mts.	19 0N	96 0E
61	Pehpei	29 44N	106 29E
61	Peiping	39 50N	116 20E
59	Pekalongan	6 53S	109 40E
16	Pekin	40 35N	89 40W
61	Peking=Peiping	39 50N	116 20E
43	Peleaga, mt.	45 22N	22 55E
29	Pelée, Mt.	14 40N	61 0W
25	Pelican Narrows	55 12N	102 55W
16	Pella	41 25N	92 55W
21	Pelly Bay	68 30N	90 20W
41	Pelopónnisos □	37 10N	22 0E
40	Peloro, C.	38 15N	15 40E
32	Pelotas	31 42S	52 23W
38	Pelvoux, Mt.	44 52N	6 20E
58	Pematangsiantar	2 57N	99 5E
66	Pemba, I.	5 0S	39 45E
22	Pembroke	45 49N	77 7W
39	Peñalara, mt.	40 51N	3 57W
32	Penas, G.de	47 0S	75 0W
19	Pendleton, Calif.	33 20N	117 28W
12	Pendleton, Oreg.	45 35N	118 50W
22	Penetanguishene	44 47N	79 55W
61	Pengpu	33 0N	117 25E
59	Pengunungan Maoke, mts.	4 0S	138 0E
61	Penki	41 48N	123 45E
36	Pennines, mts.	54 50N	2 20W
14	Pennsylvania □	40 50N	78 0W
9	Pensacola	30 30N	87 10W
24	Penticton	49 30N	119 30W
46	Penza	53 13N	45 0E
36	Penzance	50 7N	5 32W
49	Penzhinskaya Guba	61 0N	162 0E
13	Peoria, Ariz.	33 40N	112 15W
16	Peoria, Ill.	40 42N	89 36W
39	Perdido, Mte.	42 40N	0 5E
30	Pereira	4 49N	75 43W
32	Pergamino	33 52S	60 30W
38	Périgord, reg.	45 0N	0 40E
38	Périgueux	45 10N	0 42E
28	Perlas, Arch.de las	8 41N	79 7W
46	Perm	58 0N	57 10E
31	Pernambuco=Recife	8 0S	35 0W
31	Pernambuco □	8 0S	37 0W
41	Pernik	42 36N	23 2E
38	Perpignan	42 42N	2 53E
17	Perrysburg	41 33N	83 38W
16	Perryville	37 43N	89 52W
55	Persepolis	29 55N	52 50E
55	Persia=Iran ■	35 0N	50 0E
53	Persian Gulf	27 0N	50 0E
70	Perth, Australia	31 57S	115 52E
22	Perth, Canada	44 54N	76 15W
36	Perth, U.K.	56 24N	3 27W
15	Perth Amboy	43 3N	74 12W
30	Peru ■	8 0S	75 0W
16	Peru, Ill.	41 20N	89 8W
17	Peru, Ind.	40 45N	86 4W
40	Perúgia	43 6N	12 24E
47	Pervomaysk	48 5N	30 55E
46	Pervouralsk	56 55N	60 0E
40	Pésaro	43 55N	12 53E
40	Pescara	42 28N	14 13E
56	Peshawar	34 2N	71 37E
52	Petah Tiqwa	32 6N	34 53E
18	Petaluma	38 14N	122 39W
71	Peterborough, Australia	33 0S	138 45E
22	Peterborough, Canada	44 20N	78 20W
36	Peterborough, U.K.	52 35N	0 14W
24	Petersburg, Canada	56 50N	133 0W
8	Petersburg, U.S.A.	37 17N	77 26W
36	Peterhead	57 30N	1 49W
27	Peto	20 10N	89 0W
72	Petone	41 13S	174 53E
8	Petoskey	45 21N	84 55W
22	Petrolia	42 52N	82 9W
48	Petropavlovsk	55 0N	69 0E
49	Petropavlovsk-Kamchatskiy	53 16N	159 0E
31	Petrópolis	22 33S	43 9W
46	Petrozavodsk	61 41N	34 20E
46	Petsamo=Pechenga	69 30N	31 25E
42	Pforzheim	48 53N	8 43E
58	Phan Rang	11 40N	109 9E
58	Phanh Bho Ho Chi Minh	10 58N	106 40E
9	Phenix City	32 30N	85 0W
15	Philadelphia	40 0N	75 10W
41	Philippi	39 9N	80 2W
59	Philippines ■	12 0N	123 0E
15	Phillipsburg	40 42N	75 12W
24	Philomena	55 10N	111 38W
58	Phnom Penh	11 33N	104 55E
13	Phoenix	33 30N	112 10W
69	Phoenix Is.	3 30S	172 0W
15	Phoenixville	40 8N	75 31W
58	Phra Nakhon Si Ayutthaya	14 25N	100 30E
58	Phuket	8 0N	98 28E
40	Piacenza	45 2N	9 42E
31	Piaui □	7 0S	43 0W
38	Picardie, reg.	50 0N	2 15E
22	Picton, Canada	44 0N	77 8W
72	Picton, N.Z.	41 18S	174 3E
24	Picture Butte	49 53N	112 47W
26	Piedras Negras	28 35N	100 35W
40	Piemonte □	45 0N	7 30E
10	Pierre	44 23N	100 20W
67	Pietermaritzburg	29 35S	30 25E
43	Pietrosul, mt.	47 35N	24 43E
10	Pikes Pk.	38 50N	105 10W
8	Pikeville	37 30N	82 30W
32	Pilcomayo, R.	25 21S	57 42W
42	Pilsen=Plzen	49 45N	13 22E
28	Pinar del Rio	22 26N	83 40W
25	Pinawa	50 9N	95 53W
24	Pincher Creek	49 29N	113 57W
41	Pindos Óros, mts.	40 0N	21 0E
11	Pine Bluff	34 10N	92 0W
25	Pine Falls	50 34N	96 13W
24	Pine Point	60 50N	114 40W
61	Pingsiang	22 2N	106 55E
61	Pingtung	22 36N	120 30E
41	Pinios, R.	39 54N	22 45E
28	Pinos, I.de	21 40N	82 40W
43	Piotrków Trybunalsk	51 23N	19 43E
17	Piqua	49 9N	84 15W
31	Piracicaba	22 45S	47 30W
41	Piraeus=Piraievs	37 57N	23 42E
41	Piraievs	37 57N	23 42E
39	Pirineos, mts.	42 45N	0 18E
59	Piru	3 3S	128 12E
40	Pisa	43 43N	10 23E
30	Pisco	13 50S	76 5W
19	Pismo Beach	35 13N	120 40W
40	Pistóia	43 57N	10 53E
39	Pisuerga, R.	41 33N	4 52W
69	Pitcairn I.	25 5S	130 5W
44	Pite älv	65 44N	20 50W
18	Pittsburg, Calif.	38 2N	121 53W
11	Pittsburg, Kans.	37 21N	94 43W
14	Pittsburgh	40 26N	80 0W
8	Pittsfield, Ill.	39 35N	90 46W
15	Pittsfield, Mass.	42 27N	73 15W
15	Pittston	41 19N	75 47W
30	Piura	5 5S	80 45W
23	Placentia B.	47 0N	54 30W
18	Placerville	38 43N	120 48W
28	Placetas	22 15N	79 44W
15	Plainfield	42 31N	72 55W
25	Plainview	34 10N	101 40W
18	Planada	37 18N	120 19W
23	Plaster Rock	46 54N	67 24W
32	Plata, Rio de la	35 30S	56 0W
10	Platte, R.	39 16N	94 50W
16	Platteville	42 44N	90 29W
15	Plattsburgh	44 42N	73 28W
42	Plauen	50 29N	12 9E
8	Pleasantville	39 25N	74 30W
17	Pleasure Ridge Park	38 11N	85 51W
72	Plenty, B.of	37 45S	177 0E
23	Plessisville	46 14N	71 46W
41	Pleven	43 26N	24 37E
43	Plock	52 32N	19 40E
43	Ploiesti	44 57N	26 5E
41	Plovdiv	42 8N	24 44E
18	Plumas	39 46N	120 4W
36	Plymouth, U.K.	50 23N	4 9W
17	Plymouth, Ind.	41 21N	86 19W
15	Plymouth, Pa.	41 14N	75 58W
42	Plzen	49 45N	13 22E
40	Po, R.	44 57N	12 4E
61	Po Hai, B.	38 0N	120 0E
48	Pobedy, Pik	40 45N	79 58E
12	Pocatello	42 50N	112 25W
49	Podkamennaya Tunguska, R.	61 36N	90 18E
46	Podolsk	55 30N	37 30E
22	Point Edward	43 10N	82 30W
15	Point Pleasant	40 5N	74 4W
29	Pointe-à-Pitre	16 10N	61 30W
66	Pointe-Noire	4 48S	12 0E
38	Poitiers	46 35N	0 20W
38	Poitou, reg.	46 30N	0 1W
43	Pojezierze Mazurskie, reg.	53 50N	21 0E
55	Polan	25 35N	61 12E
43	Poland ■	52 0N	20 0E
46	Polesye	52 30N	28 30E
46	Polotsk	55 30N	28 50E
47	Poltava	49 35N	34 35E
19	Pomona	34 2N	117 49W
11	Ponca City	36 40N	97 5W
29	Ponce	18 1N	66 37W
19	Pond	35 40N	119 23W
21	Pond Inlet	72 41N	78 0W
*56	Pondicherry	11 59N	79 50E
40	Ponente, Rivera di, reg.	44 10N	8 20E
24	Ponoka	52 42N	113 35W
32	Ponta Grossa	25 0S	50 10W
38	Pontarlier	46 54N	6 20E
11	Pontchartrain, L.	30 12N	90 0W
34	Pontevedra	42 26N	8 40W
17	Pontiac, Ill.	40 53N	88 38W
17	Pontiac, Mich.	42 40N	83 20W
58	Pontianak	0 3S	109 15E
54	Pontine Mts.= Karadeniz Daglari	41 30N	35 0E
36	Pontrilas	51 56N	2 53W
30	Poopó, L.	18 30S	67 35W
30	Popayán	2 27N	76 36W
11	Poplar Bluff	36 45N	90 22W
27	Popocatepetl	19 10N	98 40W
45	Pori	61 27N	21 50E
24	Port Alberni	49 14N	124 48W
23	Port Alfred, Canada	48 19N	70 53W
67	Port Alfred, S.Africa	33 36S	26 55E
24	Port Alice	50 23N	127 26W
*18	Port Angeles	48 0N	123 30W
28	Port Antonio	18 10N	76 30W
22	Port Arthur, Canada= Thunder Bay	48 25N	89 10W
11	Port Arthur, U.S.A.	30 0N	94 0W
29	Port-au-Prince	18 40N	72 20W
71	Port Augusta	32 30S	137 45E
57	Port Canning	22 17N	88 48E
23	Port-Cartier	50 10N	66 50W
72	Port Chalmers	45 49S	170 38E
17	Port Clinton	41 31N	82 56W
22	Port Colborne	42 50N	79 10W
24	Port Coquitlam	49 16N	122 47W
58	Port Dickson	2 30N	101 49E
22	Port Elgin	44 25N	81 25W
67	Port Elizabeth	33 58S	25 40E
64	Port Étienne= Nouadhibou	21 0N	17 0W
66	Port-Gentil	0 47S	8 40E
64	Port Harcourt	4 40N	7 10E
21	Port Harrison= Inoucdjouac	58 27N	78 6W
70	Port Hedland	20 25S	118 35E
22	Port Hope	43 57N	78 18W
19	Port Hueneme	34 9N	119 12W
8	Port Huron	43 0N	82 28W
15	Port Jervis	41 22N	74 41W
58	Port Kelang	3 2N	101 28E
70	Port Lincoln	34 42S	135 52E
64	Port-Lyautey= Kenitra	34 15N	6 40W
*20	Port Moller	56 0N	160 50W
68	Port Moresby	9 24S	147 8E
25	Port Nelson	57 5N	92 56W
21	Port-Nouveau-Québec	58 30N	65 50W
*29	Port of Spain	10 40N	61 20W
22	Port Perry	44 6N	78 56W
71	Port Phillip B.	38 0S	145 0E
71	Port Pirie	33 10S	137 58E
65	Port Said=Bûr Saîd	31 16N	32 18E
67	Port Shepstone	30 44S	30 28E
22	Port Stanley	42 40N	81 13W
65	Port Sudan= Bur Sûdân	19 32N	37 9E
*18	Port Townsend	48 7N	122 46W
58	Port Weld	4 50N	100 38E
25	Portage la Prairie	49 58N	98 18W
29	Port-au-Prince	18 40N	72 20W
18	Porterville	36 4N	119 1W
17	Portland, Ind.	40 26N	84 59W
*9	Portland, Me.	43 40N	70 15W
*18	Portland, Ore.	45 35N	122 40W
23	Portneuf	46 42N	71 53W
39	Porto	41 8N	8 40W
32	Pôrto Alegre	30 5S	51 3W
64	Porto-Novo	6 23N	2 42E
40	Porto Tórres	40 50N	8 23E
30	Porto Velho	8 46S	63 54W
40	Portoferráio	42 50N	10 20E
18	Portola	39 48N	120 28W
36	Portsmouth, U.K.	50 48N	1 6W
15	Portsmouth, N.H.	43 5N	70 45W
8	Portsmouth, Ohio	38 45N	83 0W
8	Portsmouth, Va.	36 50N	76 20W
44	Porttipahta, L.	68 5N	26 40E
39	Portugal ■	40 0N	7 0W
32	Posadas	27 30S	56 0W
40	Potenza	40 40N	15 50E
8	Potomac, R.	39 40N	78 25W
30	Potosí	19 38S	65 50W
59	Pototan	10 56N	122 38E
42	Potsdam	52 40N	13 30E

15 Pottstown 40 15N 75 38W
15 Pottsville 40 41N 76 12W
24 Pouce Coupe 55 43N 120 8W
15 Poughkeepsie 41 40N 73 57W
19 Poway 32 58N 117 2W
13 Powell, L. 37 25N 110 45W
24 Powell River 49 53N 124 33W
61 Poyang Hu 29 10N 116 10 E
22 Poza Rica 20 33N 97 27W
42 Poznań 52 25N 17 0 E
42 Praha 50 5N 14 22 E
16 Prairie du Chien 43 3N 91 9W
24 Prairies, Coteau des 44 30N 97 0W
40 Prato 43 53N 11 5 E
41 Prepansko Jezero, L. 40 45N 21 0 E
57 Preparis North Chan. 15 12N 93 40 E
22 Prescott, Canada 44 43N 75 31W
13 Prescott, U.S.A. 34 35N 112 30W
31 Presidente Prudente 22 5s 51 25W
*9 Presque Isle 46 41N 68 1W
36 Preston 53 46N 2 42W
67 Pretoria 25 44s 28 12 E
*20 Pribilov, Is. 57 0N 170 0W
15 Price 39 40N 110 48W
47 Prikaspiyskaya Nizmennost, depression 42 20N 47 0 E
25 Prince Albert 53 15N 105 50W
25 Prince Albert Nat.Park 54 0N 106 25W
23 Prince Edward I. □ 44 2N 77 20W
24 Prince George 53 55N 122 46W
24 Prince of Wales, I., Alaska 55 47N 132 50W
71 Prince of Wales, I. Australia 10 35s 142 0 E
20 Prince of Wales I., Canada 73 0N 99 0W
24 Prince Rupert 54 20N 130 20W
14 Princess Charlotte Bay 14 15s 144 0 E
24 Princess Royal I. 52 55N 128 50W
24 Princeton, Canada 49 27N 120 30W
16 Princeton, Ill. 41 23N 89 28W
17 Princeton, Ind. 38 21N 87 34W
8 Princeton, Ky. 37 6N 87 55W
15 Princeton, N.J. 40 21N 74 40W
8 Princeton, W.Va. 37 21N 81 8W
46 Pripet-Marshes= Polesye 52 30N 28 30 E
46 Pripyat, R. 51 21N 30 9 E
30 Pritchard 30 47N 88 5W
47 Privolzhskaya Vozvyshennost 50 0N 45 0 E
17 Progreso 21 20N 89 40W
48 Prokopyevsk 54 0N 87 3 E
57 Prome 18 45N 95 30 E
38 Provence, reg. 43 40N 5 46 E
15 Providence 41 41N 71 15W
28 Providencia, I.de 13 25N 81 26W
24 Provincial Cannery 51 33N 127 37W
12 Provo 40 16N 111 37W
*20 Prudhoe Bay 70 20N 149 50W
43 Przemysl 49 47N 22 47 E
46 Pskov 57 50N 28 25 E
25 Puebla 19 0N 98 10W
10 Pueblo 38 20N 104 40W
33 Puento Alto 33 32s 70 35W
28 Puerto Armuelles 8 20N 83 10W
30 Puerto Cabello 10 28N 68 1W
28 Puerto Cortés 15 51N 88 0W
25 Puerto Montt 41 28s 72 57W
28 Puerto Padre 21 13N 76 35W
29 Puerto Plata 19 40N 70 45 E
29 Puerto Rico ■ 18 16N 66 45W
24 Puget Sd. 47 15N 123 30W
25 Pukatawagan 55 45N 101 20W
40 Pula 39 0N 9 0 E
11 Pulaski, Tenn. 35 10N 87 0W
8 Pulaski, Va. 37 4N 80 49W
12 Pullman 46 49N 117 10W
57 Punakha 27 42N 89 52 E
56 Pune 18 29N 73 57 E
56 Punjab □ 31 0N 76 0 E
30 Puno 15 55s 70 3W
33 Punta Alta 38 53s 62 4W
32 Punta Arenas 53 0s 71 0W
28 Puntarenas 10 0N 84 50W
59 Puntjak Djaja, mt. 5 0s 137 20 E
25 Purnea 25 45N 87 31 E
30 Purus, R. 3 42s 61 28W
59 Purwakarta 6 35s 107 29 E
61 Pusan 35 5N 129 0 E
72 Putaruru 38 3s 175 47 E
54 Puttgarden 54 28N 11 15 E
12 Puyallup 47 10N 122 22W
38 Puy-de-Dôme, mt. 45 46N 2 57 E
38 Puy-de-Dôme □ 45 47N 3 0 E
*18 Puyallup 47 11N 122 18W
46 Pya-ozero 66 8N 31 22 E
47 Pyatigorsk 44 2N 43 0 E

61 Pyongyang 39 0N 125 30 E
12 Pyramid, L. 40 0N 119 30W
39 Pyrénées, mts. 42 45N 0 18 E
38 Pyrénées Atlantiques □ 43 16N 0 46W
38 Pyrénées Orientales □ 42 35N 2 26 E

Q

52 Qabatiya 32 24N 35 17 E
55 Qadam 32 55N 66 45 E
54 Qarachuk 37 0N 42 2 E
55 Qasr-e Qand 26 15N 60 45 E
53 Qatar ■ 25 30N 51 15 E
65 Qattâra, Depression= Qattâra, Munkhafed . 29 30N 27 30 E
54 Qazvin 35 15N 50 0 E
65 Qena 26 10N 32 43 E
52 Quesari 32 30N 34 53 E
52 Qeshm, I. 26 50N 56 0 E
*52 Qezi'ot 30 50N 34 28 E
52 Qiryat Ata 32 48N 35 6 E
52 Qiryat Bialik 32 50N 35 5 E
52 Qiryat Gat 31 36N 35 47 E
52 Qiryat Hayyim 32 49N 35 4 E
52 Qiryat Mal'akhi 31 44N 34 45 E
52 Qiryat Shemona 33 13N 35 35 E
52 Qiryat Tiv'on 32 43N 35 8 E
52 Qiryat Yam 32 51N 35 4 E
55 Qizan 16 57N 42 34 E
55 Qolleh-ye-Damavand 36 0N 52 0 E
55 Qom 34 40N 51 0 E
55 Quchan 37 10N 58 27 E
23 Québec 46 52N 71 13W
23 Québec □ 50 0N 70 0W
24 Queen Charlotte 53 10N 132 0W
24 Queen Charlotte Is. 53 10N 132 0W
24 Queen Charlotte Str 50 45N 127 10W
71 Queensland □ 15 0s 142 0 E
*71 Queenstown 42 4s 145 35 E
67 Quelimane 17 53s 36 58 E
26 Querétaro 20 40N 100 23W
24 Quesnel 53 5N 122 30W
56 Quetta 30 15N 66 55 E
14 Quezaltenango 14 40N 91 30W
59 Quezon City 14 50N 121 0 E
38 Quiberon 47 29N 3 9W
32 Quillota 32 45s 71 16W
*56 Quilon 8 50N 76 38 E
38 Quimper 48 0N 4 9W
16 Quincy, Ill. 39 55N 91 20W
15 Quincy, Mass. 42 14N 71 0w
30 Quito 0 15s 78 35W
71 Quorn 32 25s 138 0 E

R

52 Ra'anana 32 12N 34 52 E
59 Raba 8 36s 118 55 E
64 Rabat 33 28N 6 48W
68 Rabaul 4 24s 152 18 E
16 Raccoon, R. 41 35N 93 37W
23 Race, C. 46 40N 53 18W
43 Racibórz 50 7N 18 18 E
17 Racine 42 41N 87 51W
8 Radford 37 8N 80 32W
43 Radom 51 23N 21 12 E
25 Radville 49 27N 104 17W
24 Rae 62 50N 116 3W
70 Raeside, L. 29 20s 122 0 E
32 Rafaela 31 30s 61 30W
52 Rafhao 29 42N 43 30W
40 Ragusa 36 56N 14 42 E
58 Rahaeng=Tak 16 50N 99 8 E
56 Raichur 16 10N 77 20 E
*18 Rainier, Mt. 46 50N 121 50W
25 Rainy L. 48 43N 94 29W
25 Rainy River 48 50N 89 56W
57 Raipur 21 17N 81 45 E
57 Rajahmundry 17 1N 81 48 E
56 Rajapalaiyam 9 25N 77 35 E
56 Rajasthan □ 26 45N 73 30 E
56 Rajkot 22 15N 70 56 E
57 Rajshahi □ 24 22N 88 39 E
8 Raleigh 35 46N 78 38W
52 Ram Allah 31 55N 35 10 E
52 Ramat Gan 32 4N 34 48 E
52 Ramat HaSharon 32 7N 34 50 E
52 Rambre Kyun, I. 19 0N 94 0 E
52 Ramla 31 55N 34 52 E
56 Rampur 28 50N 79 5 E
32 Rancagua 34 10s 70 50W
57 Ranchi 23 19N 85 27 E
45 Randers 56 29N 10 1 E
15 Randolph 42 10N 71 3W
70 Rangitaiki, R. 37 45s 176 53 E
57 Rangoon 16 45N 96 20 E
57 Rangoon=Rangon 16 45N 96 20 E
17 Rantoul 40 19N 88 9w

10 Rapid City 44 0N 103 0w
72 Rarotonga 21 30s 160 0w
13 Ras Dashen, mt. 13 8N 37 45 E
65 Rashid 31 21N 30 22 E
54 Rasht 37 20N 49 40 E
*20 Rat Is. 52 0N 177 30 E
40 Rathbun Res. 40 54N 93 5w
56 Ratlam 23 28N 75 0 E
24 Ratz, Mt. 57 23N 132 18w
72 Raukumara Ra. 38 5s 177 55 E
45 Rauma 61 10N 21 30 E
40 Ravenna, Italy 44 28N 12 15 E
14 Ravenna, U.S.A. 41 9N 81 15w
56 Rawalpindi 33 38N 73 8 E
22 Rawdon 46 4N 73 44w
70 Rawlinna 30 58s 125 28 E
12 Rawlins 41 50N 107 20w
22 Raymond, Canada 49 27N 112 39w
*18 Raymond, U.S.A. 46 45N 123 44w
25 Raymore 51 25N 104 31w
11 Raytown 39 0N 94 28w
38 Raz.Pte.du 48 2N 4 47w
15 Reading, U.K. 51 27N 0 57w
17 Reading, Ohio 39 14N 84 27w
15 Reading, Pa. 40 20N 75 53w
60 Rebun-To 45 40N 142 45 E
31 Recife 8 0s 35 0w
37 Recklinghausen 51 36N 7 10 E
11 Red, R., La. 31 0N 91 40w
10 Red, R., Minn. 48 10N 97 0w
15 Red Bank 40 21N 74 3w
25 Red Deer 52 20N 113 50w
25 Red Lake 51 3N 93 49w
25 Red Rock 49 58N 88 15w
16 Red Rock, L. 41 30N 93 20w
53 Red Sea 25 0N 36 0 E
10 Red Wing 44 32N 92 35w
25 Redcliff 50 5N 110 47w
10 Redding 40 30N 122 25w
19 Redlands 34 0N 117 0w
*18 Redmond 44 40N 122 7w
19 Redondo Beach 33 52N 118 26w
24 Redvers 49 34N 101 42w
24 Redwater 53 57N 113 6w
18 Redwood City 37 30N 122 15w
18 Reedley 36 36N 119 27w
42 Regensburg 49 1N 12 7 E
40 Réggio di Calabria 38 7N 15 38 E
40 Réggio nell'Emilia 44 2N 10 38 E
25 Regina 50 30N 104 35w
55 Registan, reg. 30 15N 65 0 E
21 Rehovot 31 54N 34 48 E
37 Reichenbach 50 36N 12 19 E
9 Reidsville 36 21N 79 40w
38 Reims 49 15N 4 0 E
32 Reina Adelaide, Arch. 52 20s 74 50w
25 Reindeer L. 57 15N 102 15w
39 Reinosa 43 2N 4 15w
37 Remscheid 51 11N 7 12 E
22 Renfrew 45 30N 76 40w
58 Rengat 0 30s 102 45 E
59 Renkum 51 58N 5 43 E
38 Rennes 48 7N 1 41w
12 Reno 39 30N 119 50w
15 Rensselaer 42 39N 73 44w
12 Renton 47 30N 122 9w
10 Republican, R. 39 3N 96 48w
21 Repulse Bay 66 32N 85 15w
25 Reserve 52 28N 102 39w
55 Reshteh-ye Kukha-ye Alberz, mts. 36 0N 53 0 E
32 Resistencia 27 30s 59 0w
40 Resita 45 18N 21 53 E
21 Resolution I., Canada 61 30N 65 0w
72 Resolution, I., N.Z. 45 40s 166 40 E
14 Retalhuleu 14 33N 91 46w
56 Revda 56 48N 59 57 E
24 Revelstoke 51 0N 118 0w
69 Revilla Gigedo Is. 18 40N 112 0w
24 Revillagigedo I. 55 35N 131 23w
52 Rewa 24 33N 81 25 E
46 Reykjavik 64 10N 22 0w
27 Reynosa 26 5N 98 18w
54 Reza'iyeh 37 40N 45 0 E
54 Rheden 52 0N 6 3 E
37 Rhein, R. 51 52N 6 2 E
37 Rhine=Rhein, R. 51 52N 6 2 E
10 Rhinelander 45 38N 89 29w
15 Rhode Island □ 41 38N 71 37w
67 Rhodesia ■ 20 0N 30 0 E
41 Rhodopi Planina, mts. 41 40N 24 20 E
38 Rhön, mts. 50 12N 10 0 E
38 Rhondda 51 39N 3 30w
38 Rhône, R. 43 28N 4 42 E
38 Rhône □ 45 54N 4 35 E
58 Rialto 34 6N 117 22w
58 Riau, Kepulauan 1 0N 104 30 E
58 Riau □ 0 0N 102 35 E
31 Ribeirao Preto 21 10s 47 50w
72 Riccarton 43 32s 172 37 E
19 Rice 32 15N 96 30w
10 Rice Lake 45 30N 91 42w

23 Richibucto 46 41N 64 52w
12 Richland 46 15N 119 15w
18 Richmond, Calif. 38 0N 122 30w
17 Richmond, Ind. 39 50N 84 50w
8 Richmond, Ky. 37 40N 84 20w
8 Richmond, Va. 37 33N 77 27w
22 Richmond G. 56 15N 76 17w
*18 Ridgefield 45 49N 122 45w
12 Ridgewood 40 59N 74 7w
46 Riga 56 57N 24 6 E
46 Rigas Juras Licis 57 30N 23 35 E
40 Rijeka 45 20N 14 21 E
37 Rijswijk 52 4N 4 22 E
44 Rimini 44 3N 12 33 E
23 Rimouski 48 27N 68 30w
32 Rio Cuarto 33 10s 64 25w
31 Rio de Janeiro 23 0s 43 12w
32 Rio Gallegos 51 35s 69 15w
32 Río Grande, Brazil 32 0s 52 20w
26 Rio Grande, Mexico 23 50N 103 2w
31 Rio Grande do Norte □ 5 45s 36 0w
30 Rio Grande do Sul □ 30 0s 54 0w
11 Río Grande, R. 37 47N 106 15w
66 Rio Muni □ 1 30N 10 0 E
1 Riobamba 1 50s 78 45w
27 Rioverde 21 56N 99 59w
18 Ripley 33 29N 114 40w
18 Ripon 37 44N 121 7w
52 Rishon Le Zion 31 58N 34 48 E
32 Rivera 31 0s 55 50w
15 Riverhead 40 53N 72 40w
25 Riverhurst 50 55N 106 50w
19 Riverside 34 0N 117 15w
51 Riverton 51 0N 97 0w
23 Rivière-Bleue 47 26N 69 3w
23 Rivière du Loup 47 50N 69 30w
53 Riyadh=Ar Riyad 24 41N 46 42 E
31 Rize 41 0N 40 30 E
38 Roanne 46 3N 4 4 E
9 Roanoke 37 19N 79 55w
15 Roanoke, R. 36 15N 77 20w
17 Robinson 39 0N 87 44w
25 Roblin 51 14N 101 21w
24 Robson, mt. 53 10N 119 10w
32 Rocha 34 30s 54 25w
17 Rochefort 45 56N 0 57w
17 Rochester, Ind. 42 4N 86 13w
11 Rochester, Minn. 44 1N 92 28w
15 Rochester, N.H. 43 18N 70 59w
14 Rochester, N.Y. 43 10N 77 36w
16 Rock Falls 41 47N 89 41w
9 Rock Hill 34 55N 81 2w
10 Rock Island 41 30N 90 35w
12 Rocksprings 46 55N 106 11w
*18 Rockdale 47 22N 121 28w
16 Rockford 42 20N 89 0w
71 Rockhampton 23 22s 150 32 E
*9 Rockland 44 6N 69 6w
18 Rocklin 38 48N 121 14w
8 Rockville 39 7N 77 10w
9 Rocky Mount 35 55N 77 48w
24 Rocky Mountain House 52 22N 114 44w
12 Rocky River 41 30N 81 40w
41 Ródhos 36 15N 28 10 E
18 Roebuck, B. 18 5s 122 20 E
37 Roermond 51 12N 6 0 E
37 Roeselare 50 57N 3 7 E
38 Rohnert Park 38 21N 122 42w
56 Rohtak 28 55N 76 43 E
37 Rolla 37 57N 91 46w
71 Roma, Australia 26 32s 148 15 E
40 Roma, Italy 41 54N 12 30 E
9 Rome, Ga. 34 20N 85 0w
14 Rome, N.Y. 43 14N 75 29w
30 Rondônia □ 11 0s 63 0w
2 Roraima, Mt. 5 10N 60 40w
2 Roraima □ 2 0N 61 30w
32 Rosario, Argentina 33 0s 60 50w
26 Rosario, Mexico 23 0N 106 0w
39 Rosas, G. de 42 10N 3 15 E
*29 Roseau 15 20N 61 30w
25 Rosetown 51 33N 108 0w
31 Rosetta=Rashid 31 21N 30 22 E
18 Roseville, Calif. 38 46N 121 41w
42 Roseville, Mich. 42 30N 82 56w
52 Rosh Ha'Ayin 32 5N 34 57 E
45 Roskilde 55 38N 12 3 E
1 Ross Dependency □ 70 0s 170 15w
3 Ross Sea 74 0s 178 0 E
24 Rossford 41 37N 83 33w
24 Rossland 49 6N 117 50w
42 Rostock 54 4N 12 9 E
47 Rostov 57 14N 39 15 E

Spartivento, C., Sardegna **Thanlwin Myit, R.**

40 Spartivento, C., Sardegna 38 52N 8 50E
17 Speedway 39 47N 86 15W
71 Spencer Gulf 34 30S 137 0E
72 Spenser, Mts. 42 15S 172 45E
24 Spirit River 55 47N 118 50W
33 Spitsbergen=Svalbard 78 0N 17 0E
40 Split 43 31N 16 26E
42 Splügenpass 46 30N 9 20E
12 Spokane 47 45N 117 25W
42 Spree, R. 52 32N 13 13E
18 Spring Garden 39 51N 120 46W
13 Spring Mts. 36 20N 115 43W
16 Springfield, Ill. 39 47N 89 40W
15 Springfield, Mass. 42 8N 72 37W
11 Springfield, Mo. 37 15N 93 20W
17 Springfield, Ohio 39 50N 83 48W
12 Springfield, Ore. 44 2N 123 0W
9 Springfield, Tenn. 36 35N 86 55W
23 Springhill 45 39N 64 3W
67 Springs 26 13S 28 25E
12 Springville 40 14N 111 35W
24 Squamish 49 42N 123 9W
40 Squillace 38 43N 16 35E
49 Sredinnyy Khrebet 57 0N 160 0E
49 Srednekolymsk 67 20N 154 40E
56 Sri Lanka ■ 7 0N 81 0E
56 Srinagar 34 12N 74 50E
36 Stafford 52 49N 2 9W
47 Stalingrad=Volgograd 48 40N 44 25E
15 Stamford 41 5N 73 30W
32 Stanley, Falkland Is. 51 40S 58 0W
66 Stanleyville=Kisangani 0 41N 25 11E
49 Stanovoy Khrebet 55 0N 130 0E
20 Stanton 69 45N 128 52W
*18 Stanwood 48 15N 122 23W
41 Stara Planina, Mts. 43 15N 23 0E
41 Stara Zagora 42 26N 25 39E
46 Staraya Russa 57 58N 31 10E
46 Starogard 53 55N 18 30E
14 State College 40 48N 77 52W
15 Staten I. 40 35N 74 9W
9 Statesville 35 48N 80 51W
8 Staunton 38 7N 79 4W
45 Stavanger 58 57N 5 40E
47 Stavropol 45 5N 42 0E
25 Steinbach 49 32N 96 41W
44 Steinkjer 63 59N 11 31E
23 Stellarton 45 34N 62 40W
67 Stellenbosch 33 58S 18 50E
40 Stelvio, Pso. del 46 32N 10 27E
23 Stephenville 48 33N 58 35W
10 Sterling, Colo. 40 40N 103 15W
16 Sterling, Ill. 41 48N 89 42W
46 Sterlitamak 53 40N 56 0E
42 Stettin=Szczecin 53 27N 14 27E
24 Stettler 52 19N 112 43W
14 Steubenville 40 21N 80 39W
*18 Stevenson 45 42N 121 53W
24 Stewart 55 56N 129 59W
72 Stewart, I. 46 58S 167 54E
18 Stewarts Point 38 40N 123 27W
24 Stikine, R. 56 40N 132 30W
11 Stillwater 36 5N 97 3W
12 Stillwater Mts. 39 45N 11 6W
36 Stirling 56 17N 3 57W
45 Stockholm 59 20N 18 3E
36 Stockport 53 25N 2 11W
18 Stockton 38 0N 121 20W
16 Stockton Res. 37 41N 93 45W
36 Stockton on Tees 54 34N 1 20W
36 Stoke on Trent 53 1N 2 11W
25 Stonewall 50 8N 97 19W
44 Stora Lulevatten, L. 67 20N 19 0E
45 Store Bælt, Str. 55 28N 11 0E
44 Storsjön, L. 63 12N 14 15E
44 Storuman, L. 65 13N 16 50E
42 Stralsund 54 17N 13 5E
38 Strasbourg 48 35N 7 42E
22 Stratford, Canada 43 23N 81 0W
72 Stratford, N.Z. 39 20S 174 19E
15 Stratford, U.S.A. 41 14N 73 7W
36 Stratford on Avon 52 12N 1 42W
18 Strathmore 36 9N 119 4W
22 Strathroy 42 57N 81 38W
70 Streaky, B. 32 51S 134 18E
17 Streator 41 7N 88 50W
40 Strómboli, I. 38 48N 15 12E
41 Struma, R. 40 47N 23 51E
14 Struthers 41 4N 80 38W
22 Sturgeon Falls 46 22N 79 55W
17 Sturgis 41 48N 85 25W
70 Sturt, R. 20 8S 127 24E
42 Stuttgart 48 46N 9 10E
61 Suanhwa 40 35N 115 0E
59 Subang 7 30S 107 45E
41 Subotica 46 6N 19 29E
28 Suchitoto 13 56N 89 0W
61 Suchow 34 10N 117 20E
30 Sucre 19 0S 65 15W
65 Sudan ■ 11 0N 9 0E
22 Sudbury 46 30N 81 0W
65 Sûdd 8 20N 29 30E
42 Sudety, mts. 50 20N 16 45E
65 Suez=El Suweis 29 58N 32 31E
8 Suffolk 36 47N 76 33W
21 Sugluk=Saglouc 62 30N 74 15W
58 Sukadana 1 10S 110 0E
47 Sukhumi 43 0N 41 0E
56 Sukkur 27 42N 68 52E
56 Sukkur Barrage 27 50N 68 46E
56 Sulaiman Ra. 30 30N 69 50E
53 Sulaimiya 24 11N 46 38E
59 Sulawesi □ 2 0S 120 0E
24 Sullivan Bay 50 55N 126 52W
*18 Sultan 47 51N 121 49W
59 Sulu Arch 6 0N 121 0E
59 Sulu Sea 8 0N 120 0E
58 Sumatera, I. 0 40N 100 20E
58 Sumatra, I.= Sumatera, I. 0 40N 100 20E
59 Sumba, I. 9 45S 119 35E
59 Sumbawa, I. 8 34S 117 17E
23 Summerside 46 29N 63 41W
17 Summit 41 47N 87 48W
*18 Sumner 47 12N 122 14W
47 Sumy 50 57N 34 50E
19 Sun City 33 42N 117 11W
14 Sunbury 40 52N 76 47W
58 Sunda, Selat 6 20S 105 30E
57 Sundarbans, The 22 0N 89 0E
36 Sunderland 54 54N 1 22W
22 Sundridge 45 45N 79 25W
44 Sundsvall 62 23N 17 25E
58 Sungaipenah 2 1S 101 20E
61 Sungari, R. 47 44N 132 32E
59 Sungguminasa 5 17S 119 30E
18 Sunnyvale 37 23N 122 1W
12 Superior 40 3N 98 2W
22 Superior, L. 47 40N 87 0W
54 Suphan Dagi 38 54N 42 48E
54 Sur 33 19N 35 16E
59 Surabaja 7 17S 112 45E
59 Surakarta 7 35S 110 48E
56 Surat 21 12N 72 55E
19 Surf 34 40N 120 37W
31 Surinam ■ 4 0N 56 15W
65 Surt 31 11N 16 46E
44 Surtsey, I. 63 27N 20 15W
60 Suruga-Wan 34 45N 138 30E
15 Susquehanna, R. 39 33N 76 5W
23 Sussex 45 43N 65 31W
25 Sutherland 52 15N 106 40W
56 Sutlej, R. 29 23N 71 2E
72 Suva 17 40S 178 8E
9 Suwannee, R. 29 18N 83 9W
60 Suzuka 34 55N 136 36E
33 Svalbard, I. 78 0N 17 0E
45 Svealand, reg. 59 55N 15 0E
45 Svendborg 55 14N 10 35E
46 Sverdlovsk 56 50N 60 30E
71 Swain Reefs 21 45S 152 20W
24 Swan Hills 54 50N 116 0W
17 Swan Is. 17 22N 83 57W
25 Swan River 52 7N 101 16W
36 Swansea 51 37N 3 57W
67 Swaziland ■ 26 30S 31 30E
45 Sweden ■ 67 0N 15 0E
11 Sweetwater 32 30N 100 28W
24 Swift Current 50 20N 107 45W
42 Switzerland ■ 46 30N 8 50E
71 Sydney, Australia 33 53S 151 10E
23 Sydney, Canada 46 7N 60 7W
23 Sydney Mines 46 14N 60 14W
46 Sykyvkar 61 45N 50 40E
57 Sylhet 24 43N 91 55E
24 Sylvan Lake 52 19N 114 5W
17 Sylvania 41 43N 83 42W
48 Syr Darya, R. 46 3N 61 0E
15 Syracuse 43 3N 76 9W
54 Syria ■ 35 0N 38 0E
54 Syrian Desert 31 30N 40 0E
46 Syzran 53 12N 48 30E
42 Szczecin 53 27N 14 27E
61 Szechwan □ 30 10N 106 0E
43 Szeged 46 16N 20 10E
43 Székesfehérvár 47 15N 13 25E
61 Szemao 22 50N 101 0E
61 Szeping 43 10N 124 18E
43 Szolnok 47 10N 20 15E
42 Szombathely 47 14N 16 38E

T

61 Ta Hingan Ling 48 0N 121 0E
61 Ta Liang Shan 28 50N 103 0E
55 Tabas 33 36N 56 54E
24 Taber 49 47N 112 8W
67 Table Mt. 34 0S 18 22E
66 Tabora 5 2S 32 57E
54 Tabriz 38 7N 46 20E
59 Tacloban 11 1N 125 0E
30 Tacno 18 0S 70 20W
*18 Tacoma 47 15N 122 30W
64 Tademait, plat. du 28 30N 2 30E
23 Tadoussac 48 9N 69 43W
48 Tadzhik S.S.R. □ 35 30N 70 0E
61 Taegu 35 50N 128 25E
61 Taejon 35 30N 127 22E
47 Taganrog 47 12N 38 56E
59 Tagbilaran 9 39N 123 51E
69 Tahiti, I. 17 37S 149 27W
18 Tahoe, L. 39 7N 120 3W
*18 Taholah 47 21N 124 17W
61 Tai Hu 31 10N 120 0E
61 Taichung 24 10N 120 35E
61 Taihan Shan 36 0N 114 0E
72 Taihape 39 41S 175 48E
53 Taima 27 35N 38 45E
61 Tainan 23 0N 120 15E
61 Taipei 25 2N 121 30E
32 Taitao, Pen. de 46 30S 75 0W
61 Taiwan ■ 23 30N 121 0E
52 Taiyiba 32 16N 35 0E
61 Taiyuan 38 0N 112 30E
53 Ta'izz 13 38N 44 4E
39 Tajo=Tejo, R. 38 40N 9 24W
58 Tak 16 52N 99 8E
60 Takada 37 7N 138 15E
60 Takamatsu 34 20N 134 5E
60 Takaoka 36 40N 137 0E
72 Takapuna 36 47S 174 47E
60 Takasaki 36 20N 139 0E
60 Takatsuki 34 40N 135 37E
60 Takayama 36 10N 137 5E
55 Takhar □ 36 30N 69 30E
24 Takla Landing 55 29N 125 59W
61 Takla Makan 39 40N 85 0E
32 Talca 35 20S 71 46W
32 Talcahuano 36 40S 73 10W
61 Tali, Shensi 34 48N 109 48E
61 Tali, Yunnan 25 50N 100 0E
*20 Talkeetna 62 20N 150 7W
9 Talladega 33 28N 86 2W
9 Tallahassee 30 25N 84 15W
46 Tallinn 59 29S 24 58E
53 Talo, Mt. 10 44N 37 55E
64 Tamale 9 22N 0 50W
64 Tamanrasset 22 56N 5 30E
15 Tamaqua 40 48N 75 58W
67 Tamatave 18 10S 49 23E
27 Tamazunchale 21 16N 98 47W
46 Tambor 52 45N 41 20E
64 Tamgak, Mts. 19 12N 8 35E
*56 Tamil Nadu □ 11 0N 78 15E
52 Tammun 32 18N 35 23E
9 Tampa 27 57N 82 30W
45 Tampere 61 30N 23 50E
27 Tampico 22 20N 97 50W
53 Tamra 32 51N 35 12E
61 Tamsagbulag 24 5N 6 35W
53 Tana, L. 13 5N 37 30E
44 Tanafjorden 70 54N 28 40E
58 Tanahgrogot 1 54S 116 12E
59 Tanahmerah 6 5S 140 16E
70 Tanami Desert 20 0S 129 30E
*20 Tanana 65 10N 152 15W
*20 Tanana, R. 65 10N 152 5W
67 Tananarive= Antananarivo 18 55S 47 31E
32 Tandil 37 20S 59 5W
58 Tandjung 2 10S 115 25E
58 Tandjungkarang 5 20S 105 10E
58 Tandjungpandan 2 43S 107 38E
60 Tane-ga-Shima 30 30N 131 0E
66 Tanga 5 5S 39 2E
66 Tanganyika, L. 6 40S 30 0E
64 Tanger 35 48N 5 45W
59 Tangerang 6 12S 106 39E
61 Tanglha Shan 33 0N 90 0E
61 Tangshan 39 38N 118 11E
65 Tanta 30 45N 30 57E
66 Tanzania ■ 6 40S 34 0E
61 Tapa Shan 31 45N 109 30E
27 Tapachula 14 54N 92 17W
31 Tapajós, R. 2 24S 54 41W
54 Tarabulus, Lebanon 34 31N 33 52E
65 Tarabulus, Libya 32 54N 13 11E
65 Tarabulus, reg. 30 0N 15 0E
58 Tarakan 3 20N 117 35E
40 Taranto 40 30N 17 11E
40 Táranto, G. di 40 0N 17 15E
72 Tararua, Ra. 40 45S 175 25E
72 Tarawera, L. 38 13S 176 27E
56 Tarbela Dam 34 8N 72 49E
38 Tarbes 43 14N 0 5E
30 Tarija 21 30S 64 40W
61 Tarim, R. 41 5N 86 40E
50 Tarim Basin 39 30N 85 0E
59 Tarlac 15 29N 120 35E
38 Tarn, R. 44 5N 1 6E
38 Tarn □ 43 50N 2 0E
38 Tarn-et-Garonne □ 44 5N 1 20E
39 Tarragona 41 7N 1 15E
39 Tarrasa 41 34N 2 1E
15 Tarrytown 41 5N 73 52W
54 Tarsus 36 55N 34 53E
46 Tartu 58 23N 26 43E
48 Tashkent 41 20N 69 18E
55 Tashkurghan 36 43N 67 41E
72 Tasman, B. 41 0S 173 15E
72 Tasman, Mts. 41 5S 172 35E
72 Tasman Glacier 43 45S 170 20E
*71 Tasman Peninsula 43 5S 147 50E
68 Tasman Sea 40 0S 163 0E
*71 Tasmania □ 42 0S 147 0E
43 Tatabánya 47 34N 18 26E
46 Tatar A.S.S.R. □ 55 0N 51 0E
49 Tatarskiy Proliv 54 7N 53 7E
43 Tatry, mts. 49 14N 20 0E
61 Tatung 40 8N 113 13E
32 Taubaté 23 2S 45 33W
42 Tauern, mts. 47 0N 13 12S
72 Taumaruni 38 53S 175 15E
36 Taunton, U.K. 51 1N 3 7W
15 Taunton, U.S.A. 41 54N 71 6W
42 Taunus, mts. 37 0N 35 0E
72 Taupo, L. 38 46S 175 55E
72 Tauranga 37 35S 176 11E
54 Taurus Mts.=Toros Daglari, mts. 37 0N 33 0E
*72 Taveuni, I. 16 51S 179 58W
57 Tavoy 14 5N 98 12E
36 Tay, Firth of 56 25N 3 8W
36 Tay, R. 56 25N 3 24W
49 Taymyr, Poluostrov 76 0N 104 0E
16 Taylorville 39 33N 89 18W
59 Taytay 10 45N 119 30E
61 Tayulensze 29 15N 98 1E
47 Tbilisi 41 50N 44 50E
65 Tchad, L. 13 20N 14 0E
72 Te Anau, L. 45 15S 167 45E
72 Te Kuiti 38 20S 175 11E
26 Tecoman 18 55N 103 53W
28 Tegucigalpa 14 6N 87 13W
19 Tehachapi 35 8N 118 27W
19 Tehachapi Mts. 34 56N 118 40W
55 Tehran 35 40N 51 26E
27 Tehuacán 18 20N 97 30W
27 Tehuantepec 16 10N 95 19W
27 Tehuantepec, Istmo de 17 0N 94 30W
39 Tejo, R. 38 40N 9 24W
27 Tekak 20 20N 89 30W
52 Tel Aviv-Yafo 32 3N 34 46E
52 Tel Hazor 33 2N 35 2E
52 Tel Lakhish 31 34N 34 51E
52 Tel Megiddo 32 35N 38 11E
28 Tela 15 40N 87 28W
58 Telanaipura 1 38S 103 30E
24 Telegraph Creek 57 54N 131 9W
17 Tell City 37 57N 86 46W
58 Telok Anson 4 0N 101 10E
58 Telukbetung 5 29S 105 17E
64 Tema 5 41N 0 0E
22 Témiskaming 46 43N 79 6W
58 Tempino 1 55S 103 23E
11 Temple 31 5N 97 28W
18 Templeton 35 33N 120 42W
32 Temuco 38 50S 72 50W
72 Temuka 44 14S 171 17E
56 Tenali 16 15N 80 35E
27 Tenacingo 19 0N 99 33W
27 Tenango 19 0N 99 40W
64 Tenerife, I. 28 20N 16 40W
*18 Tenino 46 51N 122 51W
70 Tennant Creek 19 30S 134 0E
9 Tennessee, R. 37 4N 88 33W
9 Tennessee □ 36 0N 86 30W
71 Tenterfield 29 0S 152 0E
31 Teofilo Otoni 17 51S 41 30W
26 Tepic 21 30N 104 54W
31 Teresina 5 5S 42 49W
59 Ternate 0 45N 127 25E
40 Terni 42 34N 12 38E
24 Terrace 54 30N 128 35W
17 Terre Haute 39 28N 87 24W
11 Terrell 32 44N 96 19W
37 Terschelling, I. 53 24N 5 20E
39 Teruel 40 22N 1 8W
67 Tete 16 13S 33 33E
64 Tetouan 35 34N 5 23W
42 Teutoburger Wald, dist. 52 10N 8 15E
40 Tevere, R. 41 44N 12 14E
11 Texarkana 33 25N 94 0W
11 Texas □ 31 40N 98 30W
11 Texas City 27 20N 95 20W
37 Texel, I. 53 5N 4 50E
11 Texoma, L. 34 0N 96 38W
27 Teziutlán 19 50N 97 30W
57 Tezpur 26 40N 92 45E
58 Thailand ■ 16 0N 101 0E
58 Thakhek 17 25N 104 45E
22 Thames, R., Canada 42 25N 82 15W
36 Thames, R. U.K. 51 24N 0 24W
56 Thana 19 12N 72 59E
56 Thanjavur 10 48N 79 12E
57 Thanlwin Myit, R. 16 31N 97 37E

Thar Desert Valdez

Map	Place	Lat.	Long.
56	Thar Desert=Great Indian Desert	28 25N	72 0E
41	Thásos, I.	40 40N	24 40E
29	The Grenadines, Is.	12 30N	61 30W
31	The Hague='s-Gravenhage	52 7N	7 14E
70	The Johnston Lakes	32 25S	120 30E
25	The Pas	53 45N	101 15W
45	The Sound, str.	50 21N	4 9W
36	The Wash	52 55N	0 15E
41	Thermaikós Kólpos	40 30N	22 47E
41	Thessalia □	39 40N	22 0E
22	Thessalon	46 15N	83 34W
41	Thessaloniki	40 38N	23 0E
23	Thetford Mines	46 8N	71 18W
25	Thicket Portage	55 25N	97 45W
45	Thisted	56 57N	8 42E
9	Thomasville, Ala.	31 55N	87 42W
9	Thomasville, Fla.	30 50N	84 0W
9	Thomasville, N.C.	35 5N	80 4W
25	Thompson	55 45N	97 52W
25	Thompson Landing	62 45N	111 7W
71	Thomson, R.	25 11S	142 53E
19	Thousand Oaks	34 10N	118 50W
24	Three Hills	51 42N	113 16W
17	Three Rivers	41 57N	85 38W
42	Thun	46 45N	7 38E
22	Thunder Bay	48 25N	89 10W
42	Thüringer Wald, mts.	50 35N	11 0E
71	Thursday, I.	10 30S	142 3E
22	Thurso, Canada	45 36N	75 15W
36	Thurso, Scotland	58 34N	3 31W
40	Tiber=Tevere, R.	41 44N	12 14E
52	Tiberias	32 47N	35 32E
65	Tibesti, plateau	21 30N	17 30E
50	Tibet, Plateau of	31 30N	85 0E
61	Tibet □	32 30N	86 0E
40	Ticino, R.	45 9N	9 14E
57	Ticul	20 20N	89 50W
57	Tiddim	23 20N	93 45E
61	Tien Shan	42 0N	80 0E
37	Tienen	50 48N	4 57E
61	Tientsin	39 10N	117 0E
32	Tierra del Fuego, I.	54 0S	69 0W
17	Tiffin	41 7N	83 11W
54	Tigris, R.=Dijilah, Nahr	31 0N	47 25E
26	Tijuana	32 32N	117 1W
49	Tiksi	71 36N	128 48E
37	Tilburg	51 34N	5 5E
22	Tilbury	42 16N	82 26W
22	Tillsonburg	42 51N	80 44W
46	Timanskiy Kryazh	65 0N	51 0E
72	Timaru	44 24S	171 15E
43	Timisoara	45 45N	21 13E
22	Timmins	48 28N	81 20W
59	Timor, I.	8 35S	126 0E
70	Timor Sea	11 0S	128 0E
64	Tindouf	27 50N	8 4W
36	Tipperary	52 29N	8 10W
18	Tipton, Calif.	36 4N	119 19W
17	Tipton, Ind.	40 17N	86 2W
52	Tira	32 14N	34 56E
41	Tiranë	41 20N	19 50E
47	Tiraspol	46 51N	29 38E
52	Tirat Karmel	32 46N	34 58E
43	Tîrgu Mureş	46 33N	24 33E
42	Tirol □	47 15N	11 20E
*56	Tiruchchirappalli	10 48N	78 41E
*56	Tirunelveli	8 44N	77 41E
25	Tisdale	52 51N	104 3W
30	Titicaca, L.	15 50S	69 20W
57	Titlagarh	20 18N	83 10E
41	Titograd	42 26N	19 14E
27	Tizimín	21 0N	88 1W
59	Tjirebon	6 44S	108 34E
26	Tlaquepaque	20 39N	103 19W
27	Tlaxcala	19 20N	98 14W
64	Tlemcen	34 52N	1 15W
59	Tobelo	1 44N	128 1E
18	Tobin	39 56N	121 7W
48	Tobolsk	58 12N	68 16E
65	Tobruk=Tubruq	32 7N	23 55E
31	Tocantins, R.	1 45S	49 10W
9	Toccoa	34 6N	83 16W
32	Tocopilla	22 5S	70 12W
46	Togliatti	53 31N	49 26E
64	Togo ■	8 0N	1 10E
60	Tohoku □	35 40N	142 0E
60	Tokara-Kaikyo	30 10N	130 10E
72	Tokelau (Union) Group, Is.	9 0S	171 45W
60	Tokushima	34 4N	134 34E
60	Tokyo	35 42N	139 46E
39	Toledo, Spain	39 52N	4 1W
17	Toledo, U.S.A.	41 39N	83 32W
39	Toledo, Montes de	39 33N	4 20W
27	Toluca	19 20N	99 50W
18	Tomales	38 14N	122 55W
64	Tombouctou	16 46N	3 1W
59	Tomini, Teluk	0 20S	121 0E
48	Tomsk	56 30N	84 58E
14	Tonawanda	43 1N	78 53W
60	Tone-Giwa	36 15N	139 30E
*72	Tonga ■	20 0S	175 0W
*72	Tonga(Friendly)Is.	20 0S	173 0W
*72	Tongatapu	21 10S	175 10W
61	Tongking, G. of	21 30N	105 0E
38	Tonlé Sap, L.	12 50N	104 0E
45	Tonsberg	59 17N	10 25E
12	Tooele	40 30N	112 20W
71	Toowoomba	27 33S	151 57E
10	Topeka	39 3N	95 40W
19	Topock	34 44N	114 28W
70	Tor, B.	35 5S	117 50E
55	Torbat-e Jam	35 14N	60 36E
23	Torbay	47 40N	52 44W
40	Torino	45 3N	7 40E
44	Torne älv	65 48N	24 8E
32	Toro, Cerro del	29 8S	69 48W
22	Toronto, Canada	43 39N	79 23W
14	Toronto, U.S.A.	40 28N	80 36W
54	Toros Daglari, mts.	37 0N	33 0E
36	Torquay	50 27N	3 31W
16	Torrance	33 50N	118 19W
39	Torremolinos	36 38N	4 30W
71	Torrens, L.	31 0S	137 45E
26	Torréon	25 33N	103 25W
15	Torrington	41 48N	73 8W
39	Tortosa	40 49N	0 31E
39	Tortosa, C. de	40 41N	0 52E
43	Torún	53 0N	18 39E
60	Tosa-Wan	33 15N	133 30E
28	Totonicapán	14 50N	91 20W
60	Tottori	35 30N	134 15E
64	Toubkal, Djebel	31 0N	8 0W
64	Touggourt	33 10N	6 0E
38	Toulon	43 10N	5 55E
38	Toulouse	43 37N	1 28E
58	Tourane=Da-Nang	16 4N	108 13E
38	Tourcoing	50 42N	3 10E
37	Tournai	50 35N	3 25E
38	Tours	47 22N	0 40E
60	Towada-Ko	40 28N	140 55E
71	Townsville	19 16S	146 48E
8	Towson	39 26N	76 34W
60	Toyama	36 41N	137 13E
60	Toyama-wan	36 50N	137 10E
60	Toyohashi	34 46N	137 23E
60	Toyonaka	34 47N	135 28E
60	Toyota	35 5N	137 9E
54	Trabzon	41 0N	39 43E
18	Tracy	37 44N	121 25W
39	Trafalgar, C.	36 11N	6 2W
24	Trail	49 6N	117 42W
45	Tranas	58 3N	14 59E
25	Transcona	49 54N	97 0W
67	Transkei □	31 20S	29 0E
67	Transvaal □	25 0S	29 0E
43	Transylvania, reg.	46 30N	25 0E
40	Trápani	38 1N	12 31E
8	Traverse City	44 45N	85 39W
25	Treherne	49 38N	98 42W
32	Treinta y Tres	33 14S	54 23W
32	Trelew	43 15S	65 20W
45	Trelleborg	55 22N	13 10E
32	Trenque Lauquen	35 58S	62 44W
36	Trent, R.	53 42N	0 41W
40	Trento	46 5N	11 8E
22	Trenton, Canada	44 10N	77 40W
17	Trenton, Mich.	42 9N	83 11W
16	Trenton, Mo.	40 5N	93 37W
15	Trenton, N.J.	40 15N	74 41W
32	Tres Arroyos	38 20S	60 20W
40	Treviso	45 40N	12 15E
*56	Trichur	10 30N	76 18E
37	Trier	49 45N	6 37E
40	Trieste	45 39N	13 45E
*56	Trincomalee	8 38N	81 15E
28	Trinidad, Cuba	21 40N	80 0W
11	Trinidad, U.S.A.	37 15N	104 30W
29	Trinidad & Tobago ■	10 30N	61 20W
33	Trinidad, I.	20 20S	29 50W
18	Trinity, R.	29 47N	94 42W
23	Trinity B.	48 0N	53 0W
12	Trinity Mts.	40 20N	118 50W
54	Tripoli=Tarabulus, Lebanon	34 31N	33 52E
65	Tripoli=Tarabulus, Libya	32 54N	13 11E
65	Tripolitania=Tarabulus, reg.	30 0N	15 0E
57	Tripura □	24 0N	92 0E
33	Tristan da Cunha, I.	37 6S	12 20W
56	Trivandrum	8 31N	77 0E
23	Trois-Pistoles	48 7N	69 10W
22	Trois-Riviéres	46 25N	72 40W
45	Trollhattan	58 17N	12 20E
44	Tromsö	69 40N	19 0E
44	Trondheim	63 25N	10 25E
44	Trondheimsfjord	63 40N	10 45E
54	Troy=Truva	39 55N	26 20E
15	Troy, N.Y.	42 45N	73 39W
17	Troy, Ohio	40 2N	84 13W
38	Troyes	48 19N	4 3E
53	Trucial States=United Arab Emirates ■	24 0N	54 30E
30	Trujillo	8 0S	79 0W
58	Trung-Phan, reg.	15 0N	108 0E
23	Truro	45 21N	63 14E
54	Truva	39 55N	26 20E
61	Tsaidam, depression	37 0N	95 0E
61	Tsangpo, R.	29 10N	95 0E
48	Tselinograd	51 10N	71 30E
47	Tsimlyanskoye Vdkhr.	48 0N	43 0E
61	Tsin Ling Shan	34 0N	107 30E
61	Tsinan	36 41N	116 59E
61	Tsinghai □	35 10N	96 0E
61	Tsingtao	36 0N	120 25E
61	Tsining	40 59N	112 59E
61	Tsitsihar	47 20N	124 0E
60	Tsu	34 45N	136 25E
60	Tsugaru-Kaikyo	41 30N	140 30E
61	Tsunyi	27 40N	107 0E
69	Taumotu Archipelago	17 0S	144 0W
32	Tubarão	28 30S	49 0W
42	Tübingen	48 31N	9 4E
65	Tubruq	32 7N	23 55E
62	Tubuai Is.	23 0S	150 0W
13	Tucson	32 14N	110 59W
46	Tula	54 13N	37 32E
27	Tulancingo	20 5N	98 2W
18	Tulare	36 15N	119 26W
18	Tulare Basin	36 0N	119 45W
30	Tulcán	0 48N	77 43W
67	Tuléar	23 21S	43 40E
52	Tulkarm	32 19N	35 2E
9	Tullahoma	35 23N	86 12W
11	Tulsa	36 10N	96 0W
30	Tulua	4 6N	76 11W
30	Tumaco	1 50N	78 45W
66	Tumba, L.	0 50S	18 0E
41	Tundzha, R.	41 40N	26 34E
61	Tungchuan	35 4N	109 2E
61	Tunghwa	41 46N	126 0E
61	Tungliao	43 42N	122 11E
61	Tungting Hu	24 10N	118 14E
64	Tunis	36 50N	10 11E
64	Tunisia ■	33 30N	9 10E
30	Tunja	5 40N	73 25W
11	Tupelo	34 15N	88 42W
57	Tura	25 30N	90 16E
61	Turfan Depression	43 0N	88 0E
40	Turin=Torino	45 3N	7 40E
66	Turkana, L.	4 10N	36 10E
54	Turkey ■	39 0N	36 0E
48	Turkmen S.S.R. □	39 0N	59 0E
29	Turks Is.	21 20N	71 20W
45	Turku	60 27N	22 14E
18	Turlock	37 30N	120 51W
37	Turnhout	51 19N	4 57E
41	Turnovo	43 5N	25 41E
43	Turnu-Severin	44 39N	22 41E
25	Turtleford	53 30N	108 50W
9	Tuscaloosa	33 13N	87 33W
14	Tuscarora Mts.	41 0N	116 20W
14	Tussey Mts.	40 25N	78 7W
49	Tuva A.S.S.R. □	51 30N	95 0E
68	Tuvalu, Is.	8 0S	176 0E
27	Tuxpan	20 50N	97 30W
27	Tuxtla Gutiérrez	16 50N	93 10W
61	Tuyun	26 5N	107 20E
54	Tuz Gölü, L.	38 45N	33 30E
54	Tuz Khurmatu	34 50N	44 45E
41	Tuzla	44 34N	18 41E
18	Twain	40 2N	121 4W
12	Twin Falls	42 30N	114 30W
11	Tyler	32 20N	95 15W
36	Tyne, R.	55 1N	1 26W
54	Tyre=Sur	33 19N	36 16E
14	Tyrone	40 40N	78 14W
40	Tyrrhenian Sea	40 0N	12 30E
48	Tyumen	57 0N	65 18E
61	Tzekung	29 25N	104 30E
61	Tzepo	36 28N	117 58E

U

Map	Place	Lat.	Long.
60	Ube	34 6N	131 20E
31	Uberaba	19 50S	48 0W
31	Uberlândia	19 0S	48 20W
58	Ubon Ratchathani	15 15N	10 50E
30	Ucayali, R.	4 30S	73 30W
25	Uchi Lake	51 10N	92 40W
60	Uchiura-Wan	42 20N	140 40E
56	Udaipur	24 36N	73 44E
45	Uddevalla	58 21N	11 55E
40	Udine	46 5N	13 10E
46	Udmurt A.S.S.R. □	57 30N	52 30E
49	Uelen	66 10N	170 0W
46	Ufa	54 45N	55 55E
66	Ugalia, R.	5 8S	30 42E
66	Uganda ■	2 0N	32 0E
12	Uinta Mts.	40 45N	110 30W
56	Ujjain	23 9N	75 43E
43	Ujpest	47 33N	19 6E
59	Ujung Pandang	5 10S	119 20E
66	Ukerewe I.	2 0S	33 0E
46	Ukhta	63 55N	54 0E
18	Ukiah	39 9N	123 13W
47	Ukrainian S.S.R. □	48 0N	35 0E
61	Ulaanbaatar	48 0N	107 0E
61	Ulan Bator=Ulaanbaatar	48 0N	107 0E
49	Ulan Ude	52 0N	107 30E
61	Ulanhot	46 5N	122 1E
56	Ulhasnagar	19 15N	73 10E
42	Ulm	48 23N	10 0E
12	Ulyanovsk	54 25N	48 25E
61	Ulyasutay	47 56N	97 28E
44	Umea	63 45N	20 20E
52	Umm el Fahm	32 31N	35 9E
53	Umm Lajj	25 0N	37 23E
54	Umm Qasr	31 39N	35 54E
*20	Umnak I.	53 0N	168 0W
67	Umtali	18 58S	32 38E
*20	Unalaska I.	54 0N	164 30W
21	Ungava B.	59 30N	67 0W
21	Ugava Pen.	60 0N	75 0W
*20	Unimak I.	54 30N	164 30W
*20	Unimak, Passage	54 35N	164 43W
17	Union City, Ind.	40 12N	84 49W
15	Union City, N.J.	40 46N	74 2W
48	Union of Soviet Socialist Republics ■	47 0N	100 0E
53	United Arab Emirates ■	24 0N	54 30E
36	United Kingdom ■	55 0N	3 0W
6-7	United States ■	37 0N	96 0W
25	Unity	52 27N	109 10W
16	University City	38 39N	90 19W
*18	Unumclaw	47 14N	122 0W
67	Uppington	28 25S	21 15E
17	Upper Arlington	40 0N	83 3W
72	Upper Hutt	41 8S	175 5E
12	Upper Klamath L.	42 16N	121 55W
10	Upper Red L.	48 10N	94 40W
64	Upper Volta ■	12 0N	0 30W
45	Uppsala	59 53N	17 42E
54	Ur	30 55N	46 25E
47	Ural, R.	47 0N	51 48E
46	Ural Mts.=Uralskie Gory	60 0N	59 0E
46	Uralsk	51 20N	51 20E
46	Uralskie Gory	60 0N	59 0E
25	Uranium City	59 34N	108 37W
60	Urawa	35 50N	139 40E
17	Urbana, Ill.	40 7N	88 12W
17	Urbana, Ohio	40 7N	83 45W
16	Urbandale	41 38N	93 48W
54	Urfa	37 12N	38 50E
54	Urmia, L.=Daryacheh-ye Reza'iyeh, L.	37 40N	45 30E
26	Uruapan	19 30N	102 0W
32	Uruguaiana	29 50S	57 0W
32	Uruguay ■	32 30S	55 30W
32	Uruguay, R.	34 12S	58 18W
61	Urumchi =Wulumchi	43 40N	87 50E
55	Uruzgan □	33 30N	66 0E
54	Usküdar	41 0N	29 5E
32	Uspallata, Paso	32 30S	69 28W
49	Ussuriysk	43 40N	131 50E
49	Ust-Kamchatsk	56 10N	162 0E
48	Ust Kamenogorsk	50 0N	82 20E
46	Ust Usa	66 0N	56 30E
42	Usti nad Labem	50 41N	14 3E
48	Ustyurt, Plato	43 0N	56 0E
28	Usulután	13 25N	88 28W
12	Utah □	39 30N	111 30W
15	Utica	43 5N	75 18W
37	Utrecht	52 3N	5 8E
60	Utsunomiya	36 30N	139 50E
56	Uttar Pradesh □	27 0N	80 0E
58	Uttaradit	17 36N	100 5E
27	Uxmal	20 22N	89 46W
30	Uyuni	20 35S	66 55W
48	Uzbek S.S.R. □	40 5N	65 0E

V

Map	Place	Lat.	Long.
67	Vaal, R.	29 4S	23 38E
44	Vaasa	63 10N	21 35E
18	Vacaville	38 21N	121 59W
56	Vadodara	22 20N	73 10E
44	Vadso	70 3N	29 50E
43	Váh, R.	47 55N	18 0E
38	Val-de-Marne □	48 45N	2 28E
38	Val-d'Oise □	49 5N	2 0E
22	Val-d'Or	48 6N	77 47W
25	Val Marie	49 14N	107 44W
43	Valahia, reg.	44 38N	25 0E
46	Valdayskaya Vozvyshennost	57 0N	33 30E
39	Valdepenas	38 43N	3 25W
32	Valdes, Pen.	42 30S	63 45W
*20	Valdez	61 14N	146 10W

Valdivia Wiesbaden

32 Valdivia 39 50s 73 14w
9 Valdosta 30 50N 83 48w
38 Valence 44 57N 4 54E
39 Valencia, Spain 39 27N 0 23w
30 Valencia, Venezuela 10 11N 68 0w
39 Valencia, G. de 39 30N 0 20E
38 Valenciennes 50 20N 3 34E
27 Valladolid, Mexico 20 30N 88 20w
39 Valladolid, Spain 41 38N 4 43w
26 Valle de Santiago 20 25N 101 15w
18 Vallejo 38 12N 122 15w
24 Valletta 35 54N 14 30E
17 Valley Station 38 6N 85 52w
22 Valleyfield 45 15N 74 8w
32 Valparaíso, Chile 33 2s 71 40w
26 Valparaíso, Mexico 22 50N 103 32w
17 Valparaiso 41 28N 87 3w
54 Van 38 30N 43 20E
70 Van Diemen Gulf 12 0s 132 0E
54 Van Gölü, L. 38 30N 43 0E
17 Van Wert 40 52N 84 35w
24 Vancouver, Canada 49 20N 123 10w
***18** Vancouver, U.S.A. 45 44N 122 41w
24 Vancouver I. 49 50N 126 30w
16 Vandalia 38 58N 89 6w
19 Vandenberg 34 41N 120 30w
24 Vanderhoof 54 1N 124 1w
45 Vänern, L. 58 47N 13 50E
22 Vankleek Hills 45 32N 74 40w
70 Vansittart, B. 14 52s 126 18E
***72** Vanua Levu, I. 15 45s 179 10E
38 Var □ 43 27N 6 18E
57 Varanasi 25 22N 83 8E
44 Varangerfjorden 69 50N 31 0E
45 Varberg 57 17N 12 20E
41 Vardar, R. 40 35N 22 50E
40 Varese 45 49N 8 50E
41 Varna 43 13N 27 56E
45 Värnamo 57 10N 14 3E
55 Vasht=Khash 28 20N 61 6E
45 Västeras 59 37N 16 38E
45 Västervik 57 43N 16 43E
44 Vatnajökull 64 30N 16 30w
45 Vättern, L. 58 25N 14 30E
38 Vaucluse □ 44 3N 5 10E
13 Vaughn 34 37N 105 12w
45 Vaxjö 56 52N 14 50E
37 Vechte, R. 52 35N 6 5E
37 Veenendaal 52 2N 5 34E
44 Vegafjorden 65 37N 12 0E
24 Vegreville 53 30N 112 3w
45 Vejle 55 47N 9 30E
40 Velebit Planina 44 50N 15 20E
46 Velikiye Luki 56 25N 30 32E
56 Vellore 12 57N 79 10E
37 Velsen 52 27N 4 40E
32 Venado Tuerto 33 50s 62 0w
38 Vendée □ 46 40N 1 20w
40 Venézia 45 27N 12 20w
40 Venézia, G. di 45 20N 13 0E
30 Venezuela ■ 8 0N 65 0w
30 Venezuela, G. de 11 30N 71 0w
40 Venice=Venézia 45 27N 12 20E
37 Venlo 51 22N 6 11E
46 Ventspils 57 25N 21 32E
19 Ventura 34 16N 119 16w
27 Veracruz 19 10N 96 10w
67 Vereeniging 26 38s 27 57E
49 Verkhoyansk 67 50N 133 50E
49 Verkhoyanskiy Khrebet 66 0N 129 0E
25 Vermilion 53 22N 110 51w
16 Vermilion, R. 41 19N 89 4w
25 Vermilion Bay 49 51N 93 24w
10 Vermillion 53 20N 110 50w
15 Vermont □ 43 40N 72 50w
24 Vernon, Canada 50 20N 119 15w
11 Vernon, U.S.A. 34 0N 99 15w
40 Verona 45 27N 11 0E
38 Versailles 48 48N 2 8E
64 Vert, C. 14 45N 17 30w
37 Verviers 50 37N 5 52E
44 Vesteralan, Is. 69 0N 15 0E
44 Vestfjorden 68 0N 15 0E
44 Vestmannaeyjar, I. 63 27N 20 15w
40 Vesuvio, mt. 40 50N 14 22E
54 Veys 31 30N 49 0E
39 Viana do Castelo 41 41N 8 50w
45 Viborg 56 27N 9 23E
40 Vicenza 45 32N 11 31E
38 Vichy 46 9N 3 26E
19 Vicksburg, Ariz 33 42N 113 42w
11 Vicksburg, Miss. 32 22N 90 56w
71 Victor Harbour 35 30s 138 37E
66 Victoria, Cameroon 4 1N 9 10E
24 Victoria, Canada 48 30N 123 25w
61 Victoria, Hong Kong 22 25N 114 15E
58 Victoria, Malaysia 5 20N 115 20E
11 Victoria, U.S.A. 28 50N 97 0w
66 Victoria, L. 1 0s 33 0E
70 Victoria, R. 15 30s 131 0E
71 Victoria □ 37 0s 144 0E
67 Victoria Falls 17 58s 25 45E
20 Victoria I. 71 0N 11 0w
28 Victoria de las Tunas 20 58N 76 59w
23 Victoriaville 46 4N 71 56w
19 Victorville 34 22N 117 18w
19 Vidal 34 9N 114 30w
42 Vienna=Wien 48 12N 16 22E
38 Vienne 45 31N 4 53E
38 Vienne □ 46 30N 0 30E
58 Viet-Nam ■ 15 0N 108 0E
59 Vigan 17 35N 120 28E
39 Vigo 42 12N 8 41w
57 Vijayawada 16 31N 80 39E
41 Vijosë, R. 40 37s 19 20E
39 Vila Real 41 17N 7 48w
38 Vilaine, R. 47 30N 2 27w
32 Villa María 32 20s 63 10w
32 Villaguay 32 0s 58 45w
27 Villahermosa 17 45N 92 50w
22 Ville-Marie 47 19N 79 26w
39 Villena 38 39N 0 52w
46 Vilnius 54 38N 25 25E
37 Vilvoorde 50 56N 4 26E
49 Vilyuy, R. 64 24N 126 26E
49 Vilyuysk 63 40N 121 20E
32 Vina del Mar 33 0s 71 30w
17 Vincennes 38 41N 87 32w
19 Vincent 34 30N 118 6w
56 Vidhya Ra. 22 50N 77 0E
61 Vinh 18 45N 105 38E
47 Vinnitsa 49 15N 28 30E
25 Virden 49 51N 100 56w
29 Virgin Is. (Br.) 18 40N 64 30w
29 Virgin Is. (U.S.) 18 20N 64 40w
10 Virginia 47 30N 92 32w
8 Virgina □ 37 45N 78 0w
8 Virginia Beach 36 54N 75 58w
18 Visalia 36 25N 119 18w
59 Visayan Sea 11 25N 124 0E
45 Visby 55 1N 8 46E
20 Viscount Melville Sd. 78 0N 108 0w
39 Viseu 40 40N 7 55w
57 Vishakhapatnam 17 45N 83 20E
38 Viso, Mte. 44 38N 7 5E
19 Vista 33 12N 117 15w
43 Vistula=Wisla, R. 54 22N 18 55E
46 Vitebsk 55 10N 30 15E
***72** Vitu Levu, I. 17 30s 177 30E
49 Vitim, R. 59 26N 112 34E
39 Vitoria, Spain 42 50N 2 41w
31 Vitória, Brazil 20 20s 40 22w
31 Vitória da Conquista 14 51s 40 51w
40 Vittório Véneto 45 59N 12 18E
26 Vizcaino, Des. de 27 40N 113 50w
57 Vizianagaam 18 6N 83 10E
37 Vlaardingen 51 55N 4 19E
46 Vladimir 56 8N 50 20E
49 Vladivostok 43 10N 131 53E
37 Vlieland, I. 53 30N 4 55E
37 Vlissingen 51 26N 3 34E
41 Vlórë 40 32N 19 28E
59 Vogelkop=Djazirah Doberai, mts. 1 25s 133 0E
66 Voi 3 25s 38 32E
47 Volga, R. 45 55N 47 52E
47 Volgograd 48 40N 44 25E
47 Volgogradskoye Vdkhr. 50 0N 45 20E
46 Vologda 59 25N 40 0E
41 Vólos 39 24N 22 59E
46 Volsk 55 57N 48 23E
64 Volta, L. 7 30N 0 15E
64 Volta Noire, R. 8 41N 1 33w
31 Volta Redónda 22 31s 44 5w
47 Volzhkiy 48 56N 44 46E
37 Voorburg 52 5N 4 24E
41 Voríai Sporádhes, Is. 39 15N 23 30E
46 Vorkuta 67 48N 64 20E
46 Voronezh 52 30N 39 30E
47 Voroshilovgrad 48 38N 39 15E
48 Vosges, reg. 48 20N 7 10E
38 Vosges □ 48 15N 7 0E
49 Vostochnyy Sayan, mts. 54 0N 96 0E
46 Votkinsk 57 0N 53 55E
46 Votkinskove Vdkhr. 57 30N 55 0E
49 Vrangelya, Ostrov 56 20N 132 10w
67 Vryburg 26 55s 24 45E
24 Vulcan 50 24N 113 15w
40 Vulcano, I. 38 25N 14 58E
46 Vyazma 55 13N 34 18E
46 Vyborg 60 43N 28 47E
43 Vychodné Běskydy, mts. 49 30N 22 0E
46 Vyshniy Volochek 57 35N 34 34E

W

37 Waal, R. 51 55N 4 30E
23 Wabana 47 38N 52 57w
17 Wabash 40 48N 85 49w
17 Wabash R. 37 46N 88 2w
25 Wabowden 54 55N 98 35w
23 Wabush City 52 55N 66 52w
65 Waco 31 33N 97 5w
65 Wâd Medani 14 28N 33 30E
37 Waddeneilanden, Is. 53 30N 6 0E
37 Waddenzee, sea 53 20N 5 5E
24 Waddington, Mt. 51 10N 125 20w
25 Wadena 51 57N 103 38w
65 Wadi Halfa 21 53N 31 19E
14 Wadsworth 41 2N 81 44w
37 Wageningen 51 58N 5 40E
71 Wagga Wagga 35 7s 147 24E
59 Wahai 2 48s 129 35E
10 Wahpeton 46 20N 96 35w
72 Waihi 37 23s 175 52E
***6** Wahiawa 21 30N 158 1w
72 Waikaremoana, L. 38 42s 177 12E
72 Waimakariri, R. 43 24s 172 42E
72 Waimate 44 53s 171 3E
25 Wainwright 52 50N 110 50w
72 Waiouru 39 28s 175 41E
72 Waipara 43 3s 172 46E
72 Waipukurau 40 1s 176 33E
72 Wairarapa, L. 41 14s 175 15E
72 Waitaki, R. 44 56s 171 7E
60 Wakasa-wan 35 45N 135 30E
72 Wakatipu, L. 45 5s 168 33E
25 Wakaw 52 39N 105 44w
60 Wakayamma 34 15N 135 15E
68 Wake I. 19 18N 166 36E
15 Wakefield 42 30N 71 4w
21 Wakeham=Maricourt 61 36N 71 58w
60 Wakkanai 45 28N 141 35E
42 Walbrzych 50 45N 16 18E
37 Walcheren, I. 51 30N 3 35E
36 Wales □ 52 30N 4 0w
22 Walkerton 44 10N 81 10w
12 Walla Walla 46 3N 118 25w
13 Wallaceburg 42 36N 82 23w
43 Wallachia= Valahia, reg. 44 38N 25 0E
15 Wallingford 41 27N 72 50w
10 Wallis, L. 32 15s 152 28E
12 Wallowa Mts. 45 20N 117 30w
36 Walsall 52 36N 1 59w
15 Waltham 42 23N 71 14w
67 Walvis Bay=Walvisbaai 23 0s 14 28E
67 Walvisbaai 23 0s 14 28E
72 Wanaka, L. 44 33s 169 7E
72 Wanganui 39 35s 175 3E
61 Wanhsien 30 50N 108 30E
67 Wankie 18 18s 26 30E
17 Wapakoneta 40 34N 84 12w
53 Warandab 7 20N 44 2E
56 Warangal 17 58N 79 45E
55 Wardak □ 34 15N 68 0E
56 Wardha 20 45N 78 39E
12 Warner Ra. 41 30s 120 20w
71 Warrego, R. 30 24s 145 21E
71 Warrego Ra. 25 15s 146 0E
17 Warren, Mich. 42 28N 83 1w
14 Warren, Ohio 41 18N 80 52w
14 Warren, Pa. 41 51N 79 8w
9 Warrington 30 22N 87 16w
16 Warrensburg 39 56N 89 4w
43 Warsaw=Warszawa 52 13N 21 0E
17 Warsaw 41 14N 85 51w
43 Warszawa 52 13N 21 0E
42 Warta, R. 52 35N 14 39E
71 Warwick, Australia 28 10s 152 1E
36 Warwick, U.K. 52 17N 1 36w
15 Warwick, U.S.A. 41 43N 71 25w
12 Wasatch Ra. 40 30N 111 15w
19 Wasco 35 36N 119 20w
8 Washington, D.C. 38 52N 77 0w
16 Washington, Ill. 40 42N 89 24w
17 Washington, Ind. 38 40N 87 8w
16 Washington, Iowa 41 18N 91 42w
16 Washington, Mo. 38 33N 91 1w
9 Washington, N.C. 35 35N 77 1w
14 Washington, Pa. 40 10N 80 15w
12 Washington □ 47 45N 120 30w
17 Washington Court House 39 32N 83 26w
16 Washington Park 38 38N 90 5w
***18** Washougal 45 35N 122 21w
37 Wassenaar 52 8N 4 24E
59 Watampone 4 29s 120 25E
8 Waterbury 41 32N 73 0w
36 Waterford 52 16N 7 8w
22 Waterloo Canada 43 30N 80 32w
10 Waterloo, Iowa 42 27N 92 20w
10 Watertown, S.D. 44 57N 97 5w
15 Watertown, N.Y. 43 58N 75 57w
17 Watertown, Wis. 43 12N 88 43w
***9** Waterville 44 33N 69 38w
15 Watervliet 42 44N 73 42w
36 Watford 51 38N 0 23w
29 Watling I. 24 0N 74 30w
25 Watrous 51 40N 105 28w
17 Watseka 40 47N 87 44w
24 Watson Lake 60 7N 128 48w
18 Watsonville 36 55N 121 45w
25 Waugh 49 40N 95 20w
17 Waukegan 42 22N 87 54w
17 Waukesha 43 0N 88 15w
10 Wausau 44 57N 89 40w
17 Wauwatsoa 43 6N 87 59w
16 Waverly 42 44N 92 29w
66 Wâw 7 45N 28 1E
11 Waxahachie 32 22N 96 83w
9 Waycross 31 12N 82 25w
9 Waynesville 35 31N 83 0w
8 Waynesboro 39 46N 77 32w
55 Wazirabad 36 44N 66 47E
15 Webster 42 3N 71 53w.
16 Webster City 42 28N 93 49w
59 Weda 0 30N 127 50E
33 Weddell Sea 72 30s 40 0w
23 Wedgeport 43 44N 65 59w
37 Weert 51 15N 5 43E
61 Weifang 36 52N 119 7E
71 Weipa 12 24s 142 0E
14 Weirton 40 25N 80 35w
8 Welch 37 29N 81 36w
67 Welkom 28 0s 26 50E
22 Welland 43 0N 79 10w
71 Wellesley, Is. 17 20s 139 30E
22 Wellington, Canada 43 57N 77 21w
72 Wellington, NZ. 41 19s 174 46E
32 Wellington, I. 49 30s 75 0w
14 Wellsville, N.Y. 42 7N 77 57w
14 Wellsville, Ohio 40 36N 80 39w
12 Wenatchee 47 30N 120 17w
61 Wenchow 28 0N 120 35E
42 Weser, R. 53 32N 8 34E
17 West Allis 43 1N 88 0w
57 West Bengal □ 25 0N 90 0E
16 West Carrollton 39 40N 84 15w
15 West Chester 39 58N 75 36w
17 West Chicago 41 53N 88 12w
19 West Covina 34 5N 117 58w
16 West Des Moines 41 35N 93 43w
28 West End 26 41N 78 58w
32 West Falkland, I. 51 30s 60 0w
17 West Frankfort 37 54N 88 55w
42 West Germany ■ 51 0N 9 0E
15 West Hartford 41 46N 72 45w
15 West Haven 41 16N 72 57w
9 West Palm Beach 26 44N 80 3w
50 West Siberian Plain 62 30N 73 0E
8 West Virginia □ 39 0N 18 0w
***9** Westbrook 43 41N 70 21w
70 Western Australia □ 25 0s 118 0E
56 Western Ghats, mts. 15 30N 74 30E
58 Western Malaysia □ 5 0N 100 0E
72 Western Samoa ■ 13 55s 172 0w
37 Westerschelde, R. 51 25N 3 45E
42 Westerwald, mts. 50 39N 8 0E
17 Westfield, Ind. 40 2N 86 8w
15 Westfield, Mass. 42 8N 72 45w
72 Westland Bight 42 55s 170 5E
24 Westlock 54 9N 113 52w
8 Weston 39 3N 80 29w
72 Westport 41 46N 171 37E
25 Westray 53 36N 101 24w
24 Westview 49 50N 124 31w
24 Wetaskiwin 52 58N 113 22w
15 Wethersfield 41 43N 72 40w
37 Wettern 51 0N 3 53E
42 Wetzlar 50 33N 8 30E
36 Wexford 52 20N 6 28w
25 Weyburn 49 40N 103 50w
36 Weymouth, U.K. 50 36N 2 28w
15 Weymouth, U.S.A. 42 13N 70 58w
72 Whakatane 37 57s 177 1E
25 Whale Cove 62 14N 93 0w
72 Whangarei 35 43s 174 21E
18 Wheatland 39 1N 121 25w
17 Wheaton 41 52N 88 6w
8 Wheeling 40 2N 80 41w
11 White, R. 33 53N 91 3w
13 White Mts., Calif. 37 30N 118 6w
15 White Mts., New England 44 10N 71 35w
65 White Nile R.= Nîl el Abyad, R. 15 38N 32 31E
15 White Plains 41 2N 73 46w
46 White Russia= Byelorussian S.S.R. □ 53 30N 28 0E
46 White Sea= Beloye More 66 0N 38 0E
17 Whitefish Bay 43 7N 87 55w
36 Whitehaven 53 33N 3 35w
24 Whitehorse 60 43N 135 3w
17 Whitewater 42 50N 88 44w
17 Whiting 41 40N 87 29w
15 Whitman 42 5N 70 56w
18 Whitney, Mt. 36 35N 118 14w
***20** Whittier 60 46N 148 48w
71 Whyalla 33 2s 137 30E
11 Wichita 37 40N 97 29w
34 Wick 58 26N 3 5w
14 Wickliffe 41 36N 81 28w
36 Wicklow Mts. 53 2N 6 24w
42 Wien 48 12N 16 22E
42 Wiesbaden 50 7N 8 17E

Acknowledgment is made to the following for providing the photographs used in this atlas.
Air India ; Australian Information Service ; Brazilian Embassy, London ; British Aircraft Corporation ; British Airways ; British Leyland ; British Petroleum ; British Rail ; British Steel Corporation ; British Tourist Authority ; Central Electricity Generating Board ; D. Chanter ; Danish Embassy, London ; Egypt Air ; Fiat (England) Ltd. ; Finnish Tourist Bureau ; Freightliners Ltd. ; H. Fullard ; M. H. Fullard ; Gas Council Exploration Ltd. ; Commander H. R. Hatfield/Astro Books ; H. Hawes ; Israeli Govt. Tourist Office ; Japan Air Lines ; Lufthansa ; M.A.T. Transport Ltd. ; Meteorological Office, London ; Moroccan Tourist Office ; N.A.S.A. (Space Frontiers) ; National Coal Board, London ; National Maritime Museum, London ; Offshore Co. ; Pan American World Airways ; Royal Astronomical Society, London ; Shell International Petroleum Co. Ltd. ; Swan Hunter Group, Ltd. ; Swiss National Tourist Office ; B. M. Willett ; Woodmansterne Ltd.